TAKING SIDES

Clashing Views on
Controversial Political Issues

D1191071

Fifth Edition

We are not afraid to follow truth wherever it may lead, nor to tolerate any error so long as reason is left free to combat it.
—Thomas Jefferson

In memory of Hillman M. Bishop and Samuel Hendel, masters of an art often neglected by college teachers: teaching.

STAFF

Jeremy Brenner	Program Manager
Brenda Filley	Production Manager
Jean Bailey	Designer
Libra Ann Cusack	Typesetting Coordinator
Diane Barker	Editorial Assistant
Lynn Shannon	Graphics Coordinator

Library of Congress Catalog Card Number: 86-71774

Manufactured in the United States of America

Fifth Edition, First Printing

TAKING SIDES

Clashing Views on
Controversial Political Issues

Fifth Edition

Edited, Selected and with Introductions by

GEORGE MCKENNA, City College, City University of New York
and
STANLEY FEINGOLD, Westchester Community College

The Dushkin Publishing Group, Inc.
Guilford, Connecticut 06437

CONTENTS

Journalist Gregg Easterbrook believes that, before Congress can lead the nation, it must be able to lead itself, and it has notably failed to do so. Brookings Institution member Gary Orfield argues that Congress does a good job of reflecting the attitudes and trends of the electorate as a whole. If Congress seems unresponsive, he says, it is not the fault of the institution but a comment on the priorities of the country at the moment.

Senator Goldwater argues that, while Congress can "declare" war, only the president can "make" war. Only the president can act with adequate force and speed to protect national security. The late Senator Javits maintains that the War Powers Act reaffirms the intention of the Framers to ensure that the effective power to make war originates in the will of Congress.

Editor Barry Crickmer argues that the interests of citizens and consumers could be better served by the forces of the profit motive than by government intervention. Journalists Martin and Susan Tolchin contend that without vigorous regulation businesses will destroy the environment and endanger lives in their single-minded pursuit of profit.

Journalist Joseph Sobran believes that the Supreme Court has inverted its original role and now wields the arbitrary power it was intended to check. Supreme Court Justice William J. Brennan, Jr., holds that judges have a duty to interpret the Constitution and to protect the democratic process.

CBS Anchor Dan Rather, argues that the "fairness doctrine" tends to chill dissent and discourage the full and robust coverage of controversial issues. Conservative activist, Elaine Donnelly, argues that the "fairness doctrine" is the only means of forcing the networks to provide some semblance of balanced news coverage.

Political scientist James Q. Wilson says that the prospect of swift and certain punishment is more likely to reduce violent crime than are social programs aimed at relieving poverty. Federal judge David Bazelon defends his position that meaningful crime control must focus on the social conditions that breed it in the first place.

Professor Walter Berns is convinced that the death penalty has a place in modern society and that it serves a need now, as it did when the Constitution was framed. Criminologist Donal MacNamara presents a ten-point argument against capital punishment, raising ethical and practical questions concerning the death penalty.

Harvard professor Glenn Loury contends that insistence on "ill-suited" civil rights strategies makes it impossible for blacks to achieve full equality in American society. Author Herman Schwartz argues that we must somehow undo the cruel consequences of racism that still plague our society and its victims.

Feminist writers, Ronnie Steinberg and Lois Haignere argue that, since certain tasks traditionally assigned to females are low-paying, we must redesign pay scales in general, according to their "comparable worth." Geoffrey Cowley, a newspaper columnist, claims that it is impossible to calculate "comparable worth," and that the effort to do so will create a confusing bureaucratic tangle and even worse inequities.

The late Senator John East says that without Contra aid the Soviets will be able to impose a military solution in Central America. Senator Christopher Dodd contends that more American military force is not the way to deal with the underlying problems of the region.

Benjamin Netanyahu, Israeli Ambassador to the United Nations, believes that the United States can sharply reduce terrorism by applying political, economic and military pressure. Conor Cruise O'Brien, former Deputy Chief of the Irish Delegation to the U.N., believes that only American moral consistency will achieve the coordinated international action that can curb terrorism.

Brzezinski, Jastrow and Kampelman believe the Strategic Defense Initiative can deflect a nuclear attack and thereby enhance the deterrent effect of our security system and reduce the likelihood of nuclear war. Bundy, Kennan, McNamara and Smith maintain that "Star Wars", holding out a false hope that a defense can be created against nuclear attack, will lead to the development of new weapons rather than arms control.

Jeane Kirkpatrick, former ambassador to the United Nations, suggests that by failing to distinguish between "authoritarian" and "totalitarian" forms of government, by concentrating on human rights violations by "friendly" regimes, we are injuring our own interests and failing to protect human rights. Alan Tonelson, associate editor of the *Wilson Quarterly*, says that we should reverse Kirkpatrick's priorities: we should put public pressure on "friendly" authoritarian regimes and work behind the scenes to stop human rights violations by Communist regimes.

PREFACE TO THE FIFTH EDITION

In the first edition of *Taking Sides* we said:

> The purpose of this book is to make a modest contribution toward the revival of political dialogue in America. What we propose to do is to examine some leading issues in American politics from the perspective of sharply opposed points of view. We have tried to select authors who argue their points vigorously but in such a way as to enhance our understanding of the issue.
>
> For each issue we have selected a pair of essays, one pro and one con. We hope the reader will examine each position carefully and then take sides.

The success of our first four editions has encouraged us to bring out this fifth, revised and expanded, version of *Taking Sides.* We have revised many issues, including the issues on Congress (Issue 4), war powers (Issue 5), the Supreme Court (Issue 7), the media (Issue 8), affirmative action (Issue 11), welfare (Issue 13), pornography (Issue 14), church and state (Issue 16), and Central America (Issue 17). We have added three new issues, "comparable worth" (Issue 12), terrorism (Issue 18), and the "Star Wars" debate (Issue 19). We have revised and brought up to date a number of our introductions and postscripts. We have also revised our introductory essay.

Despite these revisions, our basic thesis remains unchanged. We believe in public dialogue. We are convinced that the best way to guard against narrow-mindedness and fanaticism is to bring opposing views together and let them clash.

This does not mean that we consider all points of view to be equal. On the contrary, we encourage our readers to become partisans, as long as they support their positions with logic and facts, are able to make reasonable replies to opposing arguments, and are willing to revise their views if they are proven wrong.

The reader who has thoughtfully examined two antithetical views, each of which is expressed with all the evidence and eloquence that an informed advocate can bring to bear upon the argument, will also perceive that there are positions between and beyond the sharply differentiated essays that he or she has read.

In one sense, our approach resembles a series of formal debates of the kind conducted by debating teams and moot law courts. In another and more important sense, however, the conflicting arguments of this book represent something quite different. A debate is an intellectual game, in which opposition is explicit but artificial. By contrast, the essays included here were rarely written in direct response to one another. More important, they are public statements about real issues; both the political participants and the commentators are seeking the widest support for their positions. In every instance we have chosen what we believe to be an appropriate and well-reasoned statement by a committed advocate. If the argument contains an element of passion as well as reason, it is an element the student of American politics cannot afford to ignore. However, passion with substance is very different from empty rhetoric.

Although we have attempted in the Introduction to indicate the major alignments in American politics, a reflective reader of these essays will certainly realize that merely ascribing a label to a position will not dispose of it. Every analysis presented here has merit, insofar as it reflects some sense of political reality and represents a viewpoint shared by some Americans, and each analysis therefore demands to be dealt with on its own merits.

We hope that the reader who confronts lively and thoughtful statements on vital issues will be stimulated to ask critical questions about American politics. What are the highest-priority issues with which the government must deal today? What positions should be taken on these issues? What should be the attitude of Americans toward their government? To what extent, if any, does government need to be changed? How should it be organized in order to achieve the goals we set for it? What are these goals? We are convinced that a healthy, stable democracy requires a citizenry that considers these questions and participates—however indirectly—in answering them. The alternative is apathy, passivity, and, sooner or later, the rule of tyrants.

ACKNOWLEDGMENTS

We wish to acknowledge the encouragement and support given to this project by Rick Connelly, President of the Dushkin Publishing Group. We are grateful as well to Jeremy Brenner for his very able editorial supervision. We also wish to thank Dina Tritsch for calling to our attention one of the pieces on terrorism which we used in this edition. Needless to add, the responsibility for any errors of fact or judgment rests with us.

George McKenna
Stanley Feingold
New York City
October, 1986

INTRODUCTION: LABELS AND ALIGNMENTS IN AMERICAN POLITICS

Stanley Feingold
George McKenna

According to the pollsters, Americans are becoming increasingly reluctant to call themselves "liberals." More and more prefer the term "moderate," and a considerable number call themselves "conservatives." Yet this apparent shift away from "liberalism" may be misleading. Liberal commentators point out that Americans may not *call* themselves "liberal" but they *are* liberal on many key issues. Conservative commentators dispute that claim. They point out that the American people have twice elected Ronald Reagan to the presidency—the second time by a massive landslide—and have given him the highest approval ratings given to any president since Franklin Roosevelt. Reagan has been calling himself a "conservative" for a generation, and his behavior in office generally fits the "conservative" mold, so the American people have made more than a purely semantic shift away from liberalism. To this argument the liberals have a rejoinder: Americans may like Ronald Reagan, but they don't like his philosophy; indeed, liberals say, Reagan played down his "conservatism" in order to get reelected. His technique, which is the hallmark of all successful American politicians, is to paint his opponents into the corner, make them look like far-out "radicals," while characterizing himself as a "moderate" and a supporter of a "pluralistic" America.

Liberal, conservative, moderate, radical, pluralist—do these terms have any meaning? They may be useful to politicians and pollsters, but do they help us to understand opposing views on the major issues that face America today? We believe that they do, but that they must be used thoughtfully. Otherwise, the terms may end up obscuring or oversimplifying positions. Our purpose in this Introduction is to explore the basic, core meanings of the terms in order to make them useful to us as citizens.

LIBERALS VERSUS CONSERVATIVES: AN OVERVIEW

The underlying distinction between liberals and conservatives grows out of their respective views of human nature. Liberals tend toward optimism, conservatives toward pessimism (conservatives would say realism). In the eighteenth century, Jonathan Swift, author of *Gulliver's Travels*, expressed a conservative attitude when he said: "I hate and detest that animal called man, although I heartily love John, Peter, Thomas, and so forth." Shakespeare, on the other hand, anticipated the liberal view in an exclamation by one of his characters: "What a piece of work

1

is man! How noble in reason, how infinite in faculties!" (Hamlet, Act, II scene ii). Liberals have sometimes even believed in the perfectibility of humankind and have thus emphasized the need for education, a free press, political participation, and other stimuli to the mind and spirit. Although these liberal hopes have usually proven to be excessive, they have produced important social and political changes: universal public education, the extension of suffrage, primary elections, the secret ballot, and special programs to extend cultural opportunities to the poor. Liberals contend that there are virtually no limits to what people can understand and do, given a decent environment. In the Middle Ages, limitless intelligence was thought to be the property of angels; today's liberals seek to extend it to all human beings.

Conservatives scorn what they consider to be the illusions of liberals. They believe that people have limited capacities for elevating their minds and spirits, and that, limited as these capacities are, they are even more limited in some people than in others. Conservatives contend that there is a kind of natural hierarchy among people. Even American conservatives will somtimes voice some skepticism about the chief premise of the Declaration of Independence: that "all men are created equal." In terms of individual talent, conservatives believe, people are not created equal; some are naturally more intelligent than others. Conservatives tend to assume that it is the few, rather than the many, who have the mental capacity for higher education and political participation. American conservatism does not imply a yearning for the return of feudalism or government by kings or clergy, but it does inveigh against "mobocracy" and expresses concern about what happens to the political process when "the masses" get involved in it. "The time is not distant," said Gouverneur Morris at the Constitutional Convention of 1787, "when this country will abound with mechanics and manufacturers who will receive their bread from their employers. Will such men be secure and faithful guardians of liberty?" He doubted it. In more recent times, political scientist Robert Dahl has remarked that when the masses get into politics, "emotion rises and reasoned discussion declines." Though Dahl is better characterized as a "pluralist" (a term to be explained presently) than as a conservative, his view of the masses is compatible with the conservative outlook.

Let us examine, very briefly, the historical evolution of the terms "liberalism" and "conservatism." By examining the roots of these terms, we can see how these philosophies have adapted themselves to changing times. In that way, we can avoid using the terms rigidly, without reference to the particular contexts in which liberalism and conservatism have operated over the past two centuries.

Classical Liberalism

The classical root of the term "liberalism" is the Latin word *libertas*, meaning "liberty" or "freedom." In the early nineteenth century, liberals dedicated themselves to freeing individuals from all unnecessary and oppressive obligations to authority—whether the authority came from the church or the state. They opposed the licensing and censorship of the press, the punishment of heresy, the "establishment" of religion and any attempt to dictate "orthodoxy" in matters of opinion. In economics, liberals opposed state monopolies and other constraints upon competition between private businesses. At this point in its development, liberalism defined "freedom" primarily in terms of freedom *from*. It appropriated the French term *laissez-faire*, which literally means "leave to be." Leave people alone! That was the spirit of liberalism in its early days. It wanted government to stay out of people's lives and to play a modest role in general. Thomas Jefferson summed up this concept when he said: "I am no friend of energetic government. It is always oppressive."

Despite their suspicion of government, classical liberals invested high hopes in the political process. By and large, they were great believers in democracy. They believed in widening the suffrage to include every white male, and some of them were prepared to enfranchise women and blacks as well. Although liberals occasionally worried about "the tyranny of the majority," they were more prepared to trust the masses than to trust a permanent, entrenched elite. Then, as now, liberal social policy was dedicated to fulfilling every human potential and was based on the assumption that this often-hidden potential is enormous. Human beings, liberals argued, were basically good and reasonable. Evil and irrationality were believed to be caused by "outside" influences; they were the result of a bad social environment. A liberal commonwealth, therefore, was one which would remove the hindrances to the full flowering of the human personality.

The basic vision of liberalism has not changed since the nineteenth century. What has changed is the way it is applied to modern society. In that respect, liberalism has changed dramatically. Today, instead of regarding government with suspicion, liberals welcome government as an instrument to serve the people. The change in philosophy began in the latter years of the nineteenth century, when businesses—once small, independent operations—began to grow into giant structures that overwhelmed individuals and sometimes even overshadowed the state in power and wealth. At that time, liberals began reconsidering their commitment to the *laissez-faire* philosophy. If the state can be an oppressor, asked liberals, can't big business also oppress people? By then, many were convinced that commercial and industrial monopolies were crushing the souls and bodies of the working classes. The state, formerly the villain, now was viewed by liberals as a potential savior. The concept of "freedom" was transformed into something more than a negative freedom *from*; the term began to take on a positive meaning. It meant "realizing one's full potential." Toward this end, liberals believed, the state could prove to be a valuable instrument. It could educate children, protect the health and safety of workers, help people through hard times, promote a healthy economy, and—when necessary—force business to act more humanely and responsibly. Thus was born the movement that culminated in "New Deal liberalism."

3

INTRODUCTION

New Deal Liberalism

In the United States, the argument in favor of state intervention did not win a truly popular constituency until after the Great Depression of the 1930s began to be felt deeply. The disastrous effects of a depression that left a quarter of the work force unemployed opened the way to a new administration—and a promise. "I pledge you, I pledge myself," Franklin D. Roosevelt said when accepting the Democratic nomination in 1932, "to a new deal for the American people." Roosevelt's New Deal was an attempt to effect relief and recovery from the depression; it employed a variety of means, including welfare programs, public works and business regulation—most of which involved government intervention in the economy. The New Deal liberalism relied on democratic government to liberate people from poverty, oppression, and economic exploitation. At the same time, the New Dealers claimed to be as zealous as the classical liberals in defending political and civil liberties.

The common element in *laissez-faire* liberalism and welfare state liberalism is their dedication to the goal of realizing the full potential of each individual. Some still questioned whether this was best done by minimizing state involvement or whether it sometimes required an activist state. The New Dealers took the latter view, though they prided themselves on being pragmatic and experimental about their activism. During the heyday of the New Deal, a wide variety of programs were tried and—if found wanting—abandoned. All decent means should be tried, they believed, even if it meant dilution of ideological purity. The Roosevelt administration, for example, denounced bankers and businessmen in campaign rhetoric but worked very closely with them while trying to extricate the nation from the Depression. This set a pattern of pragmatism that New Dealers from Harry Truman to Lyndon Johnson emulated.

New Politics Liberalism

New Politics liberalism emerged in the late 1960s and early 1970s as a more militant and uncompromising movement than the New Deal had ever been. The civil rights' slogan, "Freedom Now," expressed the mood of the New Politics. The Vietnam peace movement demanded "unconditional" withdrawal from Vietnam. The young university graduates who filled the ranks of the New Politics had come from an environment where "non-negotiable" demands were issued to college deans by leaders of sit-in protests. There was more than youthful arrogance in the New Politics movement, however; there was a pervasive belief that America had lost, had compromised away, much of its idealism. The New Politics liberals sought to recover some of that spirit by linking up with an older tradition of militant reform, which went back to the time of the Revolution. These new liberals saw themselves as the authentic heirs of Tom Paine and Henry David Thoreau, of the abolitionists, the radical populists, the suffragettes, and the great progressive reformers of the early twentieth century.

While New Deal liberals concentrated almost exclusively on bread-and-butter issues such as unemployment and poverty, the New Politics liberals introduced what came to be known as "social issues" into the politi-

cal arena. These included: the repeal of laws against abortion, the liberalization of laws against homosexuality and pornography, the establishment of affirmative action programs to ensure increased hiring of minorities and women, and passage of the Equal Rights Amendment. In foreign policy too, New Politics liberals departed from the New Deal agenda. Because they had keener memories of the unpopular, and (for them)
unjustified war in Vietnam than of World War II, they became "doves," in
contrast to the general "hawkishness" of the New Dealers. They are
skeptical of any claim that the United States must be the leader of the
"free world," and they emphatically reject the notion that America must
seek superiority in armaments over the Soviet Union. They are not isola-
tionists (of all the political groups in America, they are probably the most
supportive of the United Nations), and they claim to be as concerned as
any other group that America's defenses be adequate. They minimize,
however, the danger to the West of an outright Soviet invasion. The real
danger, they argue, comes not from Soviet military advances but from
mutual miscalculations that could lead to a nuclear holocaust. All of the
above issues are touched upon in this book.

The schism between New Deal liberalism and New Politics liberalism
was evident during the 1984 Democratic primaries. Walter Mondale was
the candidate of organized labor, remaining old-style Democratic organization leaders, senior citizens, and others who saw the battle against the
Republicans primarily in terms of economic welfare issues. Mondale's
candidacy, then, had overtones of New Deal liberalism. Gary Hart, on
the other hand, seemed to be most popular with "yuppies" (young urban
professionals), who had come of age during the 1960s and early 1970s.
They saw economic aid to the needy as only one of a number of issues.
"Social issues" such as environmental problems, feminist concerns,
America's involvement in Central America, and, more generally, the need
to be "modern" and "relevant" were high on their agenda. In his convention speech, Hart proclaimed that "it is better to be mistaken than to
be irrelevant."

Most of the voters following the campaign were aware that the differences between Mondale and Hart were more matters of style than of
substance. Both subscribed to all of the "social issues" positions of the
New Politics. Both favored gay rights, legalized abortion, the Equal
Rights Amendment, and affirmative action programs. Indeed, these positions were written into the 1984 Democratic platform by a committee
controlled by Mondale delegates. Hart lost the nomination, but his "yup-
pie" constituency—or at least its philosophy on "social issues"—has
been increasingly dominant in the leadership circles of the Democratic
party. For example, in 1984 Ann Lewis, political director of the Democratic National Committee, said, "Gay rights is no longer a debatable issue
within the Democratic party." Before 1972, it would have been a highly
debatable issue; in 1968, it would have been unthinkable to even mention such an issue.

Conservatism

Like liberalism, conservatism has undergone historical transformation
in America. Just as early American liberals (represented by Thomas

Jefferson) espoused less government, early conservatives (whose earliest leaders were Alexander Hamilton and John Adams) urged government support of economic enterprise and government intervention on behalf of privileged groups. By the time of the New Deal, and in reaction to the growth of the welfare state since that time, conservatives have argued strongly that more government means more unjustified interference in citizens' lives, more bureaucratic regulation of private conduct, more inhibiting control of economic enterprise, more material advantage for the less energetic and less able at the expense of those who are prepared to work harder and better, and, of course, more taxes—taxes that will be taken from those who earned the money and given to those who have not earned it.

Contemporary conservatives are not always opposed to state intervention. They may support larger military expenditures in order to protect society against foreign enemies. They may also allow for some intrusion into private life in order to protect society against internal subversion and would pursue criminal prosecution zealously in order to protect society against domestic violence. The fact is that few conservatives, and perhaps fewer liberals, are absolute with respect to their views about the power of the state. Both are quite prepared to use the state in order to further *their* purposes. It is true that "activist" presidents such as Franklin Roosevelt and John Kennedy were likely to be classified as liberals. However, Richard Nixon was also an "activist," and, although he does not easily fit any classification, he was far closer to conservatism than to liberalism. It is too easy to identify liberalism with statism and conservatism with anti-statism; it is important to remember that it was liberal Jefferson who counseled against "energetic government" and conservative Alexander Hamilton who designed bold powers for the new central government and wrote: "Energy in the executive is a leading character in the definition of good government."

Neoconservatism and the New Right

Two newer varieties of conservatism have arisen to challenge the dominant strain of conservatism that opposed the New Deal. Those who call themselves (or have finally allowed themselves to be called) "neoconservatives" are recent converts to conservatism. Many of them are former New Deal Democrats, and some like to argue that it is not they who have changed; it is the Democratic party, which has allowed itself to be taken over by advocates of the New Politics. However true that may be, as neoconservatives they now emphasize themes that were largely unspoken in their earlier views. They recognize, as did the New Dealers, the legitimacy of social reform, but now they warn against carrying it too far and creating an arrogant bureaucracy. They support equal opportunity, as they always did, but now they underscore the distinction between equal opportunity and equality of result, which they identify as the goal of affirmative action programs. Broadly speaking, neoconservatism shares with the older variety of conservatism a high respect for tradition and a view of human nature that some would call pessimistic. Neoconservatives, like all conservatives, are also deeply concerned about the Communist threat to America. They advise shoring up America's defenses and resisting any movement that would lead the nation toward unilateral disarmament.

A more recent and more politically active variant of conservatism is called "the New Right." Despite the semantic resemblance between "New Right" and neoconservatism," the two differ in important ways. Neoconservatives are usually lapsed liberals, while New Rightists tend to be dyed-in-the-wool conservatives—though ones who are determined to appeal to wider constituencies than did the Old Right. Neoconservatives tend to be academics, who appeal to other similar elites through books and articles in learned journals. The New Right aims at reaching grass-roots voters through a variety of forums, from church groups to direct-mail solicitation. Neoconservatives customarily talk about politico-economic structures and global strategies; New Rightists emphasize the concerns of ordinary Americans, what they call "family issues'—moral concerns such as abortion, prayer in public schools, pornography, and what they consider to be a general climate of moral breakdown in the nation. These "family issues" are very similar to the "social issues" introduced into the political arena by the advocates of New Politics. This should not be surprising, since the rise of the New Right was a reaction to the previous success of the New Politics movement in legitimizing its stands on "social issues."

Spokesmen for the New Politics and the New Right stand as polar opposites: The former regard abortion as a woman's right; the latter see it as legalized murder. The former tend to regard homosexuality as a lifestyle that needs protection against discrimination; the latter are more likely to see it as a perversion. The former have made an issue of their support for the Equal Rights Amendment; the latter includes large numbers of women who fought against the amendment because they believed it threatened their role identity. The list of issues could go on. The New Right and the New Politics are like positive and negative photographs of America's moral landscape. For all their differences however, their style is very similar. It is heavily laced with moralistic prose; it tends to equate compromise with "selling out"; and it claims to represent the best, most "authentic" traditions of America. This is not to denigrate either movement, for the kinds of issues they address are indeed moral issues, which do not generally admit of much compromise. These issues cannot simply be finessed or ignored, despite the efforts of conventional politicians to do so. They must be aired and fought over, which is why we include some of them such as abortion (Issue 15) and church-state relations (Issue 16) in this volume.

Presidential candidates generally try to appear to be all things to all voters. In the White House, presidents often guide the ship of state by trimming their ideological sails and moving with the prevailing winds. It is all the more surprising, then, that Ronald Reagan was an avowedly conservative candidate, and proved to be a conservative president. To be sure, those who are more conservative (or, at any rate, more zealous in their conservatism) on specific issues have accused Reagan of compromising his commitments. Some right-to-lifers have not been happy with what they see as his less-than-vigorous fight against abortion; public school prayer advocates have claimed that the Reagan White House failed to press Congress for a constitutional amendment permitting in-school prayers; economic conservatives have grumbled that the White House knuckled under to congressional liberals by permitting the gasoline tax to be increased; and neoconservatives have expressed concern about Reagan's 1984 "peace" gestures to the Soviets, which, they claimed, contained overtones of appeasement. In general, however, Reagan has managed to combine the Old Right's insistence upon economic independence from government interferences with the New Right's concern with moral issues. Under Reagan, liberalism was put on the defensive; today, more than half a century after the inauguration of the New Deal, the President and his administration are expressing a different philosophy of American society.

RADICALS, REACTIONARIES, AND MODERATES

The label "reactionary" is almost an insult, and the label "radical" is worn with pride by only a few zealots on the banks of the political mainstream. A reactionary is not a conserver but a backward-mover, dedicated to turning the clock back to better times. Most people suspect that reactionaries would restore us to a time that never was, except in political myth. For many, the repeal of industrialism or universal education (or the entire twentieth century itself) is not a practical, let alone desirable, political program.

Radicalism (literally meaning "from the roots" or "going to the foundation") implies a fundamental reconstruction of the social order. Taken in that sense, it is possible to speak of right-wing radicalism as well as left-wing radicalism—radicalism that would restore or inaugurate a new hierarchical society as well as radicalism that calls for nothing less than an egalitarian society. The term is sometimes used in both of these senses, but most often the word "radicalism" is reserved to characterize more liberal change. While the liberal would effect change through conventional democratic processes, the radical is likely to be skeptical about the ability of the established machinery to bring about the needed change and might be prepared to sacrifice a "little" liberty to bring about a great deal more equality.

"Moderate" is a highly coveted label in America. Its meaning is not precise, but it carries the connotations of sensible, balanced, and practical. A "moderate" person is not without principles, but he or she does not allow principles to harden into dogma. The opposite of "moderate" is "extremist," a label most American political leaders eschew. Yet, there have been notable exceptions. When Arizona Senator Barry Goldwater, a conservative Republican, was nominated for president in 1964, he declared: "Extremism in defense of liberty is no vice! . . . Moderation in the pursuit of justice is no virtue!" This open embrace of "extremism" did not help his electoral chances; Goldwater was overwhelmingly defeated. At about the same time, however, another American political leader also embraced a kind of "extremism," and with better result. In a famous letter written from a jail cell in Birmingham, Alabama, the Reverend Martin Luther King replied to the charge that he was an "extremist" not by denying it but by distinguishing between different kinds of extremists. The question, he said, "is not whether we will be extremist but what kind of extremist will we be. Will we be extremists for hate, or will we be extremists for love?" King aligned himself with the love-extremists, in which category he also placed Jesus, St. Paul, and Thomas Jefferson, among others. It was an adroit use of a label that is usually anathema in this country.

PLURALISM

The principle of pluralism espouses diversity in a society containing many interest groups and in a government containing competing units of power. This implies the widest expression of competing ideas, and in this way, pluralism is in sympathy with an important element of liberalism. However, as Madison and Hamilton pointed out when they analyzed the sources of pluralism in the *Federalist* commentaries on the Constitution, this philosophy springs from a profoundly pessimistic view of human nature, and in this respect it more closely resembles conservatism. James Madison, possibly the single most influential member of the convention that wrote the Constitution, hoped that in a large and varied nation, no single interest group could control the government. Even if there were a majority interest, it would be unlikely to capture all of the national agencies of government—the House of Representatives, the Senate, the president and the federal judiciary—each of which was chosen in a different way by a different constituency for a different term of office. Moreover, to make certain that no one branch exercised excessive power, each was equipped with "checks and balances" that enabled any agency of national government to curb the powers of the others. The clearest statement of Madison's, and the Constitution's, theory can be found in the fifty-first paper of the *Federalist*:

> It may be a reflection on human nature that such devices should be necessary to control the abuses of government. But what is government itself, but the greatest of all reflections on human nature? If men were angels, no government would be necessary.

This pluralist position may be analyzed from different perspectives. It is conservative insofar as it rejects simple majority rule: yet it is liberal insofar as it rejects rule by an single elite. It is conservative in its pessimistic appraisal of human nature; yet pluralism's pessimism is also a kind of egalitarianism, holding as it does that no one can be trusted with power and that majority interests no less than minority interests will use power for selfish ends. It is possible to suggest that in America pluralism represents an alternative to both liberalism and conservatism. Where liberalism is majoritarian and conservatism is elitist, pluralism is anti-majoritarian and anti-elitist and combines some elements of both.

SOME APPLICATIONS

Despite our effort to define the principal alignments in American politics, some policy decisions do not neatly fit into these categories. The reader will reach his or her own conclusions, but we may suggest some alignments to be found here in order to demonstrate the variety of viewpoints.

Mainstream liberal positions are well represented among the essays in this book. In Issue 2, concerning political parties, William J. Crotty defends party reform as a liberal measure that has resulted in more representativeness and "open" conventions. This reform is opposed by Everett Carll Ladd, Jr., because it has diminished the conservative function of parties in selecting candidates. The conflict between contemporary conservatism and liberalism is clearly expressed in the opposed approaches of David Bazelon and James Q. Wilson to the question of crime (Issue 9). Wilson proceeds from a typically conservative view of man (a view that liberals call "pessimistic" and conservatives call "realistic") to the conclusion that the best way to fight crime is to imprison criminals for a long time so they cannot harm others. Bazelon, who has a more optimistic appraisal of human nature, believes that crime is a desperate yet understandable reaction to intolerable social conditions and that the best way to combat it is to reform society. More difficult to classify is the controversy considered in Issue 6: "Does Government Regulate Too Much?" Susan and Martin Tolchin's critique of deregulation is compatible with either New Deal or New Politics liberalism, but Barry Crickmer's case against regulation is reminiscent of classical liberalism or libertarianism. The same may be said of Charles Murray's case against the welfare state in Issue 13. His view is similar to that taken by such well-known conservatives as Barry Goldwater and Ronald Reagan. Opposing him on that issue is Sar Levitan, whose defense of the welfare state follows traditional "New Deal" liberal lines.

Walter Bern's defense of the death penalty (Issue 10: "Is Capital Punishment Justified?") is almost a purely conservative position. Like other conservatives, Berns is skeptical of the possibilities of human perfection and therefore regards retribution—"paying back" a murderer instead of trying to "reform" him—as a legitimate goal of punishment.

Justice William Brennan's defense of judicial activism in Issue 7 is liberal in spirit: the Constitution must be interpreted broadly, with a view to present-day realities and needs. Joseph Sobran's criticism of this approach is conservative in at least two senses. Sobran is concerned not only about the Court's method of interpreting the Constitution but also about the substance of its decisions on such questions as abortion. Many liberals regard abortion as a human right while conservatives—at least "New Right" conservatives like Sobran—consider it an act of homicide. The abortion issue is discussed more fully in Issue 15. President Reagan argues against its legalization while Beverly Harrison supports the Supreme Court decision which struck down the state laws prohibiting it.

There is a strong flavor of conservatism in the argument of James Dobson in Issue 14, which supports the position of the Attorney General's Commission on Pornography. Dobson favors the vigorous prosecution of our pornography laws. Opposing his point of view is Hendrik Hertzberg, a *New Republic* editor, who takes the liberal view that even pornography deserves the protection of the First Amendment.

Issues 17, 19, and 20—"Star Wars," Central America, and human rights—are foreign policy issues that have divided liberals and conservatives since President Reagan's first term in office. In general, liberals regard "Star Wars" and aid to the Nicaraguan rebels as militarily provocative, and they think that supporting "friendly" authoritarian regimes puts us on the wrong side of history. Conservatives insist that the first duty of statesmen is to defend their nation's security, and they regard all three policies as important means of achieving that goal.

Issue 18, on terrorism, also has liberal-conservative dimensions. The question is whether American military action is the best way to defeat international terrorism. Conor Cruise O'Brien, the Irish diplomat and scholar, takes the liberal view that only American moral consistency will bring about the coordinated international action necessary to curb terrorism. Israeli ambassador Benjamin Netanyahu takes the view, popular with many conservatives in America, that unilateral military action may be necessary to deal with terrorism.

This book has a few arguments that are not easy to categorize. Consider, for example, Issue 8, which explores the question of whether the FCC's "fairness" doctrine should be abandoned. Arguing for its abandonment is Dan Rather, the anchor for CBS Television News. Since the time of the Nixon administration in the early 1970s—if not all the way back to the 1950s—CBS News has been criticized by conservatives as left-leaning; that is the position taken by Elaine Donnelly, a spokesperson for the conservative Eagle Forum, whose view is also presented in Issue 8. Yet the opposing sides on the issue of "fairness" in broadcasting often mix together liberals and conservatives. President Reagan, for example, agrees with Dan Rather, and no one would call Reagan a liberal. On Donnelly's side are a number of liberal groups and activists, such as Common Cause and Ralph Nader.

The reader should assess the viewpoints in these essays in order to determine which are conservative, liberal, pluralist, or otherwise, and which are right or wrong. The empirical evidence supporting judgments of right and wrong is often scant. Does capital punishment deter criminals from committing murder? Does reading or seeing pornography make it more likely that men will commit rape? Even more often, evaluations of right and wrong involve value judgment; basically, one's position expresses a moral preference. (This is not to say that moral judgments are necessarily arbitrary or subjective, only that they ultimately take us out of the realm of politics and into philosophy—perhaps even into metaphysics and theology.)

Obviously one's position on the issues in this book will be affected by circumstances. After Vietnam and Watergate, for example, many who had once championed the strong presidency have adopted the opposite view. However, we would like to think that the essays in this book are durable enough to last through several seasons of events and controversies. We can be certain that the issues will survive. The search for coherence and consistency in the use of political labels underlines the options open to us and reveals their consequences. The result must be more mature judgments about what is best for America. That, of course, is the ultimate aim of public debate and decision making, and it transcends all labels and categories.

PART I
HOW DEMOCRATIC IS THE AMERICAN POLITICAL PROCESS?

"Democracy" is derived from two Greek words, demos and kratia, *meaning "people's rule." The issue today is whether the political realities of America conform to the ideal of "people's rule." Are "the people" really running this country? Or is it being run by elites not accountable to the people? Socialists say that big business runs the economy and controls the political agenda. Is that a fair charge, or is it based on simplistic premises? Political party reformers have tried to eliminate "bossism" in our party system, but their critics charge that the parties are more elitist than ever. Another issue generating controversy is the power of pressure groups, particularly that of political action committees (PACs). Are these groups undermining "people's rule," or are they—in a noisy, vulgar way—helping to make democracy work?*

Is America Ruled By an Elite?

Has Party Reform Succeeded?

Do Political Action Committees Undermine Democracy?

ISSUE I

IS AMERICA RULED BY AN ELITE?

YES: G. William Domhoff, from *Who Rules America Now?* (Englewood Cliffs, 1983)

NO: Andrew M. Greeley, from *Building Coalitions: American Politics in the 1970's* (New York, 1974)

ISSUE SUMMARY

YES: Social scientist G. William Domhoff sees American political life in terms of elite domination.
NO: Sociologist Andrew M. Greeley believes that there is no single, established center of power and points to the behavior of the system as evidence.

The United States Constitution was framed behind closed doors in 1787, and since that time there have been periodic charges that America is controlled, or is in imminent danger of being controlled, by a power elite. All representative government is necessarily government by elites (that is, small, selective ruling groups), but those who raise the specter of a power elite are charging that America is run by an *unrepresentative* elite—one that is unaccountable to the majority of voters. Almost invariably, it is added, this elite is not just political but economic. Although all industrial societies have gradations of wealth, the system of democracy is supposed to counter the weight of money with the weight of numbers. The basic contention of the elite-theorists, then, is not simply that there are rich and poor in America but that the very rich—or a small elite working in league with them—are making all the crucial decisions.

Fear of elitism has had a long history in America. Richard Henry Lee, one of the signers of the Declaration of Independence, spoke for many "anti-federalists" (who opposed ratification of the Constitution) when he warned that the proposed charter shifted power away from the people and into the hands of the "aristocrats" and "moneyites," those who "avariciously grasp at all power and property." Long after these fears were more or less quieted, there still remained a residue of suspicion that the wealthy were manipulating the machinery of government for their own purposes. Before the Civil War, Jacksonian Democrats charged Eastern merchants and bankers with usurping the power of the people. After the Civil War, a number of "radical" parties and movements revived this theme of anti-elitism. The rise of industrial monopolies, an apparent increase in political corruption, and economic hardship for Western farmers brought about the founding of the "People's Party" at the beginning of the 1890s. The "populists," as they were more commonly called, wanted economic and political reforms aimed at transferring power away from the rich and back to "the plain people." The populist assumption was that ordinary people had once possessed sovereign power in America, but it had slipped away from them.

Since the 1930s, American radicalism has been more influenced by Marxism than by populism. Like populists, Marxists emphasize the domination of America by the rich; unlike populists, Marxists do not look back with nostalgia on some golden age of democracy in America. Marxists believe America has always been dominated by the wealthy, though the domination has taken different forms at different times. Marxists also stress the class basis of domination. Instead of seeing elitism as a conspiracy of a few evil men, Marxists view it more impersonally, as a tendency inherent in capitalism.

One of the best-developed arguments disputing the populist-Marxist thesis that America is ruled by an unrepresentative elite is the argument of *pluralism*. Pluralists readily admit that there are many elites in our society. That is precisely their point: Because America contains so many groups, each has a tendency to counterbalance the power of the others. Thus, they believe, no group or coalition of groups can become an "establishment" in America.

Andrew Greeley, a priest and sociologist who teaches at the University of Arizona, argues the pluralist position in the following debate on elitism. On the other side, arguing the elitist thesis, is sociologist G. William Domhoff, who suggests that the corporate rich dominate all the decision-making positions in America.

YES

G. William Domhoff

THE POWER ELITE
AND GOVERNMENT

Members of the power elite directly involve themselves in the federal government through three basic processes, each of which plays a slightly different role in ensuring access to the White House, Congress, and specific agencies, departments, and committees in the executive branch. Although some of the same people are involved in all three processes, most people specialize in one or two of the three processes. This is because each process requires slightly different knowledge, skills, and contacts. The three processes are

1. The candidate selection process, through which members of the power elite attempt to influence electoral campaigns by means of campaign finances and favors to political candidates.
2. The special-interest process, through which specific individuals, corporations, and industrial sectors realize their narrow and short-run interests on taxes, subsidies, and regulation in dealing with congressional committees, regulatory bodies, and executive departments.
3. The policy-making process, through which the general policies of the policy-planning network . . . are brought to the White House and Congress.

The power elite involves itself in the candidate-selection process through the simple, direct, and often very unsubtle means of large campaign donations that far outweigh what other classes and groups can muster. Although the method of involvement is simple, the reason such a direct approach is possible requires a structural and historical understanding of why politics operate as they do in the United States. Only part of that understanding can be provided in this chapter, however. . . .

It is because the candidate-selection process in the American two-party system is so individualistic, and therefore dependent upon name recognition and personal image, that it can be in good part dominated by members of the power elite through the relatively simple and direct means of large campaign contributions. In the roles of both big donors and fund raisers, the same people who direct corporations and take part in policy groups play a central role in the careers of most politicians who advance beyond the local level in states of any size and consequence. "Recruitment of elective elites," concludes political scientist Walter D. Burnham, "remains closely associated, especially for the most important offices in the larger states, with the candidates' wealth or access to large campaign contributions."

The role of the wealthy donor and the fund raiser seems to be especially crucial in the nomination phase of the process. . . .

Several reforms in campaign finance during the 1970s that restricted the donation of large contributors at the national level and in some states have altered the system somewhat. . . . But these reforms have not diminished the influence of the corporate community. If anything, they have increased it quite inadvertently. In the past a handful of owners and executives would give tens or hundreds of thousands of dollars to candidates of interest to them. Now they organize luncheons and dinners at which all of their colleagues and friends are asked to give a few thousand dollars each to specific candidates and party finance committees. They also form what are called Political Action Committees (PACs) through which their stockholders and executives are asked to give up to $5,000 each year, depending upon their rank and salary in the corporate hierarchy. These committees, in turn, can contribute to all individual candidates. When a co-ordinated set of corporate PACs give to a candidate, the impact is considerable. . . .

There are other sources of campaign donations and financial favors besides the corporate community, of course, but they are neither as large nor as consistent in their donations. The role of small donations, particularly those raised through direct-mail appeals, receives considerable publicity, but it is minor when compared with that of big donors. Presidential candidate George M. McGovern raised $15 million from several hundred thousand donors in 1972, but he had to spend $4.5 of this in printing and postage, leaving him a net of only $10.5 million. By way of contrast, in the same year President Nixon raised over $19.8 million from people who gave $10,000 or more. Moreover, the McGovern campaign was dependent upon large loans from several millionaires to get its fund raising off the ground. . . .

What kinds of elected officials emerge from a political process that puts such great attention on campaign finance and media recognition? The answer is available from numerous studies. Politicians, especially those who hold the highest elective offices, are first of all people from the top 10 to 15 percent of the occupational and income ladders. Only a minority are from the upper class or corporate community, but in a majority of cases they share in common a business and legal background with members of the upper class.

Few twentieth-century Presidents have been from outside the very wealthiest circles. Theodore Roosevelt, William H. Taft, Franklin D. Roosevelt, and John F. Kennedy were from upper-class backgrounds. Herbert Hoover, Jimmy Carter, and Ronald Reagan were millionaires before they became deeply involved in national politics. Lyndon B. Johnson was a millionaire several times over through his wife's land dealings and his use of political leverage to gain a lucrative television license in Austin. Even Richard M. Nixon was a rich man when he finally attained the presidency in 1968, after earning high salaries as a corporate lawyer between

1. IS AMERICA RULED BY AN ELITE?

1963 and 1968 due to his ability to open political doors for corporate clients.

Studies of the social backgrounds and occupations of members of Congress have consistently shown that they come from the highest levels of society and are involved in the business and legal communities. A study of the Congress for 1972 found that 66 percent of the senators and 74 percent of the representatives came from the 10 percent of families with business or professional occupations, and that virtually all of the senators and representatives were themselves professional people or former business executives. Twenty percent of the senators and 5 percent of a sample of representatives were members of the upper class. Only 5 percent of the senators had been farmers or ranchers; none had been blue-collar workers. Three percent of the representatives had been farmers or ranchers, and 3 percent had union backgrounds. A comparison of these findings with a study of the Senate in the mid-1950s and the House in the early 1940s showed that there had been very little change over that time span, except for a decrease in the number of farmers and a slight increase in the number of professionals and business executives.

The stringent financial disclosure laws adopted by Congress in the mid-1970s in the aftermath of Watergate and other scandals provided detailed information on the wealth and income of senators and representatives for 1978. Changes in the law since that time suggest that it may be the best information ever to become available. Still, the information is not exact because the questionnaire required disclosure only within general ranges for each category of ownership and income. In the Senate the highest point on the ownership scale was "over $5 million"; in the House it was "over $250,000."

Nineteen members of the Senate were clearly millionaires, 10 from the Republican side and 9 from the Democratic. It was possible that another 13 or 14 were also millionaires, but the general categories did not permit accurate assessment in their cases. The largest income was that of the Republican senator from Pennsylvania, Henry J. Heinz III, with between $437,000 and $836,000. Democratic Senator Edward M. Kennedy of Massachusetts had dividend income between $288,000 and $581,000. In all, 95 of the senators had incomes from stocks or rent from real estate investments, and some held directorships or other positions in the business world. As one example, Thomas Eagleton, the Democratic senator from Missouri, continued to be a vice-president in his family's company, Missouri Pipe Fitting. He also received over $100,000 in dividends from all sources.

The less complete information on House members was nonetheless revealing in that one-third of House members had outside jobs, many in real estate or as bank directors, and 460 had income from stock or rent from real estate. At least 30 representatives were millionaires, and nearly 100 had outside incomes of $20,000 or more. Jack Brooks, a Democrat from Texas, received $56,000 in 1978 from two banks of which he was a director. Republican John J. Rhodes of Arizona, the House minority leader, was paid $32,000 for his service as a vice-president in an insurance company. The conclusions drawn by the editors of Congressional Quarterly from these data are similar to those reached by the authors of earlier studies: "With few exceptions, members of Congress were successful lawyers or businessmen before coming to Washington. Most members kept and expanded their lucrative financial investments after election to Congress."

The second general finding concerning the nature of elected officials in the United States is that a great many of them are lawyers. In 1972, for example, 70 percent of the senators and 51 percent of the representatives were lawyers, and the tion is similar for earlier times and at the state level. Of 995 elected governors for all states between 1870 and 1950, 46 percent were practicing lawyers. Twenty-five of the first 40 American Presidents were lawyers. The large percentage of lawyers in the American political system is highly atypical when compared with other countries, where only 10 to 30 percent of legislators have a legal background. An insight into this overrepresentation may be provided by comparing the United States with a deviant case at the other extreme, Denmark, where only 2 percent of legislators are lawyers. The class-based nature of Danish politics since the late nineteenth century, and the fact that political careers are not pathways to judicial appointments, are thought to discourage lawyer participation in that country. The Danish situation thus suggests that the classless nature of American political parties, combined with the intimate involvement of the parties in the judicial system, creates a climate for strong lawyer involvement in the political system.

Whatever the reasons for their involvement, lawyers are the occupational grouping that by training and career needs are ideal go-betweens and compromisers. They have the skills to balance the relationship between the corporate community that finances them on the one hand and the citizens who vote for them on the other. They are the supreme "pragmatists" in a nation where pragmatism is a central element in the self-deceiving ideology that the country has no ideology. They have an ability to be dispassionate about "the issues"

and to discuss them in legalistic ways that are confusing to all concerned. They have been socialized to be discreet, and they can claim the cloak of "lawyer-client privilege" when questioned about work for their clients that seems to overlap with their political activities.

Though some lawyers see politics as a vocation, and indeed become lawyers because they knew the law to be the best avenue to elected office, others have been quite frank in telling social scientists that they see politics as an opportunity to make the kinds of connections that will advance their law careers. Whereas businesspeople and other professionals are hampered in their careers if they take a few years off to try their hand at politics, the nature of a legal practice makes it easy and beneficial for lawyers to go into politics. Win or lose, lawyer-politicians learn the governmental system and meet potential clients. Many lawyer-legislators at the state and national level work for corporate clients while they are in office, although the practice declined dramatically at the national level after the scandals of the 1970s.

Whether elected officials are lawyers or not, the third general result of the candidate-selection process is a large number of very ambitious people who are eager to "go along to get along," in the famous advice of former House speaker Sam Rayburn. To understand the behavior of a politician, concludes political scientist Joseph A. Schlesinger, "it is more important to know what he wants to be than how he got to where he is now." This ambition, whether it be for wealth or higher office, makes politicians especially available to those who can help them rise, and such people are often members of the upper class and corporate community with money to contribute and connections to other districts, states, or regions where striving

1. IS AMERICA RULED BY AN ELITE?

candidates need new friends. Thus, even the most liberal or archconservative of politicians may develop a new circle of moderate supporters as he or she moves from the local to the congressional to the presidential level, gradually becoming more and more involved with leading figures within the power elite. . . .

The way in which Presidents rely on people from the policy groups in making appointments to government can be seen very dramatically in the varying cases of John F. Kennedy, Jimmy Carter, and Ronald Reagan. After winning an election based on promises of a "new frontier" and the image of an urbane liberalism, President-elect Kennedy called in Republican Robert Lovett, a Wall Street investment banker who was a former member of the Committee for Economic Development and the Council on Foreign Relations as well as a former Secretary of Defense. Kennedy wished to have Lovett's advice on possible appointments to the new administration. Lovett soon became, according to historian and Kennedy-aide Arthur M. Schlesinger, Jr., the "chief agent" between Kennedy and the "American Establishment." Schlesinger defined this establishment as consisting primarily of financiers and corporate lawyers who were an "arsenal of talent which had so long furnished a steady supply of always orthodox and often able people to Democratic as well as Republican administrations." Lovett seemed to be an unusual adviser for a President-elect who had promised to "get the country moving again," but Kennedy needed experienced experts to run the government. . . .

The contrast between President Carter's campaign rhetoric and his deference to the established experts was equally great. One of his main campaign themes was that as a down-home populist he was not a part of the "mess" in Washington. He was a man of the people who would bring new faces into his administration. One of his top aides, Hamilton Jordan, went so far as to promise that two of the old faces, Cyrus Vance and Zbigniew Brzezinski, would never serve in a Carter administration: "If, after the inauguration, you find a Cy Vance as Secretary of State and Zbigniew Brzezinski as head of National Security, then I would say we failed. . . . The government is going to be run by people you never heard of." Indeed, Jordan added that he would quit if Carter made such establishment appointments. A few months later, two of Carter's first appointments were Cyrus Vance—a Wall Street lawyer, director of several corporations, trustee of the Rockefeller Foundation, and member of the Council on Foreign Relations—as secretary of state, and Zbigniew Brzezinski—a foreign policy analyst and a member of the Council on Foreign Relations—as White House foreign-policy adviser. Jordan stayed on as a White House aide to Carter.

The other top appointments were equally predictable. The new secretary of defense was Harold Brown, president of the California Institute of Technology, a director of several corporations, a member of the Council on Foreign Relations, and a former appointee in the Department of Defense. The secretary of treasury was W. Michael Blumenthal, president of the Bendix Corporation and a trustee of the Rockefeller Foundation, the Council on Foreign Relations, the Committee for Economic Development, and Princeton University. Carter had come to know Vance, Brzezinski, Brown, and Blumenthal in the preceding three years as fellow participants in the Trilateral Commission, the international policy discussion group founded in 1973 to think about a new world order for the 1980s. There soon followed the news that many Trilateral members—thirteen in all—were to become members of the new administration. Journalists began to debate whether the cabinet was more connected to the Council on Foreign Relations, Rockefeller Foundation, IBM, Trilateral Commission, Coca-Cola, or Wall Street.

As with Carter, Reagan came to the Presidency with a promise to do something about all the problems that allegedly were being caused by the federal government. However, as a neoconservative he would accomplish this feat by removing the establishment figures who supposedly had caused them. Edward Meese III, who went on to serve as one of Reagan's most important White House advisers, told *Business Week* that "you will see people who have never served in Washington before and who can make a significant change in the course of government. It's like bringing a new management team to turn around a failing business."

Nonetheless, Reagan's first secretary of state was a former army officer, Alexander Haig, who had served as an aide to the secretary of defense in the 1960s and to Henry Kissinger and then President Nixon in the 1970s. He was president of United Technologies, a director of Chase Manhattan Bank, Crown Cork & Seal, Texas Instruments, and Conagra as well as being a member of the Council on Foreign Relations when he was appointed. Reagan's second appointment to that position, George Shultz, was president of the Bechtel Corporation, one of the largest construction firms in the world, and a director of Morgan Guaranty Trust. He also was a director of the Council on Foreign Relations, a former adviser to the Committee for Economic Development, and a former secretary of both labor and treasury in the Nixon administration.

The secretary of defense, Caspar Wein-berger, was a corporate lawyer from San Francisco who had served in three different positions in Washington between 1970 and 1975. He was a vice-president and general counsel of the Bechtel Corporation, a director of Pepsico and Quaker Oats, and a member of the Trilateral Commission when chosen for the position. As for the secretary of treasury, Donald T. Regan, he was the chief executive officer of Merrill, Lynch, a trustee of the Committee for Economic Development, a member of the policy committee of the Business Roundtable, and a member of the Council on Foreign Relations.

The rest of the Reagan administration also consisted of members of the corporate community who had previous government experience or visibility in the policy-planning network. To the consternation of the John Birch Society, there were many other appointees who were members of the Council on Foreign Relations in addition to Haig, Shultz, and Regan. They included the director of the CIA, the secretary of commerce, the special trade adviser, the deputy secretary of defense, and eight top-level appointments at the State Department. According to one cataloguing of over 90 advisers, consultants, and members of the Reagan administration in early 1981, 31 were members of the Council on Foreign Relations, 25 were associated with the American Enterprise Institute, 13 were affiliated with the Center for Strategic and International Studies at Georgetown University, and 12 were participants in the Trilateral Commission. . . .

Scholarly studies of cabinet appointments demonstrate in a more systematic way that the corporate community is highly overrepresented in government. However, those done by pluralists, though attesting to the presence of corporate officials in government, underestimate the actual extent of corporate involvement by placing lawyers in a separate category from businessmen even when their firms have major corporations as their clients. Fortunately, the work of sociologist Beth Mintz and political scientist Philip Burch reveals the full extent of corporate involvements.

The study by Mintz focused on the 205 individuals who served in presidential cabinets between 1897 and 1972. Defining her indicators of the "social elite" to include the 105 social clubs listed in the front of the *Social Register*, in addition to the *Social Register* itself, ... she found that 60 percent of the cabinet members were members of the upper class. Defining the "business elite" broadly in terms of service on at least one board of directors in any business corporation, or as membership in any corporation-oriented law firm, she also found that 78 percent were members of the business community. About half the cabinet officers were members of both the social and business elites as defined in this study. There were no differences in the overall percentages for Democratic and Republican administrations, or for the years before and after 1933.

The exhaustive three-volume study by Burch covers cabinet officers, diplomats, and Supreme Court justices for every administration from George Washington through Jimmy Carter. It uses a more restricted definition than the Mintz study of what Burch calls the "economic elite," but it comes to similar conclusions except in the case of the New Deal administration of Franklin D. Roosevelt. For Burch, the economic elite are those who hold executive positions, directorships, or partnerships in a large corporation or law firm "at or around" the time of government appointment, or are from families with "considerable" wealth or top-level executive or director ties. What is considered to be a large corporation or law firm varies from generation to generation with the growth of the economy.

For the years 1789 to 1861, Burch concludes that 96 percent of the cabinet and diplomatic appointees were members of the economic elite, with a great many landowners, lawyers, and merchants in the group. From 1861 to 1933, the figure was 84 percent, with an increasing number of financiers and corporate lawyers. The figures in this era varied from a low of 57 percent for the Wilson years to a high of 90 percent for the McKinley-Roosevelt-Taft era. The overall percentage fell to 64 percent for the years 1933 to 1980, with only 47 percent of the appointees during the New Deal coming from the largest of corporations and law firms. The percentages for the last three eras in the study were about the same—63 percent for the Kennedy-Johnson years, 69 percent for the Nixon-Ford years, and 65 percent for the Carter administration.

The most dramatic change uncovered in Burch's study was in appointments to the Supreme Court. From 1789 to 1937, members of the Supreme Court were primarily upper-class lawyers, many of whom had little judicial experience before their appointments. However, between 1937 and 1943 Roosevelt made eight appointments to the court, none of whom were from the corporate community. Three were law school professors with extensive government experience, and the other five had served as senators, attorneys general, or solicitor general. President Harry S. Truman continued this pattern in all four of his appointments, three of whom were former senators and one a former attorney general. Between 1952 and 1980, 9 of the 14 appointees were once again corporate lawyers, but the nature of the court had been altered nonetheless. Only 4 of the 14 had upper-class backgrounds, most had had previous judicial or government experience, and there was a strong sentiment that a variety of groups deserved some representation on the court.

One of our studies shows that corporate involvement in appointed positions in the executive branch also extends below the cabinet-level positions. Of 120 secretaries, under secretaries, and assistant secretaries in the Nixon administration, including those for the Army, Navy, and Air Force, 35 percent came from the corporate community, with another 20 percent coming from small business or small law firms. Only 28 percent had spent most of their occupational careers in government. The majority of those with government careers were serving as assistant secretaries for administration, accounting, or public relations, except in the case of the State Department, where members of the foreign service often attained significant positions.

This study also demonstrated the close relationship between government and the corporate community in another way, by determining where appointed officials go when they leave their positions. Tracing the careers of the Nixon appointees to 1979, it was found that several of the small businesspeople and lawyers, along with 7 of the 16 career employees who left government service, took positions in the corporate community as vice-presidents, trade association executives, or lobbyists. Most of those originally from the corporate community who did not retire also re-

turned to it. The corporate community not only regained most of its members who had gone to government but was infused with new members who had gained what it thought to be valuable government experience that can be of use to the corporations in the future.

The general picture that emerges from this information on the overrepresentation of members of the corporate community and policy network in appointed governmental positions is that the highest levels of the executive branch, especially in the State, Defense, and Treasury departments, are interlocked constantly with the corporate community through the movement of executives and lawyers in and out of government. Although the same person is not in government and corporate positions at the same time, there is enough continuity for the relationship to be described as one of "revolving interlocks." Corporate leaders sever their numerous directorships to serve in government for two or three years, then return to the corporate community in a same or different capacity. This system gives corporate officials temporary independence from the narrow concerns of their own companies and allows them to perform the more general roles they have learned in the policy-planning groups. However, it does not give them the time or inclination to become fully independent of the corporate community or to develop a perspective that includes the interests of other classes and groups. . . .

NO
Andrew M. Greeley

BUILDING COALITIONS

It is important that all of us who are concerned about politics realize that only on occasion can we legitimately blame a vague and shadowy "them" for our problems. Admittedly, it would be much easier if we could; then we could just sweep "them" out of office and replace them with some of "us." But one of the melancholy results of a democratic society in which power is widely diffused is that "they" turn out in the final analysis to be "we.". . .

There is a good deal to be said for the elitist viewpoint, and anyone who approaches American society with the naive notion that power is equally distributed in the population and that mere persuasive argumentation will mobilize the power in favor of social change is simply asking for trouble.

1. Some people have more power than others. The president of General Motors, for example, is likely to have more influence on decisions that are made in Washington than the assembly-line worker. The archbishop of Chicago is likewise going to have greater impact on what the Catholic Church does than the parish priest. Compared to Mayor Daley or County President George Dunne or Governor Walker or the president of the Chicago Board of Trade or of Marshall Field and Company or the *Chicago Sun-Times* I am relatively powerless about what happens in my native city. Indeed, a member of the United Steel Workers of America probably has more power than I do, because he is at least able to bring pressure on city events through his union that I am not able to bring because I lack some sort of intermediate pressure group standing between me and the city.

2. Because of the way power is distributed in American society, certain groups of men, either because of their position or because of the support they can command from large organizations, can have decisive power on specific issues, no matter what anyone else thinks. While it is rare that the combination of these

powerful men can override the strongly felt convictions of a majority of the population, it is generally unnecessary for them to try. On most issues the majority of the population, is relatively indifferent. Thus if the *Chicago Tribune* determines that there is to be a lakefront exposition hall named after their late beloved publisher, it is likely to succeed because it needs only the support of a few city leaders, and opposition to it is likely to be limited to a small segment of the population. A majority of Chicagoans probably don't care much one way or the other about the lakefront hall; if asked, they may be vaguely for it. It will be virtually impossible for the opposition to organize massive antagonism toward the idea among the general population.

3. Some extremely critical decisions are made in American society by a handful of men. For example, the decision to go ahead with the Bay of Pigs invasion and the subsequent decision to respond to the Russian intrusion of missiles into Cuba by a blockade were made by a handful of men in secret. So too, apparently, have most of the decisions in the Indochina war been made by a small group operating in secret. These men obviously do not make their decisions in complete isolation from the pressures of the wishes and opinions of the rest of society, and they also eventually run the risk of being ejected from political office if what they do displeases at least a majority of those who vote in an election. Nevertheless, most of us do not have much power in the making of foreign policy. Our influence on foreign policy is limited to what the political leadership thinks our limits of hostile response are and to our plebiscite on election day.

4. Well-organized pressure groups do exercise an influence on American society all out of proportion to the size of their membership and the representativeness of their opinions. Even though there is strong national support for gun control legislation, for example, the National Rifle Association has been successful in limiting gun control laws and in punishing senators who have dared to push too vigorously against the association. This is but one example of an incredible number of pressure groups that zealously watch social events to make sure that the well-being of their members—judged, of course, by the professional staff of the organization—is not harmed by what goes on among the political leaders.

5. David Riesman and others have called these pressure groups (which run all the way from the United States Catholic Conference to the National Education Association and include the United Steelworkers of America, the American Chamber of Commerce, and a vast variety of other thoroughly reliable and respectable institutions) "veto groups," that is, their power is most effective in preventing things from happening than in causing them to happen. The American Medical Association, for example, has effectively vetoed national health insurance for several decades, but it has not displayed much power in getting positive legislation for its own benefit. The veto groups may occasionally join forces with one another and rally around some common cause, but under normal circumstances they are much better at saying no than at saying yes.

6. But when all these concessions are made to the accuracy of the elitist analysis, one is still faced with the fact that they miss the most critical obstacle to social reform in the United States, and that obstacle is not the existence of an establishment but the relative nonexistence of one. To put the matter somewhat differently, it is the lack of concentration of power that is the real obstacle to social reform.

1. IS AMERICA RULED BY AN ELITE?

Let us take two examples. First of all, if there were an establishment of business, military, intellectual, and political leaders who did in fact exercise political control over the country, they would have gotten us out of the Vietnam war long before they did. The war was bad for business, bad for education, bad for government, bad for everyone in sight. It combined inflation with recession, alienated the youth, split the college campuses wide open, and had a rending effect on the whole fabric of American society. Furthermore, American business did not profit from the war, American political leaders did not profit from it (they generally lost elections because of it), and the American people, whose sons were killed, did not profit from it. Almost all the influential national journals were against it, and even the military muttered that it was trapped into the war by intellectual advisors of the president against their better judgment. Nevertheless, though it may have been desirable for all concerned to get us out of the war, there never existed a powerful establishment that could convene itself and announce that the war was over. The young people who vigorously demonstrated against the war were frustrated and angry because they could not communicate with the establishment to make it end the war. They might have considered the possibility that if there were an establishment, it certainly would have ended the war. The reason they can't communicate with an establishment is that there isn't one.

One can also take it as well established that the best way to cope with housing pressures in America's large cities is to distribute substantial segments of the black population in the suburban fringe that rings these large cities. Political leaders, business leaders, research experts, community leaders, virtually everyone would agree that the desegregation of the suburbs is absolutely essential for coping with problems of urban housing. Yet there does not exist in American society a group of men powerful enough to enforce such a decision over the collective opposition of all the suburban veto groups. If there were an establishment with a base of power, we would certainly have blacks in the suburbs.

The implication of the previous paragraph is that an establishment should be capable of benign as well as malign activity. Many benign actions would be very much in the self-interest of any establishment worthy of the name. That these benign things do not get done is, I think, conclusive evidence that, alas, there is no establishment. Things would be much simpler and neater if there were.

Implicit in radical criticism of the establishment is the strategy that argues that if one replaced the existing establishment with a new one composed of radical elitists and representing "the people," then one could institute benign social reforms. Professor [C. Wright] Mills* was quite explicit about that. He did not so much advocate the abolition of the power elite as making it responsible—responsible to intellectuals. But obviously it could not be made responsible to all intellectuals, so Mills decided that the power elite should be responsible to those intellectuals who happened to have the same ideas on foreign policy that he did. The power elite, in other words, will become "responsible" when it is willing to do what C. Wright Mills and his colleagues tell it to do. On the whole, I am not sure I would have liked to be governed by Professor Mills or any of his successors. I very much doubt that we could have worked out an arrangement whereby they would have been willing to

*Late professor of sociology at Columbia University and author of The Power Elite (Oxford, 1956). Eds.

26

stand for reelection. It would be interesting to see what those critics of the establishment would do if they became it. They would discover, of course, as do all government leaders, how limited their powers really are. They would probably suspect some sort of conspiracy on the part of shadowy forces still existing in the society bent on frustrating their noble plans. Like most other Jacobins before them, they would probably use force to destroy the conspiracy, only to discover that even force has its limitations as a means of effective government.

The most important obstacle to social change in the United States, then, is not the concentration of power but its diffusion. If power was concentrated sufficiently, those of us who wish for change would merely have to negotiate with those who hold the power and, if necessary, put pressure on them. But power is so widely diffused that, in many instances, there is no one to negotiate with and no one on whom to put pressure. American society has been organized from the beginning around two premises: (1)"The central guiding trend of American constitutional development has been the evolution of a political system in which all the active and legitimate groups in the population can make themselves heard at some crucial stage in the process of decision."* The second principle is a corollary of the first: (2) The larger society cannot ignore for very long what a given group considers to be its fundamental self-interest. No group, in other words, can be expected to assume the role of the permanent loser. . . .

One can fault this system of pluralism in two respects. First, one can say that it has

*Robert A. Dahl, *Preface to Democratic Theory* (Chicago: University of Chicago Press, 1956), p. 137.

failed according to its own principles; that certain disadvantaged groups are not given an adequate hearing or that society does not recognize its obligation to facilitate the development of political power in these groups. The criticism is certainly a valid one. The very nobility of the political ideal implied in American pluralism makes departures from it unfortunate and ugly, but if this is the only criticism one has to make, then the strategy is obvious: one must bargain to persuade the rest of society that its consensus must be broadened sufficiently to admit these other groups as valued and equal participants in the enterprise.

The second criticism is that given the complexities and difficulties of the modern world, the diffusion of power that exists in American society is dangerously inefficient. If one has to bargain with Polish surgeons, Latvian truckdrivers, red-necked farmers, Irish politicians, conservative black clergymen, Jewish garment makers, Swedish computer operators, Texas oil barons, Portuguese fishermen from Fall River, and cattle ranchers from Montana in order to win support for absolutely imperative social changes, then these changes will be delayed, perhaps for too long, while the evil and injustice continues. It is demeaning, degrading, and immoral to have to bargain for the elimination of clear and obvious injustice. Racism is obscene, war is obscene; both should go away without our having to bargain on the subject. A political system that distributes power so that bargaining is necessary to eliminate obscene immorality is in itself not merely inefficient but immoral. It is not proper that those who are moral and wise should be forced to negotiate with those who are immoral and stupid.

This is a logically and consistently coherent case; in effect, it advocates the abolition of the pluralistic bargaining, co-alition-forming polity that we currently have. It advocates taking the slack out of the political system and placing it in the hands of a ruling elite that would be both virtuous enough and powerful enough to accomplish quickly those social changes deemed urgent or imperative. One supposes that a strong case can be made for issues like pollution, population control, and racial injustice not to be made subject to the bargaining process, that wise and virtuous ruling elites should enforce by legislation and by police power, if necessary, the regulations that cope with these problems. The issues are so critical that there is no time to bargain with those whose intelligence and sensitivity is so deficient that they cannot see how imperative it is that action be taken with utmost speed. One can, I say, make a convincing case for such a political system, but let it be clear that it is an elite-establishmentarian system with a vengence, that it bears no similarity to what normally has been considered democracy, that it is completely at odds with the American political tradition, and completely objectionable to most Americans. . . .

If this model of American society is correct, the appropriate political strategy for those who wish to accomplish social change is not to tear down the establishment but rather to seek allies to form coalitions of various individuals and groups with some commonality of interest. These coalitions will represent an amassing of power that will be stronger than the power of those whose behavior we think is socially injurious. Thus, for example, a coalition was finally put together to force both safety and antipollution devices on the American automobile industry. It took a long time to put such a coalition together—indeed, much too long. Coalitions must be formed more rapidly if we are going to be able to cope with the critical problems that constantly arise in advanced industrial societies. The alternative to winning allies for one's cause is to impose it on the majority of one's fellow citizens whether they like it or not. Not only would this mean the end of political freedom, but it also might be extremely risky, because once we have begun to impose our will as a minority we run the risk that they may start counting noses and in full realization of our minority position, impose their will on us.

There was one thing clear in the summer and fall of 1972. Practitioners of the New Politics were as capable of misusing power as were the "corrupt bosses" whom they supposedly replaced. It did not, however, appear that they were substantially superior to the bosses in their capacity to use power intelligently. Indeed, a persuasive case could be made that as power brokers, the New Politicians were as inept as they were at everything else. Those who wish to rebuild the Democratic coalition can ill afford to be naive about the position of power in American society. Neither can they afford the naivete of raging against mythical dragons like "the establishment." There may well be certain concentrations of power in American society that the reconstructed Democratic coalition will want to break up, but it must first amass for itself a sufficient concentration of political power to be able to have a reasonable chance of winning an election and implementing its program. The builders of the new Democratic coalition must understand what their predecessors of 1972 apparently did not: One builds political power not by excluding people but by including them.

POSTSCRIPT

IS AMERICA RULED BY AN ELITE?

The arguments of both Domhoff and Greeley raise questions. Greeley freely acknowledges that America is a society with gradations of power. Just as a parish priest does not have the same power as a bishop, so ordinary citizens are less powerful than political office-holders, or assembly-line workers at General Motors less powerful than the corporation's president. Does Greeley mean to suggest that hierarchy is inherent in all political relationships? What, then, becomes of the concept of popular sovereignty? As for Domhoff, his argument seems to turn upon the number of rich people from corporate backgrounds who serve in government. But is this really relevant? People in high office are generally well-to-do, and, in America, business is an important route to wealth. But if Domhoff has gone further, if he has demonstrated that the people who govern America are not only rich but alike in their political views, if those views are contrary to the views of the majority of Americans, and if the governing elites nevertheless enforce them upon the majority, then Domhoff's argument is very telling indeed. But has he demonstrated that? No doubt Ronald Reagan, Cyrus Vance, Zbigniew Brzezinski, and George McGovern would be startled to find themselves lumped into the same "power elite."

The literature of political science and sociology contains many confrontations between elite-theory and pluralism. In his refutation of elite-theory, Greeley makes reference to C. Wright Mills' *The Power Elite* (Oxford, 1956), which is a classic statement of elite-theory. As for pluralism, Greeley cites with approval Robert Dahl and David Riesman. Dahl's *Preface to Democratic Theory* (University of Chicago Press, 1969) and *Who Governs?* (Yale, 1961) are elaborate defenses of the pluralistic thesis. Reisman's *The Lonely Crowd* (Yale, 1961) deals with a number of aspects of American society, including what he calls "veto groups." Political scientist Michael Parenti has written an American government textbook, *Democracy for the Few* (St. Martin's, 1980), based on the Domhoffian thesis that our politics and government are dominated by rich corporate elites.

One way of evaluating the pluralist and elitist perspectives on who rules America would be to study them in terms of concrete examples. We might ask, for example, what significant events have occurred in America over the past twenty years. The list would probably have to include the civil rights revolution, the Vietnam War, the rise (or reappearance) of feminism, the exposure and repercussions of Watergate, and the passage of the 1986 tax reform law. Were all these the work of one elite "establishment" or did they result from an interaction of groups in the political arena?

ISSUE 2

HAS PARTY REFORM SUCCEEDED?

YES: William J. Crotty, from *Decisions for the Democrats: Reforming the Party Structure* (Baltimore, 1978)

NO: Everett Carll Ladd, Jr., from *Where Have All the Voters Gone?* (New York, 1978)

ISSUE SUMMARY

YES: William Crotty contends that reform has opened up the political process and has given unprecedented influence to the rank-and-file party members.
NO: Everett Carll Ladd believes that since the era of reform began, the political parties have become less able to perform their primary task of providing acceptable candidates for elective office.

The present two-party system in America became fixed a century and a quarter ago, shortly after the Civil War. Until recently, the Democratic and Republican parties enjoyed great popular support. People tended to identify themselves—and their families, regions, and ethnic groups—with one of the major parties. A striking change has taken place in recent years. One-third of all adult Americans consider themselves independent, refusing to identify with either party, and that proportion is even higher among young voters.

The decline of parties is related to Vietnam and Watergate and the ways in which these events reflected unfavorably upon the parties. It may also stem from the increasing influence of television. Television makes party politics look either suspicious or ridiculous. It also focuses upon the personality of the campaigner, weakening the tie of party loyalty. The increasing mobility and sophistication of Americans weakened their ties to family, birthplace, and social class—all of which once supported party bonds as well.

Liberals and conservatives alike often deplore the absence of meaningful ideological choice between the major parties. Liberals have also bemoaned what they perceived as the undemocratic processes by which the parties chose their candidates, particularly the candidate for president. Simmering resentment came to a boil at the 1968 Democratic convention in Chicago. Bitterness within the convention, protests in the streets outside, and the use of excessive force against the demonstrators broke the party apart, and it was unable to pull itself completely together before the presidential election. However, the ill-fated convention adopted a mandate for procedural reform whose impact has changed the presidential nominating process and, with it, the character of the national parties.

Reforms initiated by a party commission went into effect at the Democratic convention in 1972. One of the major reforms called for proportional representation of women, blacks, and young people in the state delegations. This was nearly achieved in the 1972 convention—but at the price of excluding many party leaders (including prominent elected officials) from holding seats at the convention. Another major reform required that delegate votes be apportioned in accordance with the support each candidate received in the caucus or primary at which the delegates were chosen.

Because of the Democratic reforms, many states abandoned the convention and caucus methods of delegate selection in order to comply with the national party's requirements. The change affected the Republican process of delegate selection as well. As a result, thirty-seven states held primaries in 1980, as compared with seventeen in 1968. As the reformers had predicted, the changes opened up party meetings and reduced the influence of party bosses; rules for delegate selection were made specific where they had previously been vague; and minority points of view were heard in party councils where they had previously been denied. Because primaries were more numerous and received more attention, voter turnout was higher.

Perhaps the most significant consequence of the changes was the diminished importance of the convention. It had been reduced to a mere ratifying body for the candidate who was chosen in the primaries. That candidate—as was the case with the Democrats in 1972 (McGovern) and 1976 (Carter)—might receive fewer than half of the primary votes but have more than any other single candidate. In 1980, widespread dissatisfaction with the nominations of Jimmy Carter and Ronald Reagan suggested that there were leaders within both parties who might have commanded broader support both within party ranks and with independent voters. Because the Democrats believed that the give-and-take of the nominating convention was more likely to result in the designation of a nominee who was at least not unacceptable to most groups within the party, they set about reforming the reforms. The 1984 convention contained more elected party leaders who were not bound by primary votes. It is unlikely that the old convention system will be restored, but it is bound to play a more significant role than it has in the last decade.

William J. Crotty defends these reforms as the beginnings of party democracy. Everett Carll Ladd, Jr., opposes them as having contributed to the decline of the political parties.

YES
William J. Crotty

DECISION FOR THE DEMOCRATS

The year 1968 seemed predestined for sorrow. It suffered from the accumulated grievances of the preceding years, which were exacerbated by two assassinations, riots, and an administration hellbent on pursuing a major war while denying that this was its intent. It experienced a government out-of-touch with its public and neglectful, to the point of being scornful, of any and all dissent from its policies, and it witnessed a frustration born of attempting a challenge through conventional means destined to be mocked by a system unresponsive at best, closed at worst, to its pressures. The result was the explosions that shook the nation during the Chicago convention.

The "why" of Chicago is relatively easy to document. Far more difficult is tracing and evaluating the response of the political parties. The reaction of the parties, and especially the Democratic party, to the upheavals was unprecedented by any standard: it resulted in nothing less than an attempt to reshape fundamental structural mechanisms to better accommodate a diversity of views, to provide a fully representative and "open" convention, and to modernize, in line with democratic principles, procedures notoriously unreceptive to change. Whether these ambitious goals were achieved, and at what price, is another story. It is possible, though, that the reforms emanating from the convention are of far greater substantive importance than anything to emerge from that fateful election year. . . .

Party reform took second place to a lackluster general election campaign in the fall. The Humphrey campaign meandered, spiritually and organizationally, toward a November decision. The Nixon drive concentrated on packaged media presentations, carefully worded slogans designed to reassure an anxious electorate, and the presentation of a low political profile engineered to take advantage of the divisiveness within the Democratic ranks and the schisms in a tired electorate. The voters did not appear inclined to award any of the contenders with a decisive plurality. Everyone appeared relieved when

From *Decision for the Democrats: Reforming the Party Structure* Copyright ©1978, The Johns Hopkins University Press. Reprinted by permission.

the unhappiest of election years finally drew to its inevitable close.

While the victorious Republican candidate readied himself for his oath of office, another inauguration of sorts was being prepared for January, though this one received considerably less press and public attention. The efforts of a broken and dispirited party to reexamine its unhappy immediate past and to remedy its ways to insure, in the words of George Mc-Govern, that the events of 1968, and particularly the gross abuses that occurred at the Chicago convention, would never happen again, do not constitute an especially interesting story. Yet defeat—especially after an election year so debilitating for a party—can lead to a period of profound change and, in time, to a spiritual regenesis. This had happened to the Republicans after a bitter defeat in 1912, and, on a more superficial level, after their loss in 1964. In a different manner, a defeat was about to trigger a profound transformation of Democratic party procedures, one without precedent in the history of the American two-party experience. . . .

The reforms introduced a remarkable era to American politics. More was attempted, and accomplished, than can truthfully be said to have been envisioned in the decades since the Progressive movement of the early 1900s. Remarkably, the reforms had been initiated and executed by a political party that perceived itself to be in trouble. In contrast to earlier attempts at political change, the intent was to strengthen and preserve an institution of incomparable value to the American political system rather than to destroy or replace it.

The changes introduced were many. The traditional priorities of American party structure had been reversed. The national party units had attempted, with some success, to establish a code of fair and decent behavior and to have it prevail in the conduct of party business. A sense of rationality had been introduced into an incredibly complex system, and an aura of openness and equity had begun to prevail in several areas—changes in the presidential nominating process, the most significant of the national parties' duties, appeared to be an excellent foreboding of future changes in all aspects of party operations. A series of organizational structures and institutional values, little changed since the formation of the political parties over a century and a quarter earlier, were giving way to a new sense of national purpose and, it was hoped, a relevancy and responsiveness to constituent pressures, responsibilities neither party had acquitted impressively over the years.

The political implications of what the reforms were attempting to accomplish were never far from mind. The work of the reformers would effectively open the party in two regards. First, it would permit new groups to enter and make their views as to policy or candidates felt without depending on the goodwill or sponsorship of party elders whose favor they would have had to curry. Second, it would develop the foundation for establishing a permanent set of rules that would treat all with an impartiality previously unknown in party circles. It is too much to argue that such objectives were achieved by the first, and more than likely the most decisive, of the reform bursts, but a substantial beginning had been made.

Party processes were given a new legitimacy at a time when parties had begun to appear increasingly irrelevant to the solution of the main problems besetting

33

American life and when both party and the political system more broadly needed whatever support they could muster. In these terms then—and they are impressive—the reform movement, and most significantly the achievements of the McGovern-Fraser Commission, had accomplished a good deal. In its own way the reform era constituted a revolution in party operations, notable as much for its impact on traditional modes of thinking as on the structures it placed in question. One would be hard pressed to find comparable moments of achievement in the long history of political parties in this nation.

WHAT REFORM ACCOMPLISHED

The ramifications of the reform period were many. A listing of the accomplishments and their broader implications would include the following.

OPENING THE PARTY

The party was opened and, in the process, made more responsive to and representative of its rank and file. The new openness was meant to extend to all aspects of the party organization. The effort was made, for example, by the Sanford Commission, to extend procedural guarantees of fair play to party organizations from the local to the national levels. The party charter set standards and established guidelines for all manners of party deliberations. The Sanford Commission, in conjunction with the McGovern-Fraser, O'Hara, and, to a lesser extent, Mikulski commissions, attempted to restructure party institutions to make them more responsive to grassroots sentiments.

The most notable success in opening

the party to influence from the rank and file was the transformation of the presidential nominating process. The work of the McGovern-Fraser Commission, of course, was responsible for turning a relatively closed nominating process, controlled primarily by the party regulars, into one directly reflective of the concerns of those party members who chose to participate in delegate selection.

REARRANGING POWER DISTRIBUTIONS WITHIN THE PARTY

In the process of opening presidential nominations, the power relationships within the Democratic party were rearranged. Gaining increased influence were the party activitists and candidate supporters who worked during presidential election years to advance a cause, an issue, or a presidential contender with whom they identified. For the most part, these tended to be the professional people—lawyers, businessmen, teachers—and the young persons, blacks, housewives, and minority groups attracted to the party during the significant prenominating races. Losing influence were the power-wielders of the pre-1972 period: the party regulars, elected officials (governors, congressmen, senators, ·mayors, state legislators), party organizational personnel (state chairmen, national committee representatives, county chairmen), and the "fat cats," as they were called, of the business world who sought influence in politics by bankrolling candidates and campaigns and on whom the party had been heavily dependent. Also losing power in the new alignment favored by the reform procedures were the southern states and their parties, which were experiencing transformations, and the old-line factions and interest groups at the state and national levels, which had at least been consulted on nominations. These latter groups had held, in many cases, a negative veto over both candidates for the presidential nomination and the issues treated in the party platform.

The most dramatic example of the last category would have to be the labor unions. . . .The AFL-CIO continued to be a significant contributor to the congressional campaigns of Democratic candidates, but its concern with the national party affairs lessened. . . . .

THE NATIONALIZATION
OF THE PARTY

The reform movement altered the power distributions within the Democratic party in an even more fundamental way. The historic relationship between the national party and its local and state units was altered, and before reform had run its course, dramatically reversed. Traditionally, the national party exercised little real power in party matters. This role was reserved for the state and local units, the party agencies presumed to be closest to the voter. The national party appendages were relatively inactive. They occasionally provided skilled services to state and local parties in such areas as registration, polling, and getting-out-the-vote campaigns, but their contributions seldom went beyond the level of rudimentary back-up support. The national parties, of course, did hold their semi-annual national committee meetings, but these were uneventful gatherings of no particular significance to the parties at any level. The national party also supervised the arrangements for the quadrennial national convention. Here the power over the convention scheduling and agenda could be significant to the faction

controlling the national chairmanship at the time. The national party, however, had little concern over such basic practices as delegate apportionment formulas, controlled by the state parties and influenced by local political customs and power arrangements.

All of this changed abruptly, and more than anyone could ever have predicted, because of the McGovern-Fraser Commission. Building on the precedent established by the (Richard) Hughes Special Equal Rights Committee, the McGovern-Fraser Commission required the state parties to enact changes demanded by itself, the offspring of the national party. . . .

EXTENDING THE RULE OF LAW
TO PARTY AFFAIRS

Implicit in the proposals throughout the reform period was the effort to protect the interests of the individual party member and to extend and safeguard his influence in party deliberations. The intention was to remove, insofar as was possible, control over participation from the whim and caprice of individuals who happened to be in authority in a given place at a particular time. To a large extent, such an effort ran counter to the customary political efforts of using every available instrument to gain a political edge, however small, and certainly counter to the experience of the Democratic party. Traditionally, the party had resolved differences in a political give-and-take between contending party factions or candidates in any manner the combatants might devise. Manipulating rules or enforcing selective by-laws [were] among the many stratagems a party faction might use to gain its ends.

This effort to abolish the regulars' con-

35

trol over participation was not good enough for the reformers. They not only wanted an inclusiveness and an intra-party democracy in political decision-making, but they also sought an impartiality in party rules and procedures that was foreign to the historic practices of the Democrats.

The emphasis can be seen in all aspects of the reform movement. The McGovern-Fraser Commission's rules attempted to establish a model of fairness and openness in delegate selection that set the tone for future developments. The O'Hara Commission created elaborate procedures for resolving credentials committee challenges that assured clear standards of performance impartially assessed through a series of mechanisms similar to those employed by the courts. There would be briefs and counterbriefs, set times and dates for the selection meetings and for the various steps involved in adjudicating any disagreements, hearings of facts by qualified officers, and appeals made to a credentials committee and, potentially at least, to the national convention. The Credentials Review Commission carried the process a step further by attempting to provide a continuing assessment of the applicability and relevance of state party rules to the national party's reform guidelines.

Less successfully, the O'Hara Commission made efforts to open the flow of information to the individual delegates and to advance their control over presiding officials within the convention. Most dramatic of all, the Charter Commission wrote a party constitution for party affairs and established a judicial council, modeled after the Supreme Court, to codify and apply party rulings in all disputes brought before it. The Charter Commission's actions are perhaps the

ultimate steps, if they prove to be feasible, in instituting the rule of law within party councils.

REFORM AS A CONTINUING PROBLEM

One other result of the reform movement may be less obvious. The reformers extensively reviewed party processes and then rewrote the rules of behavior for the totality of national party activities. As a consequence, the reform era opened questions, once presumed settled either for better or worse or at least removed from immediate political debate, to continual reassessment. The success of the reformers in overhauling party procedures within a very few years invites others to try. The public and the party membership have now been conditioned to such reassessments. Such activity is accepted as a legitimate national party function and the authority of the party to engage in such exercises—including the enforced implementation of its directives—is no longer a subject of contention. There is much to be gained by a restructuring of procedure by any party faction that might control the national party apparatus, a national convention, or simply a reform commission. The process invites attempts at duplication. In fact, because the impressive changes brought by the McGovern-Fraser Commission serve as a model of what could be accomplished, repeated attempts to introduce new reforms (in these situations, changes intended to favor one faction or candidate) may be difficult to avoid.

For the most part, the original review of procedures and the changes introduced by the reformers were badly needed. The presidential nominating process had evolved over generations, with little rationale or logic underlying the diverse procedures utilized in the states. The reformers contended that the process was closed and arbitrary and that it gave unfair advantage to the party regulars who controlled the processes. In this broad sense, the reformers' claims were not contested by the regulars (although, of course, the measures proposed by the reformers were less well received).

No particular rules governed the operations of the national convention and its management, and the procedures were open to gross abuse. The bylaws applying to local, state, and national party organs were complex, often unrecorded, and openly manipulated by those in power. Such problems demanded some type of ordering. The reform movement attempted to accomplish this task.

The work of the McGovern-Fraser Commission and, in the wake of the post-1972 election, the Mikulski and Compliance Review commissions, indicates that no area of presidential selection can remain off limits to reevaluation and potential modification. . . .

DEBATING THE MERITS

The controversies created by the reforms are not likely to abate. The reform movement raised fundamental questions about American political parties that are not easily answered and that go to the very essence of what political parties in the United States are, or should be, about. What is a political party for? Whom does it serve? What does (or should) it stand for? Whom should it represent (and *how* should these groups, interests, and individuals be represented)? Implicit in the controversy is the question of the adaptability and adequacy of political parties—institutions developed in another age—in dealing with the pres-

sures and problems of late-twentieth-century American life. Are political parties relevant to the major concerns of contemporary American society? If not, can they be made relevant?

THE RESPONSE OF THE REGULARS

The answers that the Democratic party regulars and reformers would give to these questions should be clear enough at this juncture. The party regulars would contend that political parties are quite adequate to the demands made upon them. They would say that 1968 and its problems were exceptions to the long and basically successful exercise of party authority. If a little care is taken, the problems of that election year need not be repeated.

Political parties are electoral coalitions intended for winning elections. The achievement of this end is, by all odds, their most significant function, and all other obligations are secondary at best. The regulars would contend that a party should, of course, represent the best interests of its members, but they would go on to argue that the most effective way to do this is by winning elections. The way to pick the candidates most likely to be victorious is to give the decisive role in party affairs (including presidential nomination contests) to party and elective officeholders. These individuals have the greatest stake in the party's success as well as the knowledge and experience necessary to select the most formidable nominees representative of the party's long-run interests.

THE RESPONSE OF THE REFORMERS

Reformers would be more skeptical of the claims made on behalf of the political party. They would argue that the party has not served its membership well, that its procedures are out-dated and discriminatory, and that it has not adapted to a changing electorate and an evolving society. Their perception of the 1968 election year and its attendant difficulties would be quite different from that of the regulars. They would see that election year and the Democratic prenomination difficulties and national convention as symbolic of the internal decay that has been spreading within the party system. The 1968 election year was simply a manifestation of how serious the problems have become.

The reformers have little faith in the party regulars. They openly question the breadth of the regulars' concerns and the extent to which they accurately reflect, or possibly even consider, the sentiments of the party rank and file. Reformers differ with the party regulars on where a party's major obligations lie, and they contest the wisdom, competence, and representativeness of the party regulars. They see no particular value in entrusting the fate of the national party or control over its presidential decision-making process to an elite with which they have so little in common and which they believe to be out of touch with its constituency and with national political currents.

The reformers would argue that the grass-roots party members should be represented in all party bodies and should, to the furthest extent possible, control their deliberations. To enlarge upon this belief, reformers feel that party members who participated in the presidential primaries and caucuses should have a controlling voice in the concerns of the process. The reformers believe in a participant-oriented party, accessible to those who cared to identify with it and take part in its activities, and open to influence from below. And they seek a

party that would best represent and implement as precisely as possible the views and wishes of its membership.

The conception of an open, participant-oriented party responsive to and dependent on the good will of its rank and file is at odds with the regulars' view of a quasi-closed organization led by a somewhat inaccessible and self-perpetuating elite that would look out for the party's best interests. In fact, an open party that entrusts ultimate power over, for example, the choice of a presidential nominee to the individual party member acting in a primary or a caucus at the local level makes the need for indirect representation through local or state party organizations or elected officeholders extraneous. The reformers want a direct correspondence between the individual party member and national-level decisions, a relationship that deemphasizes the role and contributions of any intermediate agencies.

The reformers would also reject winning office as the sole end of a political party. Instead, they would contend that a party serves many functions and that perhaps its most important is adequately to represent the views of its members and to funnel these into governmental decision-making. Unless a political party responsively addresses its members' concerns about pressing social issues, its victories will be hollow. They believed that a political party has to be in direct touch with, and representative of, its grass-roots sentiments. Anything less means that the political party is not fulfilling its obligations.

The reformers would emphasize a broad set of party goals and activities (witness the party charter) than the regulars. They would argue that a party should attempt to fulfill a number of functions, from educating its membership on the issues of the day to campaigning for office, and that it should have permanent organizations active throughout the year with full-time professional staffs to serve the needs of its members. These party organizations should be open to direction from the rank and file.

While they favor a more ambitious program and a more highly institutionalized (and open) party structure, the reformers would be more skeptical of the party's operations and the adequacy of its contributions to contemporary society. They would want the party to engage in more activities while at the same time being more demanding in their assessments of the relevance and value of what the party undertakes. And they would insist (as they did) that to reach any of these goals, the Democratic party would have to be thoroughly restructured. The regulars, of course, would disagree on each and every point.

TWO MODELS OF REPRESENTATION

The two sides in the reform issues are operating from different models of political behavior. They are applying different standards of acceptable political conduct and accountability. The two models have little in common. The party regulars are advocating "a taking care of" (to borrow Hanna Pitkin's terminology) concept of representation that sees party regulars and the established interest group leaders within the Democratic coalition as the best conservators of the interests of the party and its members. . . .

The reformers would argue that a system that directly reflects rank-and-file views and allows the grass-roots participants control over party decisions, particularly over the critical choice of a

presidential nominee, is not only preferable but is the only type of procedure that will meet their concept of democratic accountability.

To the extent that direct control over party decision-making is not feasible, the reformers would opt for an "agent" theory of representation. The representative chosen by the individual party members would be given limited independence. On the major issues facing the party, he would be carefully instructed on how to perform in order to best fulfill his sponsor's wishes.

The two conceptions of representation have little in common. The issues raised, both in theoretical and practical terms, are fundamental to one's definition of a political party and the relevance of its contributions to a society. They deal with the nature of the party and its continued existence. Add to these concerns the groups displaced by the turmoil caused by the reforms and the stakes being contested in the fight for control of a national party and its nominating processes, and it is not difficult to see why the debate over reforms has continued.

The reformers won the initial battle and much of what they accomplished cannot be reversed. Nonetheless, the basic differences between the competing conceptions of what a political party is (or should be) and the manner in which it should fulfill its obligations are essentially irreconcilable. At a minimum however, political parties in the future may be judged by stricter standards of performance than in the past. Political parties should be continually called upon to prove their relevance and justify their contribution by a public that is increasingly skeptical of their value.

The reform movement accomplished a

2. HAS PARTY REFORM SUCCEEDED?

great deal in a short period of time. It managed to breathe new life into moribund party structures and to center debate on the operation of these agencies. Political parties are seldom the focus of public concern. They have grown episodically over the last century and a half to fill immediate needs. They are of immense concern quadrennially, when the various presidential contenders and their supporters attempt to bend them to their will. Between presidential elections a short-term interest is being replaced by a more customary apathy. It can be argued that during the interim between elections the hulking organizational monster that constitutes the remnants of the national party only fitfully serves any function of consequence to the electorate.

The reform movement attempted to resurrect an interest in party activities per se and to revitalize party structures and adapt them to modern concerns. . . .

Political parties had changed little in form or activity since their inception. One factor, however, had become increasingly clear: they had become spiritually exhausted and increasingly less relevant functionally to the operation of a modern democracy. The demand for organizations adequately executing the duties the parties are supposed to perform cannot be quarreled with. Critical concerns of any democratic nation include the mobilization of voters behind representative candidacies of similar policy persuasion; the selection and promotion of the most able within its ranks to positions of public responsibility; the effective representa-

tion of the views of its members; the day-to-day scrutiny of the acts of those in office; and the provision of sensible policy and candidate alternatives to an electorate it educated to the implications of official behavior. Both parties performed these functions with increasingly less ability.

In truth the parties became fractious, warring tribes, divorced from their bases of support and slavishly dependent on a president chosen from their ranks. They responded more to organized pressures and financial strength than they did to the mass of their membership. A review of party history during the last few troubled decades would make it appear that the party supporters were an inconvenience to be suffered and catered to only during national election campaigns.

Such foreboding might never have arisen above the level of irrelevant speculation had it not been for 1968. The fury unleashed by the obvious abuse of official party machinery and the ugly picture of party operations that resulted convinced most people within and without the Democratic party that change was overdue. The forces that would propel reform had been set in motion, but the events of that election year proved the catalyst. Beyond a doubt, the immediate need for remedial action had been demonstrated. Change was required; the need had been dramatized in a manner that would create the necessary reform constituency, and people were available and willing to devote themselves to the effort. So began the attempt to democratize one of the nation's oldest and most significant political institutions. . . .

NO   Everett Carll Ladd, Jr.

WHERE HAVE ALL THE
VOTERS GONE?

In October 1977 I shared with a group of civic leaders many of the complaints about the current condition of the U.S. parties. . . . Near the end of the discussion that followed my presentation, one member of the audience politely but pointedly inquired: "Do you really think that the American political system functioned better in the past than it does now, that everything is in decline?"

No, I don't. In many ways, the U.S. social and political system is now doing a better job responding to the needs of the entire citizenry than at any time in the past.

The fact remains, however, that Americans now feel notably dissatisfied with their primary public institutions. And this dissatisfaction—coming in the face of substantial achievements—seems to result in large measure from a breakdown in one critical institution designed to translate public expectations into public policy: the political parties. It is the argument of this volume that over the past decade and a half the parties have manifested a diminished capability. The party system is not functioning well. It is not doing a good job in performing those tasks which are uniquely its own. This failure carries with it serious consequences for popular confidence in the governing system. . . .

THE PERILS OF PARTY REFORM

Over the 1960s and 1970s the American party system has been performing strangely, yielding novel and all too often unfortunate results. For instance, in two of the past four presidential elections—1964 and 1972—the victors were beneficiaries of two of the greatest landslides in U.S. history. But the voters did not so much confer mandates on Lyndon Johnson and Richard Nixon as declare their opponents unacceptable. There is every indication that these negative landslides had adverse consequences for the political order. Large numbers of people felt they were without a proper choice.

Since 1964, American presidential nomination campaigns have been distinguished by the frequency of strong candidacies of a decided ideological character. Not popular with the mass constituencies of their respective parties, Goldwater, McCarthy, McGovern, and Reagan managed nonetheless either to command the nomination or come within an eyelash of doing so. And all of this happened at a time when both parties were implementing a series of momentous reforms designed to make themselves more representative!

Then, in 1976, with the Republicans at their post-Watergate nadir and presidential victory available to the opposition virtually for the asking, the Democrats— the American majority party and the oldest political party in the world— brought forth a candidate who was almost completely unknown and untried in national politics. Not more than 3 or 4 percent of the electorate could even identify Jimmy Carter six months before he was nominated for the most important of all offices. It is not surprising that the Carter campaign encountered persisting doubt and skepticism on the part of the public. The voters were dissatisfied with things as they were, but felt quite unsure whether they would be any better off with Carter in the White House. Partly for this reason, Carter's lead in the polls fell precipitously between July and October, and an election that had seemed destined to bring about the decisive retirement of a much-burdened incumbent became instead a near deadlock.

This series of strange electoral performances is chiefly the result of the pronounced weakening of American political parties that has taken place in recent decades—a process that by now has brought them to the point of virtual death as organizations. As a consequence of their increasing weakness, the parties are unable to perform a set of functions which are exclusively theirs,

and the whole political system has been rattled.

The enfeeblement of the parties has come to a head during the last decade, a span filled with partisan changes and experimentation that are conventionally billed as "reform." But if reform is understood to mean "the improvement or amendment of what is wrong," little of the sort has occurred. Reform proponents insist that the alterations have made the parties more democratic, more representative of the populace, stronger, more competitive, and generally better able to play their part in the governing process. In fact, the changes seem more to have deformed than reformed the parties. They have left the system on the whole less representative, less competitive, less able to govern.

The organizational weakness of U.S. political parties is in one sense an old story. Though Americans gave the world its first party system, they have always been highly ambivalent about the institution. Party leaders have been seen pejoratively as "bosses" and parties themselves as no better than "necessary evils." This approach to party follows in large measure from the culture's distinctive individualism, which prompts Americans to insist on their individual rights to determine electoral outcomes, and specifically on *their* rights, rather than those of party leaders, to control the nomination process.

The reform movements of the twentieth century, however, have carried the enfeeblement of parties way beyond anything required by the culture. In the early years of this century, the Progressives took a number of critical steps in that direction, particularly through their generally successful advocacy of the idea that nominations for state and local office be controlled by voters who turn out in primaries rather than by the party organization. The capacity of regulars to manage party life was decisively lessened and a theory of intraparty democracy, compatible with the old American emphasis on individual action and the suspicion of large organizations, took root to an extent not found in any other democratic system. The direct primary remains almost exclusively an American institution.

Over the last decade, a new burst of reform activity has picked up where the Progressives left off. It originated largely within the Democratic party, but in a less dramatic fashion it has engulfed the Republicans as well. And it has rendered the two great national parties unable to control the nominating process for the country's most important political office, that of president.

PARTY REFORM SINCE 1968

The current wave of party reform was set in motion by the tumultuous 1968 Democratic convention, which created two commissions, one headed by Senator George McGovern to examine and make recommendations bearing on delegates selection (a commission subsequently chaired by Representative Donald Fraser of Minnesota); the other led by Representative James O'Hara of Michigan to study convention rules and operations. Recommendations of the McGovern-Fraser Commission, implemented for the 1972 convention, proved particularly important and generated rancorous intraparty debate.

The commission insisted that *internal party democracy* was the primary value to be promoted. The changes which it was able to achieve required the state Democratic parties to "overcome the effects of past discrimination by affirmative steps" to assure the representation of blacks, women, and young people at the national conventions and other party-functions "in reasonable relationship to (the group's) presence in the population of the State." Minority views were to be represented in all slate-making sessions. Delegates were to be chosen almost exclusively through caucus and convention arrangements open to all party adherents and providing proportional representation for minority candidates, or through primaries. If a state Democratic party insisted on permitting its central committee to play a role in choosing delegates to the national convention, it was required to limit the number of delegates thus selected to not more than 10 percent of the total. Proscribed was the practice whereby "certain public or Party office holders are delegates to county, State, and National Conventions by virtue of their official position." Use of the unit rule—casting a state's delegate votes as a bloc, in the direction desired by the majority—was banned.

Party leaders in many states found the new stipulations involving the "democratized" caucuses and conventions for national delegates selection so complex and so unpalatable—the rules made these bodies available for easy manipulation by candidate supporters or issue enthusiasts and thereby greatly weakened the position of the regular leadership—that they opted instead for presidential primaries. The result was an explosion in the number of primaries, quite unforeseen by most McGovern-Fraser Commission members—from seventeen in 1968 to twenty-three in 1972 to thirty in 1976. Whereas less than half of all delegates to the 1968 convention were chosen by primaries, nearly three-fourths of the 1976 delegates were thus selected. . . .

OTHER PRECIPITANTS OF PARTY DECLINE

Reform has weakened the parties indirectly as well as directly. When nearly three-fourths of all Democratic convention delegates (and more than two-thirds of Republican delegates) are selected through primaries, for example, serious candidates have to create elaborate personal organizations to wage the costly and far-flung campaigns that are a precondition of winning. The victorious contender, once his nomination is in hand, is hardly about to disband the apparatus he put together for the primary struggle. He relies upon it and not on the party in the general election. Much attention has been devoted to the Committee to Re-Elect the President, the now-disgraced instrument of the Nixon forces in 1972. Yet for all its excesses, CREEP was in many ways the prototypical contemporary electoral organization: it was formed to serve the interest of one man; it placed these above the party's; and its substantial resources enabled it to disregard the party in contesting for the presidency.

Broad social changes have also helped to bring parties to the verge of organizational extinction. The populace is much more highly educated than ever, has many more sources of political information, clearly feels less dependent upon party as an active intermediary in the electoral process—and it is sharply and irreversibly more inclined to participate in an independent, nonpartisan basis.

The rise of the national press has also played a part in weakening the parties. Increasingly it has taken over important facets of the communications role that was once performed by party organizations. As journalist David Broder has observed, newsmen now serve as the principal source of information on what candidates are saying and doing. They act the part of talent scouts, conveying the judgment that some contenders are promising, while dismissing others as of no real talent. They also operate as race-callers or handicappers, telling the public how the election contest is going. At times they function as public defenders, bent on exposing what they consider the frailties, duplicities, and sundry inadequacies of a candidate; and in some instances they even serve as assistant campaign managers, informally advising a candidate, and publicly, if indirectly, promoting his cause.

With so much going against parties, one might have hoped for a modest dose of "countercyclical policy" to bolster a deteriorating but useful institution. Just the opposite, however, has been happening. For example, federal funding of presidential campaigns, voted into law as a means of "cleaning up" national politics, has reduced the dependency of candidates on party and on the interest groups that have served as prime building blocks of party organization. A number of proposals for further electoral reform now under consideration would have a similar effect. For example, there is strong support these days for a constitutional amendment to eliminate the electoral college and substitute direct election of the president. Whatever the proposal's overall merits, it would reduce the role of state parties by making state boundaries irrelevant to election outcomes. Candidates would become even freer to campaign without regard to the blocs, alliances, and structures that state party systems are built on.

There has been inadvertence and bad planning and just plain stupidity in all of this. But above all, the attack on political parties has come as a result of a straightforward and quite conscious pursuit of group interests. Senator McGovern for one has conceded that there are risks in "democratizing" the party, "opening it up," reducing the domination of "bosses" or "elites," and permitting "the people" to decide who the nominee will be. But he considers the risks to be worth it.

"The alternative," he says, "is a closed system where you say the elite are better able to run the country than rank-and-file citizens."

THE PEOPLE AREN'T THE WINNERS

McGovern could not be more wrong in his notion that it is "rank-and-file citizens" who benefit from party "reform" and the elite who suffer; just the opposite is the case. For a century and a half, U.S. political parties, with all their faults, have been a force for extending democracy. Can there ever have been any real doubt that, were party removed from control over presidential nominations and the public invited to fend for itself in a lightly structured selection process, the winners would not be "the people"? In fact, it has been upper-middle-class groups, not the broad mass of Americans, who have confronted the party organizations, who have held them to be unresponsive to their policy perspectives, who have attacked the legitimacy of "bosses," who have urged "democratization." And it is these highly educated, well-informed, relatively prosperous groups who have primarily benefited from party "reform," for they tend to participate in more open nomination processes at a rate that far exceeds that of "rank-and-file-citizens."

That party reform serves the interests of the upper middle class can be seen in the statistics on voter turnout in primary elections. There has been much handwringing of late about low turnout in recent general elections, but participation in them is positively robust compared with that in the primaries. In 1976, for example, in the twenty-eight states that held presidential primaries and kept statewide data on them, just 28 percent of the voting-age population went to the polls, as compared with 54 percent casting presidential ballots from those states in the November election. . . .

On the Democratic side, much has been made of George McGovern's success in capturing his party's 1972 nomination in spite of the fact that at no time during the long primary and preconvention struggle was he popular with the rank and file of his own party. The convention that formally nominated McGovern was strikingly unrepresentative of the policy preferences of the mass of Democrats, as a study by Jeane Kirkpatrick so clearly shows. When he won the nomination, Senator McGovern declared that it was "all the more precious in that it is the gift of the most open political process in our national history." One must note that this "most open political process" produced one of the most unrepresentative outcomes in our national history.

And in 1976 things remained the same in some crucial respects. To be sure, the nominee that year was a man who had clearly established himself during the primary as a centrist, popular with the party's rank and file. Yet the convention itself was as unrepresentative as it had been four years earlier. The delegates may have nominated Carter and done his bidding on the platform and related matters, but they had little in common ideologically with him or the mass of Democrats. They resembled not the rank and file, but the New Class—the young, college-educated, professional and managerial groups who have been especially advantaged by the recent recourse to "open" selection mechanisms. They stood far to the left of the rank and file, particularly on the issues of the New Liberalism—such as whether the U.S. should have a softer foreign policy vis-a-vis the Soviet Union, whether defense spending should be cut, and various social and moral questions ranging from abortion to busing. . . .

The balance of America's political experience with party "reform," however, suggests the contrary. We do need the kinds of services that only strong, autonomous party organizations can provide. By substantially removing party from nominee selection almost everywhere, we have eliminated the one institution able to practice political planning. By removing party from governance, we have aided the already strong centrifugal forces working against coherence in public policy. And even in the area of representation, where the reformers have made their proudest claims, it is at least arguable that the machinery of party achieved results superior to those of the putatively more democratic procedures that have been created in their stead.

PROTECTING AN ENDANGERED POLITICAL SPECIES

So it is high time that the nation began rethinking public policy toward the parties. They have become an endangered species, and an all-out campaign ought to be launched to protect and revive them. Direct election of the president should not be established. It would deal too severe a blow to the already tottering state and national party systems. It is possible to take care of the problem of the "faithless elector"—and to remove any real possibility that a candidate without a plurality of the popular vote might win the presidency—within the structure of the electoral college. Federal funding of elections bypasses parties too much and encourages autonomous candidacies, and it should be ended. Looking to what are strictly intraparty decisions, the recent proposal by "strong-party" advocates on the Democrats' Winograd Commission to make all Democratic governors, U.S. senators, and congressmen voting delegates to the national convention by dint of their office should be revived. It is one concrete means of acknowledging and honoring the institutional aspects of party in the presidential-selection process.

The basic change that is needed, though, is simply a renewed appreciation of what useful things parties—as institutions and not just labels—are to have around. If this should somehow come to pass, it would then be relatively easy to rebuild the parties as instruments for planning and representation within what must be recognized as a now-irreversible feature of the U.S. nominee-selection process—the widespread use of direct primaries. Restoring the organized parties to vigorous health and giving them back their central role in the presidential-selection process should be the No. 1 reform objective of the next decade.

POSTSCRIPT

HAS PARTY REFORM SUCCEEDED?

Crotty's sympathetic account makes it clear that advocates of reform wanted to increase participation by political activists, and there can be little doubt that this was accomplished. The objective was enhanced by party democracy. Ladd's critical analysis argues that this was achieved at the cost of reduced influence by party leaders and regulars and, as a result, party responsibility was diminished. It sometimes seems as if these are incompatible values: If responsibility is stressed in party organization, it is to the detriment of democratic participation, and vice versa. Can these goals be reconciled?

No student of American politics has thought longer or written more profoundly on this subject than Austin Ranney, whose *Curbing the Mischiefs of Faction* (University of California Press, 1975) expresses sympathy for the intentions of reform, criticism of the results, and skepticism about our ability to foretell what the consequences of the new reforms will be. The recent historical background to reform is examined by Everett Carll Ladd, Jr., with Charles D. Hadley in *Transformation of the American Party System,* second edition (Norton, 1978). There are provocative insights in James David Barber's, ed., *Choosing the Presidency* (Prentice-Hall, 1974) and Stephen J. Wayne's, *The Road to the White House* (St. Martin's Press, 1980). They are part of the growing literature exploring the unique way in which the United States chooses its head of state.

In his essay, Crotty concludes: "The reform movement constitutes but a beginning." Others are advocating still other reforms, including the establishment of a single nation-wide presidential primary (or, alternatively, four regional primaries to replace the numerous individual ones), and public financing of congressional elections. The critics of reform seek to restore an independent, deliberative role to the national convention, and the Democratic party has already begun to move in that direction.

ISSUE 3

DO POLITICAL ACTION COMMITTEES UNDERMINE DEMOCRACY?

YES: Elizabeth Drew, from *Politics and Money* (New York, 1983)

NO: Robert J. Samuelson, from "The Campaign Reform Failure," *The New Republic* (September 5, 1983)

ISSUE SUMMARY

YES: Political journalist Elizabeth Drew believes that through lavish expenditures to candidates and members of Congress, political action committees corrupt the democratic political process. She contends their undesirable influence could be curbed by public financing of congressional election campaigns.
NO: Economist-journalist Robert Samuelson maintains that it would be as futile to attempt to reduce the influence of money as it would be undesirable to restrict free speech and political organization. To suppress PACs would curtail the democratic process, he claims.

Half a century ago, American folk humorist Will Rogers observed that then it took a lot of money even to *lose* an election. What would Will Rogers say if he were alive today?

Using television as a medium of communication and persuasian has greatly increased the expenditures in election campaigns. In 1980, according to the most comprehensive study of that election year, over $1.2 billion was spent in behalf of all candidates. Nearly half of this was spent on national elections: $275 million on the presidential election and $239 million on the elections for the House of Representatives and the Senate. In fact, for every voter who went to the polls on Election Day $15 was spent trying to reach him or her. Is that too high a price to pay to make the democratic electoral process work?

More controversial than the amount of money spent in politics is its source. Political action committees have become a major factor in financing American election campaigns. PACs (as they are called) have proliferated in recent years, with more than one hundred new special-interest groups being founded each year. It is estimated that there are now more than 3,500 PACs, representing almost every conceivable political interest.

By raising money from political sympathizers, association members, and public solicitations, PACs have provided the funds with which candidates reach the public. It is estimated that PACs spent more than $80 million on campaigns in 1982, when there was no presidential election. In 1984 at least ten incumbent Senators (in both parties) received more than $300 thousand in PAC money. Some members of Congress have taken no chances on winning an existing PAC's approval and have created their own. The Congressional Club, founded by Republican Senator Jesse Helms of North Carolina, raised nearly $5 million in 1983 alone.

Legislators are divided on the influence of PACs. Democratic Representative Barney Frank of Massachusetts has said: "You can't take thousands of dollars from a group and not have it affect you." But Democratic Representative Joseph Addabbo of New York disagrees: "PACs aren't buying anything, and I'm not selling." Critics argue that PAC money in recent years probably influenced congressional votes to maintain high dairy price supports and not to require warranties on used cars. On the other hand, defenders of PACs maintain that they are less interested in influencing members of Congress opposed to their point of view than in electing new members who are sympathetic.

PACs are not a new phenomenon. Pressure groups or, as founding father James Madison called them, factions have always been part of the political process and to eliminate them would be to destroy liberty itself. What Madison hoped for was the broadest participation of interest groups, so that compromises among them would result in an approximation of the national interest.

What was true at the time of our nation's founding may no longer be true, according to Elizabeth Drew, who chronicles American politics for *The New Yorker.* She fears that money can "buy" candidates, elections, and crucial votes on the floor of Congress. What defenders of PAC independence fear, as economist-journalist Robert J. Samuelson points out, is that inhibiting the ability of interest groups to provide financial support for candidates and causes violates the First Amendment guarantees of free speech and political action. Efforts to limit spending in presidential elections have failed dismally, argue these critics, and there is no reason to believe that limits on congressional campaigns will succeed any better.

There is no disagreement on the proposition that money has changed our politics. The question is whether the vast expenditures have corrupted the system and what, if anything, can be done about it.

YES   Elizabeth Drew

POLITICS AND MONEY

There have always been "interests" in this country which have sought to influence public policy, and there always will be, and always should be. Legislators have to look after the various interests of the area they represent and work out the political equation among their constituencies. In *The Federalist Papers,* Madison wrote of the natural inclination of man to form factions, and said that the consequent "instability, injustice, and confusion introduced into the public councils have, in truth, been the mortal diseases under which popular governments have everywhere perished." Since to remove the causes of "the mischiefs of faction" would be to destroy liberty, Madison wrote, the alternative was to control their effects. He offered the hope that in the republican form of government which was being established, the number of conflicting factions would make it difficult for any particular one to dominate, or for those with a "common motive" to "discover their own strength and to act in unison with each other." But, realistic as Madison was, he could only extrapolate from the society he saw and, happily for him, could not anticipate the sophisticated organizing of almost every conceivable interest, the skills that factions would develop in promoting such interests, and the systematized raising and contributing of large sums of money in order to influence public policy.

From *Politics and Money* ©1982, Elizabeth Drew (Macmillan) originally in The New Yorker.

In earlier periods of our history, some nationally based interests—steel, the railroads—assumed that it was only prudent business practice to own legislators and to influence the election of Presidents. Some of the more energetic fund raisers were awarded Cabinet positions and ambassadorships—a tradition that has not exactly died. The scandals over the power of the trusts, and over the manipulations of Mark Hanna, the Ohio mining magnate who was responsible for the nomination of William McKinley in 1896 and, for a time, literally for the fortune of the Republican Party, were factors leading to the reform movement of the early twentieth century. Hanna, a pioneer in the field, raised millions for the Republican Party by systematically assessing banks and corporations. Robert La Follette's reform movement grew out of these scandals, and it was in reaction to them that President Theodore Roosevelt made some farseeing proposals. In a message to Congress in 1905, Roosevelt proposed that all corporate contributions to politics be banned. In 1907, he went further, and proposed the public financing of campaigns, saying, "The need for collecting large campaign funds would vanish if Congress provided an appropriation for the proper and legitimate expenses of each of the great national parties. Then the stipulation should be made that no party receiving campaign funds from the Treasury should accept more than a fixed amount from any individual subscriber or donor; and the necessary publicity for receipts and expenditures could without difficulty be provided." In 1907, Congress passed the Tillman Act, which prohibited corporations and banks from making contributions to campaigns for federal office, and over the next few years Congress passed some fairly toothless legislation requiring the filing of reports of certain campaign contributions. Then, in 1921, came the Teapot Dome scandal, leading to the Federal Corrupt Practices Act of 1925, which continued the existing prohibitions on contributions by corporations and banks, and required the reporting of campaign receipts and expenditures, but the law was infinitely evadable and was never really enforced.

By 1970, there was such consternation over the rising costs of campaigns—political advertising on television had now become commonplace—that Congress passed a bill to limit the amount that could be spent for television and radio advertising, but Richard Nixon vetoed the measure, siding with broadcasters, who argued that it discriminated against them. The following year, Congress came close to completing action on a more comprehensive bill, which required, among other things, that all federal candidates disclose the sources of their campaign funds, but its final enactment was delayed until 1972, so that members of Congress and Presidential candidates could raise more money before the new disclosure requirements went into effect. The 1971 law dealt with what were seen as major problems at that time by limiting the amount that candidates (and their families) could spend on their own campaigns—there had been a couple of notable spenders in 1970—and limiting the amount that candidates could spend on political advertising. It also came at the question of costs from another direction, by requiring that television and radio stations charge their lowest rates for political advertising in the periods immediately preceding primaries and general elections. Common Cause, the citizen's lobby, which had been founded in 1970 and had made campaign financing one of its major issues, tried to get Congress to enact a limit on contributions, but the idea met with little interest.

At the same time, organized labor took the first of a series of steps to secure its own role in the political process—steps that led ultimately to the universe of political-action committees, or PACs. In 1972, labor leaders asked Congress to simply codify what was then understood to be existing law. Labor unions and corporations had been specifically barred from making direct contributions to political campaigns, but the law had been interpreted to mean that labor could use dues and corporations could use treasury funds to administer political committees that would raise voluntary contributions from their members or employees for the election of candidates for public office. In the nineteen-forties, labor had begun to establish political-action committees, to try to offset unlimited contributions by wealthy individuals. A few trade and professional associations had also established political-action funds—the American Medical Association, the dairy cooperatives, and something called the Business-Industry Political Action Committee, or BIPAC, which was founded in 1963. (BIPAC was begun by the National Association of Manufacturers in response to the A.F.L.-C.I.O.'s Committee on Political Education, or COPE.) And a very few corporate political-action committees had been set up. But labor was concerned that its right to establish political-action committees would be challenged by the Nixon Administration's Justice Department, so it backed an amendment to the 1971 bill which stated that the prohibition of direct contributions of treasury money by unions and corporations did not prevent them from establishing PACs using voluntary contributions. The amendment also said that union dues and corporate-treasury money could be used

for "nonpartisan" get-out-the-vote drives and for communicating with members and stockholders about politics. Labor failed to consider that business had the resources to overtake it.

Not long afterward, in the course of the Watergate disclosures, it became clear that many corporations hadn't needed to establish political-action committees because they were maintaining secret funds for the financing of federal campaigns. The public was scandalized by such revelations as that Nixon's campaign committee, the Committee for the Re-Election of the President, had raised almost seventeen million dollars from only a hundred and twenty-four contributors, who gave more than fifty thousand dollars each, and that over $1.7 million had been received from people who were given ambassadorships.

And so in 1973 Congress went at the subject of campaign financing again, and in 1974 it passed the comprehensive law providing for the public financing of Presidential campaigns (the Senate had also approved public financing of congressional campaigns, but this was blocked in the House); placing limits on contributions by individuals and committees for all campaigns for federal office; limiting overall expenditures by congressional as well as Presidential campaigns (this replaced the 1971 ceiling on political advertising); and prohibiting expenditures by individuals and groups outside campaigns—independent expenditures. Cash contributions of over a hundred dollars were prohibited—an important restriction. A Federal Election Commission was established to enforce the federal election laws. The 1974 limits on independent expenditures, the overall spending limits on congressional campaigns, and the 1971 limit on spending by individual candidates using their own funds were later struck down by the Supreme

Court (*Buckley* v. *Valeo*); in essence, the Court equated freedom of speech with the spending of money.

Two widely held misconceptions about what happened in 1974 are that the provision in the law which gave political-action committees their great sendoff was backed only by labor, and that its consequences were unforeseen. The provision was in fact a joint effort by labor and business. (The U.S. Chamber of Commerce and BIPAC, among others, were involved.) It stemmed from a suit brought by Common Cause in 1972 against the T.R.W. corporation, which had established a political-action committee. The suit was brought under a section of the Corrupt Practices Act which prohibited government contractors from making direct or indirect campaign contributions. T.R.W. dissolved the fund, and the suit was dropped. But labor, which had contracts with the government to train workers, became alarmed, and, joined by business, nearly succeeded in 1972 in rewriting that section of the law to allow government contractors to have PACs. In 1974, they succeeded.

Fred Wertheimer, the president of Common Cause, says, "The PAC provision was part of a much larger fight, but we as well as labor and business were paying attention to it. We could see that we were establishing a dual system, with public financing of Presidential campaigns and private financing of congressional campaigns. We knew where we were headed."

On December 31, 1974, there were approximately six hundred political-action committees. By November, 1982, there were about thirty-four hundred—an increase of almost five hundred percent. Between 1980 and 1982 alone, there was an increase of twenty-five percent. In 1976, political-action committees spent about twenty-three million dollars on congres-

sional races. In 1982, they contributed about eighty million dollars—an increase of forty-five percent over two years earlier, and a total increase of two hundred and forty-eight percent in six years. And in each succeeding election, PACs have contributed a higher percentage of the winners' funds. In 1982, the average House winner received over a third of his money from PACs; more than one hundred members received over half of their funds from PACs. In 1974, there were eighty-nine corporate PACs; by 1982 there were fourteen hundred and ninety-seven, while labor had three hundred and fifty. Trade associations, such as the A.M.A. and the National Association of Realtors, had six hundred and thirteen political-action committees. The rest were PACs maintained by "independent" groups, by cooperatives, and by single-interest ideological groups.

There were attempts—in 1976, 1977, and 1978—to legislate public financing of congressional campaigns; some came close in one chamber or the other, but all of them ultimately failed. In 1979, the House of Representatives passed legislation to limit to seventy thousand dollars the overall amount that a House candidate could accept from PACs. The legislation was not brought to the floor in the Senate, because Republican leaders threatened to conduct a filibuster against it.

One person who saw the possibilities of the 1974 law was Guy Vander Jagt, who in 1975 became the chairman of the National Republican Congressional Committee—the campaign committee for electing Republicans to the House. Vander Jagt, a representative from Michigan, says, "In 1975, I spent most of the year trying to get businesses and industries to establish PACs. I worked with the Chamber of Commerce and with the National Associa-

3. DO POLITICAL ACTION COMMITTEES UNDERMINE DEMOCRACY?

tion of Manufacturers, and I travelled the country giving my Paul Revere speech: 'Wake up, America, wake up. There's a war going on—a war that will determine the economic future of this country, and you aren't involved.'" His cry of alarm was clearly heeded. . . .

There are things that can be done about the effect of money on our political system once the nature and the extent of the problem are recognized. The impact of the need for money on congressional behavior has been dramatic. First, there is no question that we have a political system in which politicians' access to money is vital and, in more cases than not, decisive. Richard Wirthlin, the Republican pollster, says, "Money not only can make the difference but can make a huge difference." He continues, "People make decisions based upon the way they see the world, and the way they see the world is conditioned by the information they have; and money can influence not only the information they have but also the perceptions they have, and therefore influences who wins and loses." Second, it is clear that the politicians' anxiety about having access to enough money corrodes, and even corrupts, the political system. It is clear that the effect on them is degrading and distracting at best. At the least, politicians increasingly consider how their votes will affect their own—and their opponents'—ability to raise money. At worst, votes are actually traded for money. It is clear that we are at some distance from the way the democratic process is supposed to work. The most fundamental question is, What kind of electoral process would give us the best kind of representation—the best at representing the public interest and producing public officials who, on the basis of experience and judgment, would make decisions that would not always represent

passing public attitudes or be affected by financial contributions? Finally, it is clear that the system for funding Presidential campaigns with public money, in order to make them reasonably competitive and removed from the pressures of private interests, isn't working as it was intended to.

The broad outlines of what could be done to deal with all these things are: first, a system of public financing of congressional campaigns, which would include limits on what could be spent for the campaigns and a ceiling on the overall amount that any member could accept from political-action committees; second, a radical approach to political advertising, the costliest component of campaigns, which would include a ban on the purchase of air time and a provision for free air time; third, a reimposition of the limits on expenditures by independent committees, and other measures to close the loopholes being exploited by Presidential campaigns. Variations on all these proposals are possible, and objections to all of them are plentiful. Some of the proposals would be difficult to work out, but if the same amount of energy and ingenuity went into making the law effective that has gone into finding ways around it, the difficulties could be resolved. The point is not to try to establish a perfect political system but to try to get the system back closer to what it was intended to be.

Two of the proposals—those dealing with independent committees and political advertising—require some consideration of what the First Amendment is really about. Moreover, when the Supreme Court first ruled that limits on independent expenditures were unconstitutional, it found no history of abuse, which is understandable, since up to that point there were no limits on contributions. In the Buckley case, a prohibition on independent expenditures was held unconstitutional with only one dissenter—Justice Byron White. In its ruling in the Schmitt case, six years after Buckley, the Court was evenly divided on the question of independent expenditures by groups on behalf of publicly financed Presidential candidates, with one member unable to participate because of an apparent conflict of interest. Therefore, it would seem that the constitutional issue is no longer the settled question that people thought it was when the Court ruled in the Buckley case.

The Buckley decision was an odd one, because at the same time that it equated money with speech and held that limits on independent *expenditures* were unconstitutional, it held that limits on *contributions* to candidates were constitutional. Its rationale was that expenditures did not pose the same danger as contributions. But if one has an absolute right to spend unlimited amounts of money for a political candidate outside the candidate's campaign, why can't one contribute whatever one wants to the candidate? Archibald Cox, the professor of constitutional law at the Harvard Law School, who also served as Special Prosecutor during Watergate and is chairman of Common Cause, argued both the Buckley case and the Schmitt case, as well as other First Amendment cases before the Court. Cox says he thinks that it is at least a fifty-fifty possibility that all that the framers of the Constitution had in mind when they wrote the First Amendment was a prohibition on prior censorship, and that some people argue that the possibility is much greater. In any event, he says, one need not resort to that argument to get at the problem of the First Amendment and independent expenditures.

Cox explains the Court's apparent contradiction in the Buckley decision by saying he believes that what the Court had in mind when it considered independent expenditures was, say, a group of professors taking an ad in a newspaper, or an individual flying around the country making speeches in support of a candidate, or even someone buying fifteen or thirty minutes of television time on behalf of a candidate. Therefore, when Cox argued the Schmitt case he suggested that the Court could limit the effect of its finding in the Buckley case by stipulating that it was not thinking in terms of large organizations making independent expenditures, which they have funded by a money-raising effort, and which, as he pointed out, "even without consultation, it's no great trick to coordinate." He suggested that one way to deal with the proposition that spending money equals free speech would be to say that there are lots of different kinds of expenditures, and perhaps money is speech in the instance of a person spending money to publish or broadcast his own thoughts, while it is an entirely different thing when an organization raises money from all over the country and spends it to broadcast. The difference, he said, is that the money is collected nationally, and that it is used for much speech but few ideas. As for the Court's argument that independent expenditures do not create the risk of corrupting public policy, Cox replied that that may be true in the case of an individual who spends for his own personal expression, or of the group of professors, but it is not true in the case of groups that raise and spend millions on behalf of a candidate.

Cox suggests a new way of looking at our elections—a way that could be most helpful in clarifying our thinking about them. He says that an election ought to be treated like a town meeting or an argument before the Supreme Court. As he puts it, there are some forums where, to have meaningful, open debate, you see to it that everyone gets an equal allocation of time and a fair chance to express his point of view. "No one considers that a restriction on freedom of speech," Cox says.

If we redefine what we mean by "freedom of speech," and uncouple the idea of "the marketplace of ideas" from the idea of "the free market," we can begin to get back to how the political system was supposed to work. It is one thing to establish a system that guarantees contending factions an opportunity to express their views, and quite another to auction off the system to those factions that can afford to pay for the most time to express them—not to mention the secondary effects that such an auction system has. Whether or not the person who has the most broadcast time always prevails, it is demonstrable that the power and the cost of political broadcasting distort the political process.

A way to guarantee contending factions a chance to have their say, turn our elections into more of a fair fight, lower the amount of money that is spent on campaigns, and raise the level on which they are fought would be to prohibit political advertising and provide the candidates with free air time. This may sound like a radical concept, but in fact America is one of the very few countries in the world that allow any purchase of television time for political broadcasts; no Western European nation does. And, while we are at it, we could consider requiring that most of the free broadcast time be in segments of not less than, say, five or ten minutes. (In Great Britain, the major parties are currently required to broadcast in segments of a minimum of five or ten minutes.) This would make it necessary for candidates to actually say something, in contrast to the one-minute or thirty-second spots, which are uninformative at best and misleading at worst. (An argument has been made that you can tell what a candidate is like from his television spots, but that requires the public to be able to sort out fact from fiction when it doesn't necessarily have the information; and it puts the burden on the opponent to refute the spots—often something that cannot be done in thirty seconds or a minute. The answer is usually more complicated than the charge.) Arrangements would also have to be made to assure that the free time offered would be when people were likely to be watching—but this, too, could be worked out.

The essential point is that under this proposal the contenders would have a fair chance to be heard, without having to scramble to outspend their opponents for broadcasting—the most expensive and the most influential element of a campaign. Cox thinks that such a proposal could be upheld constitutionally. There would, of course, be stiff opposition to it. The broadcasters would oppose it, for obvious reasons; but the ownership of broadcasting stations is among the most lucrative businesses in America. A fallback position would be for the government to pay a portion of the cost of this broadcast time as part of a publicly financed system for congressional campaigns. (In effect, the government already does this for the publicly financed Presidential campaign.) But there is no point in adopting a fallback position until the fairest and most sensible plan has been tried. Whenever the idea of free broadcast time is brought up, a lot of sand is thrown in the air about such things as what to do in a media market like New York or Los Angeles, where there may be a number of races, or, alternatively, what to do in races where there are no media markets. Surely the mind of man can figure out some answer. When I was talking about this with Robert Dole, the chairman of the Senate Finance Committee, who, on the basis of what he had encountered in his efforts to write more equitable tax laws, is in favor of diminishing the role of money in campaigns, he said, "If they can figure out the tax code, they can figure this out." There are several paths of thinking that those trying to devise a solution might take. One is to keep in mind that the stations in the large media markets are among the most profitable ones. Another is that congressional candidates in areas like New York and Los Angeles often don't buy media time now, because they think it isn't worth it to pay for a broadcast that takes in so much more territory than their district. There is no particular reason that they should be given the means to start broadcasting where they did not do it before. But, in any case, they could be given air time without great financial risk to the stations. Another point to keep in mind is that cable television allows politicians to narrow the size of the audience they are trying to reach, and a number of politicians are already using cable, which is far less expensive than most traditional broadcast outlets. Or, in a media market with a number of candidates, the candidates could be given some free mailings instead. This, too, could be taken care of under a public financing scheme.

Common Cause has been advocating the granting of free response time to a candidate who has been attacked by an independent committee, its theory being that as long as such expenditures are allowed, this will neutralize the effect. If the attack came in the form of direct mail, the candidate could receive a subsidy to respond. But it is not out of the question that the courts will ban expenditures by the large-scale independent committees that have been springing up, especially if there is a system of public financing of congressional campaigns.

The idea of public financing of congressional campaigns has been gaining an increasing number of adherents. An aide to the House leadership said that what he witnessed during the consideration of the 1982 tax-increase bill had made him a convert to the idea. When I asked him why, specifically, he replied, "The long lines of suitors and the access they had." A number of people believed that the Ninety-seventh Congress reflected the impact of the pressure of money, in its various forms, more than any Congress before it. And this sense of things led a number of people who had never before subscribed to the idea of public financing of congressional campaigns to decide that the system had to be changed. A former member of Congress said to me recently, "I used to be against public financing. I thought raising money was an important way to build a campaign, to get people committed. But then I began to see how the present system was corrupting even the best of them on the Hill. And they gin each other up: they see that others are doing it, and say, Why not? It became very depressing to watch. And I changed my mind about public financing." Actually, the public-financing schemes would still allow for private participation.

A number of proposals for a system of public financing have been put forward by members of Congress as well as by Common Cause. They have been sponsored by both Republicans and Democrats. They have several common characteristics. They would provide, for the candidates in the general election, a matching system similar to that which obtains in the Presidential-primary system, and would impose spending limits. (The question of public financing of congressional primaries has been set aside as something to be worked out, if necessary, once a system for the general elections is in place.) It is possible to consider spending limits without a public-financing system, but this, too, would require a change of opinion on the part of the Supreme Court; and there would always be the problem of setting the limits high enough to make candidates viable and low enough to give them a chance of not being utterly at the mercy of contributors and fund raisers. Just as the Presidential-primary system matches private individual contributions of two hundred and fifty dollars, the congressional system would match contributions of a hundred dollars. A bill sponsored by David Obey, a Democratic representative from Wisconsin and a late convert to the idea of public financing, would limit to ninety thousand dollars the total amount of matching money for a candidate for the House. Individuals would still be allowed to contribute a thousand dollars. Some of those who favor public financing would consider allowing higher individual contributions in exchange for an agreement on such a scheme. The proposals for public financing also contain a limit on the total amount a candidate could accept from political-action committees. So private money would not be driven out of the congressional campaigns—it would just be brought under control. And members of Congress would be freed from the anxiety and fear—and corruption—that accompany the present race for money. Obey's bill would limit to ninety thousand dollars the amount that candidates for the House could accept from PACs. His bill does not deal with Senate races, but others have proposed setting limits for Senate races on the basis of a state's population. A bill sponsored by Representatives Mike Synar, Democrat of Oklahoma; Jim Leach, Republican of Iowa; and Dan Glickman, Democrat of Kansas, would limit the amount that House can-

didates could accept from PACs to seventy-five thousand dollars, while the amount that Senate candidates could accept would vary with the size of the state—from seventy-five thousand to five hundred thousand. But the problem with simply limiting the amount that can be received from PACs, without dealing with the larger context, is that the interests that give through PACs would simply turn around and give through individual contributions—as independent oil largely does now. Common Cause and some people on Capitol Hill would also lower the amount that a PAC could contribute to an individual: from ten thousand dollars per election cycle—five thousand for the primary and five thousand for the general election—to half that amount. Obey's bill would limit campaign spending in a congressional general election to a hundred and eighty thousand dollars—a figure that seems unrealistically low and appears to be a negotiating position. The bill would also limit personal and immediate-family expenditures to twenty thousand dollars for those who participate in the public-financing plan. If a candidate chose not to accept public financing but to spend large amounts of his own money, or to exceed the spending limits, the spending limits on his opponent would be lifted, and the opponent would receive double the amount in matching funds. Obey would provide free television time for a candidate to respond to an independent group's attack, or additional public financing equal to the amount of the independent expenditures for television; and he would also offer to match other independent expenditures that amounted in the aggregate to more than five thousand dollars.

If in fact there would remain imbalances as a result of labor's efforts to get people registered and to the polls, it is not beyond the mind of man to figure out a solution to this, either. (It is to be remembered that both labor and business are now allowed to spend unlimited amounts to communicate with their own members or employees on political matters. Moreover, such organizations as the Chamber of Commerce conduct get-out-the-vote drives, and business is developing other ways to compete with labor.) The possibilities range from prohibiting these activities—which doesn't seem very healthy—to improving the registration system or designing a system under which the parties play the major role in these activities. One possibility would be to allow the parties to raise money for such activities (as was done in 1979 for the Presidential campaign)— and, in both Presidential and congressional campaigns, to impose limits and an effective reporting system. This way, soft money could be brought under control, and the two problems would be dealt with at once.

Two arguments made against public financing are that it would amount to an incumbent-protection act, since incumbents enjoy certain advantages, and that it would guarantee a challenger enough money to give an incumbent a disconcertingly stiff race. (The second argument is one that people on Capitol Hill make very quietly.) Both arguments, of course, can't be true. And if public financing amounted to an incumbent-protection act, it would have passed long since, unless Congress is an uncommonly noble institution. Moreover, most of the public-financing schemes have taken it into account that a highly restrictive spending limit would prevent challengers from competing effectively. Fred Wertheimer, the president of Common Cause, points out that the first two incumbent Presidents to run under the system of public financing of Presidential campaigns—Ford and Carter—both lost. As for the advantages of incumbency,

Common Cause has brought legal action against abuse of the franking privilege. Wertheimer adds, "Incumbency has its pluses and its minuses." He says, "The key is to have a system that allows a challenger to compete. That's really all we can do, and that's all we should do."

Leach refers to the proposal to limit PAC contributions as "a kind of domestic SALT agreement between big business and big labor." In introducing his bill, Obey said, "We do not object to people accepting PAC contributions. But the size of these contributions moved around the nation by unseen hands in Washington office buildings can determine the politics of Wisconsin or Montana or Vermont or any other state in the Union. We do object to that." The lines between the representative and his constituents have been disturbed, if not yet completely cut. Elections are determined in increasing measure by forces outside the district and the state.

A number of Republicans think that it is not against the interests of their party to support a public-financing system. Barber Conable, a Republican representative from New York, who is among them, says, "Large contributions tend to come to incumbents; by the nature of things, our party will have more challengers." One Republican political consultant says, "Republicans who oppose public financing—and the great majority do—say, 'How can we overcome the numerical disadvantage of being a Republican?' I don't think that's a valid objection. It is true that Republicans are in the minority, but that is not an argument for opposing public financing. Privately, their argument is 'We can blow them out by outspending them.' My view is that if the money represents an unfair advantage it ought to be eliminated. Where is the ethics or morality in saying the system ought to be maintained because it

59

benefits you, if the advantage is inherently unfair?"

It has been argued that the public financing of congressional campaigns would be costly. However, most of the proposals call for it to be paid for out of the voluntary dollar checkoff on tax returns, which might be raised to two dollars—so the system would be self-financed. Another dollar a year seems a small price to pay. (One estimate, based on recent campaign costs, is that the system would cost about eighty million dollars per two-year election cycle.) The more important point is how expensive it is *not* to have public financing and some limit on PAC contributions, and how risky it is *not* to restore the Presidential-election system to the way it was supposed to work. The costs are everywhere—throughout the tax code and the federal budget. They turn up in everything from the Pentagon budget to medical bills. In effect, as we go about our daily lives,

buying food, gasoline, and medicine, and as we pay our taxes, we are paying for the current system of financing campaigns.

And there are less tangible but more important costs. We are paying in the declining quality of politicians and of the legislative product, and in the rising public cynicism. We have allowed it to become increasingly difficult for the good people who remain in politics to function well. What results is a corrosion of the system and a new kind of squalor—conditions that are well known to those who are in it and to those who deal with it at close range. The public knows that something is very wrong. As the public cynicism gets deeper, the political system gets worse. Until the problem of money is dealt with, the system will not get better. We have allowed the basic idea of our democratic process—representative government—to slip away. The only question is whether we are serious about trying to retrieve it.

NO

Robert J. Samuelson

THE CAMPAIGN REFORM FAILURE

The United States invented modern democracy and has practiced it longer and more successfully than any other nation. For all its flaws, it works remarkably well. While mediating among the jumbled interests of a geographically, ethnically, racially, religiously, and economically diverse nation, it has preserved both freedom and stability. When asked about their political leaders, Americans (according to public opinion polls) often hold their noses. But when asked about their political system, they overwhelmingly express intense pride.

Any discussion of money's role in politics needs to start with these fundamentals, because the critics of the status quo do not simply argue that the current system of campaign financing is imperfect. Increasingly, they contend that it menaces the American democratic achievement itself. As Elizabeth Drew concludes in her short book, *Politics and Money:* "We have allowed the basic idea of our democratic process—representative government—to slip away. The only question is whether we are serious about trying to retrieve it."

To advance this argument is to shoulder a heavy burden. It does not suffice to demonstrate that money plays an important and not always healthy role in politics. No one has ever doubted that. Nor does it suffice to show that the current system is flawed. Almost everyone concedes that. The burden that Drew and other reform advocates assume is to persuade that money has attained unprecedented leverage over government behavior. And more: that there are possible reforms that would represent substantial improvements without aggravating current deficiencies or creating new ones.

The argument fails—utterly. . . .

There are two reasons, nevertheless, for treating Drew's tract seriously. The first is that it elicits agreement from large numbers of influential people. Many journalists, congressmen, and lawyer-lobbyists—all powerful opinion-makers

3. DO POLITICAL ACTION COMMITTEES UNDERMINE DEMOCRACY?

about Washington—seem to accept that money is corrupting politics. Typical is this prepublication plaudit from *Washington Post* reporter Bob Woodward: "No one else has had the guts or the determination to open up this subject. Brilliant reporting. As a reporter, I am embarrassed I didn't find this story myself."

Even if the "story" is untrue—which it is—its constant repetition gives the appearance of truth and shapes public opinion. Drew's *New Yorker* series is but one example of a general media drumbeat of criticism. (See, for instance, Mark Green's "Political PAC-man," TNR, December 13, 1982.) Played often enough and loud enough, the theme of corruption acquires respectability. It aggravates the very problem the reformers purport to be curing: the loss of public confidence in elected officials and governmental institutions. The aim, of course, is campaign reform.

And therein lies the second cause for concern. For the logic of campaign reform implies fundamental, not cosmetic, changes. It strikes at a basic constitutional tenet: free speech. If free speech includes the right to seek political influence, it involves the right to spend. The Supreme Court took this position in *Buckley* v. *Valeo* (a 1976 case challenging the 1974 election law), and it is simply common sense. If I am unhappy with my legislator, am I to be prevented from spending money in an effort to convince others of my position? If I want to influence my government, am I to be prevented from spending money to do so? And what more natural way than working to elect people who share my views?

Problems obviously surface. Representative democracy presumes to represent people, not dollars. Moreover, people do not speak only as individuals but also as organized groups—interest groups. And

interest groups are unequal in size, wealth, and, usually, influence. This part of the problem is not new. James Madison recognized it years ago. Calling interest groups "factions," he argued that their power would be limited by natural conflicts and the mechanics of government. The division of power among two legislative houses and the executive and judicial branches would require compromise, groups acting "in unison with each other." But if the provisioning of money has now become so vital to politics that Madison's balance is lost, then irreconcilable conflicts arise among traditional values. Either free speech (including free spending) is compromised or the representative nature of democracy is eroded.

Drew is convinced that we have reached this juncture and, therefore, entertains radical revisions in free speech. She argues that we need to "redefine what we mean by 'freedom of speech,' and [to] uncouple 'the marketplace of ideas from the idea of the 'free market.' " In practice, she favors more public financing for campaigns and tighter controls on private campaign spending. Justifying these, she approvingly summarizes an argument made by former Solicitor General Archibald Cox, a chairman of Common Cause who has argued campaign law cases. Cox, she writes,

> suggested that one way to deal with the proposition that spending money equals free speech would be to say that there are lots of different kinds of expenditures, and perhaps money is speech in the instance of a person spending money to publish or broadcast his own thoughts, while it is an entirely different thing when an organization raises money from all over the country and spends it to broadcast. The difference, he said, is that the money is collected nationally, and that it is used for much speech but few ideas.

A measure of reformers' obsession is that they have descended to these meaningless and essentially antidemocratic distinctions. Individuals may have a right to "free speech," but organizations (collections of individuals) may have a lesser right. Some speech is good, but speech devoid of "ideas" (whose ideas?) may not be. Organizations locally financed may be more deserving than those nationally financed. Happily, however, we have not reached the juncture that Drew and other reformers suggest. To be sure, the political system is changing—it always is and always has—but the changes have not demolished representative government, including Madison's safeguards.

No one seriously disputes that campaign (as opposed to legislative) politics needs more money than ever before. The critical questions are whether money's new role fundamentally distorts politics and the opportunities for representation and influence. . . .

Like most campaign reformers, Drew is most agitated by the rise of PACs, especially business and trade association PACs. It's true that these PACs have assumed a larger share of total campaign financing. But this is partially the doing of the campaign reform law itself. Aside from legitimizing PACs, it also restricted, probably unintentionally, even modest individual giving. Between 1974 and 1982, prices roughly doubled, meaning that 1974's $1,000 contribution was worth only about $500 in 1982. This almost certainly made it more essential for Congressmen to accept money from PACs and more attractive for politically active individuals to give to them.

Even so, PACs' total share of campaign funds has probably not risen as quickly as commonly assumed. Individual fundraising still accounts for the lion's share of con-

gressional funds. In 1982, PACs accounted for about 29.3 percent of the total for *winning* candidates, up from 22 percent in 1976. In the House, the proportion rose from 25.6 percent to 34.2 percent; the comparable Senate figures were 14.8 percent in 1976 and 21.9 percent in 1982. And even these figures do not imply anything about legislative influence, because PACs are remarkably diversified. They come in all sizes, shapes, and flavors. In 1980, corporate PACs accounted for about a third of the total and labor PACs for about a quarter; but there were also PACs from trade associations (also about a quarter), PACs set up by independent political groups, agricultural cooperatives, and members of Congress (including Republicans and Democrats, liberals and conservatives). In total, Democratic candidates received slightly more from PACs than Republicans—$42.8 million against $36.4 million—because labor PACs favored Democrats by an 18 to 1 margin. . . .

The acid test lies in legislation. What happens in Congress? An example of Drew's tunnel analysis involves oil provisions in the massive 1981 tax cut. As she portrays it, these resulted primarily from a "bidding war" for oil campaign contributions. Although the original White House tax bill contained a small pro-oil section, the Democrats sweetened it considerably. They hoped, Drew says, to reclaim their share of oil money, which she says had shifted heavily to the Republicans. The Republicans retaliated by sweetening the proposal even further. When the bidding was over, the bill contained tax relief, rising to $3.6 billion in fiscal 1986, for oil interests. Thus, money moves legislation.

There was indeed a bidding war, but of a different sort: over votes more than contributions. At the time, the House was torn between White House and Democratic tax bills. Both contained significant individual and business cuts, although the amounts and the distributions differed. The real question was power: could the Democrats control the House, where they were nominally the majority party? Once the House leadership decided it wanted a Democratic bill at all costs, the swing Congressmen who would determine the bill's fate acquired enormous bargaining power. And this group—consisting heavily of conservative Democrats, quickly labeled "Boll Weevils," and including many from oil states—used its power accordingly.

Of the forty-eight Democrats who ultimately voted for the Reagan tax bill (the Republicans ultimately prevailed), twelve came from Texas, Louisiana, and Oklahoma. In 1980, these three states accounted for 61 percent of U.S. oil production. Although Drew discusses the bill as if it benefited only oil producers, much of the tax relief went to royalty owners, who own land on which oil is produced for a fee (usually 12.5 percent). Estimates of royalty owners vary from five hundred thousand to 2.5 million—the smaller number is probably more accurate—but they're concentrated in oil-producing states. As one Hill staffer puts it: "Oil filters down throughout the whole district. Even people who don't have a direct interest in oil have an indirect interest, because of its economic importance. You get a political orientation that is pro-oil." But had the Democratic leadership contested the White House tax proposal with a philosophical alternative—conceding tactical defeat, instead of being bludgeoned into submission—the Boll Weevils would never have acquired negotiating leverage.

An even more important omission mars Drew's account. No one denies that independent oil producers have long used campaign contributions to further their own ends. But if anything, their influence was waning in the 1970s. For most of the decade, the government controlled domestic oil prices and prevented producers from reaping most benefits of higher world oil prices. When controls were finally removed—having been opposed by most economists and by Europe and Japan, which saw low prices feeding America's oil gluttony—Congress limited producers' gains by imposing a windfall-profits tax in 1980. The entire 1981 struggle was to lighten, not eliminate, provisions of the windfall tax. The independent producers and royalty owners were fighting a rearguard action. They did influence policy—but only at the margin. In the 1981 tax bill, the oil provisions accounted for 1.5 percent of the total estimated revenue loss.

Most of Drew's other examples founder on similar complications. She cites the efforts of the American Medical Association to have Congress prevent the Federal Trade Commission from reviewing potentially price-fixing practices of professional associations. But, as Drew offhandedly notes, the A.M.A. proposal failed. She cites an effort by maritime interests to have more oil transported in American vessels. But that failed, too. She cites passage (also as part of the 1981 tax law) of the All Savers Certificate for savings and loans associations, a scheme she rightly describes as ill conceived. But its approval stemmed not so much from campaign contributions as other factors: first, the identification of the savings industry with housing; and second, widespread fears that, if the industry wasn't helped, numerous bankruptcies would result. In case after case, the actual story is more complicated than Drew's story.

Her list also omits most major issues: Social Security defense policy, Medicare and medical costs, overall economic management. No one has yet seriously contended that campaign contributions dominate policies in these areas, though surely "special interests" are involved. The issues are simply too entangled in popular passions, prejudices, and conflicting political philosophies. Individual defense projects may subsist on vested interests—nothing new—but overall defense spending clearly reflects other pressures.

Far from being "brilliant" journalism, Drew's reporting is precisely the kind that young reporters ought to be warned away from vigorously. It involves selective and misleading use of evidence, an overreliance on self-serving quotes, and an absence of critical analysis. She approvingly quotes a favorite one-liner by Senator Robert Dole, Republican of Kansas: "There aren't any Poor PACs, or Food Stamp PACs or Nutrition PACs or Medicare PACs." But, of course, there is a food stamp program, a Medicare program, and a substantial array of welfare programs. They were enacted because they were thought to be good ideas and, even if recently trimmed, they survive because people still believe them to be good ideas and because they have substantial constituencies.

Just because moneyed interests swarm all over Capitol Hill (and they do) does not mean that money rules the roost. In fact, PACs tend to check each other. When one interest organizes a PAC, competing interests do likewise. Even then, there are other checks on their power. One is the spotlight of public attention focused by the press, groups like Common Cause, and other politicians. Another is the obstacle course of enacting any legislation. American democracy is still working to accommodate conflicting interests and ideals. It is not perfect, but the Madisonian mechanisms have survived.

A charitable observer might convict

Drew and fellow reformers of nothing more than sloppy analysis. Like Drew, most reformers are intelligent and well intentioned. Their numbers include energetic and reflective younger members of Congress. Nor is their unease and outrage difficult to understand. Their analysis springs from their nerve endings. Just as some people dislike fast-food restaurants, they detest the taste and feel of the new politics. Drew does not like Washington's nightly fundraisers. She thinks it demeaning, degrading, and distracting that elected representatives spend their time dealing with anything so crass as money. She abhors the lobbyists infesting Capitol Hill with their wads of PAC funds. It simply offends her sensibilities.

But this distaste produces a mentality far more threatening to the national political tradition than the sins of campaign finances. The attempt to deny money's new place in politics is futile—just as it was futile to deny the emergence of big city machines—but the effort entails heavy costs. The most obvious is the smothering of campaigns in bureaucratic tedium. Alexander drily observes that federal election law increasingly resembles the tax law, with the Federal Election Commission "doing for politics what the Internal Revenue Service does for taxes." This, he notes, "increases the need for professionals—accountants, lawyers and other skilled individuals—to help candidates" comply with complex regulations, and it may "chill enthusiasm for citizen participation . . . since nonknowledgeable amateurs may easily violate the law."

A more serious defect is to undermine the moral authority of political leaders and the political process. If one lesson emerges clearly from Drew's account, it is the impossibility of enacting campaign reform laws that will not be speedily subverted.

3. DO POLITICAL ACTION COMMITTEES UNDERMINE DEMOCRACY?

The ease with which the limits on Presidential spending were evaded—via "independent expenditures" and state party spending—underscores that. Because politics now increasingly requires spending (as opposed to volunteer efforts or organizational commitment), legislated restrictions invite circumvention. If spending through one channel is curtailed, it will simply pop up—with some delay and difficulty, perhaps—elsewhere. The capping of individual contributions and the skyrocketing of PAC spending is but one example.

To enact laws whose failure can be predicted is an act of extreme political and legal irresponsibility. It means government creates unrealistic and unmaintainable moral standards. Candidates and political professionals are immediately thrust into unavoidably compromising positions. They can strictly abide by the letter and spirit of the law—an act of high virtue and possibly political suicide. Or they can examine the law to see how it can be stretched, twisted, and avoided. Perhaps, in the first flush of reform, virtue prevails. But as time passes and evasions become more widespread, the taboos against them diminish and the necessity of conforming increases. The participants in this process become steeped in either cynicism or guilt. When the public recognizes the gap between enacted standards of behavior and actual practices, esteem for elected officials suffers. Reformers fan the disillusion, declaring politics "corrupt" and proclaiming they are trying to reestablish the government's moral authority. Actually, they are unwittingly destroying it. . . .

Coping with these contradictions risks intruding on free speech, a subject Drew treats casually. At some points, she ambiguously suggests limits on political groups that, simply put, she just doesn't like. For example, she deplores the activities of the National Conservative Political Action Committee and the Congressional Club, a PAC maintained by Senator Jesse Helms, Republican of North Carolina. The massive activities of these groups, she argues, go "beyond political expression . . . they manipulate people's desire for political expression, and in a way that deliberately distorts the issues." These groups, she says, "are not the same as grass-roots movements that form around an issue. These committees are highly skilled, directed organizations that use people's feelings about certain issues to gain influence."

This is a mind-boggling train of thought. NCPAC and the Congressional Club differ from "grass-roots movements that form around an issue," yet they "use people's feelings about certain issues to gain influence." Can anyone make sense of that? To follow Drew's thinking to its logical conclusion is to suggest rules for restricting what she believes is demagoguery (as opposed to legitimate political expression) and inappropriate "highly skilled, directed organizations" (as opposed to appropriate "grass-roots" groups). Somehow, one suspects, these are distinctions never contemplated by the Founding Fathers.

Ultimately, the cause of reforming campaign finances leads to dead ends because it clings to a primitive, unrealistic, and even undesirable view of representative government. "Special interests" is one of those over-used phrases that is simultaneously descriptive and deceptive. It is descriptive in the sense that the interests of these groups are usually narrow and often selfish. It is deceptive in the pejorative implication that the term naturally carries. The burden—and the glory, too—of modern American democracy is the proliferation of these groups. Their expansion is the natural result of the post-Depression growth of government spending and authority. If democracy is people's right to be heard on issues that engage their interests and emotions, then government's growth could have had no other effect. Because government interferes more, it is interfered with more. Because the nature of its intervention has become more narrow and detailed, so has the nature of the political reaction.

The inevitability of special interests and their political activism underlines the permanent importance of one campaign reform enacted in the early 1970s: disclosure of election contributions. Secret free speech is an illogical and almost comical concept. The disclosure of contributions not only exposes the motives of politicians to public scrutiny but also enables competing interests to mobilize. But, otherwise, most campaign reforms represent a futile effort to reverse irreversible trends. Supposing, against all logic, that the campaign activities of "special interests" could be curbed, would that end the problem? Of course not. It would simply intensify Washington lobbying and grass-roots campaigns to influence specific decisions. Banks' successful effort to repeal the withholding of interest and dividends may be a forerunner of this sort of effort.

More important, the prejudice against special interests strikes at the heart of the democratic process. One person's special interest is another's crusade. The function of politics is not only to govern in the general interest and to reconcile differences among specific interests; it is also to provide outlets for political and social tensions. People often accept governmental outcomes with which they disagree if they feel they had a chance to influence the process. In a nation as diverse as the United States, it is unhealthy to place too many restrictions on these outlets. The risk is making people believe that government is even more inaccessible and unresponsive than they already do.

No one, of course, should pretend the resulting system is problem-free. It isn't. The growth of government authority and political activism has led to severe tensions, most obvious to Congressmen. They are overburdened with work, confronted with more issues than they can possibly master, pestered by more constituencies than can possibly be satisfied, and—given the certainty of disappointed suitors—presented with the constant threat of organized opposition to their reelection. Within Congress, the multiplication of government programs and interest groups has made the creation of enduring coalitions more difficult. Combined with other changes—declining party loyalty, the weakening of parties and (within Congress) committee chairmen, the fading of Depression-era attitudes—these shifts have made politics more difficult and less secure. Power has been fragmented or, in Drew's word, splintered. At the same time, powerful and often contradictory popular expectations of government performance have emerged concerning everything from Social Security to the environment.

The convergence of these trends—the diffusion of power and increased public demands—accounts for much of government's floundering and failure over the past decade. On the one hand, government faces paralysis: a collision of competing interests so severe that nothing happens. (In late 1982, one Congressman described Congress's inability to revise the Clean Air Act to Drew this way: "The stalemate has been caused 50 percent by industry and 50 percent by environmentalists. Congressmen on the committee say, 'Hey, do we really have to act on this this year?' ") On the other hand, there looms the sort of pervasive contradiction that compels government to act in ways that are ultimately self-defeating. The clearest illustration is the tax system: the proliferation of special tax provisions has reduced public confidence in the system, while simultaneously spurring new demands for more special relief which, once enacted, further erode public confidence.

The picture can be dispiriting. In part it reflects the inability of political leaders—of both parties—to find new themes that cut across the special interests of individuals, groups, and corporations and provide a new basis for building coalitions. This is the ongoing drama of government, but it should not be mislabeled. The system is struggling, but it is not corrupt.

POSTSCRIPT

DO POLITICAL ACTION COMMITTEES UNDERMINE DEMOCRACY?

Congress has dealt fitfully with the issue of improper political influence, as Elizabeth Drew demonstrates when tracing legislative action from a 1907 bar on corporate contributions to the 1974 law establishing public financing of presidential campaigns. However, the issue does not die.

What is improper influence? When is a monetary contribution a valid expression of political support, and at what point does it become a corrupt act, unduly influencing the behavior of a public official? On the one hand, democracy demands free expression and participation, including the right to expend effort and money on behalf of issues and candidates. On the other hand, there is the risk that vast sums of money will provide radically unequal access for different points of view and that underfinanced candidates will not reach their potential audiences.

Herbert Alexander has been the leading scholar chronicling the influence of money in American elections since 1960. His latest study is *Financing the 1980 Election* (Lexington Books, 1983). An up-to-date survey of the influence of PACs is undertaken in "Is Congress for Sale?" by Jeffery L. Sheler with Robert F. Black, *U.S. News & World Report* (May 28, 1984).

Other countries succeed in setting strict limits on campaign spending. Can we do it without inhibiting political expression? Should we substitute public financing of congressional elections? Or do we accept PACs as a vigorous expression of political freedom? In short, do PACs undermine or do they underline democracy?

PART II
DOES AMERICAN GOVERNMENT GOVERN WELL?

The Constitution gives us three governing organs: President, Congress, and the Supreme Court. Over the years our government has generated another organ with a life of its own: the bureaucracy. Finally, it is arguable that the mass media have become at least a quasi-governing power.

How well do these organs work? Have some become too powerful and others too weak? The clear intent of the Constitution is that President, Congress, and the Supreme Court should be "co-equal" branches, but in recent years critics have charged that the President has over-shadowed Congress. Other critics focus their criticism upon the Supreme Court, which, they charge, has been exceeding its legitimate powers. And what of the mass media? Have newspapers, maga-zines, radio and TV become a collective governing organ of the nation? If so, do they need some sort of "reform"? Or would such "reform" really amount to repression? The arguments in this section demonstrate that there are no easy answers.

Is Congress Too Weak?

Has Congress Restricted Presidential War Powers Too Much?

Does the Government Regulate Too Much?

Does the Supreme Court Abuse Its Power?

Regulating Media: Is the "Fairness Doc-trine" Unfair?

71

ISSUE 4

IS CONGRESS TOO WEAK?

YES: Gregg Easterbrook, from "What's Wrong With Congress?" *The Atlantic Monthly,* December 1984

NO: Gary Orfield, from *Congressional Power: Congress and Social Change* (New York, 1975)

ISSUE SUMMARY

YES: Journalist Gregg Easterbrook believes that, before Congress can lead the nation, it must be able to lead itself, and it has notably failed to do so.
NO: Brookings Institute member Gary Orfield argues that Congress does a good job of reflecting the attitudes and trends of the electorate as a whole. If Congress seems unresponsive, he says, it is not the fault of the institution but a comment on the priorities of the country at the moment.

Can Representative Government Do the Job? was the title of a thoughtful 1945 book, and many Americans remain uncertain about the answer to that question. Putting the question bluntly, we may ask: Is Congress strong enough?

There is a widespread belief that Congress is a clumsy, unwieldy institution. The structure of Congress impresses (or depresses) its critics as being a horse-and-buggy vehicle in a jet age. Power is fragmented among many committees in the absence of national parties, which might impose discipline on legislators and coherence on legislation. Within the committees, the chairmen have the power; until recently, chairmen were chosen strictly on the basis of seniority (length of service) rather than for their leadership abilities. Woodrow Wilson called America "a government by the chairmen of standing committees of Congress." Although much power has since shifted to the president, congressional chairmen remain subject to few checks.

Perhaps the decline of Congress in this century is partly due to its outmoded structure, but it is easy to see how the two World Wars, the Korean and Vietnam wars, and the Great Depression, as well as other issues that transcend national boundaries, contributed to the decline. Increasingly, we have looked to the president rather than to Congress for inspiration, initiative, and leadership. The president, after all, is an individual, and we can personalize his power; we can identify him and identify *with* him, while Congress remains a faceless abstraction.

The president can act with a promptness and decisiveness that the two houses and their 535 members cannot. He alone is nationally elected and may, therefore, come closer to being a tribune of the people. He alone possesses the power of life and death as the negotiator of international relations and commander-in-chief of the armed forces.

It was not surprising, therefore, that liberals looked to the president for the bold action that was not forthcoming from a lethargic and leaderless Congress. But many who had supported presidential dominance eventually ended up warning against the "Imperial Presidency" as a result of Watergate, the abuse of power, the evidence of unnecessary presidential secrecy and calculated deceit, and a new awareness of unchecked presidential decision making.

The fear that presidential power may be abused has kindled the hope that representative government can be improved. Toward that end, the seniority system (at least for Democrats) is no longer a certain route to committee chairmanships. The requirement of open committee meetings and increased access to once-confidential files has increased public (particularly the press') scrutiny of governmental behavior. Congress has set up its own budget committees, and the War Powers Act was designed to inhibit presidential warmaking in the absence of a congressional declaration of war.

Perhaps, as Gary Orfield suggests, what is necessary is not technical reform but political will—that is, a public desire to have Congress exercise its power more vigorously. Orfield holds that it is not fair for reformers to criticize Congress for not adopting programs that most Americans have not indicated support for. On the other hand, Gregg Easterbrook lists a variety of shortcomings—the fragmentation of legislative power, the inability to modernize the budget process, the proliferation of lobbies—which appear to contribute to the decline of congressional power.

YES
Gregg Easterbrook

WHAT'S WRONG WITH CONGRESS?

Representative Michael Synar, of Oklahoma, swears that this actually happened: He was addressing a Cub Scout pack in Grove, Oklahoma, not far from his home town of Muskogee. Synar asked the young boys if they could tell him the difference between the Cub Scouts and the United States Congress. One boy raised his hand and said, "We have adult supervision."

Is anyone in charge on Capitol Hill? October's two-week-long melodrama over shutting down the government was not an isolated instance. Recently Congress voted for a $749 billion package of tax cuts, and only a few months later was locked in debate over a constitutional amendment for a balanced budget. The House voted in favor of Ronald Reagan's plan to almost double the number of nuclear warheads in the U.S. arsenal, and not long after voted in favor of the nuclear freeze. Only once in the past six years has Congress finished the budget appropriations before the beginning of the fiscal year; many spending bills have not been completed until months after the spending they supposedly control has begun. Long periods of legislative stalling are followed by spasms in which bills are passed with wild abandon, and these often contain "unprinted amendments" whose contents congressmen have never had an opportunity to read. Many provisions of "tax leasing" became law that way, as, in 1981, did the phone number of a woman named Rita. Rita's number had been scribbled in the margin of the only copy of an amendment being voted on, and the following day it was duly transcribed into the printed copy of the bill.

"The system is a mess, and what's amazing is how many members of Congress are fully aware that the system is a mess," says Alan Dixon, a senator from Illinois. Congress has, of course, seemed out of control at many points in the past. During the late 1930s, as signs of war grew, Congress was synonymous with irresponsibility; during the McCarthy era, with cowardice. In 1959 it ground to a halt over the minor issue of Dwight Eisenhower's nomination of Lewis Strauss as secretary of commerce and the even less important issue of an Air Force Reserve honorary promotion for the actor Jimmy Stewart. Through the 1960s it huffed and puffed about the Vietnam War, but never failed to approve funds for the fighting. In 1972, after hours of acrimonious debate, it voted to raise the federal debt ceiling for a single day. A degree of built-in vacillation was part of the Founding Fathers' plan for the legislature. But have recent changes in the structure both of U.S. politics and of Congress as an institution pushed Congress across the fine line separating creative friction from chaos?

"Congress today is a totally different institution from what it was when I arrived, in 1961," says Morris Udall, of Arizona, one of the House's senior members. "The magnitude of change is no illusion." The end of the seniority system; the arabesque budget "process" and other time-consuming new additions like the War Powers Act; the transformation from party loyalty to political-action-committee (PAC) loyalty; the increased emphasis on media campaigning; the vogue of running against Washington and yet being a member of the Washington establishment; the development of ideological anti-campaigns; a dramatic increase in congressional-subcommittee power and staff size, and a parallel increase in the scope and intensity of lobbying—all are creations of the past fifteen years. Some have served to make the nation's legislature more democratic and to improve its contact with the public. Others have made congressmen more frantic and timorous. But every change has in some respect caused Congress to become more difficult to run. Right now there isn't anyone in charge, and there may never be again.

EVERYWHERE A MR. CHAIRMAN

Hardly anyone laments the dismantling of the seniority rules—not even people like Udall, who would benefit if the old system still existed. From roughly the turn of the century until 1975 rank was based solely on how many years a member had been in Congress. The chairman of a committee could create or disband subcommittees, choose the subcommittee chairmen (often choosing himself), dictate when the subcommittees held hearings and whether bills were "referred" to them, hire the committee staff, and exert total control over when the committee itself would hold hearings or report bills to the floor. All these powers rested exclusively with twenty to twenty-five men in each chamber; others in Congress could wield power only by outvoting the senior members on the floor, and then only when the senior members permitted such votes to occur.

Seniority had long been considered unassailable, for the reason that senior members would use their powers to block any reform. But by the late 1960s the resistance of the southern committee chairmen to the obvious need for civil-rights reform had eroded seniority to the point at which challenges became possible. Every two years, as a new Congress was convened and new internal rules were passed, younger members would press for further concessions. "In 1971 we managed to pass a resolution saying that seniority would not be the sole criterion for chairmanship and that there ought to be a vote," Udall explains. "It was vaguely worded and we didn't try to take the issue any further. In 1973 for the first time, we held such votes. Every chairman was retained, but it established the precedent—that there had to be a vote. Then in 1975 we won."

4. IS CONGRESS TOO WEAK?

It was a pivotal year for the structure of Congress. Ninety-two new representatives, mostly Democrats—the "Class of '74"—had been elected to the House in the wake of Watergate. Government institutions in general were in a state of low regard. Conservative southerners had been shamed by how long they had stood by Richard Nixon; and two powerful old-school committee chairmen, Wilbur Mills,, of the Ways and Means Committee, and Wayne Hays, of the House Administration Committee, were going off the deep end. The Class of '74 provided the extra margin of votes needed to end seniority in the House. Three entrenched chairmen—Wright Patman, of the Banking Committee, F. Edward Hebert, of Armed Services, and W.R. Poage, of Agriculture—were overthrown. More significant in the long run, a "subcommittee bill of rights" was passed. Essentially, subcommittees won the right to hold hearings on any subject at any time. Committee members would be able to "bid" for subcommittee chairmanships; full committee chairmen could no longer control these slots or hold more than one subcommittee chairmanship themselves. Each subcommittee chairman would get funds for at least one staff aide who would work for him personally, not for the committee. The total number of subcommittees would be expanded. A similar though more genteel sequence of change took place in the Senate.

The autocracy of the chair broken, Congress was transformed from an institution in which power was closely held by a few to an institution in which almost everyone had just enough strength to toss a monkey wrench. In 1964 there were forty-seven meaningful chairmanships available in the House and Senate. Between the dispersion of subcommittee posts and the increase in the total number of committees and subcommittees, 326 Mr. Chairman positions were available in 1984. Allowing for those who hold more than one chairmanship, 202 of Congress's 535 members—38 percent—are now in charge of something.

More than any other factor, the deregulation of subcommittees has increased Congress's workload and decreased its cohesion. In 1970, before the change, congressional committees held an average of twenty-three meetings a day, and it remains at that level today. Senators now average twelve committee and subcommittee assignments each. With the trend toward "government in the sunshine" the number of closed committee hearings has dropped substantially—from 35 percent of all hearings in 1960 to seven percent in 1975. This serves the public's right to know but also increases the amount of time congressmen spend posturing for public consumption instead of saying what they think, which is practical only in closed hearings. The subcommittee bill of rights established "multiple referral," under which several subcommittees could consider the same bill or topic. The result is increased redundancy, more speechifying, and almost unlimited potential for turf fights.

According to John Tower, chairman of the Senate Armed Services Committee, "Our committee spends a large proportion of its time trying to fend off competition from other committees and monitoring what the other committees are doing." In the Senate the Armed Services, Appropriations, Governmental Affairs, Budget, Foreign Relations, and Veterans' Affairs committees all have an interest in military legislation; subcommittees of the same committe may also have overlapping jurisdictions, such as the Arms Control and European Affairs subcommittees of Foreign Relations. Multiple subcommittees each with multiple jurisdictions are a primary cause of the dizzy progression of non-events in Congress. Headlines like SENATE MOVES TO BAN IMPORTS and HOUSE HALTS FUNDS often refer to subcommittee actions that will be modified many times before they take effect or, more likely, vanish without a trace. Some sort of milestone was achieved last June when both the International Economic Policy Subcommittee of the Senate Foreign Relations Committee and the International Trade Subcommittee of the Senate Finance Committe held hearings covering the same topic—Japanese auto imports—on the same day, at the same time, with many of the same witnesses.

Driving the system is the unleashed desire of congressmen to be in command of something—anything. Culture shock for new congressmen arriving in Washington can be severe. Having just won a grueling electoral test and bearing the status of big wheels at home, in Washington they discover that they are among thousands of potentially important people competing for influence and attention. Young congressmen also find themselves assigned to cramped, dingy offices with Naugahyde furnishings and no majestic view of the Capitol dome. The yearning for a Washington badge of recognition and the additional perquisites that would make Capitol Hill life what they imagined it to be can set in almost immediately.

A chairmanship is particularly important because television is permitted in hearing rooms. Almost from the onset of television, congressmen have realized the promotional potential of the carefully scripted hearing: the McCarthy and Kefauver hearings of the 1950s, which were among the first "television events," made their eponyms famous.

Fame may be an elusive goal, but pub-licity is not. The proliferation of networks and newscasts meshes perfectly with the proliferation of Capitol Hill hearings. Congress itself is difficult for television to cover, because no single person is in charge and few actions are final. A well-done hearing, in contrast, has a master of ceremonies, a story line, and an easily summarized conclusion when a witness commits a gaffe, announces a "policy shift," or clashes angrily with committee members. Hearings, unlike floor action, also allow congressmen to introduce props—the masked witness being a perennial favorite, piles of money or gimmicks like chattering teeth being reliable avenues to television coverage.

Once created, a subcommittee takes on a life of its own, if for no other reason than that the staff must justify its existence. In 1970 the House Committee on the District of Columbia had fifteen staff members; today it has thirty. The Senate Rules Committee had thirteen staff members in 1970 and today has twenty-seven. The House Appropriations Committee has more than twice as many staff members as it had in 1970, and the Merchant Marine and Fisheries Committee's staff has risen from twenty-one to eighty-nine. Debra Knopman, a former staff aide to Senator Daniel Moynihan, says, "The staffs are so large everybody wants to have his say and leave his own little stamp. Pretty soon the weight of people wanting attention becomes greater than the force moving the legislation, and the whole thing grinds to a halt."

Staff allegiance is to the subcommittee chairman rather than to the overall purpose of the legislature, and bickering with members of other staffs becomes a primary means of self-advancement. While the top jobs in congressional offices pay well—$46,000 to $56,000 a year—the average pay is only $25,000; between the low salaries and hectic working conditions, turnover in congressional offices runs at a rate of 40 percent a year. A staff of bright, inexperienced people will work harder and produce more good ideas per salary dollar spent than an older, trained staff, but it will also lack an institutional memory, demand more attention, and make more mischief, mostly in the form of turf fights.

The proliferation and redundancy of committees has produced a proliferation of redundant committees to study the problem. In the past decade the Senate has appointed three internal-reform study groups: the Stevenson Committee (named after the former Illinois senator Adlai Stevenson III), the Pearson-Ribicoff Study Group (run by retired senators James Pearson, of Kansas, and Abraham Ribicoff, of Connecticut), and a committee now meeting under the chairmanship of Senator Dan Quayle, of Indiana. Stevenson recommended a simplified system that would combine overlapping committees. Pearson and Ribicoff recommended that all subcommittees be abolished: that committees like the Small Business Committee and the Select Committee on Aging, which exist mainly to mollify interest groups, be subsumed into larger committees; and that the pairs of committees most frequently at each other's throats—the Armed Services and Foreign Relations committees, and the Budget and Appropriations committees—be merged.

None of the major Stevenson or Pearson—Ribicoff recommendations were enacted. The feudalistic system may prove in the long run more resilient than the seniority system, because now the number of congressmen with a stake in preventing change is much greater. Merging the Armed Services and Foreign Relations committees, for example, would eliminate one of the glamorous "A" committee chairmanships that are tickets to instant promi-

nence, to say nothing of eliminating about ten subcommittee chairmanships. When Howard Baker, the retiring majority leader, appeared before the Quayle committee last July to present a summing up of his years of leading the Senate, only two senators were present to hear him. All the rest had schedule conflicts.

THE BUDGET THAT WOULDN'T DIE

The way Congress spends money was converted into a "process" with the passage, in 1974, of the Congressional Budget and Impoundment Control Act. Its immediate purpose was to prevent Richard Nixon from "impounding," or refusing to spend, money that Congress had appropriated. But the Budget Act also had a long-term goal: solving a structural defect in Congress's spending machine.

Before 1974 the House and Senate each had three kinds of committees involved with the budget: authorizing, appropriating, and revenue. The authorizing committees, like Agriculture, Transportation, Energy, and Interior, are the most familiar; they "authorize" federal activity by writing legislation in their subject areas. But though they can start or end programs, they cannot approve expenditures—only the two appropriating committees can do that. Since the amount spent on a program usually determines that program's effect on policy, the potential for overlapping and disputation is boundless. Neither authorizing nor appropriating committees, meanwhile, have the power to raise the money that backs up the checks—only the Finance Committee, in the Senate, and the Ways and Means Committee, in the House, do. Because of this separation it became all too easy for authorizing and appropriating committees to ignore the fiscal consequences of their actions—getting the money was somebody else's job—and for the revenue committees, in turn, to demand that the other fellow crack down on spending.

During the 1950s and 1960s, when deficits were relatively stable, this state of affairs was tolerable. According to Robert Giaimo, who served in the House from 1958 to 1980 and was the Budget Committee chairman in the late 1970s, "No one, including myself, in Congress in the 1960s ever asked what anything would cost. All we thought about was, Does this sound like a good program? Can we get it through?"

The budget process was intended to bring together the questions of how much to spend, how to spend it, and where the funds would come from with a single resolution that would both guide Congress and impose a series of spending ceilings to control the deficit. Congress would have, say, a certain ceiling for transportation, and if it wanted to add funds to subway construction, it would have to remove a like amount from highways.

Ideally this would have been accomplished through some merging of the authorizing, appropriating, and revenue committees. But merger would have required that at least two powerful chairmen, plus many subcommittee chairmen, surrender their posts. So an entirely new procedural tier, the budget committees, complete with two important new chairmanships, was set on top. The result is what Howard Baker calls "a three-layer cake." In theory, on receiving the President's budget requests, in early winter, the budget committees quickly produce a nonbinding first resolution to set general ceilings. Then the authorizing committees write policy-setting legislation within those ceilings, and the appropriating commit-

tees—after learning of the authorizing committees' policy objectives—award the money. Near the end of this cycle the budget committees produce a second resolution to reconcile the inevitable differences between what the budget ceilings allow and what the committees are actually spending. This resolution is binding, and after it is passed, in theory the remaining pieces fall smoothly into place.

In practice the budget process isn't working anything like that. Budget resolutions have become the subjects of such contention that this year the first resolution, due on May 15, wasn't passed until October 1—even though it was nonbinding. Appropriating and authorizing committees work concurrently and nearly year-round, the appropriating committees choosing dollar amounts before, from the standpoint of policy, they know how the money will be used. The Budget Act breaks down spending into functional categories different from those employed by the committee structure, so when a budget resolution is being debated, wrestling goes on over which portion of which ceiling should apply to which committee, a procedure known as "crosswalk." Thus the process leads to a continuous frenzy of activity but few decisions that count.

In order to prepare the fiscal 1984 defense budget, the Senate Appropriations Committee held seventeen days of hearings, producing about 5,300 pages of testimony. The Senate Armed Services Committee held twenty-seven days of hearings on the defense budget and called 192 witnesses, many of whom also appeared before the Appropriations Committee to make the same statements. The Senate Budget Committee held hearings on the subject as well, producing two resolutions that had to be debated and voted on by the full Senate.

Meanwhile, in the House, the Armed Services, Appropriations, and Budget committees were duplicating this work, and the full chamber was voting on a different budget resolution. And none of it was final.

When the defense bill itself came to the Senate floor, it sparked weeks of debate; the (different) House bill caused a similar swirl on the floor. Even after that the defense budget wasn't finished. A House-Senate conference committee had to be created to resolve the discrepancies between the two versions, and then the conference-committee bill had to be debated and voted on by both chambers. Spending levels for the Defense Department weren't finally set until mid-November of 1983, seven weeks after the fiscal year had begun.

Last summer Howard Baker was negotiating simultaneously with various factions on the defense authorization bill and the defense appropriations bill and with a House-Senate conference committee deadlocked on the defense sections of the budget resolution. In other words, he was trying to arrive at three different versions of the same number—none of which would be final. "This is crazy," Baker told the Quayle committee, in a plaintive tone. "It makes absolutely no sense."

The endless budget deliberations have also been a driving force behind a dramatic increase in the number of recorded votes on the floor. In 1960 the House staged 180 roll-call votes, or 0.7 votes per working day. In 1970 there were 443 votes, or 1.3 per working day, and in 1980 there were 1,276 votes—3.9 each day. (In the Senate roll calls have increased from 1.5 a day in 1960 to 3 a day in 1980.)

The sheer logistics of staging four roll-call votes a day are imposing, because congressmen are rarely on the chamber floor, or even in the Capitol. When roll-call votes are signaled, congressmen must drop what they are doing (usually attending committee meetings at one of the congressional office buildings several hundred yards from the Capitol), race to the floor, vote, and race back. It is considered political suicide to miss roll-call votes, even when the subjects are trivial (in recent years the House voted 305 to 66 to establish Mother-in-Law Day and 388 to 11 to permit the International Communication Agency to distribute a slide show called *Montana: The People Speak*) or when the votes are likely to be overturned later. Since low attendance has an instant negative connotation, one of the easiest ways for a challenger to attack an incumbent congressman is to hammer at a "bad attendance record" on floor votes—a tactic that avoids the issue of whether the congressman might have made more meaningful use of his time. . . .

MULTIPLE LOBBYING

There are so many lobbyists today largely because there are so many opportunities to lobby. The breakdown of the seniority system and the weakening of congressional leadership has drastically increased the number of people on whom the touch must be put.

A well-informed veteran lobbyist says, "There used to be two to five guys on each side [House and Senate] who had absolute control over any category of bills you might want. All you had to do was get to them. Now getting the top guys is no guarantee. You have to lobby every member on every relevant subcommittee and even [lobby] the membership at large."

Another lobbyist, Eiler Ravnholt, who was for twelve years the administrative assistant to Senator Daniel Inouye, of Hawaii, and who now represents the Hawaiian Sugar Planters Association, adds that it has become necessary to lobby the expanded staff as well. "In the present environment congressmen spend so much time campaigning that they have no choice but to cede much of the legislative authority to their staffs," Ravnholt says. "During the 1960s it was not unusual to walk into the Senate library and see Sam Ervin sitting at a desk, researching a bill. Ervin was an exception,, but not that much of an exception; until fairly recently many congressmen played active roles in the legislative detail work. Now they can't. Nobody can. The staff does the detail work, and so you must lobby the staff." And where before there were a few important individuals on the House and Senate staffs, now there are thousands.

And thousands of lobbyists. There are 6,500 registered lobbyists in Washington (twelve for every congressman), but the figure does not include trade-association officers, lawyers working on retainer to clients, or liaison officials of corporations with Washington offices. The generally accepted total is about 20,000, or thirty-seven lobbyists for every congressman. Determined interest groups often hire several lobbyists, whose contacts grant access to different sectors of Congress. Brewers pressing for a beer-distribution-monopoly bill have, for example, hired the firm of Wagner and Baroody (all-purpose lobbying), Kip O'Neill, son of Tip O'Neill (access to Democrats), the former congressman John Napier, of South Carolina (access to Republicans), and Romano Romani, a former aide to Senator Dennis DeConcini (access to senators). So many lobbyists in Washington now represent so many overlapping interests that a sub-specialty has sprung up—lobbying among lobbyists.

The budget process has been a veritable boon to the lobbying profession. With multiple votes, there is a steady progression of brush fires for lobbyists to stamp out—increasing their clients' anxiety and willingness to pay high fees—and also many more opportunities for a lobbyist to make his case. "Now they can wear you down," Senator Patrick Leahy, of Vermont, says. "You might be able to hold out for the public interest on the first, second, third, fourth, fifth votes, but on the sixth vote they're back again, and many give in." . . .

NO FUN ANYMORE

"I often feel that by the time I arrived in Congress, in 1974, the fun was over," Representative Gradison says. "All the landmark legislation, the laws that were exciting and glorious to take part in, had been passed. Now the bills were beginning to fall due, and there would not be glorious work for us, just the struggle to pay those bills."

Through the 1960s and early 1970s Congress made history time and again: the Civil Rights Act; the Voting Rights Act; the Clean Air and Water acts; Medicare and Medicaid; the Resource Conservation and Recovery and Toxic Substances Control acts, which started federal action against toxic wastes; new federal housing programs and aid to education; the successful battles against Nixon and the seniority system; public financing for presidential races; disclosure laws for federal candidates and officials—the list goes on.

Twenty years ago a congressman looking at the nation saw *wrongs*, like legally sanctioned discrimination, that could be righted simply by changing the law. It can be argued that today's political horizon is far different. There are many intractable dilemmas, but few open-and-shut cases such as raw pollution being pumped into a stream. Most current social problems don't have self-evident solutions of the type that Congress could codify in bills and announce tomorrow. Stopping the poll tax against blacks was one thing; moving an entire generation out of the ghetto and into the economic mainstream is quite another, and it's not at all clear how that can be done.

Congressmen face, instead, the tasks of reining in dramatic programs of previous Congresses and cutting the deficit, which are neither politically glamorous nor pleasant tasks. "They build statues and name schools after people who promote great programs," Representative Bill Frenzel, of Minnesota, says. "They never build statues for people who have to say no."

Indeed, what with the fragmentation of Congress, the inherent unpleasantness of cutbacks, and the eye-glazing vista of deficits of $172 billion, it becomes difficult for congressmen to take seriously the idea that any one particular cut matters. Everybody's taking what they can get—why should my program be the one to suffer when the deficit is so vast? What difference could another few hundred million possibly make?

Traditionally, congressmen find it easiest to advocate a bold new spirit of austerity in someone else's state or district. But there is a sense in which congressmen do not even mind excessive spending in other districts: it creates an atmosphere in which overspending is the norm and money for pet programs is less likely to be challenged.

In June, when the $18 billion water-projects authorization bill was about to go to the House floor, James Howard, of New Jersey, the chairman of the Public Works Committee, circulated a roster of the House with black spots next to the names of members in whose districts were programs he planned to attack if they voted against the water bill. Included in the Public Works Committee's bill was $189 million for a dam in the district of the committee's ranking Republican, Representative Gene Snyder, of Kentucky. Representative Harold Wolpe, of Michigan, who got a black dot, told T.R. Reid, of *The Washington Post,* "You always hear rumors in the cloakroom that they'll kill your project if you dare to oppose anybody's else's, but this is the first time I've ever seen them put it on paper. . . . It's extraordinarily blatant." The more spending in general, the more for my district: everybody does it. Any congressman who goes after another congressman's program knows his will be attacked in turn, both by the congressman and by the program's PACs and lobbyists. Even a congressman who might be willing to accept a cut in his own district knows that in the present undisciplined environment he would be played for a sucker; no other congressman would join in the sacrifice.

This attitude helps explain why, for example, nearly every congressman favors cutting the defense budget in the abstract but votes to preserve the individual programs that make up that budget. In 1983 Congress *added* $4.6 billion to the Pentagon appropriations that President Reagan had asked for. Defense lobbyists in particular are adept, when budget showdowns approach, at avoiding any discussion of whether their projects are the efficient or otherwise proper choice, and at framing the issues strictly in terms of jobs: Congressman, this vote represents 2,000 jobs for your district. Any government expenditure creates jobs—the question is what jobs are best for the nation when national needs, finances, and policies are weighed. But this question is seldom posed to an individual congressman. The question posed is, Do you want these jobs in your district today or not? Do you want your name on them or not? . . .

[E]xcept in the unlikely event of a new détente, the message of politics in the 1980s must be, Expect less—either less Social Security and Medicare and lower pensions or less income after taxes.

In the 1920s society lived well beyond its means and pretended that tomorrow would never come. Is the United States Congress, in its present state, able to deal with tomorrow? Can it take the message to the voters that they should in every way expect less? . . .

Here are some possibilities congressional leaders might consider:

Committee structures should be combined and simplified; particularly, the quadruple budget/appropriations/authorization/revenue sequence should be reduced by at least one phase. The most logical and least turf-destructive reductions would be to combine the budget committees with the revenue committees, putting the combined groups in control of overall revenue-versus-appropriations ratios, and to eliminate the appropriations committees. Money and policy amount to the same thing. Why must Congress pretend otherwise?

Seniority-system reforms should be reeled back somewhat—not to return to the stagnant old days but to stop the tail from wagging the dog.

Congressmen should receive a substantial raise and in return be required to forsake all forms of outside income. They are supposed to function as judges of society's needs; they should be as far above reproach (and influence) as judges.

There should be an absolute freeze on present federal-spending levels, extending to all entitlement programs and defense. If Congress wanted to allocate more money to one program, it would have to take some away from somewhere else. Congressmen cannot hope to reverse the "everybody does it" mentality of deficit increases without a political tool—a means by which they can argue to constituents (in simple, twenty-second terms) that they would like to give them more but just can't. There is nothing in the original social compacts of Social Security and other entitlement programs that confers a "right" to perpetual increases or to benefits for those who don't need them; those "rights" are political creations of Congress, and can be reversed.

A pay-as-you-go law should be enacted. Advocated by Senator John Glenn and others, pay-as-you-go would be a direct means of accomplishing what the budget process attempts to accomplish indirectly: tying government revenues to spending. Any legislation allocating new funds would at the same time have to provide a source for those funds, in the form of either a tax increase or a deduction from another program. When a person buys something, he considers the purchase not in the abstract but in light of how much he has to spend and what will be left over for other purchases. Businesses act the same way. Only government separates the question of what to spend from what is affordable. Pay-as-you-go would have far more teeth than the strictly symbolic balanced-budget amendment, which would require Congress to balance the budget unless, on an annual basis, it voted otherwise. The balanced-budget amendment would add another showy "process" but no actual discipline.

Budgets should be drawn up on a two-year cycle to reduce duplication. Multi-year procurement cycles should be employed for the development and manufacture of complicated items like weapons. Military contractors may feed at the public trough in a shameless manner, but in their behalf it should be said that changing their instructions regularly, as Congress is prone to do, does not make for efficient business. To help longer-cycle budgets work, Congress should devise a "this time we really mean it" clause that could prevent budget decisions from being constantly reopened for tinkering.

Lobbyists should be denied access to the Capitol. Of course lobbyists are not all sinister; most are simply doing their job. But the number of supplicants gathered round to demand handouts makes it difficult for congressmen to think clearly. Imagine lobbyists for parties in a lawsuit allowed in to see the judge—how credible would his decision be? And having lobbyists crowd outside the chambers of the House and Senate, flashing thumb signs to congressmen like coaches issuing orders to Little Leaguers, is a national disgrace.

There should be a cap on total campaign expenditures for each candidate. The existence of PACs and interest groups is far less corrupting than the need to raise great and ever-greater sums. If House races were limited to, say, $100,000 and Senate races to $500,000, the temptation to pander would be greatly reduced. Also, all campaign funds unspent after a given election should either be returned to donors or be contributed toward retiring the federal debt. If there were a cap on what congressmen could spend and no way for them to hoard what they didn't spend, fund-raising would be far less addictive than it is today. Restraining nonconnected and soft-money groups would not be as easy as restraining congressmen. But at least this proposal would get the

congressmen out of fund-raising and back to their responsibilities.

What can be done to restrain indirect spending on campaigns when the Constitution guarantees freedom of speech? Preserve that freedom by limiting all advertising *to speech.* Whether by candidates or by representatives of soft-money or ideological groups, only *speech,* in which an actual, real, named, identifiable person stands and talks, would be permitted. No electronic graphics; no talking cows; no actors pretending to be men in the street; no sunset walks along the beach. Banning Madison Avenue-style advertising from politics has been advocated by Curtis Gans, the director of the Committee for the Study of the American Electorate. The Supreme Court ruled in 1976 that money used to buy time on or space in communication media equates to the freedom of speech. This ruling has caused many people to think that the Gans approach would be held unconstitutional. But what do special effects, actors, and graphics have to do with any freedom we hold dear? Their purpose is to evade political debate, not advance it. Let money be used to buy TV spots, but only ones that hold to a standardized format, in which real candidates or real spokesmen for groups stand before the same solid-color background and state their ideas—whatever those ideas might be—with absolute privilege. This would surely satisfy the Founding Fathers, reduce the cost of campaigning, and by the way return the focus of politics to the issues.

The congressional calendar should be fixed, making it harder to put off decisions over and over again. A quarter system might be appropriate. During three quarters of the year congressmen would not be permitted to shuttle home to campaign but would be required to stay in Washington and attend to their work. During the fourth quarter Congress would shut down, and congressmen could return to their districts to find out for themselves what is happening there. During this time they could also hold away-from-Washington hearings—an art that died with television and instant access to publicity—in order to hear testimony from average Americans, not members of the Washington expert set.

None of these reforms would be easy to implement, especially those that involve intrusions upon existing turf and perquisites. But if congressmen cannot govern Congress, how can they hope to govern the country?

In 1984 several governors were begged by national party officials to run for Senate seats; all refused, seeing no reason to surrender jobs where they could accomplish something useful in order to submit themselves to the 535-ring circus that is Congress. A generation ago the idea of politicians who would rather avoid joining the Senate would have been outrageous; now it seems perfectly reasonable. Congress, unique among our government institutions, has control over its own fate—it can't blame another branch of the government for its condition. Before Congress can lead the nation, it must be able to lead itself.

NO

Gary Orfield

CONGRESSIONAL POWER

POPULAR STEREOTYPES OF CONGRESS

Americans continually proclaim their pragmatic flexibility and realism. Yet they maintain the oldest set of stable political institutions in the world and repeatedly describe the operations of that structure in terms of seldom challenged myths. These myths include a view of Congress as a declining and hopelessly fragmented body trying with little success to cope with the expansive and even dangerous power of a stronger institution, the Presidency.

Even in early 1974, when, with the deepening of the Watergate crisis, respect for Presidential authority approached its modern low point Congress was seen in even more intensely unfavorable light. While the polls showed that only a fourth of the public approved of the job President Nixon was doing, they also showed that Congress had the respect and approval of only one American in five. Even Congress's impressive performance in the impeachment proceedings, which forced President Nixon's resignation, has produced little confidence that Congress can play a major positive role in the formation of national policy.

The assumptions about the sorry state of Congress have often been so pervasive that observers don't even bother to look at the evidence. This book will argue that the popular stereotype is fundamentally wrong. Congress is alive and well, at least in the field of domestic policy. If it is not progressive, it is usually reasonably representative and responsive. As public opinion changes, as Presidents define their constituency in different ways, and political circumstances gradually alter the membership of the House and Senate, Congress has been moving away from its traditional conservative or passive role in the development of national policy. This change became quite apparent with the beginning of the Nixon Administration. As the President moved sharply to the right on social policy, and the Supreme Court was largely neutralized by a series of four conservative appointments, Congress

Excerpted from *Congressional Power: Congress and Social Change*, by Gary Orfield. Copyright ©1975 by Harcourt Brace Jovanovich, Inc. Reprinted by permission of the publishers.

often remained the most progressive of the three branches in dealing with social policy issues.

The early 1970s did not see Congress become a seedbed for liberal activism. Although the legislative branch was now often more responsive to new social needs than the other principal institutions of government, there were still very broad and important areas of inaction and stalemate in domestic policy. This analysis will show that there is nothing in the institutional structure of Congress which renders the legislative branch either weak or conservative. In fact, Congress regularly exercises more power than it is credited with, and the ideological impact of its participation shifts from issue to issue and from political circumstance to political circumstance.

Our political system's lack of responsiveness to some of the very real social crises that preoccupy many intellectuals is not inherent in the Congressional process. Congressional reformers are simply wrong when they claim that institutional changes will produce "good" responses to the environmental problem, to inequitable taxation, irrational urban policies, and other major difficulties. The basic problem is more fundamental, and arises from the fact that the major progressive political force in this society, the activist liberal wing of the Democratic Party, is almost always a minority. Reformers spread the illusion that different procedures within Congress would produce answers to problems most Americans simply don't want to face. So long as Congress is a representative body, it is highly unlikely to produce decisive answers to controversial questions before public opinion accepts the necessity of action. . . .

THE CHANGING PRESIDENCY

The Presidency, political scientists have often said, is inherently progressive because the Presidential election system has a built-in liberal bias, while Congressional power grows out of an electoral structure that magnifies local concerns. A number of Presidential campaigns during the past several decades have been organized around competition for the big blocks of electoral votes in the large urbanized states. At the same time Congressional malapportionment over represented rural areas in the House, while the lightly populated nonindustrial states have always been greatly overrepresented in the Senate.

Most political scientists have argued that the great importance of the big, closely divided states in Presidential elections has magnified the political influence of the urban minorities concentrated in these states. The political situation, analysts argued, made the President the natural spokesman for minority and urban needs. This very argument was used by some Congressional liberals in 1969 against adoption of a Constitutional amendment for direct election of the President.

Whatever the historical validity of these assertions, they no longer hold. In the 1964, 1968, and 1972 Presidential campaigns the GOP candidates wrote off the black vote and operated on the assumption that the real swing vote was in the suburbs. The Republican nominees saw the black vote, not as a swing vote, but as an integral locked-in element of the Democratic Party base. Turning their backs on the declining central-city electorate, they looked to the suburbs. In dramatic contrast to previous elections, the GOP adamantly refused to concede the South to the Democrats. By following a strategy that ignored the urban ghettos and put primary importance on the Southern and Border states, the Republicans were altering the Presidential political base from a source of liberal leverage to a collection of forces desiring to slow and reverse social changes already underway. . . .

THE DECLINE OF CONSERVATIVE POWER IN CONGRESS

While a new interpretation of the Presidential constituency was taking hold in the minds of many, something quite the opposite was beginning to become evident in Congress. As the 1970s began, the big cities enjoyed reasonable representation and growing seniority power within Congress. As political competition in the South spread and produced real challenges in former one-party districts, a growing proportion of the safe, stable, one-party districts that remained were located in the central cities, where Democratic voters frequently constitute overwhelming majorities. Given the continuing decline in central city population and the ten-year time lag before a new reapportionment, the relatively liberal central-city constituencies were destined to have increasing overrepresentation in the House as the 1970s advanced. . . .

The Senate was now seldom in the control of the old, rigidly conservative coalition of Southern Democrats and Republicans. On a number of issues it was now possible to form a moderate-liberal majority in support of social policy proposals.

THE UNCHANGING CRITICISM OF CONGRESS

Congress was changing, but perceptions of Congress remained largely fixed. Denunciations of Congressional ineptitude and legislative stalemate continued to proliferate. Inside and outside of Congress, critics said that only basic reforms could preserve Congress's intended role as a major force in American government. Even while they were sending their local incumbents back to Washington in great numbers, the American people expressed extremely low regard for Congress as an institution.

Characteristically, both the criticisms of Congress and the proposed cures are usually stated in institutional terms. We are told that the Congressional structure is inefficient or unresponsive, or that the rules screen out the competent and stifle innovation. Implicitly, however, the criticisms are political. When a critic says that Congress is not responsive, he obviously has in mind some set of national needs he believes Congress should respond to. Often these are the needs of an oppressed social group or of important decaying public institutions like the central cities and their school systems. The reform proposals often implicitly assume that procedural changes would release a suppressed progressive majority, likely to take a far more activist role in the provision of governmental services. This assumption may well be incorrect.

While the claim that certain major institutional features of Congress imposed a conservative bias on the legislative process has considerable historic validity, the recent picture is unclear. With a few notable exceptions, which run in both liberal and conservative directions, recent Congresses have rather accurately reflected the values and the confusion of the public in dealing with major issues of social change.

If the interpretation offered here is correct, liberals are unlikely to accomplish much by reforming Congressional procedures. The sobering reality is that the real obstacles are not so much on Capitol Hill as in the society as a whole. While tinkering with legislative arrangments may permit some minor improvements, basic social reforms probably require a political movement able to change public values.

Most of the time, we have the Congress we really want and the Congress we deserve. We send the same members back to Washington time after time. Congress is inherently neither liberal nor conservative. Its political tendencies change with the times, with political circumstances, with the delayed responses of the seniority system, and with tides of public opinion. In social policy battles of the early 1970s, Congress became relatively more progressive and activist than the Presidency.

RECENT AREAS OF CONFRONTATION

The interplay of Presidential and Congressional influences can be examined by closely looking at the development of policy in three broad areas—civil rights, education, and employment—during the period from the late Johnson Administration through the early portion of President Nixon's second term. These issues, analyzed in the central portion of this study, and others discussed in less detail thereafter, obviously cannot adequately represent the whole sweep of domestic social policy. Each, however, is a prominent and long standing political question on which there were relatively clear progressive and conservative positions. By looking at the development of several issues through a large number of legislative battles spanning several years, one obtains a more realistic portrait of the policy

process than by merely examining the legislative history of one or a few bills.

The civil rights section will underline the limits of Presidential authority and the power of the Congressional veto when the President tries to reverse reforms that are already part of established law. Though he invested considerable time and prestige and intensely pressured his Congressional supporters, the President met a series of costly defeats. Even though he drew on his leadership role to deepen and exploit racial polarization, the President encountered successive frustrations.

In education policy the President's main objectives were to reduce the federal support for education and to renounce most of the existing federal leverage on state and local school systems. Congress, on the other hand, pressed each year for higher funding and retention of the federal requirements in the Great Society legislation. It was Congress that prevailed—only modestly in the financial struggle, but much more clearly in the protection of the legislative framework.

While the civil rights and school policy battles often involved legislative vetoes of conservative White House initiatives, the development of a new jobs policy is best seen as an important Democratic Party effort to initiate a new domestic policy from a Congressional base, in the face of strong Presidential oppostion. Study of this effort provides an opportunity to reflect on both the possibilities and the limitations of Congressional policy initiation during a period of executive hostility. . . .

THE NEED FOR REASSESSMENT OF CONGRESS

We must stop thinking in terms of

institutional stereotypes and unexamined assumptions. Both scholars and activists need to devote more attention to reassessing the contemporary reality and future possibilities of Congressional policy initiatives. They need to think less in terms of a handful of visible new bills, and more in terms of the whole array of Congressional influences that help shape policy in a given area. It is time for critics to rethink their wildly overoptimistic promises about Congressional reform, and to recognize that Congress often only reflects the indecision or contradictory desires of the local publics and the local political structures.

It is a delusion for liberals to think that there is a hidden majority for basic social reform somewhere inside Congress that could be liberated by a few institutional reforms. Activist liberals must begin with the realization that they have only a minority in Congress, particularly in the House. On some issues, in fact, a more democratic House might be an even less progressive House. If strong progressive programs are to prevail in Congress, their supporters must first prevail in elections.

CONGRESS AND SOCIAL POLICY: A SUMMARY

The United States has been passing through a period of massive social and economic change during the past decade. Congress has played an extremely important role in shaping the uneven governmental responses to those changes. Contrary to popular cliches, the nation has not entered a period of an imperial Presidency and a passive Congress, nor has deadlock totally paralyzed action in most areas of policy.

The past decade has brought profound changes in the position of blacks, women, and young people in the social and political system. The major civil rights laws were a powerful response to the central shame of American democracy, governmental enforcement of the racial caste system of the South. After decades of resistance, Congress not only passed these laws, but strengthened them and then protected them from a hostile President. Congressional action has been crucial to the women's movement's attack on concepts of female status ingrained in Western culture. Congressional action making eighteen-year-olds full citizens has had little visible immediate impact, but will surely make the political system more open and responsive to young people.

After Congress approved the vast expansion of the federal role in domestic programs in the 1960s, the determined efforts of a conservative President to reverse the trend tested the real dispositions of the Democratic Congress. The period found even the more conservative elements of the legislative branch operating more progressively than the President. This was very apparent, for example, in the massive Social Security boosts approved by the Ways and Means and the Senate Finance committees, and in the continual rejection of the President's meager education and health budgets by both Appropriations committees. In most cases Congress led the executive branch in responding to new ecological issues and in creating new tools for control of the economy.

The period of the late 1960s and early 1970s witnessed simultaneously the advance of sweeping claims of Presidential powers, and the decline of the real strength of the Presidency. During the period between the end of the Second World War and the late 1960s, Presidents enjoyed great latitude in the conduct of foreign policy and military affairs. This freedom of action, and the bipartisan Congressional support that sustained it, began to erode when rising opposition to the Vietnam War destroyed the Johnson Presidency. At first it affected the margins of international power, such as foreign military assistance, but by the early 1970s it had produced serious Congressional pressures to restrain the military apparatus and to subject Presidential action to legislative control. War powers legislation—passed over a Presidential veto—and some reductions in the defense and foreign aid budgets began to cut into the muscle of executive leadership; 1973 saw the extraordinary spectacle of Congress forcing the end of military action in Cambodia by cutting off funds, and Congress rejecting trade legislation central to the policy of detente with the U.S.S.R.

The Nixon period witnessed the resurgence of some long neglected legislative powers in domestic affairs, and the most striking Congressional rejection of a President's domestic program in decades. In the major Supreme Court nomination fights, Congress resumed an active role in the constitution of the highest Court, a power that had lain dormant for most of the twentieth century. When the early phases of the Watergate scandal indicated grave improprieties in the executive branch, Congress acted both through a massive investigation and through insistence on an independent special prosecutor to force revelation of the most serious corruption in American history. When the investigation came under Administration attack, very heavy Congressional pressure persuaded the President to retreat. Eventually he was forced to leave office.

The success of the legislators in resisting a sustained, intense White House fight against serious investigation of the scandals and in helping the press educate the public, and forcing the President to yield unprecedented personal records was a tribute to the vitality of Congress. The experience seemed certain to increase both Congressional power and Congressional vigilance for some time to come. Anyone who doubts the continuing reality of Congressional power need only read the transcripts of the extraordinary White House tapes that President Nixon was forced to release by pressure from the House Judiciary Committee. Amid all the plots and the bitter, candid criticisms of men and institutions, it is evident that President Nixon and his chief advisors retained a fear of Congressional power. While their discussions are full of plans to thwart the independence and manipulate the operations of various governmental institutions, the mass media, and the criminal justice system, there is a continual recognition of the limited power the White House can exercise over Congress.

In 1974 the House Judiciary Committee began the impeachment process for the second time in American history. The process had been virtually forgotten since Congress failed to impeach Andrew Johnson after the Civil War, but now it worked. Only when impeachment and conviction seemed certain did the President resign. The revival of Congress's ultimate weapon surely lends strength to the legislative branch, and diminishes the power and autonomy of future Presidents.

Presidential power rests to a substantial degree on the sense of respect and legitimacy accorded to the office of the

4. IS CONGRESS TOO WEAK?

President. One certain effect of the Watergate scandal and the President's resignation has been to weaken that respect for some time to come, thus increasing the relative power of Congress.

While the Watergate disaster dramatized Congress's investigatory power and resurrected the idea of impeachment, its drama often obscured more mundane facts about the period. In the long and often unpublicized domestic policy struggles of the period, Congress responded to intense and singleminded White House pressure without yielding its role.

The period of Presidential reaction on social policy under President Nixon showed that the close tie between Congress and various organized constituencies could have liberal as well as conservative consequences. Coming to office with the belief that he had a mandate to reverse many of the domestic innovations of the Great Society, the President encountered determined resistance from Congress. Congress responded by rejecting a higher portion of Nixon legislative proposals than those of any recent President, even though Nixon presented a relatively slim set of innovations. Only by stretching executive powers and spending his political authority in bitter confrontations with Congress over vetoes and impoundments was the President able to slow the momentum of those programs. Eventually, the price to be paid was strong Congressional attempts to cut back on the powers of the executive branch.

In arguing that Congress possesses a substantial capacity to initiate new national policies, and that those policies may well be more "progressive" or "responsive" than positions taken by a

President, this book certainly does not mean to support another false view of Congress. While Congress may be *relatively* more activist than a conservative President, it can hardly be described as a liberal institution. The major liberal force in American politics is the Northern and Western wing of the Democratic Party. Only when political circumstances give that wing of the party an operating majority in Congress (a rare circumstance) or predominant influence in the executive branch (a more common occurrence) does that institution become the primary focus for policy innovation.

During the Nixon Administration Congress succeeded in putting a few major new social issues on the national agenda, and in protecting much of the Great Society framework. On many other issues, however, its record was far more mixed. Design of new housing policies, for example, was long stalled by a stalemate within Congress, as well as by one between Congress and the White House. Congress delegated vast powers over the economy to the executive branch without making basic policy decisions. Congress preserved existing civil rights laws, aimed primarily at the classic Southern forms of discrimination, but proved incapable of developing policies to cope with the intensifying racial separation of the urban North. There were few significant new ideas in education policy in the legislation of the early 1970s, and the intense national discussion of health care needs yielded little on Capitol Hill. Efforts to reform the tax structure or to alter the basic assumptions of welfare policy were largely barren. The list goes on and on.

Judged against the national goals of activist liberal groups, or even against the Democratic Party platform, the record of

Congress was fundamentally inadequate. Congress has not responded forcefully to a number of evident social needs. The obstacle has been sometimes the President, and sometimes Congress itself.

The important thing to remember is that the failings criticized by activists are usually not failings produced by the structure or procedures of Congress, but by the vision of its members. The shortcomings—and many of the achievements—result from reasonably effective Congressional representation of widely held and often contradictory values of the public and of the members' active and important constituents. The unwillingness to move forward in some significant areas of social policy reflects far less the inadequacies of Congress as an organization than the failure of middle-class Americans to recognize that any social crisis exists. The basic reason why neither Congress nor the President is truly liberal is that liberalism normally represents a minority position in the United States—a fact often obscured by the assumption that the Democratic Party is a liberal party, rather than an exceedingly broad coalition.

Much of the national movement for extensive Congressional reform is based on false assumptions. Reform and rationalization of committee jurisdiction, chairmen's powers, the budget process, Congressional staff capacity, etc., may produce a more efficient legislative body, more equitable to individual members, and perhaps better able to compete with the executive branch. These are worthwhile goals, but they are not likely to transform the substance of Congressional decisions. Reformers who promise an institutional answer to a political question are likely to be disappointed. There are no shortcuts. Probably the only way to

build a new Congress is to undertake the hard political work necessary to send new men and women to Capitol Hill.

Although Congress is neither the liberal institution some would wish, nor the conservative institution many believe it to be, it is a powerful force in the construction of national policy. While the political circumstances of depression, wars and international crises, and a burgeoning executive branch have often served to magnify the Presidency, the remarkable fact is that Congress has preserved the Constitutional model of fragmented power through an era of serious parliamentary decline in most Western nations. If anything, the political scandals of the early 1970s have only reinforced this model, increasing public support for the assertion of Congressional authority....

In a society experiencing rapid social and political change, the major democratic institutions reflect shifting constituencies and evolving political alliances. At the present time these forces tend to be moving Congress away from its very conservative past, and the Presidency away from the historical circumstances that once made the White House the powerful spokesman for urban minorities. The very heavy dependence of GOP Presidential candidates on Southern support and the growing power in the House of liberal Democrats from safe one-party urban seats are two signs of these changes. Nothing suggests, however, that there is anything permanent or historically inevitable about these changes. The time has come for students of American politics to recognize the limits of institutional generalizations based on the political circumstances of the recent past.

The abuses of Presidential power

93

4. IS CONGRESS TOO WEAK?

revealed by the Watergate scandals have tended to replace the popular image of the beneficience of Presidential power with a popular fear of the abuse of executive authority. The long established tendency of progressives to look to the White House for responsive leadership is being replaced by a judgment that the President is excessively powerful, and by a tendency to look to Congress for salvation. Both images assume that the President possesses vast, even excessive powers. While this is surely true in the fields of foreign policy, military affairs, and national security, it is not true in the development of the nation's social policy. Thus, for example, institutional changes intended to reduce the power of a corrupt executive branch may have the consequence of constricting the already limited power of a future liberal President to initiate and implement major social reforms.

It has been a disservice—and one currently conducive to a crushing disillusionment with politics—for academics to spread the belief that Presidential power is better than Congressional power. (What they actually meant was that during the period between the early 1930s and the mid-1960s, the Presidency was usually controlled by the Democratic Party, and that the President tended to respond to a more liberal constituency than that of the Congressional leadership.) It would, of course, be equally misleading to assume that Congressional power is better, more progressive, or less corrupt.

It is vital to realize that the making of national domestic policy takes place in a context of genuinely divided power, and that the Congress as well as the President possesses both the ability to initiate and the power to veto major policy changes. The system works well when there is a clear consensus in the country, or clear control of both branches by the dominant wing of either party. Usually these conditions are not present and the system is biased either toward compromise and incremental change, or toward confrontation and inaction. The Nixon period clearly shows that the modern Presidency can be quite as efficient an engine of negative social policy as was Congress during certain earlier progressive Administrations.

It is only fair to recognize that much of the criticism that has been aimed at Congress has been misdirected. It is really criticism of the inefficiencies and delays built into the American Constitutional system, and of the nebulous and often contradictory ideological bases of the alliances that constitute the national political parties. Failure to correctly identify these underlying causes leads one to misjudge the solutions.

The people of the United States generally have the kind of legislative body they want and deserve. It is a Congress that has the power to take decisive action, but most of whose members rarely believe the public demands such change. It is an evolving institution and an increasingly representative one. It has great power but rarely selects leaders who use that power with energy, skill, and imagination. With a few significant exceptions, the altering of its internal rules will not change its decisions much. Congress is likely to be a moderately progressive institution in the next years. If it is to be much more than that—or less—its membership must be significantly changed.

POSTSCRIPT

IS CONGRESS TOO WEAK?

Democratic President Harry Truman castigated a "do-nothing" Republican Congress, while Republican President Ronald Reagan criticized an obstructionist Democratic House of Representatives. Presidents often find Congress to be, if not too strong, at least too independent. Champions of Congress, on the other hand, deplore the absence of sufficient power to keep the president in line. (See Issue 5: "Has Congress Restricted Presidential War Powers Too Much?")

James MacGregor Burns has argued (most recently in *The Power to Lead: The Crisis of the American Presidency,* Simon and Schuster, 1984) that nothing less than a fundamental constitutional change could lead to a more effective exercise of power. Although Easterbrook shares many of Burns' criticisms of Congress, he spells out specific reforms which would enhance legislative power.

Orfield contends that Congress is constantly changing, even in the absence of substantial reform. If the national legislature is less liberal than some reformers wish it might be, Orfield argues, it is because the American people by and large want it that way.

The Reagan administration once again demonstrated that Americans look to the president and not to Congress for leadership. This is also true of students of American politics. Consequently, books on Congress are far fewer than those on the presidency. An outstanding new book is Arthur Maass' *Congress and the Common Good* (Basic Books, 1984), which describes, analyzes, and defends the role of Congress in the democratic political process. In sharp contrast, Mark Green's *Who Runs Congress?* (Bantam/Grossman, revised 1975) is a muckraking survey that dwells upon what's wrong—and concludes that a great deal is. Students seeking up-to-date information on Congress and legislative issues will find no more reliable sources of information than the *Congressional Quarterly Weekly Report* and the annual *Congressional Quarterly Almanac.*

Easterbrook believes that reform is necessary to reduce the volume of legislation, simplify the committee system, curb the lobbyists, and assume legislative control of the budgetary process. Orfield maintains that change is not only possible but constantly takes place. He concludes that we generally get the kind of Congress we deserve.

Critics and defenders might agree that the caliber of Congress depends in large part on the concern of the electorate. Then the issue becomes how to motivate the American people to desire and elect a better Congress.

ISSUE 5

HAS CONGRESS RESTRICTED PRESIDENTIAL WAR POWERS TOO MUCH?

YES: Senator Barry Goldwater, Republican, Arizona, from Senate debate on September 28, 1983

NO: Jacob K. Javits, from "War Powers Reconsidered," *Foreign Affairs* (Fall 1985)

ISSUE SUMMARY

YES: Senator Goldwater argues that, while Congress can "declare" war, only the President can "make" war. Only the President can act with adequate force and speed to protect national security.
NO: Former Senator Javits maintains that the War Powers Act reaffirms the intention of the Framers to ensure that the effective power to make war originates in the will of Congress.

"The Congress shall have power ... to declare war." Article I, Section 8 of the United States Constitution goes on to assert that Congress can raise and support armed forces. However, Article II, Section 2 asserts: "The President shall be Commander in Chief of the Army and Navy." As in so many other areas of power, the Framers of the Constitution sought to give an appropriate role to both the national legislature and the Chief Executive.

In historical practice Presidents have often acted without a congressional declaration of war. When the Southern rebels attacked Fort Sumter, President Lincoln did not wait for Congress to act. From George Washington to Ronald Reagan, American Presidents have called the armed forces into action to repel attack or to discourage it.

However, it is only since the end of World War II that American Presidents have engaged our troops in large-scale wars in the absence of a congressional declaration. American soldiers fought in Korea obstensibly as part of a United Nations force. In Vietnam, the United States engaged in one of the costliest wars in its history without a declaration of war. The American invasion of Grenada was quickly over, but it was undertaken without any presidential consultation with Congress.

Tension between the Congress and the President as to the appropriate exercise of the power to wage war reached a climax during the Vietnam War. After an alleged incident involving an American ship in the Gulf of Tonkin, off the coast of Vietnam, President Lyndon Johnson sought and was given authority to conduct policy in Vietnam. The 1964 Tonkin Resolution, which was passed by a nearly unanimous vote, gave the President wide latitude in conducting a war that became increasingly controversial over the next decade, as its cost in lives grew and the hope of successful resolution grew dim.

After the negotiation of a cease fire in Vietnam, the War Powers Resolution was adopted in 1973, reflecting the criticisms of members of Congress who wished to reassert congressional authority and to prevent the United States from again engaging in a long and bloody war without congressional approval.

The War Powers Act was adopted into law over the veto of President Richard Nixon. It calls for consultation with Congress before armed forces are introduced into combat and for prompt reports by the President to Congress on the need for the nature of American involvement in hostilities. The heart of the War Powers Act is a stipulation that the President cannot employ American troops in hostilities for more than sixty days without obtaining congressional approval.

Those who support the War Powers Act see it as redressing the imbalance between the President and Congress, checking the power of the President to engage the United States in war without a commitment by Congress. At the same time, the War Powers Act implicitly acknowledges that Presidents have often employed our armed forces without congressional consultation, and that they will continue to do so. The "sixty days" provision further recognizes the necessity for swift emergency action where the nations's security requires a prompt response to danger.

American armed forces have been employed abroad in the Middle East, most particularly in Lebanon, in Southeast Asia, in the abortive effort to rescue American hostages in Iran, in Grenada, and elsewhere. None of these actions was preceded by a congressional resolution, although most were followed by presidential reports to Congress under the War Powers Act. Whether these or other incidents circumvent the law or uphold its spirit is part of the debate. Those who support the War Powers Act deeply believe that it upholds the principles of American constitutional government. Those who would repeal it believe as fervently that it inhibits the power of the President to defend our system of government.

YES   Barry Goldwater

A SOUND LEGISLATIVE POWER?

I do not agree with any declaratory provisions of the Resolution that imply the War Powers Resolution is a binding law. I do agree that we must find a way out of any potential impasse in foreign affairs between the Executive and Legislative Branches.

It would be the height of folly for us to stand here debating legal technicalities and political theory, while in Lebanon the Marines are getting shot at. What we need at this moment of crisis in Lebanon is support for a bipartisan foreign policy, not a constitutional confrontation between the Congress and the President.

This is no time for our nation to be fighting internally over the interpretation of the War Powers Resolution, a legislative measure that uses general, undefined terms and is probably the most unconstitutional measure Congress has ever passed.

Congress should never attempt to impose an artificial time limit on the deployment of United States military units. It is the height of nonsense to tell forces who are shooting at you that no matter what they do, you will pull out by a date certain.

The Democratic Caucus Resolution stands in contrast with the position taken by a Democratic President, Harry Truman, who in June of 1950 sent American troops to try and hold the area around Pusan after South Korean forces collapsed under a massive attack by North Korea. The late Dean Acheson, then Secretary of State, has reported President Truman briefly

From the *Congressional Digest*, November 1983, pages 267-275.

considered asking for a Congressional Resolution approving what the United States was doing in Korea.

Dean Acheson advised the President not to go to Congress and the President agreed that this should not be done. Mr. Acheson gave the following explanation: "It seemed to me if, at this time, action was pending before the Congress, by which hearings might be held, and long inquiries were being entered into as to whether or not this was the right thing to do, or whether the President had the authority to do it, or whether he needed Congressional authority for matters of that sort— we would be doing about the worst thing we could possibly do for the support of our troops and for their morale."

Mr. Acheson's advice is relevant to our debate today. I wish my Democratic friends in the Senate would heed the counsel that a Democratic Secretary of State gave to his President at an important moment of history, when fast decisions, not an impasse, were required.

If the War Powers Resolution had been in effect in the 1940's, President Roosevelt would have stood in violation of the law after April 15 of 1941, when he placed troops in Greenland. President Roosevelt would have violated the War Powers Resolution after July 7 of 1941, when he stationed over 8,000 Marines in Iceland with orders to defend what was then a British base, being operated by the British against the Nazis.

If these actions did not reach the level of the deployment of American forces into hostilities, then most certainly what happened on September 6, 1941, would have started a clock moving for the withdrawal of American naval units from hostile waters, under the interpretation used by the Democratic Caucus today. On September 6, the American destroyer "Greer" was traveling through the American defense zone on a mail run to Iceland when it encountered a German U-boat, which launched two or three torpedos at the "Greer." The "Greer" dodged them and dropped a circle of depth charges around the U-boat.

President Roosevelt announced that the "time for active defense is now" and said that: "From now on, if German or Italian vessels of war enter the waters, the protection of which is necessary for American defense, they do so at their own peril." To clear up any doubt, Secretary of the Navy Knox declared publicly on September 15, 1941, that "the Navy is ordered to capture or destroy by every means at its disposal Axis-controlled submarines or surface raiders in these waters."

If the matter of Presidential authority had come before Congress for debate, Congress would likely have listened to the voices of appeasement and defeatist elements who would not unite, who would not rearm and who would not consider sacrifices of any kind for our individual or collective security.

History proves that we can have no assurance Congress will act when a firm response is needed. Congress would have created an even greater world crisis if the War Powers Resolution had been in effect to tie the hands of Presidents Roosevelt and Truman.

History shows it is wrong for Congress to interfere with tactical military decisions of the President. It is wrong for Congress to usurp the President's direction of the day-to-day operations of foreign policy. It is dangerous and foolish to put a narrow interpretation on the word "hostilities."

I support the Baker resolution because it will avoid a constitutional confrontation with the President at a time when the marines are being shelled and fired upon in Lebanon.

Now, this is not to say I have changed my mind about the fact that the marines should not be in Lebanon. I have not altered my opinion.

Instead I am saying that Congress cannot and should not try to legislate the marines out of Lebanon. We do not have the constitutional authority to order them out.

The President has the last word over the deployment and use of the existing Armed Forces no matter what Congress might do today. I am happy to support the Baker resolution because it is an alternative to the far worse proposal by the Democratic Party Caucus which would attempt to usurp the reins of military direction from the President.

Also, I should mention that, in my opinion, section 2(b) of the Baker resolution, which would trigger section 4(a)(1) of the war powers resolution, does not mean a thing. We will not make an unconstitutional piece of legislation valid by simply referring to it in a second piece of legislation. The war powers resolution is probably the most unconstitutional measure Congress has ever passed and it will remain unconstitutional even if we pass the Baker resolution with section 2(b) in it and the President signs it.

I would like to discuss the general subject of the war powers and the folly of congressional efforts to tie the President's hands in making military decisions.

Look at what happened in 1975 when President Ford asked Congress to join with him in the decision to evacuate Americans from Saigon. As you will recall, Congress never granted his request.

Caught between the choice of strict adherence to the 1973 statutory prohibition on U.S. activities in, over, or from off the shores of Indochina and his duty to uphold the lives and interests of his countrymen and women, President Ford ignored the legislative restriction and took into his own hands the protection of Americans.

Weeks later, while Congress was still tied up with its debate on the matter, President Ford announced that the Indochina evacuation was completed. Then, he pleaded for funds to pay for purely humanitarian assistance and transportation of refugees, but Congress rejected this request the very next day.

This episode reveals all too clearly the inability of Congress to act decisively in time of need. I mentioned an earlier moment in history when Congress also neglected its duties. It was a time when only the strong actions of President Franklin Roosevelt, taken independently of Congress, enabled this Nation to aid Great Britain and thereby defend our own security before Pearl Harbor ...

The fact is that the United States, as the strongest free nation in the world, has a stake in preventing totalitarian conquest. The President has a duty to resist challenges in the early stages and cannot wait until the challenge is so clear that the cost of resistance is prohibitive.

The danger in the war powers resolution and any other legislative effort like it which is intended to restrict the President's defense powers is that it takes away all flexibility to deal with unforeseen events. The failure of Congress to approve even humanitarian legislation to support the evacuation of American citizens from Saigon offers convincing proof that Congress cannot be counted on to deal quickly with future problems as the need arises. Unlike the President, an assembly of 535 Secretaries of State does not rush to decision.

Anyone who reviews history will know

that Presidents have always exercised independent defense powers, whether or not their statutory authority was clear, and occasionally, in the face of direct Congressional restrictions. In fact, Presidents have used force or the imminent threat of force on more than 200 occasions without any Congressional declarations of war.

George Washington settled this issue, when, as our first President, he ordered his Secretary of State, Thomas Jefferson, to threaten Spain with military force if she would not open the Mississippi River to navigation by American citizens. When he became President, Thomas Jefferson sent a squadron of armed ships into the Mediterranean without any Congressional authority, with orders to sink, burn and destroy vessels which may threaten American commerce. Only half a year after he issued his military orders and four months after a naval blockade and battle had occurred did Jefferson inform Congress.

Jefferson gave an indication of the principle which guided his decision-making, when he wrote on September 20, 1810, that:

"A strict observance of the written laws is doubtless one of the high duties of a good citizen; but it is not the highest. The laws of necessity, of self-preservation, of saving our country when in danger, are of higher obligation."

Jefferson's concise statement summarizes why the Framers vested the President with independent powers to act for the safety of the nation. The majority of Framers had served in the army of militia during the War of Independence and they were intimately familiar with the restrictions which the Continental Congress had imposed on General Washington's activities, restrictions they knew had nearly lost the American Revolution. It was in order to

correct this known weakness of the Articles of Confederation that the Framers made the President the "Commander-in-Chief" under the new Constitution.

We can also turn to the words of the Framers themselves. For example, George Mason said at the Virginia Convention to ratify the Constitution:

"Although Congress are to raise the army . . . the President is to command without any control."

Mason refused to sign the original Constitution because it did not include a Bill of Rights, but he attended the Constitutional Convention of 1787 and was active in shaping the final document. He knew what it meant.

The active role of governors in putting down civil disorders just prior to the Constitutional Convention of 1787, the evolution in early State constitutions from weak executives to strong executives, the memory of interference by the Continental Congress with military decisions of General Washington, and the entire course of practice under the Constitution from the Administration of President Washington to the current Administration of President Reagan, all demonstrate beyond any reasonable doubt that the power to employ the existing forces of the United States in defense of United States citizens and the survival of our country, in reaction to foreign dangers, was and is vested with the President.

Yes, Congress is given certain of the defense powers. Congress has the power of the purse. Congress can "declare" war. But the text of the Constitution does not say that Congress "makes" war, and the Framers specifically rejected such a proposal.

This does not mean that Congress is without any leverage. Congress can reduce the size of the Army, Navy, Marines or Air

101

Force. Congress can prevent the construction of any additional nuclear aircraft carriers by not appointing the money. The Senate can reject Presidential appointments of Ambassadors or Executive officers of the Defense and State Departments. But once the military forces are established and equipped, it is for the President alone to decide how to deploy and use those forces.

NO

Jacob K. Javits

WAR POWERS RECONSIDERED

We live at a juncture where U.S. foreign policy is at higher risk than at any point since the end of the Vietnam War. Great and sometimes confused and countervailing interests are at stake in Nicaragua; indeed, across Central America. The Persian Gulf is a tinderbox, which could be engulfed in the flames of Islamic fundamentalism. And we have seen the Middle East's coastal plain torn and fragmented to the point of anarchy in Lebanon.

Beirut, once the Paris of the Middle East, today gives full and paradoxical expression to all of the tensions that threaten to rip apart the structures of colliding civilizations. We sense, somehow, that society as we have known it since the Enlightenment is under siege by forces beyond our comprehension. There is no place on earth, whether along the East German border, the dividing line between North and South Korea, or even south of the line between Mexico and the United States, in which we do not sense uncertainty and the potential for violence. It is because we have reached this point, at which conflict threatens to overwhelm the comity that marks civilized society, that we must ensure that steps taken to protect ourselves and our institutions do not, in themselves, become violations of what we are and wish to continue to be.

The War Powers Resolution of 1973 remains one of the firmest supports of our determination that the American people will decide their own fate. I am grateful to have played a central role in the formulation of that resolution. It was the first legislation in our history to establish a statutory framework in which Congress and the president could function so as to give meaning to the constitutional authority over war.

In one sense it was—and is—a question of the paramountcy of the civilian over the military; the power of Congress to declare war, which is civilian, and the power of the president, as commander in chief, which is military. We cannot place the great question of war or peace in the hands of a single human being, not even our president. But we are so crowded by our sense of assault that the temptation is great to turn to an individual surrogate to shield us. . . .

5. HAS CONGRESS RESTRICTED WAR POWERS TOO MUCH?

II

Our Constitution's Founding Fathers could have had no grasp of the enormous changes and frightening potential of uncontrolled armed conflict in the late twentieth century. But, much to their credit, the statesmanship they exercised produced a document that has lived for two centuries beyond its conception. No other written constitution has survived in such good health over anything approaching a similar span of time.

Those eighteenth-century farmer-politicians had a sense that the fundamental values of a republic can be given effective expression only if the mechanisms of government interlock in such a way as to assure a system of checks and balances that permits action, flexibility and—in grave matters—the bedrock expression of the common will. That is why, among all the other splendid architectural structures within the Constitution, we find the president accorded the powers of "Commander in Chief of the Army and Navy of the United States" (Article II, Section 2) and the Congress empowered with the constitutional responsibility "to declare war" (Article I, Section 8).

The constitution-makers thus divided the responsibility for engagement in armed conflict between the executive and legislative branches of the government. There can be little doubt that their objective here, as elsewhere, was to maintain an unresolved tension between the institutional authority of the two branches, the executive and legislative, thereby leaving the political decision to the people.

The Founders, being men of the eighteenth century when monarchy still flourished, recognized the power of the intense symbolism that would be attached to the office of the president. The person who occupied that post, although designated as the head of a single branch of government, would be accorded recognition as the expression of the nation. In the presidency, fellow citizens would see themselves as "a people." For over 200 years, this extra-constitutional dimension to the president's authority has tipped the scales whenever there has been an issue between Congress and the president over the authority to engage in armed conflict. There can be no doubt, however, that the constitutional intention was to endow the president with all the powers that ultimately adhere to a military commander but, at the same time, to withhold from him the ultimate authority on the gravest political decision of whether to "declare war."

One can certainly make the case that the restrictions on the power to make war, in the actuality of committing the nation to war, have been successfully flouted by presidents from the days of the Barbary pirates to yesterday's headlines. On most of these occasions, Congress has backed away from a confrontation with the chief executive as to the constitutional settlement of the question.

One can also make the argument that these violations of constitutional principle have, in and of themselves, changed the meaning of the Constitution. Certainly, if one actually subscribes to the notion that "to declare war" is simply a formality and was so regarded when it was written into the Constitution as a guiding principle, there is little to discuss about the power to declare war. In this case, we are then, constitutionally, citizens of a republic in which the chief executive may risk American lives at any time, at any place on earth, at his own discretion.

I believe the weight of our history strongly implies just the opposite. Further, and of even greater consequence, the presidential incursions on the war powers of the Congress have always been covert and gradual—strongly implying that the men who have violated this congressional power were uneasy over the right and the consequences of their actions. In the 200 or so instances of exercise of presidentially ordered force against foreign enemies, we have yet to see an acknowledgement by the chief executive that he is committing the nation to war. We have had "police actions"; we have had "surgical strikes"; we have had "invitations to assist." We have had, in other words, a bad case of euphemism-itis. For war is war; and the loss of life, the expenditure of treasure and the agony of the people, as we all have good reason to know, is occasioned by acts of war and not by anything else.

I noted earlier that the Constitution's flexibility was one of the most important gifts made to posterity by the political craftsmen who shaped our institutions. Unfortunately, we have seen that flexibility used to far greater effect in this arena by presidents than by Congress. The manipulative potential in the presidential office is so large that to challenge it under the international gun has taken political courage beyond that of the Congress as an institution through much of our history. The legislative branch has, time and again, been reactive to events as shaped by outside forces, and by presidential initiatives and responses as a function of the president's self-perceived authority as commander in chief.

III

Progress has been made in reestablishing congressional authority, although the constitutional struggle continues.

In 1973, an undeclared war in Vietnam that caused greater agony in the United States than any event since the Civil War was drawing to an unhappy and grotesque conclusion. We were forced for the first time in our history to acknowledge a military defeat. Fifty thousand American lives, and countless numbers of Vietnamese lives, bled away in Indochina.

It was this tragic war that finally forced Congress to a succession of acts that limit the president's power to impose his military writ as he so chooses. The culmination of that effort was the War Powers Resolution, which passed both houses of Congress in November 1973, but only after both houses overrode President Nixon's veto by the requisite majorities of two-thirds. This veto was symptomatic of the position of presidents who resist any curb on their power to commit the nation to war. The veto was overridden because of the urgent need of the people to establish some restraint on the presidency and to safeguard the constitutional responsibility vested in the Congress to declare war, a power to be exercised by the Congress alone without any presidential consent or signature.

Under the War Powers Resolution, the president must consult with Congress "in every possible instance" *before* introducing the armed forces "into hostilities or into situations where imminent involvement in hostilities is clearly indicated by the circumstances." Under Section 4(a)(1), the president must report to Congress on the status of U.S. troops in such situations. Section 5(b), perhaps the engine of the resolution, requires the president to withdraw such troops within 60 to 90 days unless Congress authorizes their continued presence. He must, in any case, withdraw them immediately if directed to do so by a concurrent congressional resolution, which is not subject to a presidential veto. Recently, however, the Congress did make

105

such action subject to a presidential veto when in October 1983 it gave President Reagan authority to keep the marines in Lebanon for up to 18 months.

The War Powers Resolution did not, and does not, guarantee the end of presidential war, but it does present Congress with the means by which it can stop presidential war if it has the will to act. The resolution does not represent an effort to tie the president's hands or to deny him his rightful powers—as previous presidents have charged. Rather, the legislation provides the method by which the Congress and the president can render a collective judgment on the question of whether to risk war.

IV

Nevertheless, I must express my misgivings as to the effectiveness of the War Powers Resolution thus far: the resolute will of Congress is the issue here.

The fact is that the last three Presidents—Messrs. Ford, Carter and Reagan—have consulted with the Congress on occasion, sometimes reluctantly and even grudgingly; the consultations have varied greatly in quality from good to superficial. Also, the record shows that presidents took military measures without the effective prior consultation with Congress that is required under the resolution.

President Ford's actions in the Mayaguez incident in 1975 cost the lives of 40 U.S. marines. In the event, it developed that the ill-fated rescue attempt was unnecessary. In this case the President consulted with a mixed group of members of the House and Senate foreign relations committees after the orders had been issued to the marines to engage in combat and while they were on their way to Southeast Asia. The President did, however, report

to the Congress under the War Powers Resolution on this occasion.

In connection with the actions of President Ford in 1975 when U.S. troops and American, Vietnamese and Cambodian civilians were evacuated from Saigon and Phnom Penh, again there was a pass at consultation. It is fair to add that the situation was dire and that statutory law gave some accommodation to the use of troops for these evacuations.

President Carter's unsuccessful rescue attempt of our hostages held in Iran was also undertaken with no real prior consultation with Congress. It was said only that a guarded reference was made on the subject to Senator Robert C. Byrd (D-W.Va.), the majority leader, a day before the action took place. This was justified on the grounds that secrecy was vital to the operation and that it was humanitarian. But secrets have been kept in the Congress; for example, the Manhattan Project, which invented the atomic bomb; and the danger of leaks is just as real in the White House as it is in the Congress, as history has shown.

President Reagan's deployment of U.S. marines to Beirut in 1982 and 1983 involved substantial disregard of the War Powers Resolution, when viewed in its totality. When the President first acted in August 1982 to deploy the marines in Beirut to assure the evacuation of the Palestine Liberation Organization fighters, there was real consultation with the House and Senate foreign relations committees. But when the marines were redeployed after the assassination of President Bashir Gemayel of Lebanon and the massacres of the Sabra and Shatila Palestinian refugee camps, the avoidance of the War Powers Resolution began, until a final showdown with the Congress when the marines began to suffer casualties in August of 1983. When the President spoke to the Congress during this latter period, he was careful to skirt the War Powers Resolution in defining his authority, and rather referred to his "constitutional authority with respect to the conduct of foreign relations and as Commander in Chief."

There was considerable comment in the press and in Congress regarding the President's distinct avoidance of the impact of the War Powers Resolution in his communication with Congress. The actions he was taking were clearly subject to the operative section of the resolution which gives the Congress the power to compel a withdrawal within 60 to 90 days of U.S. armed forces who were obviously engaged in hostilities due to military necessity. The Congress could have compelled such action by itself in invoking that provision of the resolution. In fact, the foreign relations committee chairman, Senator Charles Percy (R-Ill.), and the ranking member, Senator Claiborne Pell (D-R.I.), wrote the President specifying such action. It was only the force of public opinion that finally made the President come to terms on this subject with the Congress.

Then, in reporting to Congress, the President did cite the War Powers Resolution, but took care not to cite the section of the act under which he made the report. In so doing, the President refrained from triggering the time clock that would give him only 60 to 90 days to keep the troops in Lebanon without congressional authority. In this case, public opinion and congressional will compelled the President and the Congress to work out a compromise.

The President was given authority by Congress by a joint resolution in October 1983 to keep the U.S. marines in Lebanon for up to 18 months; he also accepted the fact that if Congress wanted them to be withdrawn sooner, he would have to sign an appropriate resolution to that effect (the Congress could also override by a two-thirds vote of each house). On the other hand, the President conceded that the War Powers Resolution was applicable.

It is significant that an amendment to limit the time to six months was narrowly defeated in committee. The delay in getting the use of the War Powers Resolution and the length of time given in the compromise resolution was inordinately long for such an operation, considering the limit of 60 to 90 days.

This compromise resolution showed congressional reluctance to invoke the War Powers Resolution in a timely way, and according to its terms. Looking back on the death of 241 U.S. marines, because of a suicide truck bombing by terrorists, one wonders whether that tragedy of October 23, 1983, might have been averted if the legislative clock under the War Powers Resolution had been running.

President Reagan's actions with respect to Nicaragua have caused great concern about compliance with the War Powers Resolution. U.S. troops in substantial numbers have engaged in war exercises in Honduras with Honduran troops on the border with Nicaragua. Mines have been sown in Nicaraguan waters and the ships of other nations endangered, and "contras," rebels fighting Nicaraguan forces, have been supported under the commander in chief's authority. Here, too, is a mixed bag, as Congress has voted non-military aid for the contras.

Perhaps the clearest example, thus far, of presidential indifference to the statutory obligation to consult with Congress on war has been our action in Grenada, desirable as this may have been. Senator Charles McC. Mathias, Jr. (D-Md.), a ranking member of the Senate Foreign Relations Committee, has noted that "congressional leaders were simply called to the Oval Office and told that the troops were under way. That is not consultation. The Prime Minister of Great Britain was advised about the invasion before the President told the Speaker of the House of Representatives or the Majority Leader of the Senate."

If a president had treated the Congress in such a preemptory fashion with regard to any other constitutional mandate, he would have faced an angry legislature jealous of its prerogatives and refusing to allow them to be whittled away. But, in the matter of the greatest power of them all— the authority to put our people at war— Congress has been relatively reluctant in asserting its rightful obligation.

I can bear witness, myself, to the inadequate resolve displayed in such matters by well-intentioned legislators. The pressure of the threat of armed conflict is such that even I found myself willing to compromise, to lean in the direction of the presidency, by giving either more time or a wider latitude of discretion to presidential actions than warranted by the specific provisions of the War Powers Resolution. I was one of those who endorsed President Ford's Mayaguez action, although at one level I had to know that there was no rationale in the context of the War Powers legisla-

tion that should justify a president's dispatching marines into a combat situation and *then* reporting to Congress. In the dispute over the use of marines in Lebanon, the effort once more was to put the onus on those who would restrain a president. The President resisted invoking the War Powers Resolution, but Congress threatened to withhold funds. The resulting compromise was too favorable to presidential incursion on congressional war powers.

I recall all of these episodes with deep sadness, for they underline the overweening power of the presidency in periods of crisis. The reluctance to challenge the president is founded in an awareness that he holds, in large degree, the fate of the nation in his hands. We all wish to assist and sustain the presidency. But I have come to the conclusion that the awesome nature of the power over war in our time should require us to withhold, in relevant cases, that unquestioning support of the presidency. This, despite the fact that when U.S. troops are under fire it may appear that a legislator is foot-dragging when he or she questions whether a particular legal requirement has been observed. Such a legislator runs the risk of being attacked for "nitpicking." The overwhelming temptation is to wait and see, to let the dust settle. I believe that this dust will never settle. . . .

POSTSCRIPT

HAS CONGRESS RESTRICTED PRESIDENTIAL WAR POWERS TOO MUCH?

Both Goldwater and Javits quote Thomas Jefferson in support of their positions. Both quotations represent Jefferson fairly. In principle, Javits reminds us, Jefferson applauded the check which Congress would apply to the President's ability to wage war. In practice, Goldwater points out, Jefferson did not hesitate to use American armed forces without congressional action if he believed that their employment was in the interest of American national security.

The War Powers Resolution has become the focal point of a debate as to the respective powers of Congress and the President, but it does not seem to have changed the nature of the debate. Even the supporters of the resolution concede, as Javits does, that "avoiding the War Powers Resolution's intent has become more the rule than the exception." Javits points out how difficult it would be politically for members of Congress to question the President's compliance with the resolution, while American armed forces were engaged in combat.

The larger questions are explored in Cecil V. Crabb, Jr. and Pat M. Holt, *Invitation to Struggle: Congress, the President and Foreign Policy* (Congressional Quarterly Press; 1980). The War Powers Resolution was the subject of extensive hearings conducted by the Committee on Foreign Affairs of the House of Representatives in 1982. Senator John G. Tower provides an informed perspective in "Congress versus the President: The Formulation and Implementation of American Foreign Policy," in the Winter 1981-82 issue of *Foreign Affairs*.

ISSUE 6

DOES THE GOVERNMENT REGULATE TOO MUCH?

YES: Barry Crickmer, from "Regulation: How Much Is Enough?" Nation's Business (March 1980)

NO: Susan and Martin Tolchin, from Dismantling America (Houghton Mifflin, (1983)

ISSUE SUMMARY

YES: Editor Barry Crickmer argues that the interests of citizens and consumers could be better served by the forces of the profit motive than by government intervention.

NO: Martin and Susan Tolchin contend that without vigorous regulation businesses will destroy the environment and endanger lives in their single-minded pursuit of profit.

Government regulation of economic decision making is as old as the Interstate Commerce Commission, which was established in 1887 to regulate railroad rates. The Sherman and Clayton Antitrust Acts of 1890 and 1914 respectively, as well as the law establishing the Federal Trade Commission in 1914, were also designed to outlaw unfair methods of business competition.

Congress later established regulatory agencies to set standards for natural (or socially useful) monopolies, such as electric power companies and radio and television stations. Between 1920 and 1940, it set up the Federal Power Commission, the Federal Communications Commission, and the Civil Aeronautics Board. The national government also created the Federal Reserve System in 1913 and the Securities and Exchange Commission in 1934 (after the stock market crash) to regulate the investment of capital in industry and banking practices generally.

Although governmental regulation of commerce on behalf of the public interest was introduced as early as the Pure Food and Drug Act of 1906 (now administered within the Department of Health and Human Services), most activity within this area is relatively recent. The Equal Employment Opportunity

Commision was established in 1965. The Environmental Protection Agency, the Occupational Safety and Health Administration, and the National Highway Traffic Safety Administration were all created in 1970. The Consumer Product Safety Commission was set up in 1973, and the Office of Surface Mining Reclamation and Enforcement (within the Department of the Interior) came into being in 1977. With these and other newly-established agencies, the federal government assumed a wide-ranging responsibility to protect all persons against certain hazards that unrestrained private economic enterprise might otherwise create.

The rules written by these regulatory bodies have changed our lives in many ways, altering the food we eat, the cars we drive, and the air we breathe. Their defenders have applauded the protection that has been provided against profit-motivated predators who would otherwise adulterate our food, endanger our safety, and pollute the environment in order to maximize profits.

On the other hand, many investigators have joined businessmen in condemning government's movement into these areas, making the following arguments. One: Regulation inhibits production by suppressing innovation and discouraging risk-taking, resulting in declining employment. Two: Regulation invariably overregulates by setting standards for every aspect of manufacture when it could set overall objectives that businesses could meet in whatever ways they devise. Some economists maintain that government would accomplish more by assessing fees or taxes to discourage certain activities rather than fixing rigid standards. Three: Regulation costs too much in business compliance expenditures, which are passed on to the consumer, and in increased government payrolls. If government regulation drives a company out of business, the standard of living for those affected will go down. That is to say, the costs outweigh the benefits.

These indictments of the regulatory process were voiced by President Reagan in his 1980 campaign for the presidency. Not surprisingly, when he entered office in 1981 he sought to restrain what he considered to be excessive regulation. His proposed restraints on regulatory agencies called for initiating periodic reviews of their activities, allowing either house of Congress to veto proposed new regulations, and requiring economic impact analyses before new rules could go into effect.

The lines of this argument are clearly drawn in the following essays. Barry Crickmer argues that the objectives of safety and health, as well as productivity, will be better achieved in the absence of government regulation. Susan and Martin Tolchin are deeply concerned that the Reagan administration's thrust toward deregulation will reverse all the progress that has been made in protecting workers, consumers, and the environment.

YES

Barry Crickmer

REGULATION: HOW MUCH IS ENOUGH?

Federal regulation is often called inflationary. irritating. costly. and even farcical. But that's not the worst that can be said of it. The worst is that it isn't working.

The development. methodology. philosophy. and results of federal intervention in the marketplace fit Sir Ernest Benn's definition of politics as "the art of looking for trouble. finding it everywhere. diagnosing it wrongly. and applying unsuitable remedies."

For all the billions of dollars the regulatory agencies have spent and the billions more they have caused to be spent. there is surprisingly little evidence that the world is any better off than it would have been without federal tinkering.

NEEDLESS EXPENSE

Economist Murray Weidenbaum observes that "virtually every study of regulatory experience from trucking to pharmaceuticals to pensions indicates both needless expense and ineffective operations or. worst yet. counterproductive results."

For the old-line. economic regulatory agencies. the evidence of ineffectiveness has convinced even liberals to favor trimming or abolishing their powers. Presidential candidate Edward M. Kennedy (D-Mass.) points proudly to his role in deregulating the airlines. Even Federal Trade Commission Chairman Michael Pertschuk has been extolling the virtues of free market incentives.

But the newer. health-safety-social-environmental regulators still have vigorous defenders. although the defense is of necessity based more on what it is hoped they will do than on what they have done so far.

TYPICAL PROBLEMS

The first to document the failure of health and safety regulation may have been University of Chicago economist Sam Peltzman. He is certainly one of the pioneers in the field.

Dr. Peltzman did a cost-benefit analysis of the more stringent drug regulations that followed the thalidomide tragedy in Europe.

The Food and Drug Administration was an appropriate target for this seminal work published in 1973-74. Historically, the FDA belongs with the older single-industry regulators; by mission, it resembles the newer health and safety agencies. Further, some of its key problems are typical of most health and safety regulation.

Dr. Peltzman found that the new drug rules were costing American consumers three or four times as much as the economic benefits they produced. He also suggested that a too-cautious approach to approval of new drugs might foreclose or delay lifesaving advances in pharmaceutical technology.

Following Dr. Peltzman's work came a study by William M. Wardell, professor of pharmacology, toxicology, and medicine at the University of Rochester.

Dr. Wardell compared post-thalidomide drug development in the United States and Great Britain, which has fewer restrictions on new drugs. He demonstrated that lives were being saved in Britain and lost in the United States because of the more conservative U.S. policy toward new drugs. The British benefit not only from the more rapid introduction of valuable new drugs, he found, but also from the development of safer substitutes for potentially hazardous drugs in use.

It is easy to understand the FDA's caution. The damage done by a drug that should have been banned is visible and dramatic. The suffering and death that could have been prevented by a drug that was never developed are invisible and conjectural. Bureaucrats can hardly be blamed for trying to minimize known risk at the expense of unknown benefit. This dilemma is endemic to public-sector health safety regulation.

AUTO SAFETY

After making his point about drug regulation, Dr. Peltzman turned to auto safety. In a study published in 1975, he found that "essentially nothing in the post-1965 behavior of the total death rate can corroborate the idea that safety devices provide the kind of lifesaving suggested in safety literature."

A year later, the General Accounting Office reported that auto safety equipment mandated between 1966 and 1970 seemed to have reduced the risk of death and injury significantly, while that required after 1970 has produced no further improvement.

Other critics charge that federal auto safety regulations raise repair costs and waste gasoline.

It appears that the National Highway Traffic Safety Administration didn't know when to stop, stopped too soon, or should never have started.

In its seven years of existence, the Consumer Product Safety Commission has produced a handful of standards dealing with such threats as matchbook covers and swimming pool slides, inadvertently put a company out of business because of a typographical error in a list of hazardous toys, and arrested nine allegedly unsafe trash bins at a

113

shopping center outside Washington, D.C.—in a daring daylight raid, as crime reporters say.

The trash cans went peacefully, if not quietly.

The incident prompted commission officials to search for a less cumbersome way to enforce their safety standards.

The Occupational Safety and Health Administration, like the traffic safety agency, is a very active agency with little to show for its activity. At least four major studies—including one by the Chamber of Commerce of the United States—failed to find any significant OSHA impact on the existing trend of industrial fatalities. Unlike the traffic safety agency, however, OSHA does not even try to subject its rules to cost-benefit analysis.

Similar evidence could be cited concerning the failures of the Environmental Protection Agency, the Energy Department, and other major and minor federal regulators. "The history of regulation is a history of disappointment," Harvard professors Albert Nichols and Richard Zeckhauser observe in a *Public Interest* article.

WHY DOES REGULATION FAIL?

The question is, why? Why has the direct and indirect expenditure of more than $100 billion a year on federal regulation failed to produce results commensurate with the effort? Or in some cases, any positive results at all?

Is the federal government trying to do the impossible? Or is it trying to do the possible in an impossible way? The answer is probably a little of both.

Many of the newer regulatory programs were ill-conceived and ill-considered. Typically, each got started after a single-interest pressure group succeeded in creating a wave of hysteria over an alleged crisis.

When this happens, most members of Congress quickly jump on the reform bandwagon. Those who don't may get crushed under its wheels. Says Rep. George Hansen (R.-Idaho): "It's very hard in Congress to vote against mother and home. And how do you vote against something labeled clean meat, safety, and health?"

The news media—especially television—build pressure for quick fixes because they tend to focus on problems that can be presented dramatically, rather than on the comparatively dry analyses of possible solutions. Also, representatives of single-interest groups always have something quotable to say, so they get lots of publicity. Through such exposure, special-issue crusaders develop what Mr. Weidenbaum calls the power of arrogance. Soon, as authors Nichols and Zeckhauser put it, "the appetite for favorable results is . . . so enormous that the probability of success seems almost irrelevant," and the most far-reaching laws are passed with little thought to the consequences.

When OSHA was formed, they point out, no evidence was presented that even relatively modest gains could be achieved.

A similar pattern prevailed during adoption of the tough auto emissions standards of 1970. Congress passed that bill with little debate. And yet, "few people seem to have had any idea of what was in the legislation," said Howard Margolis, a research fellow at the Massachusetts Institute of Technology, writing in *Public Interest*.

"Even a superficial examination of available information" would have shown that the costly new standards could make very little difference in air pollution levels.

The same phenomenon is discussed by economists Dorothy Tella and Paul MacAvoy in an analysis written for the U.S. Chamber's Council on Trends and Perspective:

"The rapid growth of health, safety, and environmental regulation in the late 1960s and early 1970s is not easy to explain. The market failures cited to justify new regulation did not show up then for the first time, and at least some of the indicators . . . that prompted Congress to regulate . . . were explained almost wholly by demographic factors beyond the reach of the regulatory process. . . .

"In every case where Congress chose to regulate, there were alternatives— court penalties for polluters, tax penalties for employers with poor safety records, government-funded information programs. In general, better arguments could have been made for the alternatives than for agency controls."

If the health and safety regulators were created in response to nonexistent crises, it is not surprising they have made little impact on mortality rates.

SAFER AND HEALTHIER

Certainly, health and safety problems do exist and will continue as long as human beings remain fallible. Even so, statistics confirm that the American public is far safer and healthier today than in past years.

Moreover, the same statistics show that most of the progress occurred well before the advent of the health and safety agencies. The general accident rate, for example, peaked at 94.1 fatalities per 100,000 people in 1907, then began a long, steady decline until leveling off at about 20 per 100,000 after 1957.

This long-term improvement in safety suggests another hypothesis to explain the poor record of federal regulators. The private sector is motivated by profits to seek safer working conditions and products. That profit incentive will reduce the accident and disease rate to the lowest level consistent with an efficient allocation of resources.

The federal government is then left with trying to achieve dramatic safety gains when fine-tuning is all that can reasonably be expected.

The theory is difficult to prove because, as long as any hazards remain, they can always be attributed to business misfeasance. But it is not hard to demonstrate the stong profit incentive in improving safety.

Unsafe working conditions can deprive an employer of trained workers, increase insurance costs, and raise wages for dangerous work. Unsafe products expose the manufacturer to civil suit, higher insurance costs, and loss of patronage to competitors.

However, there is no free market incentive for pollution control. Control costs raise prices without increasing the value of a product to the consumer, and a manufacturer who bears the costs of pollution control voluntarily suffers a competitive disadvantage. Consequently, there is agreement on the need for government action to limit pollution. The disagreement comes over the means.

In passing, though, government itself does not show in its own activities a concern for the public interest superior to that of the private sector. Federal facilities are among the worst polluters, from the Tennessee Valley Authority to the Capitol Power Plant. OSHA's offices have

6. DOES THE GOVERNMENT REGULATE TOO MUCH?

violated OSHA's standards. The Equal Employment Opportunity Commission has been found guilty of racial discrimination. Government and private employees alike were exposed to asbestos dust before its harmful effects were known.

People will make mistakes, whether they are in public or private enterprise. But neither pleas of human fallibility nor complaints about cost deter some health and safety regulators from demanding perfection.

"Every worker has a fundamental human right to a safe and healthful workplace," asserted Labor Secretary Ray Marshall in a speech (in 1979). Absolutely safe? Perfectly heathful? On the previous page of his text, the Labor Secretary sagaciously observed that "it is much easier, when dealing with environmental and occupational health, to fall back upon demagoguery. . . ."

Joan Claybrook, administrator of the traffic safety agency, shows a similar lack of perspective.

Accused of requiring more safety than the consumer wants to buy, she replied in *Regulation* magazine that "producers who know how to make a product safer have an obligation to do so, and if they do not fulfill that obligation, then government must take it on . . . the sanctity of life has the highest value in our society."

That statement, praiseworthy on its surface, is the kind of mother-and-home phrase that troubles many legislators. There are many ways to save lives and improve health, but, unfortunately, the government has no rational, established method for choosing among them.

"Why should the government spend almost $30,000 per year to keep a kidney patient alive," University of Virginia professor Steven E. Rhoads asked in *Public Interest*, "and yet not pay for mobile cardiac units that can provide an additional life-year for as little as $1,765?"

At the other end of the scale, the chemical industry has calculated that OSHA's proposed limits on worker exposure to benzene would eliminate one case of leukemia every six years, at a cost of $300 million each.

CURIOUS INCONSISTENCIES

A society never has enough resources to do everything that everyone would like to do. But OSHA and its brethren are not responsible for weighing their own plans against alternative uses of resources outside their spheres of influence. Thus, OSHA's efforts to save lives, like the FDA's, may result in a net loss of lives. This lack of a guiding philosphy and a coordinating authority also results in some curious inconsistencies.

Consider the CAT scanner, a very effective and expensive type of X-ray machine.

Federal health planners say physicians and hospitals are acquiring more of these devices than are needed, thereby wasting money. So the government wants to limit their number. In this case, cost-effectiveness is considered more important than the comfort, convenience, and perhaps even safety of the patients affected.

Contrast that policy with OSHA's proposed factory noise controls. OSHA wants employers to silence noisy machinery at great cost, rather than require workers to wear protective earplugs at modest cost.

The protective ear gear is uncomfortable, and workers might not wear it, says OSHA.

So in the case of noise standards, comfort and convenience are more important than cost-effectiveness.

PHILOSOPHICAL CHOICE

Beyond the economic trade-offs, there is a difficult philosophical choice between freedom and safety. Is an adult citizen a peer of the realm or its ward?

Sometimes society permits informed adults to participate in hazardous activities, vocational and avocational. And sometimes the law is used to limit or forbid such decisions.

"Why . . . do we find ourselves serenely contemplating a person's plan to climb a dangerous Himalayan peak at the same time that we propose making it illegal for her to buy a can of Tab?" asked University of California geneticist William R. Havender in a *Regulation* article.

There is little government objection to test pilots, firefighters, police, military personnel, and athletes accepting the risks of their trades.

Yet, industrial workers must apparently be protected from all risk, regardless of cost and their willingness to accept those risks in return for high pay and other benefits. In personal behavior, the government has attempted to force motorcycle riders to wear protective helmets on the ground that deaths and injuries impose costs on society. But if medical authorities are correct, far higher costs are imposed on society by those who smoke, eat, and drink to excess.

PERSONAL COMPULSION

Why do the regulators pick on the motorcycle riders? Perhaps because the motorcycle vote is relatively small.

"The resort to personal compulsion is a last resort when politicians fear that the public will not pay the cost of programs pushed on behalf of abstract principles," said Harvard Law School professor Charles Fried in *Regulation*. And he deplores "the moral obtuseness that treats people as public utilities."

Prof. Fried is not alone in his concern that freedom is endangered by well-meaning regulators. That point is often made.

But the regulators also raise some troubling questions. Are citizens always aware of the risk inherent in a product or occupation? If not, how can they make rational decisions? Dare we take chances with potentially hazardous environmental contaminants that may cause irreversible damage that does not show up for decades? And where environmental or genetic risk is involved, who represents the interests of future generations?

Americans need to make some painful choices about the priority of first principles. Until there is an agreed-upon basis for making trade-off decisions, it will remain impossible to know how much or how best to regulate.

In the words of Washington Gov. Dixie Lee Ray, a former federal regulator herself: "The reality is that zero defects in products plus zero pollution plus zero risk on the job is equivalent to maximum growth of government plus zero economic growth plus run-away inflation. That's what we have."

NO
Susan and Martin Tolchin

SILENT PARTNER:
THE POLITICS OF DEREGULATION

I don't know anybody who believes in dirty air or dirty water.
> —Irving Shapiro, former chairman of the board of the Du Pont Company

Regulation is the key to civilized society.
> —The late Jerry Wurf, president of the American Federation of State, County, and Municipal Employees

Century-old Anaconda, Montana, in the foothills of the well-named Bitterroot Range of the Rocky Mountains, became an instant ghost town on a crisp September morning in 1980. With little warning to its fifteen hundred employees, some of whose fathers and grandfathers had worked for the company, the Anaconda Copper Company closed the smelter that was as old as the town itself, and its reason for existence. The smelter had processed the copper ore mined in Butte, twenty-eight miles southeast, and the smelted copper was then sent by rail to a refinery in nearby Great Falls. The refinery was also closed soon afterward.

The company announced that because of the high cost of complying with government regulations, it would henceforth ship its copper to Japan, where it would be refined and smelted before being returned to the United States, a round trip of about fourteen thousand miles. Anaconda had recently been acquired by the ARCO Oil Company, which claimed that compliance with federal and state standards would cost between $300 and $400 million. At a press conference called to announce the closing, the president of the company explained that the decision was reached after "exhausting every option available" to bring the smelter into compliance with environmental, health, and work place regulations, but the costs of compliance were "prohibitive."

It was part of a pattern in which overregulation was blamed for reducing the United States to an underdeveloped nation, whose minerals were taken by industrialized nations that in turn sent back finished products. This was a reversal of the industrial imperialism that had sent America and other industrial powers roaming the world for natural resources, exploiting their less-developed neighbors and intervening in their internal political and fiscal affairs. The emergence of a potent Japanese lobbying effort in the nation's capital, and its influence on legislation and regulation, is testimony that the United States is considered by some ripe for the picking, and on the verge of joining the industrial have-nots. Like the closing of the steel mills in Youngstown, Ohio, Anaconda highlighted a new trend that has disturbing implications for the national defense, as well as an estimated total nationwide cost of $125 billion in lost production and more than two million jobs.

Skeptics, and there were many, contended that the closing was really triggered by a costly labor dispute preceded by decades of poor management, when technological improvements were shunned in favor of the pursuit of profits. These skeptics cited a short-term approach, in which managers were encouraged to regard their positions as stepping stones to more prestigious and lucrative appointments, rather than developing long-term loyalties to institutions and rejecting immediate profits in favor of capital investments and long-term growth. As early as 1972, *Forbes* magazine observed that "Anaconda's problems seem to have stemmed directly from its corporate style of life; its patrician stance, its attitude of affluence." A major corporate blunder had been the company's failure to foresee the nationalization of its extensive copper mines in Chile by the government of Salvador Allende, which marked the beginning of a steady decline in Anaconda's fiscal fortunes. "The company was making so much money in Chile that they let their domestic operations go a little flat," said L.R. Mecham, vice president of Anaconda.

Mecham added that labor troubles were a major factor in the closings. The plant had been idle since July, due to a nationwide strike against the copper industry.

"Montana was notorious for having some of the worst labor practices in the country," he said.

The ranks of the skeptics also included government regulators, who argued not only that the costs of complying with regulations were far lower than the company's figures, but that they were willing to negotiate flexible timetables for meeting those standards. Challenging Anaconda's figures, the federal Environmental Protection Agency (EPA) put the price tag at about $140 million; the Occupational Safety and Health Administration (OSHA) added another $3 million to the estimate. Roger Williams, a regional administrator of EPA, said the finality of the decision came as a "complete surprise" to him because of Anaconda's earlier commitment to retrofit its existing facilities to meet air pollution requirements. "The company's past failure to investigate options with EPA," he wrote, "coupled with the company's ability to quickly secure profitable contracts with foreign industry piques my interest, and I'm sure the public's, in knowing the reasons behind the company's decision."

The real reasons, that is. For regulation had become the national whipping boy, and it was easier to lay the blame at the feet of faceless bureaucrats in Washington than on mismanagement, the greed of organized labor, the worldwide decline of the copper industry, or the fact that copper smelting's most valuable by-product—sulfuric acid—had become virtually unmarketable in the United States. "They have used the closing as a political tool, to send a message to Congress about the Clean Air Act," said Steve Rovig, an aide to Senator Max Baucus, Democrat of Montana. . . .

Similarly, the American automobile industry blamed its precipitous decline, not on its high prices, oversized cars, or shoddy products, but on the raft of government regulations intended to improve the safety and fuel efficiency of the vehicles and perhaps make them more marketable. No matter that Japan overcame its long-standing reputation for shoddy production by applying rigorous standards of quality control, standards that were abandoned during the same period by Detroit. And how do the steel, copper, and auto industries reconcile their tendency to make regulations the scapegoat with the cold fact that their foreign competitors, most notably Japan, also live with stiff regulations, particularly in the environmental field?

By the late 1970s, complaints of excessive regulation had become management's all-purpose cop-out. Were profits too low? Blame regulation. Were prices too high? Blame regulation. Were inadequate funds and manpower earmarked for research and development? Blame regulation for sapping both funds and manpower. Was American industry unable to compete with foreign competitors? Blame regulation.

In a highly technological society such as ours, the need for increased regulation is manifest. It is inconceivable to think of "lessening the regulatory burden," as some put it, at a time when private industry has the power to alter our genes, invade our privacy, and destroy our environment. A single industrial accident in the 1980s is capable of taking a huge toll in human life and suffering. Only the government has the power to create and enforce the social regulations that protect citizens from the awesome consequences of technology run amuck. Only the government has the ability to raise the national debate above the "balance sheet" perspective of American industry. This is not to dismiss the many socially conscious businessmen who are concerned with the public interest, but, unfortunately, they do not represent the political leadership of the business community. After all, the "bottom line" for business is making a profit, not improving the quality of the environment or the work place. Its primary obligation is to its shareholders, not to the community at large.

Complaints against regulation have become a standard lament of American business, not without some justification. Horror stories abound. Federal bureaucrats were designing everything from toilet seats to university buildings. Small companies complained that they were drowning in paperwork and were being "regulated out of business." Douglas Costle, a former administrator of the Environmental Protection Agency in the Carter administration, estimated that his agency's regulations alone increased the Consumer Price Index by four-tenths of one percent each year, while estimates of the total cost of regulation exceeded $100 billion a year.

The complaints focused on what are known as social regulations, regulations not geared to a specific industry but to the general public. Regulations falling into this category included those whose benefits were designed to provide clean air and water, safety in the work place, product safety, pure food and drugs, and protection for the consumer in the marketplace. Their goals were ambitious, but expensive to implement. . . .

TAKING CHARGE OF REGULATION

The long simmering battle against regulation finally found a champion during the 1980 presidential campaign. Ronald Reagan, en route to the White House, needed little prodding. Once a television host and lecturer for the General Electric Company, he had made a political career of championing the virtues of free enterprise, and had vowed during the campaign to "get the government off the backs of the people." Responding to this deeply bipartisan antiregulatory mandate, the new President initiated a crusade against government regulation and quickly laid the groundwork for the direction of regulation in the 1980s. To Reagan and his allies, the future lay in deregulation, or the removal of regulations from the books whenever possible in order to allow market forces to operate in their stead. Barely a week after his election, Ronald Reagan promised to dismantle existing regulations, and to freeze all new rules for at least a year after his inauguration. In living up to the spirit of his campaign promises, Reagan gave the American people a chance to see for themselves what life would be like without the onerous hand of big government.

The President's appointment of Murray Weidenbaum to chair the Council of Economic Advisers was an important choice, both substantively and symbolically, in the President's war against the regulators. A well-known economics professor at Washington University in St. Louis, Weidenbaum's major distinction was his philosophic opposition to the excesses of regulation. "The encroaching of government power in the private sector in recent years has been massive [and] self-defeating," he wrote prior to his appointment. Afterward, he frequently exhorted federal regulators: "When you have nothing to do, undo."

There is no question, of course, that a President and a Congress can change regulatory priorities. The question is whether such changes are in the interests of a highly technological society, in which private industry has the power to inflict widespread damage to life and health. Additional questions of particular relevance to President Reagan concern administrative

procedures. While a President is empowered to change these procedures, with the help of Congress, questions have been raised about whether President Reagan adhered to traditional procedure governing the regulatory process, and the extent to which "undoing regulation" through procedural change has acted to the detriment of society.

The new President was so successful in capitalizing on his public relations victory over regulation that the system virtually reeled from its impact. Environmental protection became a thing of the past, as the EPA studiously ignored the laws and regulations dealing with clean air and water, as well as hazardous waste. Mine deaths shot up as regulations governing the safety of the mines were slowly dismantled through budget cuts and lack of enforcement. Through a program of consistent neglect, worker safety followed a similar path, victim of a more relaxed OSHA. No area of social protection was left untouched by White House efforts to unravel the regulations, the agencies, and the process. Even the nuclear regulators were encouraged to speed up the permit-granting process for nuclear plants by "streamlining" safety regulations.

What had taken years to build was dismantled in the first twelve months of the Reagan administration. Following the dictum that the marketplace could better evaluate the public's needs than government, Reagan trusted his friends in the business community to determine air quality, public safety, and a variety of other social questions far outside their realm of expertise. But the nation had become too complex for a return to this version of nineteenth-century laissez-faire capitalism, as became all too apparent early in the deregulation program. Nobody said anything about dead miners when discussing the burdens of regulation; no one reminded the public that not all industrialists would voluntarily clean up the local waterways and air without big government's interference. More than likely, the midnight dumpers were too busy finding new landfills for their illegal toxic wastes to make speeches about overregulation; now, with lax enforcement, they could probably operate in broad daylight.

It soon became apparent that in dismantling regulation, the President was dismantling America. Regulation is the connective tissue, the price we pay for an industrialized society. It is our major protection against the excesses of technology, whose rapid advances threaten man's genes, privacy, air, water, bloodstream, lifestyle, and virtual existence. It is a guard against the callous entrepreneur, who would have his workers breathe coal dust and cotton dust, who would send children into the mines and factories, who would offer jobs in exchange for health and safety, and leave the victims as public charges in hospitals and on welfare lines. "The child labor laws or the abolition of slavery would never have passed a cost-benefit test," said Mark Green, a public interest advocate, referring to the theory that now dominates regulatory decision making.

Regulations provide protection against the avarice of the marketplace, against shoddy products and unscrupulous marketing practices from Wall Street to Main Street. They protect legitimate businessmen from being driven out of business by unscrupulous competitors, and consumers from being victimized by unscrupulous businessmen. "Regulation is the key to civilized society," said the late Jerry Wurf, president of the American Federation of State, County, and Municipal Employees. The extent to which we take regulations for

granted in our daily lives is reflected by the confidence with which we drink our water, eat our food, take our medication, drive our cars, and perform hundreds of other tasks without thought of peril. This provides a striking contrast to the situation in many Third World nations, devoid of regulations, where those tasks can be performed only with extreme care. (Indeed, there is evidence that some of those countries adhere to United States regulations in the absence of their own government protections. The Squibb representative in Egypt, for example, said in 1979 that he could not market his company's drugs in that country unless they had been cleared by the United States Food and Drug Administration.)

In responding so agreeably to the critics of regulation, the politicians so quick to deregulate forgot that it was the very same process that prevented thalidomide—a tranquilizer prescribed to pregnant women that caused birth defects—from reaching the United States marketplace. A conscientious FDA medical officer, Frances Kelsey, spotted the drug and held it up, unimpressed with the fact that it had already been approved by the West German regulators. Critics also forget that regulations have helped to restore the Great Lakes, which ten years ago were on their way to a polluted oblivion, and have brought the nation more breathable air by reducing sulfur emissions by 17 percent since 1972. And although the Anaconda Copper Company complained bitterly about EPA regulations, lung disease in western Montana declined significantly after the copper company took its first steps toward compliance with air quality standards.

When social regulation works, its benefits are invisible. It is hardly newsworthy, or even noticeable, that the nation's air and water have become considerably cleaner over the last decade, a regulatory development that could be viewed as a stunning success. So could the Consumer Product Safety Commission's regulations that changed the design of cribs and significantly reduced the number of crib deaths by strangulation.

The problem is that those who breathe and those whose lives were saved by a safer crib have no trade association to applaud the unseen and unheralded benefits of the regulatory process—when it is working well. They have no Political Action Committee to reward politicians who support the regulatory system, or to punish those who attack it. Indeed, most people are unaware that regulations play any role in their well-being. No constituency with significant power has developed over the years to bolster, promote, reinforce, and expand these "public goods." Yet this is another reason the regulatory process was created in the first place: to protect those public goods and those who benefit from them. Indeed, ever since the first United States Congress gave the President the power to make rules for trading with the Indians, regulation has grown geometrically, often with the enthusiastic support of Congress and the President, because it represented a system that held the promise of protecting the public against the incursions of more narrowly focused interests. "We created the regulatory agencies to do what we don't have time to do," said the late Sam Rayburn, when he was Speaker of the House. . . .

The social regulatory agencies have become the government's orphans, attacked by both management and labor. Management contends that the cost of compliance will erode profits, while labor fears that it could cost jobs and lead to the destruction of entire industries. In an increasing number of cases, management and labor have joined forces to fight the regulatory agencies, producing formidable alliances. In one successful effort, the grain millers union fought side by side with management against the FTC's antitrust efforts to break up the giant cereal companies. In cases like this, who is left to provide the support network and the constituency so necessary to an agency's effective survival?

In this harsh political climate, it is no wonder that leadership on all fronts is in short supply. When President Carter claimed credit for returning salmon to the Columbia River, few applauded his efforts in cleaning up that once polluted waterway. When he attempted to intervene to cut the cost of environmental regulation, he was quickly branded an "enemy of the environment" by an army of critics. Nor did he find many friends among members of the business community, who faulted him for not moving fast enough to dismantle the regulatory process.

Both Congress and President Reagan learned the political lessons of the past, finding it was much easier to correct regulatory "excesses" by dismantling an agency, by reducing its budget to a point that renders it virtually ineffective, than to address the issue at hand.

Throwing the baby out with the bath water became a familiar pattern. It was guaranteed to stop an agency that had failed to work efficiently, that was perhaps working too efficiently, or that was working against the interests of a powerful industry. When certain members of Congress began receiving complaints against the FTC, they mounted such a successful campaign to hold up its appropriations that the agency was forced to close down for a few days in the spring of 1980. By 1981, another consumer agency, the Consumer Product Safety Commission, less vigorous than the FTC but equally offensive to business interests, fought valiantly to stay alive, even on its paltry budget of $40 million a year.

Congress regards its interventions as part of its legitimate oversight function to monitor the regulatory agencies. This has more than a grain of truth to it. A closer look reveals, however, that Congress bears considerable responsibility for the current state of siege that confronts the agencies, as well as for the volatility of regulatory politics in general. With its ambiguous mandates, increasingly detailed legislation, vulnerability to special interests, and increased involvement in the budget process, Congress has reinforced the uncertainty surrounding regulation and done little to improve its troubled future.

What few citizens realize is that all regulation stems from a statutory base. Agencies do not regulate on the basis of whim. OSHA did not initiate the guarantee of a safe work place for every worker; Congress wrote the enabling legislation that created the agency and gave it that far-reaching mandate. It was also Congress that set the goals for air quality standards, not the EPA, although both Reagan and Congress eleven years later threatened to reduce the EPA's power during the renewal of the Clean Air Act—essentially penalizing the agency for doing its job.

Under the guise of responding to pressures, Congress is acting out a charade. The members bask in the applause when they are credited with giving the nation clean air and a safe work place, but recoil from the anger of those who must bear the brunt of the high cost of regulation. . . .

WHO BENEFITS AND WHO LOSES?

The most serious consequence of the trend to deregulate is the dismantling of the social regulations, which provide a connective tissue between the needs of the public and private sectors. Private industry is entitled to make a profit, but its employees are entitled to their health and safety, their consumers are entitled to safe and well-made products, and the public is entitled to have its air, water, and quality of life safeguarded.

The rapid pace of technological advances has given industry awesome tools with which to alter our genes, invade our privacy, and even destroy our lives. It is difficult, therefore, to regard the current dismantling of regulation as anything but an aberration, a trend that will soon be reversed. One can thus expect increased pressures on government for protection against forces over which individuals have less and less control. And one would certainly expect those forces to be resisted by the affected industries. That conflict will be resolved in the political arena, which will be the ultimate arbiter in the current attempt at dismantling America. . . .

POSTSCRIPT

DOES THE GOVERNMENT REGULATE TOO MUCH?

Any consideration of social regulation by government must assess both costs and benefits. Society must ask how much it is willing to pay to avoid a given risk, just as workers will demand increased wages for running a greater risk. Most people are likely to agree that there are some benefits that merit the cost, and some costs that outweigh the benefits. Crickmer does not make many concessions, but he does acknowledge that pollution controls are necessary and that earlier automobile safety requirements did make a difference in reducing deaths and injuries. On the other side, Susan and Martin Tolchin concede that before Reagan came into office "federal bureaucrats were designing everything from toilet seats to university buildings." Although both essays aknowledge that the other side may have a point or two in its favor, the two remain sharply opposed to one another. This is true even when they quote the same economist: Murray L. Weidenbaum.

Weidenbaum has written a comprehensive account of government regulation: *Business, Government, and the Public* (Prentice-Hall, 1977). His survey and case studies cover consumer products, the environment, and job and automobile safety. Harold Seidman, in *Politics, Position and Power,* second edition (Oxford, 1975), maintains that conflicts between the regulatory agencies and the elected branches rarely turn on questions of substantive reform or administrative efficiency but are essentially political conflicts between opposing interests. Herbert Kaufman's *Red Tape: Its Origins, Uses, and Abuses* (Brookings Institution, 1977) clearly and briefly explains why bureaucratic institutions, including regulatory agencies, create so many obstacles to compliance.

The world is a dangerous place. The supporters of governmental regulation believe that in the absence of such controls we will face greater hazards and that more dangers will be loosed upon us by unscrupulous entrepreneurs. The opponents hold that we will more surely be strangled by red tape and impoverished by the regulatory costs that make prices higher when they do not actually make production unprofitable. It is tempting to counsel moderation between the extreme principles, but it is difficult to apply moderation in practice. Take, as an example, the debate on the peaceful development of nuclear energy. Neither side will be happy with a compromise that means small-scale utilization of atomic power. Such a policy will not fulfill the hopes of those who see nuclear energy as a solution for the energy crisis, and it will not allay the fears of those who see it as a threat to the lives of millions of people living near nuclear plants. Yet it is possible that, in this field as in others, the give and take of politics will dictate solutions that satisfy neither side and that keep the issue of regulation alive.

ISSUE 7

DOES THE SUPREME COURT ABUSE ITS POWER?

YES: Joseph Sobran, from "Minority Rule," *National Review,* December 31, 1985

NO: William J. Brennan, Jr., from "The Constitution of the United States: Contemporary Ratification," Georgetown University, Washington, D.C., October 12, 1985

ISSUE SUMMARY

YES: Journalist Joseph Sobran believes that the Supreme Court has inverted its original role and now wields the arbitrary power it was intended to check.
NO: Supreme Court Justice William J. Brennan, Jr., holds that judges have a duty to interpret the Constitution and to protect the democratic process.

Although the Supreme Court has declared fewer than one hundred Acts of Congress unconstitutional, judicial review (the power to exercise this judgment) is a critical feature of American government. It extends to all law—not simply federal law—and includes not only statutes but the actions of all agents of governmental power.

The power of judicial review consists not only of a negative power to invalidate acts contrary to the Constitution but equally (and far more frequently) of a positive power to give meaning and substance to constitutional clauses and the laws enacted in accordance with constitutional power. Finally, individual cases have impact and reverberation, which may profoundly influence the future direction of law and behavior. To take a prominent example, when the Supreme Court reinterpreted the equal protection clause of the Constitution's Fourteenth Amendment in 1954, it changed forever the legal and social patterns of race relations in the United States.

Some limitations on judicial review are self-imposed, such as the Court's refusal to consider "political questions"—that is, questions better decided by the elective branches rather than the courts. But it is the Supreme Court that decides which questions are political. The Supreme Court has been notably reluctant to curb a president's extraordinary use of emergency power in wartime and has done so rarely.

Still other limitations on judicial review derive from the judicial process, such as the requirement that the party bringing a case to court (any court) must have sufficient "standing" as an aggrieved party to be heard. Some laws do not appear to give any contesting party the basis for bringing a suit. Other laws rarely present themselves in an appropriate form for judicial decision, such as the ordinary exercise of presidential power in foreign relations. These exceptions qualify, yet do not really negate, the spirit of Alexis de Tocqueville's observation of nearly a century and a half ago that "scarcely any political question arises in the United States that is not resolved, sooner or later, into a judicial question."

Judicial review is exercised by state courts and inferior federal courts as well as by the United States Supreme Court, but the last word is reserved to the latter. When a power so vast is exercised in controversial areas, the judiciary cannot claim immunity from criticism, and it does not receive it. Critics have argued that the framers of the Constitution did not intend for so great a power to be possessed by so unrepresentative (unelected) an organ of government. The Court has been chided for going too far, too fast (by law enforcement agencies protesting the measures dealing with the rights of accused persons, for example) and for not going far enough, fast enough (by civil rights activists working for racial equality). In the 1930s, liberals castigated the "nine old men" for retarding social progress by invalidating major New Deal measures. In the 1950s, conservatives pasted "Impeach Earl Warren" (then Chief Justice) stickers on their car bumpers, and they bemoaned the Court's "coddling" of Communists and criminals. In the 1980s, some critics viewed the Supreme Court headed by Chief Justice Warren Burger as being less sympathetic to enforced integration, women's rights, the defense of accused persons, and the protection of socially disapproved expression.

Whether the framers intended that the courts should exercise the power of judicial review or not, they now possess it. They are not going to relinquish it, and it is unimaginable that Congress will ever take it away. The issue is, therefore, not whether there should be judicial review, but how much? Should judges act on issues of social policy where legislatures have failed to act? Do courts perform a democratic function in upholding the rights of minorities, which are ultimately the rights of all, even against the power of the majority? Or do they serve democracy better by having questions of social change to be decided by the people's representatives?

Journalist Joseph Sobran is convinced that the Supreme Court has usurped power which belongs to the elective branches. Supreme Court Justice William J. Brennan, Jr., is equally persuaded that the Court, in upholding liberty and justice for all, has upheld the principles of the Constitution.

YES   Joseph Sobran

JUDICIAL POWER IS MINORITY RULE

In January 1973, the United States Supreme Court handed down the most astonishing ruling in its history: it effectively struck down as unconstitutional the abortion laws of all fifty states.

This ruling made abortion on demand a fact of life in America, and abortion clinics sprang up across the nation overnight. An enormous new grass-roots political movement sprang up in response. The controversy over abortion has been one of the most heated and bitter in the annals of American politics. After all, the Court acted in defiance of a deeply rooted part of the Western moral tradition. Yet liberals expected the nation to acquiesce instantly and condemned anti-abortion protest as "divisive." The entire pro-life movement, which until *Roe* v. *Wade* had generally prevailed through the normal legislative process, was accused of trying to "impose its views" on the country; liberals made no such charge, however, against the majority of the Court, which had committed an exercise of what Justice Byron White, in his dissent, called "raw judicial power."

There was a further irony in the Court's ruling. Precisely because the substantive issue of abortion aroused great moral passion, the procedural oddity of the decision attracted little notice. The Court had struck down the laws of all fifty states—not only the most restrictive, but even the most permissive. This was far more sweeping than its famous ruling in *Brown* v. *Board of Education,* which affected the laws of only a dozen states, and had far more popular moral sentiment on its side.

In *Roe,* as opposed to *Brown,* the Court virtually held that *every state legislature in the nation had acted in violation of the Constitution.* This had a remarkable implication: it meant that none of the states had understood the original agreement among themselves. All had been acting inconsistently with the federal social contract without knowing it until, of course, the U.S. Supreme Court set them straight.

But that was not all. The Court's own constitutional qualms about legal restrictions on abortion were themselves a novelty. One would think there might have been earlier qualms—at the time the abortion laws were first passed in the nineteenth century, in legislative debates along the way, in scholarly articles in the law journals, in earlier lower-court rulings. But apparently there were none, ever. The abortion issue had been debated on its substantive merits, but never in terms of constitutionality.

So *Roe* in effect held not only that popular and legislative majorities had always been wrong, *but that no minority had ever been right.* That was the measure of the Court's arrogance. "Discovering," in its anfractuous way, a "right to privacy," which itself is nowhere explicit in the Constitution, the Court found the "right" to abortion in the "penumbra" of this phantom—and swept away a whole century of diverse legislation whose common denominator was a minimal regard for the personhood of unborn human beings.

If the subject had been less inflammatory than abortion—if, say, the Court had struck down the traffic laws of all fifty states—our primary attention would have been given to the formal absurdity of the Court's claim to have discerned the true meaning of the Constitution for the first time. *Roe* marked the pinnacle of the Court's assumption not so much of unique expertise as of oracular authority.

It might be supposed that the Constitution was singularly opaque, if its meaning could elude so many generations of citizens, legislators, scholars, and judges. And it might be wondered how the Court was able so suddenly to achieve true insight into that deeply hidden meaning. But although the Court's reasoning seemed dubious even to some liberal scholars who themselves favored legal abortion as a matter of public policy, the ruling stood. For like so many of the Court's flashes of constitutional vision, *Roe* happily coincided with the current liberal agenda, which mandated abortion on demand.

For a generation the Court implemented the liberal agenda on social poliicy in the name of preserving (or somehow "expanding") constitutional rights. It struck down legislation or simply dictated policy in the areas of public-school prayer, aid to private schools, racial segregation, police arrest procedures, legislative districting, pornography, birth control, and abortion. Apart from *Roe,* the Burger Court has generally avoided radical innovations, but it has generally conserved the radical innovations of its predecessors, qualifying some of them without contradicting any of them. This practice has only increased the public's confusion about the Court's role, but it has been purposeful: a Court that accused its predecessors of simple error would damage its own institutional authority, just as a pope would damage the authority of the papacy. From the Court's point of view, it is better strategy to pretend that the Court has maintained an overall consistency than to acknowledge that (to take the obvious example) the Warren Court bequeathed the nation a substantial body of bogus constitutional law.

What has made this mess possible? One factor is that the liberal community, so powerful in the academy and mass communications, has run interference for the Court as long as the Court has promoted the liberal agenda—especially those parts of the agenda that would have a hard time getting through the legislative process. Liberals in other branches of government have been happy to have the Court performing this service, thus sparing them the

129

risks of advocating legal pornography and abortion before the voters. It is much easier for them to shrug that the "interpretation" of the Constitution is the Court's prerogative under the Constitution itself, and to tell angry constituents that it would be improper for the legislative branch to interfere with the independence of the judiciary.

In addition, Americans have become sadly ignorant of their own Constitution and abjectly deferential to the supposed expertise of the Court. They have accepted the judicial mystique and the crippling ground rules it imposes on them. Most of them are totally unaware that the Constitution was intended as a social contract to which any citizen might appeal, that their own ancestors regularly adverted to it in legislative debate, and that it is only recently that it has been supposed that the interpretation of the Constitution was the special preserve of the judicial branch of government.

But thanks to the judicial mystique, American self-government has been seriously eroded. Major changes in our way of life (the omnipresence of pornography is testimony enough) can now be imposed by a body of nine unelected officials, answerable to nobody. Not only is the Court spared the necessity of facing either the voters or a reappointment proceeding: its members are nearly unremovable. The so-called "checks and balances" hardly inhibit it at all, since few citizens, even among conservatives, have the stomach for impeachment proceedings against an individual Justice, let alone against a majority of the Court. There are no day-to-day mechanisms for correcting the Court's errors, real or perceived, corresponding to the veto or the votes to override that enable the executive and legislative branches to control each other's individual acts. Far

from having "separate and equal" status with the other two branches, the Court enjoys a kind of superiority, even supremacy. . . .

Something else has happened to enlarge the Court's power, which Publius could not have foreseen. Since 1925, the Court has used a dubious interpretation of the Fourteenth Amendment to "incorporate" the Bill of Rights into state constitutions. In a progressive and piecemeal way, it has held that the states are bound as much as Congress to observe the separation of church and state (though this is not a personal right), the free exercise of religion, the freedom of speech and of the press, the privilege against self-incrimination, and so forth. (It is an interesting anomaly—and a tip-off to the ideological motivation of the "incorporation" process—that the Court has not required the states to respect the right to keep and bear arms.)

By means of the incorporation doctrine, the Court has assumed a wide power to strike down state and local legislation. And in fact it strikes down state and local laws about a hundred times as often as federal legislation. (This is another tip-off: the states, unlike Congress, have no ready means of striking back at the Court even if they want to.)

And so the Supreme Court, conceived originally as a *check* on federal expansion, has turned judicial review into an *instrument* of federal expansion. Since the New Deal especially, the Court has materially assisted the centralization of power and the weakening of the original federal system. Publius would be aghast.

Furthermore, though the fact is seldom noticed, the Court's recent career is even more remarkable for the federal legislation it has let pass than for the state and local laws it has struck down. The clear implication of Article I, Section 8, in conjunction with the Tenth Amendment, is that Congress is essentially limited to the powers explicitly conferred on it in the Constitution—or why enumerate them? The meaning of the Tenth Amendment has been debated endlessly (and there is some room for latitude on the question whether Congress can be strictly limited to its explicit powers), but it is unreasonable to suppose that Congress was to be able to assume new powers at its pleasure. Publius, after all, points out that the powers of Congress are "few and defined," while the powers remaining to the states are "numerous and indefinite." Yet the selective function of the "activist" Court has made the Tenth Amendment nearly a dead letter. Congress now legislates about anything it is in the mood to legislate about.

This means that the original federal system is now in ruins. The Tenth Amendment was more than an afterthought; in fact it is logically prior to the first eight amendments. (Willmoore Kendall described the First Amendment as nothing more than the Tenth Amendment as applied specifically to the areas of religion and speech.)

It is worth recalling Publius's apprehensions about the Bill of Rights. He argued that a bill of rights might be necessary under a monarchy or despotic form of government, in which the powers of the state were general and unlimited, and freedom could only be achieved by specifying a few exceptions to this power. But under a free government, which had only such powers as were explicitly conferred on it by the people, freedom was the rule and those powers were the exception. If the government had no authority to regulate the press, he argued, it was superfluous to stipulate that the government must respect the freedom of the press: "For why declare that things shall not be done which there is no power to do?" Such rights would confuse people about the basic presumption that the government did *not* have a general and unlimited power, by implying that it did.

Such objections were taken seriously, and the Ninth and Tenth Amendments were framed to meet them. As Kendall says, the Tenth contains in miniature the whole theory of the Constitution. Its desuetude is a constitutional calamity. The Federal Government now has a general and unlimited power, to which the Bill of Rights offers only a handful of exceptions. Under the original plan, the creation of a socialist regime in Washington would have been impossible; now it can be voted, or smuggled, into existence.

Most Americans have only a vague knowledge of the Constitution, and they tend to identify it with a few provisions in the Bill of Rights as construed by liberal Justices and publicists. The liberal interpretation is so thoroughly established that even a Justice as conservative as William Rehnquist can't challenge it except in a few details. No reform is possible without a virtual renaissance of constitutional understanding. To put the problem in a few words, the Constitution is now widely identified with its corruptions. . . .

Liberalism has succeeded in perverting the judiciary in order to impose its will on the majority. Since many parts of its agenda could never have mustered a majority in their favor, it has adopted the insidious strategy of identifying its agenda with "constitutional values." As the record shows, this strategy at least deserves high marks for cunning.

But nobody should be fooled. The Court "discovered" these values in the Constitution at just the same time the or-

7. DOES THE SUPREME COURT ABUSE ITS POWER?

gans of liberal propaganda were pushing them, and those Justices who dominated the Court at the peak of its liberalism— William O. Douglas, Hugo Black, William Brennan, Thurgood Marshall—were also, in their personal lives, passionate advocates of liberal causes. They were promoting their own policy references when they pretended to be reading the Constitution and they got away with it. Their bad history and bad logic have been copiously exposed; their bad legacy remains in the body of constitutional law, and we are left to cope with it as we may.

If we set aside the merits of the abortion issue itself, *Roe v. Wade* stands as an especially clear case of the Court's imposing a novel minority agenda, a liberal fad, under the pretense of pursuing the intimations of the Constitution itself. I repeat: *constitutional* objections were practically never heard in America until the advocates of legal abortion decided on the strategy of smuggling their cause into law via the judiciary. Then the Court obligingly "discovered" in the Constitution what had never before been suspected of residing there: a right to abort. In order to do this, the Court had to pretend that every legislature that had ever considered the issue had misunderstood the Constitution, and it had to be able to count on widespread passivity before its usurpations of power. It was able to do both.

By such devices the Court performs an innovative role while it affects to perform a conservative one. It enlists our reverence for the Constitution in order to make us indiscriminately deferential to the Constitution's current interpreters. In a final inversion of the original constitutional plan, the modern Court has FORCE and WILL, but not judgment. The perversion of the judicial branch marks a pretty complete triumph of factional politics over the kind of republican government envisioned by the generation of Washington, Jefferson, Hamilton, and Madison.

NO

William J. Brennan, Jr.

JUDICIAL DEFENSE
OF THE CONSTITUTION

. . . The Constitution is fundamentally a public text—the monumental charter of a government and a people—and a Justice of the Supreme Court must apply it to resolve public controversies. For, from our beginnings, a most important consequence of the constitutionally created separation of powers has been the American habit, extraordinary to other democracies, of casting social, economic, philosophical and political questions in the form of law suits, in an attempt to secure ultimate resolution by the Supreme Court. In this way, important aspects of the most fundamental issues confronting our democracy may finally arrive in the Supreme Court for judicial determination. Not infrequently, these are the issues upon which contemporary society is most deeply divided. They arouse our deepest emotions. The main burden of my twenty-nine Terms on the Supreme Court has thus been to wrestle with the Constitution in this heightened public context, to draw meaning from the text in order to resolve public controversies.

Two other aspects of my relation to this text warrant mention. First, constitutional interpretation for a federal judge is, for the most part, obligatory. When litigants approach the bar of court to adjudicate a constitutional dispute, they may justifiably demand an answer. Judges cannot avoid a definitive interpretation because they feel unable to, or would prefer not to, penetrate to the full meaning of the Constitution's provisions. Unlike literary critics, judges cannot merely savor the tensions or revel in the ambiguities inhering in the text—judges must resolve them.

Second, consequences flow from a Justice's interpretation in a direct and immediate way. A judicial decision respecting the incompatibility of Jim Crow with a constitutional guarantee of equality is not simply a contemplative exercise in defining the shape of a just society. It is an order—supported by the full coercive power of the State—that the present society change in a fundamental aspect. Under such circumstances the process of deciding can be a lonely, troubling experience for fallible human beings conscious that their

From, "The Constitution of the United States: Contemporary Ratification," by Justice William J. Brennan. Presented at symposium, Georgetown University, Washington, DC, October 12, 1985.

best may not be adequate to the challenge. We Justices are certainly aware that we are not final because we are infallible; we know that we are infallible only because we are final. One does not forget how much may depend on the decision. More than the litigants may be affected. The course of vital social, economic and political currents may be directed.

These three defining characteristics of my relation to the constitutional text—its public nature, obligatory character, and consequentialist aspect—cannot help but influence the way I read that text. When Justices interpret the Constitution they speak for their community, not for themselves alone. The act of interpretation must be undertaken with full consciousness that it is, in a very real sense, the community's interpretation that is sought. Justices are not platonic guardians appointed to wield authority according to their personal moral predelictions. Precisely because coercive force must attend any judicial decision to countermand the will of a contemporary majority, the Justices must render constitutional interpretations that are reviewed as legitimate. . . .

There are those who find legitimacy in fidelity to what they call "the intentions of the Framers." In its most doctrinaire incarnation, this view demands that Justices discern exactly what the Framers thought about the question under consideration and simply follow that intention in resolving the case before them. It is a view that feigns self-effacing deference to the specific judgments of those who forged our original social compact. But in truth it is little more than arrogance cloaked as humility. It is arrogant to pretend that from our vantage we can guage accurately the intent of the Framers on application of principle to specific, contemporary questions. All too often, sources of potential enlight-

enment such as records of the ratification debates provide sparse or ambiguous evidence of the original intention. Typically, all that can be gleaned is that the Framers themselves did not agree about the application or meaning of particular constitutional provisions, and hid their differences in cloaks of generality. Indeed, it is far from clear whose intention is relevant—that of the drafters, the congressional disputants, or the ratifiers in the states?—or even whether the idea of an original intention is a coherent way of thinking about a jointly drafted document drawing its authority from a general assent of the states. And apart from the problematic nature of the sources, our distance of two centuries cannot but work as a prism refracting all we perceive. One cannot help but speculate that the chorus of lamentations calling for interpretation faithful to "original intention"—and proposing nullification of interpretations that fail this quick litmus test—must inevitably come from persons who have no familiarity with the historical record.

Perhaps most importantly, while proponents of this facile historicism justify it as a depoliticization of the judiciary, the political underpinnings of such a choice should not escape notice. A position that upholds constitutional claims only if they were within the specific contemplation of the Framers in effect establishes a presumption of resolving textual ambiguities against the claim of constitutional right. It is far from clear what justifies such a presumption against claims of right. Nothing intrinsic in the nature of interpretation—if there is such a thing as the "nature" of interpretation—commands such a passive approach to ambiguity. This is a choice no less political than any other; it expresses antipathy to claims of the minority to rights against the majority.

Those who would restrict claims of right to the values of 1789 specifically articulated in the Constitution turn a blind eye to social progress and eschew adaptation of overarching principles to changes of social circumstance.

Another, perhaps more sophisticated, response to the potential power of judicial interpretation stresses democratic theory: because ours is a government of the people's elected representatives, substantive value choices should by and large be left to them. This view emphasizes not the transcendant historical authority of the framers but the predominant contemporary authority of the elected branches of government. Yet it has similar consequences for the nature of proper judicial interpretation. Faith in the majoritarian process counsels restraint. Even under more expansive formulations of this approach, judicial review is appropriate only to the extent of ensuring that our democratic process functions smoothly. Thus, for example, we would protect freedom of speech merely to ensure that the people are heard by their representatives, rather than as a separate, substantive value. When, by contrast, society tosses up to the Supreme Court a dispute that would require invalidation of a legislature's substantive policy choice, the Court generally would stay its hand because the Constitution was meant as a plan of government and not as an embodiment of fundamental substantive values.

The view that all matters of substantive policy should be resolved through the majoritarian process has appeal under some circumstances, but I think it ultimately will not do. Unabashed enshrinement of majority will would permit the imposition of a social caste system or wholesale confiscation of property so long as a majority of the authorized legislative body,

fairly elected, approved. Our Constitution could not abide such a situation. It is the very purpose of a Constitution—and particularly of the Bill of Rights—to declare certain values transcendent, beyond the reach of temporary political majorities. The majoritarian process cannot be expected to rectify claims of minority right that arise as a response to the outcomes of that very majoritarian process. As James Madison put it:

> "The prescriptions in favor of liberty ought to be levelled against that quarter where the greatest danger lies, namely, that which possesses the highest prerogative of power. But this is not found in either the Executive or Legislative departments of Government, but in the body of the people, operating by the majority against the minority." (I Annals 437).

Faith in democracy is one thing, blind faith quite another. Those who drafted our Constitution understood the difference. One cannot read the text without admitting that it embodies substantive value choices; it places certain values beyond the power of any legislature. Obvious are the separation of powers; the privilege of the Writ of Habeas Corpus; prohibition of Bills of Attainder and ex post facto laws; prohibition of cruel and unusual punishments; the requirement of just compensation for official taking of property; the prohibition of laws tending to establish religion or enjoining the free exercise of religion; and, since the Civil War, the banishment of slavery and official race discrimination. With respect to at least such principles, we simply have not constituted ourselves as strict utilitarians. While the Constitution may be amended, such amendments require an immense effort by the People as a whole.

To remain faithful to the content of the Constitution, therefore, an approach to interpreting the text must account for the existence of these substantive value choices, and must accept the ambiguity inherent in the effort to apply them to modern circumstances. The Framers discerned fundamental principles through struggles against particular malefactions of the Crown; the struggle shapes the particular contours of the articulated principles. But our acceptance of the fundamental principles has not and should not bind us to those precise, at times anachronistic, contours. Successive generations of Americans have continued to respect these fundamental choices and adopt them as their own guide to evaluating quite different historical practices. Each generation has the choice to overrule or add to the fundamental principles enunciated by the Framers; the Constitution can be amended or it can be ignored. Yet with respect to its fundamental principles, the text has suffered neither fate. Thus, if I may borrow the words of an esteemed predecessor, Justice Robert Jackson, the burden of judicial interpretation is to translate "the majestic generalities of the Bill of Rights, conceived as part of the pattern of liberal government in the eighteenth century, into concrete restraints on officials dealing with the problems of the twentieth century." (Barnette, 319 U.S. at 639).

We current Justices read the Constitution in the only way that we can: as Twentieth Century Americans. We look to the history of the time of framing and to the intervening history of interpretation. But the ultimate question must be, what do the words of the text mean in our time. For the genius of the Constitution rests not in any static meaning it might have had in a world that is dead and gone, but in the adaptability of its great principles to cope with current problems and current needs. What the constitutional fundamentals meant to the wisdom of other times can-

not be their measure to the vision of our time. Similarly, what those fundamentals mean for us, our descendants will learn, cannot be the measure to the vision of their time. This realization is not, I assure you, a novel one of my own creation. Permit me to quote from one of the opinions of our Court, *Weens v. United States*, 217 U.S. 349, written nearly a century ago:

"Time works changes, brings into existence new conditions and purposes. Therefore, a principle to be vital must be capable of wider application than the mischief which gave it birth. This is peculiarly true of constitutions. They are not ephemeral enactments, designed to meet passing occasions. They are, to use the words of Chief Justice John Marshall, 'designed to approach immortality as nearly as human institutions can approach it.' The future is their care and provision for events of good and bad tendencies of which no prophecy can be made. In the application of a constitution, therefore, our contemplation cannot be only of what has been, but of what may be."

Interpretation must account for the transformative purpose of the text. Our Constitution was not intended to preserve a preexisting society but to make a new one, to put in place new principles that the prior political community had not sufficiently recognized. Thus, for example, when we interpret the Civil War Amendments to the charter—abolishing slavery, guaranteeing blacks equality under law, and guaranteeing blacks the right to vote—we must remember that those who put them in place had no desire to enshrine the status quo. Their goal was to make over their world, to eliminate all vestige of slave caste.

Having discussed at some length how I, as a Supreme Court Justice, interact with this text, I think it time to turn to the fruits of this discourse. For the Constitution is a sublime oration on the dignity of man, a bold commitment by a people to the ideal of libertarian dignity protected through law. Some reflection is perhaps required before this can be seen.

The Constitution on its face is, in large measure, a structuring text, a blueprint for government. And when the text is not prescribing the form of government it is limiting the powers of that government. The original document, before addition of any of the amendments, does not speak primarily of the rights of man, but of the abilities and disabilities of government. When one reflects upon the text's preoccupation with the scope of government as well as its shape, however, one comes to understand that what this text is about is the relationship of the individual and the state. The text marks the metes and bounds of official authority and individual autonomy. When one studies the boundary that the text marks out, one gets a sense of the vision of the individual embodied in the Constitution.

As augmented by the Bill of Rights and the Civil War Amendments, this text is a sparkling vision of the supremacy of the human dignity of every individual. This vision is reflected in the very choice of democratic self-governance: the supreme value of a democracy is the presumed worth of each individual. And this vision manifests itself most dramatically in the specific prohibitions of the Bill of Rights, a term which I henceforth will apply to describe not only the original first eight amendments, but the Civil War amendments as well. It is a vision that has guided us as a people throughout our history, although the precise rules by which we have protected fundamental human dignity have been transformed over time in response to both transformations of social condition and evolution of our concepts of human dignity.

Until the end of the nineteenth centu-

ry, freedom and dignity in our country found meaningful protection in the institution of real property. In a society still largely agricultural, a piece of land provided men not just with sustenance but with the means of economic independence, a necessary precondition of political independence and expression. Not surprisingly, property relationships formed the heart of litigation and of legal practice, and lawyers and judges tended to think stable property relationships the highest aim of the law.

But the days when common law property relationships dominated litigation and legal practice are past. To a growing extent economic existence now depends on less certain relationships with government—licenses, employment, contracts, subsidies, unemployment benefits, tax exemptions, welfare and the like. Government participation in the economic existence of individuals is pervasive and deep. Administrative matters and other dealings with government are at the epicenter of the exploding law. We turn to government and to the law for controls which would never have been expected or tolerated before this century, when a man's answer to economic oppression or difficulty was to move two hundred miles west. Now hundreds of thousands of Americans live entire lives without any real prospect of the dignity and autonomy that ownership of real property could confer. Protection of the human dignity of such citizens requires a much modified view of the proper relationship of individual and state.

In general, problems of the relationship of the citizen with government have multiplied and thus have engendered some of the most important constitutional issues of the day. As government acts ever more deeply upon those areas of our lives once marked "private," there is an even greater need to see that individual rights are not

7. DOES THE SUPREME COURT ABUSE ITS POWER?

curtailed or cheapened in the interest of what may temporarily appear to be the "public good." And as government continues in its role of provider for so many of our disadvantaged citizens, there is an even greater need to ensure that government act with integrity and consistency in its dealings with these citizens. To put this another way, the possibilities for collision between government activity and individual rights will increase as the power and authority of government itself expands, and this growth, in turn, heightens the need for constant vigilance at the collision points. If our free society is to endure, those who govern must recognize human dignity and accept the enforcement of constitutional limitations on their power conceived by the Framers to be necessary to preserve that dignity and the air of freedom which is our proudest heritage. Such recognition will not come from a technical understanding of the organs of government, or the new forms of wealth they administer. It requires something different, something deeper—a personal confrontation with the well-springs of our society. Solutions of constitutional questions from that perspective have become the great challenge of the modern era. All the talk in the last half-decade about shrinking the government does not alter this reality or the challenge it imposes. The modern activist state is a concomitant of the complexity of modern society; it is inevitably with us. We must meet the challenge rather than wish it were not before us. . . .

As I interpret the Constitution, capital punishment is under all circumstances cruel and unusual punishment prohibited by the Eighth and Fourteenth Amendments. . . .

This is an interpretation to which a majority of my fellow Justices—not to mention, it would seem, a majority of my fellow countrymen—does not subscribe.

Perhaps you find my adherence to it, and my recurrent publication of it, simply contrary, tiresome, or quixotic. Or perhaps you see in it a refusal to abide by the judicial principle of *stare decisis,* obedience to precedent. In my judgment, however, the unique interpretive role of the Supreme Court with respect to the Constitution demands some flexibility with respect to the call of *stare decisis.* Because we are the last word on the meaning of the Constitution, our views must be subject to revision over time, or the Constitution falls captive, again, to the anachronistic views of long-gone generations. I mentioned earlier the judge's role in seeking out the community's interpretation of the Constitutional text. Yet, again in my judgment, when a Justice perceives an interpretation of the text to have departed so far from its essential meaning, that Justice is bound, by a large constitutional duty to the community, to expose the departure and point toward a different path. On this issue, the death penalty, I hope to embody a community striving for human dignity for all, although perhaps not yet arrived. . . .

If we are to be as a shining city upon a hill, it will be because of our ceaseless pursuit of the constitutional ideal of human dignity. For the political and legal ideals that form the foundation of much that is best in American institutions—ideals jealously preserved and guarded throughout our history—still form the vital force in creative political thought and activity within the nation today. As we adapt our institutions to the ever-changing conditions of national and international life, those ideals of human dignity—liberty and justice for all individuals—will continue to inspire and guide us because they are entrenched in our Constitution. The Constitution with its Bill of Rights thus has a bright future, as well as a glorious past, for its spirit is inherent in the aspirations of our people.

POSTSCRIPT

DOES THE SUPREME COURT
ABUSE ITS POWER?

In the debate over the scope of judicial power, there are those who advocate judicial activism and those who support judicial self-restraint. The former want to use judicial power to fulfill constitutional purposes; the latter yield to the popularly elected branches of the government and to the people. Neither position should be pushed too far. Neither school of thought is so activist that it would allow judicial initiative in areas where the courts have not been asked to render decisions nor so self-restraining that it would withdraw entirely the power of the courts to declare the acts and actions of elected officials unconstitutional.

In *The People and the Court* (Macmillan, 1960), Charles L. Black, Jr., carefully developed the argument that judicial review is compatible with—and the best safeguard of—constitutional government. Eugene V. Rostow, in *The Sovereign Imperative* (Yale, 1962), has gone further, maintaining that judicial review serves to keep the other branches of government democratic. The late Alexander Bickel was possibly the most influential and profound critic of judicial review in recent times. In *The Least Dangerous Branch* (Bobbs-Merrill, 1962) and *The Majority of Consent* (Yale, 1975), Bickel has argued that relying too much on judicial power increases the risk of committing injustice in the name of moral duty. Archibald Cox, who was the original Watergate prosecutor, has written an account of *The Role of the Supreme Court in American Government* (Oxford, 1976) that combines the virtues of thoughtfulness and brevity.

Debate on the scope of judicial power does not deter judges from continuing to render decisions in cases involving such controversial issues as compulsory busing, preferential treatment for minorities, the right of abortion and the power of the states to outlaw it, women's rights, unions' rights, and the president's right of executive privilege. Tocqueville's observation that "scarcely any political question arises in the United States today that is not resolved, sooner or later, into a judicial question" does not seem like an overstatement today. However, a Supreme Court that boldly entertains bitterly divisive issues cannot escape becoming a subject of political controversy itself.

ISSUE 8

REGULATING THE MEDIA: IS THE "FAIRNESS DOCTRINE" UNFAIR?

YES: Dan Rather, from Address to *US Senate Committee on Commerce, Science, and Transportation,* September 28, 1982

NO: Elaine Donnelly, from Address to *US Senate Committee on Commerce, Science, and Transportation,* January 30, 1984

ISSUE SUMMARY

YES: CBS anchor Dan Rather argued that the "fairness doctrine" tends to chill dissent and discourage the full and robust coverage of controversial issues.
NO: Conservative activist Elaine Donnelly argues that the "fairness doctrine" is the only means of forcing the networks to provide some semblance of balanced news coverage.

The First Amendment puts it in unequivocal language: "Congress shall make no law . . . abridging the freedom of speech, or of the press." But press freedom has always hinged on more than the commands of the Constitution. The theory behind it was concisely stated in 1919 by Supreme Court Justice Oliver Wendell Holmes, Jr. The "best test of truth," Holmes said, "is the power of the thought to get itself accepted in the competition of the market." The purpose of the First Amendment, therefore, is to promote "free trade in ideas." When ideas, opinions, and assertions are allowed to compete with one another, we the people can then decide which view is more nearly correct. If the government interferes in the process by censorship or punishment of free expression, it deprives us of the only sure means of separating truth from error.

What Holmes and other defenders of press freedom took for granted back in 1919 was America's rich variety of newspapers. Indeed, in the America of his time almost every city in the country had competing newspapers, and the big cities had several. They all had their biases, and some of them were full of nonsense, but that was the whole point: the public could compare points of view, could see opinions collide, and could therefore sort out truth from error.

Suppose, however, that there were not thousands of newspapers, but only three. Suppose, further, that even those three did not really compete with one another. (They might compete in comics or sports coverage but not in ideas). Finally, suppose that the three papers refused to print readers' criticism of their news or editorials. In that situation, would not the "free trade in ideas" be curtailed? The press would be free of government control, but it would be doing its own censoring, depriving its readers of diverse viewpoints.

Critics charge that the above model in many ways describes American TV. On a nationwide basis, TV news and entertainment are largely in the hands of three networks, ABC, NBC, and CBS. They "compete" with one another commercially, but—again, according to their critics—their news slant is pretty much the same.

For the past half-century or more, the government has, at least to some degree, sided with the critics. The government characterizes the electronic media as being of "limited access." The limited access does not necessarily result from the desire to limit competition; it results simply from the nature of electronics. There are only so many broadcasting "bands" to go around, and the government gives each station the exclusive right to broadcast within its assigned frequency. In return, it demands that the stations operate in the "public interest."

What is the "public interest"? The Communications Act of 1934 says it must include a diversity of viewpoints. For example, it requires stations which endorse political candidates to allow "equal time" for the endorsement of competing candidates. More fundamentally, it sets up a Federal Communications Commission (FCC), and gives it the power to make and enforce rules for broadcasters. Acting on that authorization, the FCC in 1949 promulgated its "fairness doctrine." Not to be confused with the "equal time" rule, the "fairness doctrine" requires radio and TV stations to air controversies and to allow at least some time—not necessarily equal time—to diverse and competing viewpoints.

The doctrine was challenged by a radio station during the 1960s. The station refused to broadcast an FCC-ordered reply to one of its political messages, and the case wound up in the Supreme Court. In a landmark decision, *Red Lion Broadcasting Co.* v. *Federal Communications Commission* (1969), the Court upheld the "fairness doctrine." In its opinion, written by Justice Byron White, the Court said that the purpose of the First Amendment is "to preserve an uninhibited marketplace of ideas in which truth will ultimately prevail." Therefore, we cannot "countenance monopolization of that market, whether it be by the Government itself or a private licensee." The broadcasters' right of free speech must not be allowed to deprive audiences of diverse viewpoints. "It is the right of the viewers and listeners, not the right of broadcasters, which is paramount. . . ."

In recent years the FCC has come close to abandoning the "fairness doctrine." The Reagan-appointed FCC commissioners have made no secret of their distaste for government regulation, and they have interpreted "fairness" so loosely that it is now enough if a broadcaster consigns dissenting views to the small hours of the morning. Even in this diluted form, the "fairness doctrine" is unacceptable to broadcasters, who consider it an abridgment of press freedom. They would like to see it formally abolished, along with the "equal time" rule. In the following selections, taken from testimony before the Senate Commerce Committee, CBS anchor Dan Rather makes a case for abolition, while Elaine Donnelly, a representative of a conservative group called "Eagle Forum," argues for continued regulation.

YES

Dan I. Rather

FREEDOM FROM
GOVERNMENT RESTRAINT

I am grateful for the opportunity to appear here today because there is no issue that I feel more strongly about than the one we are now considering. That is the assurance of the full protection of the First Amendment to the electronic press. Although my strong feelings on this subject stem partly from the fact that I am now primarily a broadcast journalist, they go beyond these professional concerns.

I would like to emphasize that I am here as an individual, as a citizen. I am not here to engage in a special pleading on behalf of myself nor my colleagues in broadcast journalism. And I certainly do not mean to tell you that we, any more than our colleagues in the print press, are infallible in our efforts to bring the public news fairly and accurately, or that those efforts should not be subject to criticism and scrutiny both by the public and by other journalists.

But I am here to say as strongly as I know how that any Government role in overseeing the journalistic decisions of broadcasters is fundamentally at odds with the concept of a free press.

Perhaps we reporters say too often that the First Amendment guarantee of a free press is not intended to confer special privileges on us, but rather to protect the rights of the public we serve. But if that statement has become a cliche—I hope it has not, but if it has, it is because it expresses a basic truth.

The framers of the First Amendment understood the necessity of divorcing the power to govern from the right and responsibility to inform the people about the affairs of Government. They would never have dreamed of establishing a Government agency as the judge of the "fairness" of the very newspapers which were meant to act as a check against the abuses of Government power.

And that was not because they always liked what they saw in the newspapers of their day. Thomas Jefferson, for example, deplored "the malignity, the vulgarity, and the mendacious spirit" of the press of his time, but he considered

From, statement by Dan Rather to US Senate Committee on Commerce, Science and Transportation, *Hearings on Freedom of Expression,* September 28,30, and November 19, 1982.

these to be "evils for which there is no remedy." "Our liberty depends on the freedom of the press," Jefferson wrote, "and that cannot be limited without being lost."

I would like to think that the spirit that characterizes the press of today—both print and broadcast—is far different from that of the newspapers of Jefferson's era, as he saw that spirit. I have 20 years of experience with the commitment to fairness and accuracy which motivates my colleagues at CBS News, and I am very proud of that commitment. But the fundamental point remains the same: All our basic liberties depend for their survival on freedom of the press—not freedom so long as the ruling majority thinks the press is right, but freedom from all Government restraint.

It is ironic, therefore, that as we approach the 200th anniversary of the Bill of Rights, the medium on which the public most relies for its news and information must still answer to a Government agency empowered to decide on the fairness, balance, and responsibility of its reporting on public events.

We are fortunate that those charged with the regulation of broadcasting have been, by and large, civilized and sensitive men and women who have attempted to perform their function with due regard for First Amendment values. But the security of our freedoms cannot be allowed to depend on good fortune alone.

Let us be clear about what Government power to regulate broadcast content means. It is a power exercised most prominently through the fairness doctrine and the so-called equal time law. It means that a politically appointed body—the Federal Communications Commission—is continually called upon to decide whether broadcasters have been fair and balanced in their

coverage of the most highly charged issues of the day.

While that is bad enough in itself, it is made even worse by the fact that television and radio stations must regularly apply to the Government for the right to remain on the air. So, if the FCC determines that a particular station has not met Government-approved standards of fairness, that station can be permanently silenced by the Government.

How would we feel if this situation were to exist with respect to our daily newspapers? I think we would find it intolerable, even if the possibility of such draconian Government were confined solely to the realm of theory. Unfortunately, however, history teaches us that Government efforts to intimidate the press are not always just the stuff of which nightmares are made.

To any future administration intent on bending the broadcast media to its will, not only the fairness doctrine, but the entire licensing process, could serve as a subtle but powerful instrument of Government coercion. And the prospect of such Government coercion is made all the more frightening because it is most likely to occur during times of national trauma, when the need for a free and uninhibited press is most critical.

There is, therefore, a very real tension between the entire concept of Government licensing and a broadcast press which is truly independent. We need not dwell on this, however, to conclude that the most direct kinds of regulation of broadcast content—such as the fairness doctrine and equal time provision—should have no place in a society that is rightfully proud of having the freest press in the world.

Journalists should not have to justify what they publish, to even the most well-intentioned Government. Nor should the presentation of a controversial report result in their being required to cull through newsroom files to prove to a Government bureaucracy that the "other side" has also been presented. Such Government scrutiny, it seems to me, is fundamentally incompatible with the robust and independent press which the first amendment was designed to foster.

I can assure you, Senator, that all this has a definite, if subtle, impact on the real world of broadcast journalism. When I was a young reporter, I worked briefly for wire services, small radio stations and newspapers, and I finally settled into a job at a large radio station owned by the *Houston Chronicle*. Almost immediately on starting work in that station's newsroom, I became aware of a concern which I had previously barely known existed— the FCC.

The journalists at the *Chronicle* did not worry about it; those at the radio station did. Not only the station manager but newspeople as well were very much aware of this Government presence looking over their shoulders. I can recall newsroom conversations about what the FCC implications of broadcasting a particular report would be. Once a newsperson has to stop and consider what a Government agency will think of something he or she wants to put on the air, an invaluable element of freedom has been lost.

At CBS, when the claim is made that our coverage of a complex issue has not been "balanced," when someone goes to the FCC and demands equal time, the problem is largely handled by management and lawyers. But such complaints often involve extensive litigation before the Commission and the courts, costing many thousands of dollars—sometimes hundreds of thousands of dollars—and ab-

sorbing hours of management time and effort.

How will the small broadcaster, without the economic resources of a CBS, react to the threat of such costly and time-consuming legal proceedings? Will there not be a temptation to steer clear of controversy, so as to avoid these burdens?

It is bad enough that broadcasters are subject to such inhibitions. But recent technological advances lend compelling new urgency to the task of extending full First Amendment protection to the electronic media. As you pointed out, we are rapidly approaching the day when newspapers, books, and magazines will be available in many homes on the television screen. While it may seem inconceivable that such technological change would lead to the imposition of content controls on traditional print journalism, the only sure way to prevent this is by making clear that the First Amendment means what it says—for the electronic as well as the printed press.

Indeed, the very technological change which makes it more vital than ever that electronic journalism achieve full First Amendment citizenship, at the same time undermines the traditional rationale for regulating broadcast content. Whatever arguments might have been made in the past about the scarcity of broadcast frequencies, there are now more than 10,000 television and radio stations in the United States, almost six times the number of daily newspapers. In addition, such emerging technologies as cable television, direct satellite-to-home broadcasting, and subscription TV promise to increase enormously the diversity of viewing choices available to the public.

But the public does not depend on television and radio alone for news and commentary on public affairs. It also receives information from books, magazines, and newspapers, not to mention the countless other institutions in this pluralistic society—educational, civic, religious, and professional—which play an essential role in shaping public awareness and opinion.

With all these competing sources, it strikes me as not a little fantastic to argue that Government regulation is needed to keep broadcast journalism honest. In the final analysis, it is the pluralism of our society which provides us our surest defense against the abuse of freedom of the press.

As I noted at the outset, none of us in the print or broadcast press can claim that we always achieve perfect accuracy, fairness, and balance in our reporting. On those occasions when we do fall short, we expect to be called to account for our errors by the public and by our peers, just as newspapers and magazines are. But this process of criticism and review is one in which the Government can have no proper role, for the dangers inherent in such Government intervention are far greater than those posed by occasional journalistic excess.

CBS News, I want to emphasize again, is committed to accuracy and fairness in news reporting and will remain so, whether or not there is a fairness doctrine or an equal time law. Our ultimate judges, of course, will be the millions of people who watch and listen to our news broadcasts every day. I do not believe they would fail to recognize bias or distortion for very long, and my experience bears that out.

Once again, the words of Thomas Jefferson are instructive.

> As yet we have found it better to trust the public judgment, rather than the magistrate, with the discrimination between truth and falsehood. And hitherto the public judgment has performed that office with wonderful correctness.

Insuring the full protection of the First Amendment to the electronic press would constitute a renewed vote of confidence in the intelligence and judgment of the American public and a renewed commitment to the First Amendment faith of our Founding Fathers. That vote and that renewed commitment are long overdue, and I hope they will come soon.

The CHAIRMAN. Mr. Rather, thank you. . . .

I am curious. You used the word "trauma" in your statement. You said that this coercion "is most likely to occur during times of national trauma." Could you elaborate on that?

Mr. RATHER. Senator, I think the record is fairly clear, for example—and this is only one example—that the press was under considerable attack by the administration during the Watergate era and the press was also under considerable political pressure during the Vietnam war, pressure not only from the Republican and Democratic administrations. But I do not think we have to chronicle those incidents that occurred then or at other points in our history to appreciate the dangers that exist here.

The point is that as long as we have the current system of regulation, the potential for abuse is going to be there, whether it manifests itself as it did during the Watergate era or during the Vietnam war period. The regulation of a politically appointed agency is something that every journalist feels at one time or another over his shoulder if he is working in broadcast journalism.

As long as a politically appointed agency has the power to put broadcasters out of business, we are going to have to live with the possibility that some future administration will try to exploit that. I said in my statement I think it is too risky to rely on our good luck that such a situation will not arise, and that is why I think it is essential to assure the electronic press the complete independence from Government to which the press as a whole is insured, in my judgment, under the First Amendment.

The CHAIRMAN. Let me ask you this in terms of making editorial judgments. A story breaks and you must make a decision as to whether or not you want to put it on the news that night, and you realize there may be some potential for fairness doctrine complications.

You probably think twice about it, but do you consult with lawyers or with higher management at that stage and say, ladies and gentlemen, what do you think? Should we go with this or not? From your standpoint, what kind of ramifications are there for the entire company?

Mr. RATHER. Frankly, I do not do that. But I work at CBS News. We do not do that. We make a judgment is this a story for us, and in general, this is a vast oversimplification, but what we do is we run it and then we let the management and the lawyers worry about it.

But again I emphasize that at CBS News, rightly or wrongly, we consider ourselves an institution with a past, with a tradition, with resources and experience that local station newsrooms simply do not have—perhaps I should say by and large they do not have. So the reality for me at CBS News is quite a bit different than the reality that I know and experienced at local stations.

The answer to your question is no. We do not do that at CBS News, but at local radio and television stations it happens on a day-in and day-out basis. Many times the local station news director simply does not know where the boundaries are. He does not have any idea. He has been there a short period of time, in some cases. He does not know what the station manage-

ment's view is. He does not know who the lawyers are for the station. And the temptation is very large to say, well, what do we do about this. Do we run it or don't we run it?

Now that is the reality when you work in a local station newsroom. There are exceptions to that, of course, but that is what we are dealing with on a day-to-day basis, far less at the networks—a place like CBS News—than in local station newsrooms and small chain newsrooms.

The CHAIRMAN. I think I have visited all of the local radio stations in Oregon many times and my initial observation is that no one is getting rich running small radio stations in relatively small towns. They work pretty hard at it. Normally, the owner is involved in the running of it, and questions must go through that owner's mind from time to time: If indeed I air this and if indeed the FCC complains, it is going to cost me $5,000 or $10,000, and I simply cannot afford it.

Mr. RATHER. Well, there is that. It is also he just does not want the trouble. I do not underplay that at all. And increasingly the appearance of lawyers in newsrooms and even having to think about lawyers in newsrooms—when I first started in this business—in fact, for a very long time, until recently—no journalist that I knew, nor did I, very often thought of lawyers at all. Now, one is forced to think of lawyers fairly often. One reason is that it has become so expensive just to defend yourself. Even if you have a very good case, the cost of defending yourself can be enormous. We are talking about the cost in dollars.

Now for that local station operator in Oregon or Texas or where have you, it is not just a case of dollars. It is a case of he may get in trouble in the community. Someone may not know the details, but they will say, well, somebody has attacked you under the fairness doctrine. Well, yes, we are fair. We try to be fair in our newsroom.

Those conversations go on, but the temptation—and this is the point—the temptation is to say, look, I am not looking for trouble. I do not want any trouble and to signal the newsroom—if indeed not to say to the newsroom—do not handle anything that is hot. Zoning ordinances come to mind. I have some experience with that.

Somebody said, look, you want to do a documentary on zoning ordinances. Why do you want to do a documentary on zoning ordinances? I said, well, it is fairly important. Yeah, but a lot of people feel strongly about that; why don't you do something about the Salvation Army.

These are real conversations, and that is the danger to say far less of a CBS News than it is in a local station newsroom, and these dangers are real.

The CHAIRMAN. Let me ask you a further issue that has presented itself and you can tell me if it is a valid concern.

I am getting more and more complaints from local radio stations and, to some extent, local television stations, about having to provide free time to groups that are on the other side of issues where proponents have bought time. . . .

Mr. RATHER. Well, of course, this is a fairly common complaint among those of us who work in broadcast journalism. I do not mean this case specifically, but the whole business of having to provide equal time.

Journalistically, if you stop and think about it, it is a very good example of why the Government should not be in the business of regulating a journalistic enterprise,

that the print press is free to use its journalistic judgment—underscore "journalistic judgment"—in presenting whatever debates between major candidates or in-depth coverage of their position it thinks will help inform the public. That is a judgment made by the editors of a newspaper.

Now the kinds of cases that you are describing, what comes into play is this hovering, the possibility of Government interference and what it creates, again, it creates the mood and atmosphere, a texture of operating that says do not give anybody any time because you may really catch it.

Now for us where it really comes into play is in Presidential elections. As we all know, there are dozens of fringe candidates in a Presidential election, and it can make it nearly impossible to come to grips with saying, look, let's have a debate between the major candidates in this election. That can be impossible to do because you have these equal time divisions. . . .

Ideally, the editor in a broadcast newsroom should be able to make his judgments the same way a person on a newspaper does, and that is that if he wants to run on the front page—the newspaper man wants to run on the front page the debate—put "debate" in quotation marks, if you will—between the two major candidates or three major candidates, he can do so, and put everybody else, if he chooses to do so, on page 5 or 6.

In broadcasting, you cannot do that. I fully understand the argument and the concern of people who say well, it is a little bit different in broadcasting. My answer is yes, it is a little bit different, but it should not be. . . .

NO   Elaine Donnelly

PROTECTING THE PUBLIC INTEREST

. . . . Arguments for the deregulation of television may sound very persuasive, but only from the perspective of those fortunate few who happen to own or control television stations. It is understandable that broadcasters want even more power and the right to be accountable to no one, but I cannot understand why the interests of the two other parties concerned in this matter have been almost totally ignored in the testimony presented to date before this committee.

Mr. Chairman, I appreciate this opportunity to remind the members of this Committee that broadcasters do not own the First Amendment, even if they think they do.

Actually, there are three groups with an interest in the concept of free expression: (a) Broadcasters; (b) Individuals and candidates who need access to the airwaves; and (c) Members of the general public who need to be informed as citizens and voters. All three groups are important, but the U.S. Supreme Court ruled in 1969 (*Red Lion Broadcasting* vs. *FCC*) that the rights of the third group—the public—are paramount.

Please remember that broadcasters are in a position to greatly diminish the first amendment rights of the other two groups. New technologies that are not universally available do not change the fact that no one can gain access to television unless the time is given or sold to them by station-managers.

As an activist woman who has been involved in the public debate surrounding a number of controversial issues of public importance, I know from personal experience how easy it is for a broadcaster to deny free expression to those whose views do not agree with the "media elite." Let me give you just one concrete example. At the end of over ten years of debate over the proposed Equal Rights Amendment, a survey of the official video record of evening network news programs showed that out of 11 hours of total coverage from March, 1972, to June, 1982, 95 percent of the time was devoted to spokespeople for the pro-ERA side, while opponents appeared only 5 percent of the time.

From, statement by Elaine Donnelly, on Behalf of Eagle Forum, to US Senate Committee on Commerce, Science and Transportation, *Hearings on Freedom of Expression Act of 1983*, January 30, February 1 and 8, 1984.

This shocking record of biased coverage on that issue alone demolishes the self-serving testimony of network correspondents like CBS's Dan Rather who appeared before this Committee last year to complain about the unfairness of the Fairness Rules. Dan Rather, the National Association of Broadcasters, and the other media moguls that you have heard from are not just ordinary citizens. Their power to influence public opinion by setting the agenda of public discussion is far "more equal" than that of the rest of us.

It was bad enough that the opponents of ERA enjoyed only 5 percent of the network coverage over a period of ten years, but it was even more hurtful that in most of the coverage overall of those difficult years, the broadcast media managed to almost totally conceal from the American people the important and undisputed information that passage of ERA would have resulted in the drafting of women for combat duty in a future war. If it were not for the Fairness Rules that the women of Eagle Forum invoked at the local level, as a means to exercise our rights of free speech, it is entirely possible that the ERA would have been ratified without any real public understanding of its true effects. That would have been unfair to women, and to the general public which still has the paramount right to be informed about this and other issues of the day.

Incidentally, this same argument could be made by proponents of ERA, if their side has been the one that was held to only 5 percent of the network news coverage. The Fairness Rules are neutral in their impact—available to liberals and conservatives, pros and cons alike—no matter what the issue might be.

Mr. Chairman, the Supreme Court ruled that censorship of a medium not open to all is no more acceptable than censorship by the government. Nevertheless, statements in favor of concepts such as objectivity in journalism, professional ethics, fairness, and the responsibility of broadcasters to serve the public interest by allowing conflicting viewpoints to be heard are conspicuously absent in your hearing record to date. The Supreme Court upheld the minimal Fairness Rules as a means to protect the true "marketplace of ideas," which should not be confused with the lucrative commercial marketplace of broadcasting.

The testimony you have heard about new technologies such as Teletext and Direct Broadcast Satellites is most intriguing, but it does not change the fact that surveys show that over 65 percent of the people still get most of their information from conventional "free" television. This percentage is not likely to change because space-age technologies are expensive, and the demand for them is already leveling off because of that expense. Mr. Chairman, we cannot afford to become a nation of information "haves" and "have nots."

Joel Chaseman, President of the Post-Newsweek Stations, Inc., suggested in a speech before the Town Hall of California (Los Angeles, January 27, 1981) that "the Federal Communications Commission has become a home for technology hedonists, falling in love with each new development they meet, committed to none, apparently believing that invention is the mother of necessity." Mr. Chaseman declared in that speech that it is the height of bureaucratic arrogance to suggest that the First Amendment rights of the public will be served if only every household is wired for cable TV at the rate of at least $16.50 per month (for starters), or if everyone buys a home computer or an earth station costing several hundred dollars plus an additional monthly charge. The suggestion that ordinary people will have to pay dearly for access to diverse points of view on television is tantamount to suggesting that everyone has the right to vote, but only if they can afford to pay a poll tax for the privilege.

Please remember that the broadcasting networks enjoy a unique monopoly that already distorts the marketplace of ideas in a way that cannot be equalled by the print media. Among local newspapers, even those owned by the big publishing conglomerates, there is no equivalent to the impact and dominance of the network news programs. Local newspapers can set their own agendas of editorial discussion, and choose from a vast spectrum of additional "op-ed" pieces from columnists that reflect the wide diversity of opinion on national issues of the day. Time rules that are necessary ensure fair elections and an informed electorate. If [proposed legislation] is enacted, stations would be free to sell all of their time just before a local, state, or national election to one Party's nominees, at bargain rates, to the exclusion of all the other Party's candidates from the President on down. How would the public be served if broadcasters could use their monopoly of the airwaves to endorse candidates, allow personal, unanswered attacks against opposing candidates, and to censor those opposing candidates right off the air without any responsibility to anyone?

By contrast, the networks offer only one commentator per program, such as Bill Moyers on CBS and John Chancellor on NBC. Affiliate station managers who usually limit their editorials to local issues are no competition for the media giants; nor are the cable stations and community access programs that are midgets in the world of the media elite. It is important to

remember, too, that the same giants that have dominated the communications industry to date, such as Time, Inc., Warner-Amex, Westinghouse, and networks such as ABC are now using their considerable economic clout to take over cable TV and other systems, in the same way that many newspapers have been swallowed up by the big conglomerates.

The testimony you have heard about how much easier it supposedly is to buy a television station than it is to buy a newspaper is entirely beside the point. What about the First Amendment rights of those who are not in a position to buy either?

99.9 percent of the candidates and issue advocates in this country can always buy a paid newspaper ad or produce their own publication, but they cannot have access to television unless someone gives or sells the time that is needed. . . . The deregulators' suggestions that people who are being censored out of the media should go out and buy a TV or radio station is the modern electronic equivalent of Marie Antoinette's "Let them eat cake."

EQUAL TIME RULES

In addition to abolishing the Fairness Doctrine that relates to the coverage of controversial issues of public importance, [proposed legislation] would abolish the Equal Time rules that are necessary to ensure fair elections and an informed electorate. If [that were] enacted, stations would be free to sell all of their time just before a local, state, or national election to one Party's nominees, at bargain rates, to the exclusion of all the other Party's candidates from the President on down. How would the public be served if broadcasters could use their monopoly of the airwaves to endorse candidates, allow personal, unanswered attacks against opposing candidates, and to censor those opposing candidates right off the air without any responsibility to anyone?

Would any Senator on this Committee be content to buy commercial time for his next campaign on a dozen 5-mile radius low-power stations, instead of the most-watched network affiliate stations in the state? That kind of effective censorship . . . would constitute a violation of your First Amendment rights of free expression, and there is no way that that would serve your interest or that of the public.

The Equal Time rules have sometimes been cumbersome, and it has been necessary to adjust and reinterpret their meaning from time to time in order to protect the rights of both the major and minor candidates. However, the total elimination of Equal Time rules would serve only to expand the power of broadcasters, moneyed interests, and those who have favor with the decidedly liberal media elite. (For a scholarly analysis of the liberal leanings of the recognized media elite, see the 1983 Lichter/Rothman study published in *Public Opinion*.) Our entire system of free and fair elections could be permanently distorted as a result.

THE EXAGGERATED COMPLAINTS OF BROADCASTERS

In my opinion, the various complaints of station managers and broadcasters that have been expressed before this Committee are utterly unconvincing.

Anyone who takes the time to study the Fairness Rules as printed in the Federal Register can see just how minimal they really are. For example, the Fairness Doctrine does not require equal time, and the FCC's skimpy record of enforcement

demonstrates that station managers have little to fear from the bureaucrats in Washington. Actually, anyone who has filed a legitimate complaint with the FCC knows that the Commission is one of the weakest and most ineffective agencies in the government. Contrary to the impression given by some of your previous witnesses, the government does not monitor what goes on the air; the broadcaster—not the government—has the sole right to decide how the general principles of fairness in the public interest are to be met. The only reason that the rules work at all is because they serve as a useful standard and starting point for cooperation between station managers, those who seek access to the media, and the general public that has a right to expect free access to the "marketplace of ideas."

If a station manager feels that it is too much to ask that he allow the public to hear a variety of opinions, then he should exercise his option to sell the station to one of the many applicants who would like to take his place.

Witnesses before your Committee have expressed great alarm at the prospect that electronically-transmitted newspapers are threatened by an all-powerful bureaucracy that could step in and tell them how to run their newspaper. I have not encountered so much paranoia since I read the story of Chicken Little. Even if the Supreme Court upheld this fearsome intrusion into the realm of the print media (and it hasn't), Congress would have all the power in the world to resolve the problem.

The sky is not about to fall on the *Wall Street Journal* or *USA Today*. There is no reason for panic, or legislation that ignores the interests of the majority while catering to the wildest fears of the powerful minority.

Mr. Chairman, the Fairness Rules of today are carefully balanced to protect the rights of broadcasters as well as other parties with an interest in the First Amendment. If these reasonable guidelines to protect the public interest are sacrificed on the altar of the commercial marketplace, the true marketplace of ideas would be narrowed to serve the interests of only those with power, influence, or popularity among the media elite.

POSTSCRIPT

REGULATING THE MEDIA:
IS THE "FAIRNESS DOCTRINE" UNFAIR?

At one point in her testimony, Elaine Donnelly remarks that cable TV stations are being taken over by large corporations "in the same way that many newspapers have been swallowed up by the big conglomerates." By calling attention to monopolization in the newspaper industry, Donnelly raises a tricky question: would she favor a "fairness doctrine" for newspapers? That would really open up a can of worms, though the Supreme Court has perhaps sealed the can forever by a 1974 decision (*Miami Herald* v. *Tornillo*) striking down a Florida statute which would have compelled newspapers in some circumstances to print readers' replies.

The "fairness doctrine" and the Supreme Court's *Red Lion* decision upholding it are explored at length by former CBS News president Fred Friendly in his book, *The Good Guys, the Bad Guys, and the First Amendment* (Random House, 1975). In the book Friendly argues for a looser interpretation of "fairness," which has in fact become FCC policy. On the other hand, Kevin Phillips, a former Nixon administration aide, thinks the doctrine should be strengthened. See his *Mediacracy: American Parties and Politics in the Communications Age* (Doubleday, 1975), and his article, "Controlling Media Output," in the November/December 1977 issue of *Society*.

Liberals and conservatives often change sides on the issue of regulation, depending on what is being regulated. If the topic is, say, the manufacture of automobiles, depend on liberals to favor stiff regulation in "the public interest," and be assured that conservatives want to protect "free enterprise." But change the topic to the media and watch the sudden switch: now it is the liberals who extol the virtues of "free enterprise" and the conservatives who champion regulation in "the public interest." This does not have to mean that either side is inconsistent; after all, making words and pictures is somewhat different than making cars. Still, what is startling is the *attitudinal* switch: quasi-socialists suddenly sound like earnest exponents of *laissez-faire,* and vice-versa.

PART III
SOCIAL CHANGE IN AMERICA: HOW MUCH AND WHAT KIND?

It is difficult to imagine any topic which is more emotional and devisive than that of social morality today. Whatever consensus once existed on such topics as public school prayer, pornography, abortion, and race-consciousness, that consensus has been shattered in recent years as Americans have taken opposing views— and, what is more important, taken those competing views into Congress, state legislatures, and our nation's courts. Each side tends to personalize the issues, and, all too often, villify those who disagree with them.

These issues generate intense passions but they need calm reflection if they are ever to be resolved. Taken as a whole, the arguments in this section may help us see both sides of some very stormy debates.

Will Tougher Sentencing Reduce Crime?

Is Capital Punishment Justified?

Is Affirmative Action Reverse Discrimination?

Should Workers Be Paid According to "Comparable Worth"?

Does Our Welfare System Hurt the Poor?

Should Pornography Be Protected as Free Speech?

Should Abortion Be Outlawed?

Should We Have a "Wall of Separation" Between Church and State?

155

ISSUE 9

WILL TOUGHER SENTENCING REDUCE CRIME?

YES: James Q. Wilson, from *Thinking About Crime* (New York, 1983)

NO: David Bazelon, from "Solving the Nightmare of Street Crime," *USA Today* (January 1982)

ISSUE SUMMARY

YES: Political scientist James Q. Wilson says that the prospect of swift and certain punishment is more likely to reduce violent crime than are social programs aimed at relieving poverty.
NO: Federal judge David Bazelon defends his position that meaningful crime control must focus on the social conditions that breed it in the first place.

Crime is a major social problem in America, and most Americans suspect that it is growing worse. Everyone, except perhaps criminals themselves, wants to eliminate crime. The question is: how?

The problem is serious and complex. In fact, even the federal crime index does not give a precise idea of the incidence of major crime. (Major crimes are identified by the Federal Bureau of Investigation as criminal homicide, forcible rape, robbery, aggravated assault, burglary. larceny over $50, and auto theft.) It is even uncertain whether the incidence of major crimes has increased strikingly in recent decades or whether it is because more crimes are being reported by victims (perhaps because of the increase in personal, automobile, and home insurance) and being better recorded by police.

However, some aspects of crime in the United States are indisputable. Crime is widespread but is more concentrated in urban areas. It is disproportionately committed by the young, the poor, and members of minority groups. The commission of some crimes (those that require public knowledge of the activity, such as prostitution, drug selling, and gambling) involve the corruption of law-enforcement officials. The rates for some crimes, particularly violent crimes, are much higher in the United States than in many other countries. For example, there are more criminal homicides in New York City (where the rate of homicide is lower than that of a number of other American cities) than in all of Great Britain or Japan, which have nine and fifteen times the population of New York, respectively.

There is little dispute about the increased public awareness of the problem, and the widespread fear that people—particularly parents and older people—feel in high-crime areas. Something needs to be done; but what? Reform society? Reform criminals? Some would deal with crime's "root causes," but as yet we do not know what those root causes are. Others think the solution lies in the severity of punishment, as in the slogan, "Lock them up and throw away the keys!

Not only is imprisonment constitutionally (and morally?) questionable, but it raises questions even as it resolves others. Who should be imprisoned? For how long, and for what crimes? Most of the Watergate criminals, whose offenses endangered the American electoral process, were sent to country-club prisons for a matter of months. Lower-class criminals usually serve their longer terms in much bleaker surroundings. Is our system of justice biased in favor of white-collar and well-connected criminals? Even if it is not, or even if the bias is corrected, are most prisons serving the purposes they are supposed to serve? Do they really deter crime, or do they serve as schools for criminals, making them more hardened? Are there perhaps more "enlightened" ways of dealing with crime in America?

These are some of the questions touched upon by United States Court of Appeals Judge David Bazelon and political scientist James Q. Wilson in the selections following. As will be seen, their answers are quite different from one another.

YES   James Q. Wilson

THINKING ABOUT CRIME

The average citizen hardly needs to be persuaded that crimes will be committed more frequently if, other things being equal, crime becomes more profitable than other ways of spending one's time. Accordingly, the average citizen thinks it obvious that one major reason why crime has increased is that people have discovered they can get away with it. By the same token, a good way to reduce crime is to make its consequences to the would-be offender more costly (by making penalties swifter, more certain, or more severe), or to make alternatives to crime more attractive (by increasing the availability and pay of legitimate jobs), or both.

These citizens may be surprised to learn that social scientists who study crime are deeply divided over the correctness of such views. While some scholars, especially economists, believe that the decision to become a criminal can be explained in much the same way as we explain the decision to become a carpenter or to buy a car, other scholars, especially sociologists, contend that the popular view is wrong—crime rates do not go up because would-be criminals have little fear of arrest, and will not come down just because society decides to get tough on criminals.

This debate over the way the costs and benefits of crime affect crime rates is usually called a debate over deterrence—a debate, that is, over the efficacy (and perhaps even the propriety) of trying to prevent crime by making would-be offenders fearful of punishment. But the theory of human nature that supports the idea of deterrence—the theory that people respond to the penalties associated with crime—also assumes that people will take jobs in preference to crime if the jobs are more attractive. In both cases, we are saying that would-be offenders are rational and that they respond to their perception of the costs and benefits attached to alternative courses of action. When we use the word "deterrence," we are calling attention to only the cost side of the equation. No word in common scientific usage calls attention to the benefit side of the equation, though perhaps "inducement" might serve.

The reason scholars disagree about deterrence is that the consequences of committing a crime, unlike the consequences of shopping around for the best price on a given automobile, are complicated by delay, uncertainty, and ignorance. In addition, some scholars contend that many crimes are committed by persons who are so impulsive, irrational, or abnormal that even if delay, uncertainty, or ignorance were not attached to the consequences of criminality, we would still have a lot of crime.

Imagine a young man walking down the street at night with nothing on his mind but a desire for good times and high living. Suddenly he sees a little old lady standing alone on a dark corner, stuffing the proceeds of her recently cashed Social Security check into her purse. Nobody else is in view. If the young man steals the purse, he gets the money immediately. The costs of taking it are uncertain—the odds are at least ten to one that the police will not catch a robber, and even if he is caught, the odds are very good that he will not go to prison, unless he has a long record. On the average, no more than three felonies out of a hundred result in the imprisonment of the offender. In addition, whatever penalty may come his way will come only after a long delay—in some jurisdictions, a year or more might be needed to complete the court disposition of the offender, assuming he is caught in the first place. Moreover, this young man might, in his ignorance of how the world works, think the odds against being caught are even greater than they are, or that delays in the court proceedings might result in a reduction or avoidance of punishment.

Compounding the problem of delay and uncertainty is the fact that society cannot feasibly increase by more than a modest amount the likelihood of arrest, and though it can to some degree increase the probability and severity of prison sentences for those who are caught, it cannot do so drastically, by, for example, summarily executing all convicted robbers, or even by sentencing all robbers to twenty-year prison terms. Some scholars note a further complication: the young man may be incapable of assessing the risks of crime. How, they ask, is he to know his chances of being caught and punished? And even if he does know, perhaps he is driven by uncontrollable impulses to snatch purses whatever the risks.

As if all this were not bad enough, the principal method by which scholars have attempted to measure the effect of deterrence on crime has involved using data about aggregates of people (entire cities, counties, states, and even nations) rather than about individuals. In a typical study, the rate at which, say, robbery is committed in each state is "explained" by means of a statistical procedure in which the analyst takes into account both the socio-economic features of each state that might affect the supply of robbers (for example, the percentage of persons with low incomes, the unemployment rate, the population density of the big cities, the proportion of the population made up of young males) and the operation of the criminal-justice system of each state as it attempts to cope with robbery (for example, the probability of being caught and imprisoned for a given robbery, and the length of the average prison term for robbery). . . .

The best analysis of [problems] in statistical studies of deterrence is to be found in a 1978 report of the Panel on Research on Deterrent and Incapacitative Effects, which was set up by the National Research

159

9. WILL TOUGHER SENTENCING REDUCE CRIME?

Council (an arm of the National Academy of Sciences). That panel, chaired by Alfred Blumstein, of Carnegie-Mellon University, concluded that the available statistical evidence (as of 1978) did not warrant any strong conclusions about the extent to which differences among states or cities in the probability of punishment might alter deterrent effect. The panel (of which I was a member) noted that "the evidence certainly favors a proposition supporting deterrence more than it favors one asserting that deterrence is absent," but urged "scientific caution" in interpreting this evidence.

Other criticisms of deterrence research, generally along the same lines as those of the panel, have led some commentators to declare that "deterrence doesn't work," and that we may now get on with the task of investing in those programs, such as job-creation and income maintenance, that *will* have an effect on crime. Such a conclusion is, to put it mildly, premature.

One way to compensate for errors in official statistics relating to crime rates is to consider other measures of crime, in particular reports gathered by Bureau of the Census interviewers from citizens who have been victims of crime. While these victim surveys have problems of their own (such as the forgetfulness of citizens), they are not the same problems as those that affect police reports of crime. Thus, if we obtain essentially the same findings about the effect of sanctions on crime from studies that use victim data as we do from studies that use police data, our confidence in these findings is strengthened. Studies of this sort have been done by Itzhak Goldberg, at Stanford, and by Barbara Boland and myself, and the results are quite consistent with those from research based on police reports. As sanctions become more likely, both sets of data suggest, crime becomes less common.

It is possible, as some critics of deterrence say, that rising crime rates swamp the criminal-justice system, so that a negative statistical association between, say, rates of theft and the chances of going to prison for theft may mean not that a decline in imprisonment is causing theft to increase but rather that a rise in theft is causing imprisonment to become less likely. This might occur particularly with respect to less serious crimes, such as shoplifting or petty larceny; indeed, the proportion of prisoners who are shoplifters or petty thieves has gone down over the past two decades. But it is hard to imagine that the criminal-justice system would respond to an increase in murder or armed robbery by letting some murderers or armed robbers off with no punishment. Convicted murderers are as likely to go to prison today as they were twenty years ago. Moreover, the deterrent effect of prison on serious crimes like murder and robbery was apparently as great in 1940 or 1950, when these crimes were much less common, as it is today, suggesting that swamping has not occurred.

Still more support for the proposition that variations in sanctions affect crime can be found in the very best studies of deterrence—those that manage to avoid the statistical errors described above. In 1977, Alfred Blumstein and Daniel Nagin published a study of the relationship between draft evasion and the penalties imposed for draft evasion in each of the states. After controlling for the socio-economic characteristics of the states, they found that the higher the probability of conviction for draft evasion, the lower the evasion rates. This is an especially strong finding, because the study is largely immune to the problems associated with other analyses of deterrence. Draft evasion is more accurately measured than street crimes, and draft-evasion cases could not have swamped the federal courts in which they were tried, in part because such cases made up only a small fraction (about 7 percent) of the workload of these courts, and in part because federal authorities had instructed the prosecutors to give high priority to these cases. For all these reasons, Blumstein and Nagin felt they could safely conclude that draft evasion is deterrable.

White-collar crime can also be deterred. In the late 1970s, Michael Block, Fred Nold, and J.G. Sidak, then at Stanford, investigated the effect of enforcing the antitrust laws on the price of bread in the bakery business. When the government filed a price-fixing complaint against colluding bakery firms, and when those firms also faced the possibility of private suits claiming treble damages for this price-fixing, the collusion ended and the price of bread fell.

Another way of testing whether deterrence works is to look not at differences among states or firms at one point in time but at changes in the nation as a whole over a long period of time. Historical data on the criminal-justice system in America are so spotty that such research is difficult to do here, but it is not at all difficult in England, where the data are excellent. Kenneth I. Wolpin, of Yale, analyzed changes in crime rates and in various parts of the criminal-justice system (the chances of being arrested, convicted, and punished) for the period 1894 to 1967, and concluded that changes in the probability of being punished seemed to cause changes in the crime rate. He offered reasons for believing that this causal connection could not be explained away by the argument that the criminal-justice system was being swamped.

Given what we are trying to measure—changes in the behavior of a small number of hard-to-observe persons who are responding to delayed and uncertain penalties—we will never be entirely sure that our statistical manipulations have proved that deterrence works. What is impressive is that so many (but not all) studies using such different methods come to similar conclusions. More such evidence can be found in studies of the death penalty. Though the evidence as to whether capital punishment deters crime is quite ambiguous, most of the studies find that the chances of being imprisoned for murder do seem to affect the murder rate. Even after wading through all this, the skeptical reader may remain unconvinced. Considering the difficulties of any aggregate statistical analysis, that is understandable. But, as we shall shortly see, the evidence from certain social experiments reinforces the statistical studies. . . .

Two well-known changes in sentencing practices are the so-called Rockefeller drug laws in New York and the Bartley-Fox gun law in Massachusetts. In 1973, New York State revised its criminal statutes relating to drug trafficking in an attempt to make more severe and more certain the penalties for the sale and possession of heroin (the law affecting other drugs was changed as well, but the focus of the effort—and the most severe penalties— were reserved for heroin). The major pushers—those who sold an ounce or more of heroin—would be liable for a minimum prison term of fifteen years and the possibility of life imprisonment. But the law had some loopholes. Someone who had sold an ounce could plea bargain the charges against him down, but no lower than to a charge that would entail a mandatory one-year minimum prison sentence. Police informants could get probation instead of prison, and persons under the age of sixteen were exempt from the mandatory sentences. A provision that was made part of some amendments passed in 1975 exempted from the law persons aged sixteen to eighteen. A group was formed to evaluate the effect of this law. The authors of its report, issued in 1977, found no evidence that the law had reduced the availability of heroin on the streets of New York City or reduced the kinds of property crime often committed by drug users. Of course, it is almost impossible to measure directly the amount of an illegal drug in circulation, or to observe the illicit transactions between dealers and users, but a good deal of circumstantial evidence, gathered by the study group, suggests that no large changes occurred. The number of deaths from narcotics overdoses did not change markedly, nor did admissions to drug-treatment programs or the price and purity of heroin available for sale on the street (as inferred from buys of heroin made by undercover narcotics agents).

The explanation for this disappointing experience, in the opinion of the study group, was that difficulties in administering the law weakened its deterrent power, with the result that most offenders and would-be offenders did not experience any significantly higher risk of apprehension and punishment. There was no increase in the number of arrests, and a slight decline in the proportion of indictments resulting in conviction. Offsetting this was a higher probability that a person convicted would go to prison. The net effect was that the probability of imprisonment for arrested drug dealers did not change as a result of the law—it was about one imprisonment per nine arrests both before and after passage of the law. On the other hand, the sentences received by those who did go to prison were more severe. Before the law was passed, only 3 percent of persons imprisoned for selling an ounce or more of heroin received a sentence of three years or more. After the law went into effect, 22 percent received such sentences. Perhaps because sentences became more severe, more accused persons demanded trials instead of pleading guilty; as a result, the time needed to dispose of the average drug case nearly doubled.

Does the experience under the Rockefeller law disprove the claim that deterrence works? The answer is no, but that is chiefly because deterrence theory wasn't satisfactorily tested. If "deterrence" means changing behavior by increasing either the certainty or the swiftness of punishment, then the Rockefeller law, as it was administered, could not have deterred behavior, because it made no change in the certainty of punishment and actually reduced its swiftness. If, on the other hand, "deterrence" means changing behavior by increasing the severity of punishment, then deterrence did not work in this case. What we mainly want to know, however, is whether heroin trafficking could have been reduced *if* the penalties associated with it had been imposed more quickly and in a higher proportion of cases.

Severity may prove to be the enemy of certainty and speed. As penalties get tougher, defendants and their lawyers have a greater incentive to slow down the process, and those judges who, for private reasons, resist heavy sentences for drug dealing may use their discretionary powers to decline indictment, accept plea bargains, grant continuances, and modify penalties in ways that reduce the certainty and the celerity of punishment. The group that evaluated the Rockefeller law suggested that reducing severity in favor of certainty might create the only real possibility for testing the deterrent effect of changes in sentences.

The Bartley-Fox gun law in Massachusetts was administered and evaluated in ways that avoided some of the problems of the Rockefeller drug laws. In 1974, the Massachusetts legislature amended the law that had long required a license for a person carrying a handgun, by stipulating that a violation of this law would entail a mandatory penalty of one year in prison, which sentence could not be reduced by probation or parole or by judicial finagling. When the law went into effect, in April of 1975, various efforts were made to evaluate both the compliance of the criminal-justice system with it and the law's impact on crimes involving handguns. James A. Beha, II, then at the Harvard Law School, traced the application of the law for eighteen months, and concluded that, despite widespread predictions to the contrary, the police, prosecutors, and judges were not evading the law. As in New York, more persons asked for trials, and delays in disposition apparently increased, but in Massachusetts, by contrast with the experience in New York, the probability of punishment increased for those arrested. Beha estimated in 1977 (at a time when not all the early arrests had yet worked their way through the system) that prison sentences were being imposed five times more frequently on persons arrested for illegally carrying firearms than had been true before the law was passed. Owing to some combination of the heavy publicity given to the Bartley-Fox law and the real increase in the risk of imprisonment facing persons arrested while carrying a firearm without a license, the casual carrying of firearms seems to have decreased. This was the view expressed to interviewers by participants in the system, including persons being held in jail, and it was buttressed by a sharp drop in the proportion of drug dealers arrested by the Boston police who,

at the time of their arrest, were found to be carrying firearms. . . .

Deterrence and job-creation are not different anti-crime strategies; they are two sides of the same strategy. The former increases the costs of crime; the latter enhances the benefits of alternatives to criminal behavior. The usefulness of each depends on the assumption that we are dealing with a reasonably rational potential offender.

Let us return to our original example. The young man is still yearning for the money necessary to enjoy some high living. Let us assume that he considers finding a job. He knows he will have to look for one; this will take time. Assuming he gets one, he will have to wait even longer to obtain his first paycheck. But he knows that young men have difficulty finding their first jobs, especially in inner-city neighborhoods such as his. Moreover, he cannot be certain that the job he might get would provide benefits that exceed the costs. Working forty hours a week as a messenger, a dishwasher, or a busboy might not seem worth the sacrifice in time, effort, and reputation on the street corner that it entails. The young man may be wrong about all this, but if he is ignorant of the true risks of crime, he is probably just as ignorant of the true benefits of alternatives to crime.

Compounding the problems of delay, uncertainty, and ignorance is the fact that society cannot feasibly make more than modest changes in the employment prospects of young men. Job-creation takes a long time, when it can be done at all, and many of the jobs created will go to the "wrong" (i.e., not criminally inclined) persons; thus, unemployment rates among the young will not vary greatly among states and will change only slowly over time. And if we wish to see differences in unemployment rates (or income levels) affect crime, we must estimate those effects by exactly the same statistical techniques we use to estimate the effect of criminal-justice sanctions.

The problem of measurement error arises because we do not know with much accuracy the unemployment rate among youths by city or state. Much depends on who is looking for work and how hard, how we count students who are looking only for part-time jobs, and whether we can distinguish between people out of work for a long period and those who happen to be between jobs at the moment. Again, since inaccuracies in these data vary from place to place, we will obtain biased results.

The problem of omitted factors is also real, as is evident in a frequently cited study done in 1976 by Harvey Brenner, of Johns Hopkins University. He suggested that between 1940 and 1973, increases in the unemployment rate led to increases in the homicide rate. But he omitted from his analysis any measure of changes in the certainty or the severity of sentences for murder, factors that other scholars have found to have a strong effect on homicide.

Finally, the relationship between crime and unemployment (or poverty) is probably complex, not simple. For example, in a statistical study that manages to overcome the problems already mentioned, we might discover that as unemployment rates go up, crime rates go up. One's natural instinct would be to interpret this as meaning that rising unemployment causes rising crime. But rising crime might as easily cause rising unemployment. If young men examining the world about them conclude that crime pays more than work—that, for instance, stealing cars is more profitable than washing them—they may then leave their jobs in favor of crime. Some young men find dealing in drugs more attractive than nine-to-five jobs, but, technically, they are "unemployed."

Perhaps both crime and unemployment are the results of some common underlying cause. In 1964, the unemployment rate for black men aged twenty to twenty-four was 12.6 percent; by 1978, it was 20 percent. During the same period, crime rates, in particular those involving young black men, went up. Among the several possible explanations are the changes that have occurred where so many young blacks live, in the inner parts of large cities. One such change is the movement out of the inner cities of both jobs and the social infrastructure that is manned by adult members of the middle class. The departure of jobs led to increased unemployment; the departure of the middle class led to lessened social control and hence to more crime. If we knew more than we now know, we would probably discover that all three relationships are working simultaneously: for some persons, unemployment leads to crime; for others, crime leads to unemployment; and for still others, social disintegration or personal inadequacy leads to both crime and unemployment. . . .

The hope, widespread in the 1960s, that job-creation and job-training programs would solve many social problems, including crime, led to countless efforts both to prevent crime by supplying jobs to crime-prone youths and to reduce crime among convicted offenders by supplying them with better job opportunities after their release from prison. One preventive program was the Neighborhood Youth Corps, which gave to poor young persons jobs during the afternoons and evenings and all day during the summer. An evaluation of the results of such programs among poor blacks in Cincinnati and Detroit found no evidence that participation in the Youth

Corps had any effect on the proportion of enrollees who came into contact with the police. Essentially the same gloomy conclusion was reached by the authors of a survey of a large number of delinquency-prevention programs, though they reported a few glimmers of hope that certain programs might provide some benefits to some persons. For example, persons who had gone through a Job Corps program that featured intensive remedial education and job training in a residential camp were apparently less likely to be arrested six months after finishing their training than a control group. . . .

The best and most recent effort to identify the link between employment and crime was the "supported-work" program of the Manpower Demonstration Research Corporation (MDRC). In ten locations around the country, MDRC randomly assigned four kinds of people with employment problems to special workshops or to control groups. The four categories were long-term welfare (Aid to Families with Dependent Children) recipients, school dropouts, former drug addicts, and ex-convicts. The workshops provided employment in unskilled jobs supplemented by training in job-related personal skills. The unique feature of the program was that all the participants in a given work setting were people with problems; thus the difficulties experienced by persons with chronic unemployment problems when they find themselves competing with persons who are successful job-seekers and job-holders were minimized. Moreover, the workshops were led by sympathetic supervisors (often themselves ex-addicts or ex-convicts), who gradually increased the level of expected performance until, after a year or so, the trainees were able to go out into the regular job market on their own. This government-subsidized work in

a supportive environment, coupled with training in personal skills, was the most ambitious effort of all we have examined to get persons with chronic problems into the labor force. Unlike vocational training in prison, supported work provided real jobs in the civilian world, and training directly related to what one was paid to do. Unlike work-release programs, supported work did not immediately place the ex-convict in the civilian job market to sink or swim on his own.

Welfare recipients and ex-addicts benefited from supported work, but ex-convicts and youthful school dropouts did not. Over a twenty-seven-month observation period, the school dropouts in the project were arrested as frequently as the school dropouts in the control group, and the ex-offenders in the project were arrested *more* frequently (seventeen more arrests per 100 persons) than ex-offenders in the control group.

The clear implication, I think, of the supported-work project—and of all the studies to which I have referred—is that unemployment and other economic factors may well be connected with criminality, but the connection is not a simple one. If, as some people assume, "unemployment causes crime," then simply providing jobs to would-be criminals or to convicted criminals would reduce their propensity to commit crimes. We have very little evidence that this is true, at least for the kinds of persons helped by MDRC. Whether crime rates would go down if dropouts and ex-convicts held on to their jobs we cannot say, because, as the supported-work project clearly showed, within a year and a half after entering the program, the dropouts and ex-convicts were no more likely to be employed than those who had never entered the program at all—despite the great and compassionate efforts made on their

9. WILL TOUGHER SENTENCING REDUCE CRIME?

behalf. Help, training, and jobs may make a difference for some persons—the young and criminally inexperienced dropout; the older, "burned-out" ex-addict; the more mature (over age thirty-five) ex-convict. But ex-addicts, middle-aged ex-cons, and inexperienced youths do not commit most of the crimes that worry us. These are committed by the young chronic offender. . . .

Some may agree with me but still feel that we should spend more heavily on one side or the other of the cost-benefit equation. At countless scholarly gatherings, I have heard learned persons examine closely any evidence purporting to show the deterrent effect of sanctions, but accept with scarcely a blink the theory that crime is caused by a "lack of opportunities." Perhaps they feel that since the evidence on both propositions is equivocal, it does less harm to believe in—and invest in—the "benign" (i.e., job-creation) program. That is surely wrong. If we try to make the penalties for crime swifter and more certain, and it should turn out that deterrence does not work, then we have merely increased the risks facing persons who are guilty of crimes in any event. If we fail to increase the certainty and swiftness of penalties, and it should turn out that deterrence does work, then we have needlessly increased the risk of being victimized for many innocent persons. . . .

But we cannot achieve large reductions in crime rates by making sanctions very swift or very certain or by making jobs very abundant, because things other than the fear of punishment or the desire for jobs affect the minds of offenders, and because while we say we want a speedy, fair, and efficient criminal-justice system, we want other things more.

The behavior of most of us is affected by even small (and possibly illusory) changes

in the costs attached to it. We are easily deterred by a crackdown on drunk driving, especially if it is highly publicized, and our willingness to take chances when filling out our tax returns is influenced by how likely we think an audit may be. Why, then, should we not see big changes in the crime rates when we make our laws tougher?

The answer is not that, unlike the rest of us, burglars, muggers, and assaulters are irrational. I am struck by the account given in Sally Engle Merry's book, *Urban Danger,* of her extended interviews with youthful offenders in a big-city neighborhood she observed for a year and a half. She found that these young men had a sophisticated, pragmatic view of their criminal enterprises, even though they were neither "white-collar" criminals nor highly professional burglars. They distinguished carefully between affluent and less-affluent targets, spoke knowledgeably about the chances of being caught in one part of the district as opposed to another, understood that some citizens were less likely to call the police than others, knew which offenses were most and which were least likely to lead to arrest and prosecution, and had formed a judgment about what kinds of stories the judges would or would not believe. Though many committed crimes opportunistically, or in retaliation for what they took to be the hostile attitudes of certain neighbors, they were neither so impulsive nor so emotional as to be unaware of, or indifferent to, the consequences of their actions. . . .

Chronic offenders may attach little or no importance to the loss of reputation that comes from being arrested; in certain circles, they may feel that an arrest has enhanced their reputation. They may attach a low value to the alleged benefits of a legitimate job, because it requires punctuality, deferential behavior, and a forty-hour week, all in exchange for no more money than they can earn in three or four burglaries carried out at their leisure. These values are not acquired merely by trying crime and comparing its benefits with those of non-criminal behavior; if that were all that was involved, far more of us would be criminals. These preferences are shaped by personal temperament, early familial experiences, and contacts with street-corner peers—by character-forming processes that occur in intimate settings, produce lasting effects, and are hard to change.

Whereas the drinking driver, the casual tax cheat, or the would-be draft evader, having conventional preferences, responds quickly to small changes in socially determined risks, the chronic offender seems to respond only to changes in risks that are sufficiently great to offset the large benefits he associates with crime and the low value he assigns to having a decent reputation. Changing risks to that degree is not impossible, but changing those risks permanently and for large numbers of persons is neither easy nor inexpensive, especially since (as we saw in Wayne County, with the felony firearm statute, and in New York, with the Rockefeller drug law) some members of the criminal-justice system resist programs of this kind.

One third of all robberies committed in the United States are committed in the six largest cities, even though they contain only 8 percent of the nation's population. The conditions of the criminal-justice system in those cities range from poor to disastrous. *The New York Times* recently described one day in New York City's criminal courts. Nearly 4,000 cases came up on that day; each received, on the average, a three-minute hearing from one of seventy overworked judges. Fewer than one case in two hundred resulted in a trial. Three quarters of the summonses issued in the city are ignored; 3.7 million unanswered summonses now fill the courts' files. It is possible that some measure of rough justice results from all this—that the most serious offenders are dealt with adequately, and that the trivial or nonexistent penalties (other than inconvenience) imposed upon minor offenders do not contribute to the production of more chronic offenders. In short, these chaotic courts may not, as the *Times* described them, constitute a "system in collapse." But could such a system reduce the production of chronic offenders by increasing the swiftness, certainty, or severity of penalties for minor offenders? Could it take more seriously spouse assaults where the victim is reluctant to testify? Or monitor more closely the behavior of persons placed on probation on the condition that they perform community service or make restitution to their victims? Or weigh more carefully the sentences given to serious offenders, so as to maximize the crime-reduction potential of those sentences? It seems most unlikely. And yet, doing some or all of these things is exactly what is required by any plan to reduce crime by improving deterrence. For reasons best known to state legislators who talk tough about crime but appropriate too little money for a big-city court system to cope properly with lawbreakers, the struggle against street crime that has supposedly been going on for the last decade or so is in large measure a symbolic crusade.

I have written at length elsewhere about the obstacles that prevent more than small, planned changes in the criminal-justice system. Given the modest effect that changes will have on the observable behavior of chronic offenders, we may want to supplement improvements in the criminal-justice system with programs that would reduce the causes of crime. When I published the first edition of *Thinking*

167

9. WILL TOUGHER SENTENCING REDUCE CRIME?

About Crime, in 1975, I argued that a free society lacked the capacity to alter the root causes of crime, since they were almost surely to be found in the character-forming processes that go on in the family. The principal rejoinder to that argument was that these root causes could be found instead in the objective economic conditions confronting the offender. Labor-market or community conditions may indeed have some effect on the crime rate, but since I first wrote, the evidence has mounted that this effect is modest and hard to measure and that devising programs—even such extraordinary programs as supported work—that will have much impact on repeat offenders or school dropouts is exceptionally difficult.

By contrast, a steadily growing body of evidence suggests that the family affects criminality and that its effect, at least for serious offenders, is lasting. Beginning with the research of Sheldon and Eleanor Glueck in Boston during the 1930s and 1940s, and continuing with the work of Lee Robins, William and Joan McCord, and Travis Hirschi in this country, Donald West and David Farrington in England, Lea Pulkinnen in Finland, Dan Olweus in Norway, and many others, we now have available an impressive number of studies that, taken together, support the following view: Some combination of constitutional traits and early family experiences accounts for more of the variation among young persons in their serious criminality than any other factors, and serious misconduct that appears relatively early in life tends to persist into adulthood. What happens on the street corner, in the school, or in the job market can still make a difference, but it will not be as influential as what has gone before.

If criminals are rational persons with values different from those of the rest of us,

then it stands to reason that temperament and family experiences, which most shape values, will have the greatest effect on crime, and that perceived costs and benefits will have a lesser impact. For example, in a society where people cannot be under continuous official surveillance, the pleasure I take in hitting people is likely to have a greater effect on my behavior than the occasional intervention of some person in a blue uniform who objects to my hitting others and sets in motion a lengthy and uncertain process that may or may not result in my being punished for doing the hitting.

In a sense, the radical critics of America are correct. If you wish to make a big difference in crime rates, you must make a fundamental change in society. But what they propose to put in place of existing institutions, to the extent that they propose anything at all except angry rhetoric, would leave us yearning for the good old days when our crime rate may have been higher but our freedom was intact.

There are, of course, ways of re-organizing a society other than along the authoritarian lines of radical Marxism. One can imagine living in a society in which the shared values of the people, reinforced by the operation of religious, educational, and communal organizations concerned with character formation, would produce a citizenry less criminal than ours is now without diminishing to any significant degree the political liberties we cherish. Indeed, we can do more than imagine it; we can recall it. During the latter half of the nineteenth century, we managed in this country to keep our crime rate lower than it might have been in the face of extensive urbanization, rapid industrialization, large-scale immigration, and the widening of class differences. We did this, as I have argued elsewhere ("Crime and American Culture,"

The Public Interest, Winter, 1982), by investing heavily in various systems of impulse control through revival movements, temperance societies, uplift organizations, and moral education—investments that were based on and gave effect to a widespread view that self-restraint was a fundamental element of character.

These efforts were designed to protect (and, where necessary, to replace) the family, by institutionalizing familial virtues in society at large. The efforts weakened as the moral consensus on which they were based decayed: self-expression began to rival self-control as a core human value, at first among young, well-educated persons, and eventually among persons of every station. Child-rearing methods, school curricula, social fashions, and intellectual tendencies began to exalt rights over duties, spontaneity over loyalty, tolerance over conformity, and authenticity over convention.

The criminal-justice system of the nineteeth century was probably no swifter or more certain in its operations than the system of today, at least in the large cities, and the economy was even more subject to booms and busts than anything we have known since the 1930s. The police were primitively organized and slow to respond, plea bargaining was then, as now, rife in the criminal courts, prisons were overcrowded and nontherapeutic, and protection against the vicissitudes of the labor market was haphazard or nonexistent. Yet these larger social processes may have had a greater effect on crime rates then than they do today, because then, unlike now, they were working in concert with social sentiments: society condemned those whom the police arrested, the judge convicted, or the labor market ignored. Shame magnified the effect of punishment, and perhaps was its most important part.

Today, we are forced to act as if the degree of crime control that was once obtained by the joint effect of intimate social processes and larger social institutions can be achieved by the latter alone. It is as if we hope to find in some combination of swift and certain penalties and abundant economic opportunities a substitute for discordant homes, secularized churches, intimidated schools, and an ethos of individual self-expression. We are not likely to succeed.

Nor are we likely to reproduce, by plan, an older ethos or its accompanying array of voluntary associations and social movements. And, since we should not abandon essential political liberties, our crime-control efforts for the most part will have to proceed on the assumption—shaky as it is—that the things we can change, at least marginally, will make a significant difference. We must act as if swifter and more certain sanctions and better opportunities will improve matters. Up to a point, I think, they will, but in reaching for that point we must be prepared for modest gains uncertainly measured and expensively priced.

Brighter prospects may lie ahead. By 1990, about half a million fewer eighteen-year-old males will be living in this country than were living here in 1979. As everyone knows, young males commit proportionately more crimes than older ones. Since it is the case in general that about 6 percent of young males become chronic offenders, we will in 1990 have 30,000 fewer eighteen-year-old chronic offenders; if each chronic offender commits ten offenses (a conservative estimate) per year, we will have a third of a million fewer crimes from this age group alone. But other things may happen as well as the change in numbers. A lasting drop in the birthrate will mean that the number of children per family will remain low, easing the parental problem of supervision. A less youthful society may be less likely to celebrate a "youth culture," with its attendant emphasis on unfettered self-expression. A society less attuned to youth may find it can more easily re-assert traditional values and may be more influenced by the otherwise marginal effects of improvements in the efficiency of the criminal-justice system and the operation of the labor market. Natural and powerful demographic forces, rather than the deliberate re-establishment of an older culture, may increase the values of those few policy tools with which a free society can protect itself. In the meantime, justice requires that we use those tools, because penalizing wrong conduct and rewarding good conduct are right policies in themselves, whatever effect they may have.

NO

David L. Bazelon

SOLVING THE NIGHTMARE OF STREET CRIME

The nightmare of street crime is slowly paralyzing American society. Across the nation, terrified people have altered their lifestyles, purchasing guns and doubling locks to protect their families against the rampant violence outside their doors. After seething for years, public anxiety is now boiling over in a desperate search for answers. Our leaders are reacting to these public demands. In New York, Gov. Hugh Carey proposed the hiring of more police officers and prosecutors; in California, Attorney General Deukmejian has asked the legislature for immediate adoption of a package of new law enforcement bills.

A recent address by the Chief Justice of the United States has helped to place this crisis high on the public agenda. Speaking before the American Bar Association in February, Chief Justice Warren Burger described ours as an "impotent society," suffering a "reign of terror" in its streets and homes. The time has come, he declared, to commit vast social resources to the attack on crime—a priority comparable to the national defense.

Some have questioned whether a sitting Chief Justice should advocate sweeping changes in the criminal justice system and others have challenged his

From "Solving the Nightmare of Street Crime," by David Bazelon. Reprinted from *USA Today*, January 1982. Copyright ©1982 by Society for the Advancement of Education.

particular prescriptions, but I believe the prestige of his office has focused the nation's attention on issues critical to our future. We should welcome this opportunity to begin a thoughtful and constructive debate about our national nightmare.

In this debate, public concern is sure to generate facile sloganeering by politicians and professionals alike. It would be easy to convert this new urgency into a mandate for a "quick fix." The far-harder task is to marshall that energy toward examining the painful realities and agonizing choices we face. Criminologists can help make our choices the product of an informed, rational, and morally sensitive strategy. As citizens and as human beings, they have a special responsibility to contribute their skills, experience, and knowledge to keep the debate about crime as free of polemics and unexamined assumptions as possible.

I would like to outline some avenues of inquiry worthy of exploration. I offer no programs, no answers. After 31 years on the bench, I can say with confidence that we can never deal intelligently and humanely with crime until we face the realities behind it. First, we must carefully identify the problem that so terrorizes America. Second, we should seek to understand the conditions that breed those crimes of violence. Finally, we should take a close look at both the short- and long-term alternatives for dealing with the problem.

TYPES OF CRIMES AND WHO COMMITS THEM

A reasoned analysis must begin by asking: What is it that has our society in such a state of fear? Politicians, journalists, and criminal justice professionals who should know better speak rather generally about "crime in America" without specifying exactly what they mean. There are, in fact, several distinct types of crimes and people who commit them.

Consider white-collar crime. This category embraces activities ranging from shoplifting to tax fraud to political corruption. It is undoubtedly a phenomenon of the gravest concern, costing society untold billions of dollars—far more than street crime. To the extent that such crimes appear to go unpunished, they breed disrespect for law and cynicism about our criminal justice institutions. Yet, as costly and corrosive as such crimes are, they do not instill the kind of fear reflected in the recent explosion of public concern. White-collar crimes, after all, are committed by the middle and upper classes, by "[p]eople who look like one's next-door neighbor," as sociologist Charles Silberman puts it. These people do not, by and large, threaten our physical safety or the sanctity of our homes.

Nor do the perpetrators of organized crime. After all, hired guns largely kill each other. The average citizen need not lock his doors in fear that he may be the object of gang warfare. Organized crime unquestionably does contribute to street crime— the most obvious connection is drugs—but organized crime has certainly not produced the recent hysteria.

Nor do crimes of passion cause us to bolt our doors so firmly at night. That would be like locking the fox *inside* the chicken coop. Clearly, it is the random assault of *street* crime—the muggings, rapes, purse snatchings, and knifings that plague city life—which puts us all in such mortal fear for our property and lives.

Once we focus on the kind of crime we fear, the second step in a constructive analysis is to identify those people who commit it. This is no pleasant task. The real roots of crime are associated with a constellation of suffering so hideous that, as a society, we can not bear to look it in the face. Yet, we can never hope to understand street crime unless we summon the courage to look at the ugly realities behind it. Nobody questions that street criminals typically come from the bottom of the socioeconomic ladder—from among the ignorant, the ill-educated, the unemployed, and the unemployable. A recent National Institute of Justice study confirms that our prison population is disproportionately black and young. The offenders that give city dwellers nightmares come from an underclass of brutal social and economic deprivation. Urban League president Vernon Jordan calls them America's "boat people without boats."

It is no great mystery why some of these people turn to crime. They are born into families struggling to survive, if they have families at all. They are raised in deteriorating, overcrowded housing. They lack adequate nutrition and health care. They are subjected to prejudice and educated in unresponsive schools. They are denied the sense of order, purpose, and self-esteem that makes law-abiding citizens. With nothing to preserve and nothing to lose, they turn to crime for economic survival, a sense of excitement and accomplishment, and an outlet for frustration, desperation, and rage.

Listen to the words of a 15-year-old ghetto youth:

> In Brooklyn you fall into one of two categories when you start growing up. . . . First, there's the minority of the minority, the "ducks" or suckers. These are the kids who go to school every day. They even want to go to college. Imagine that! School after high school! . . . They're wasting their lives waiting for a dream that won't come true.

> The ducks are usually the ones getting beat up on by the majority group—the "hard rocks." If you're a real hard rock you have no worries, no cares. Getting high is as easy as breathing. You just rip off some duck. You don't bother going to school, it's not necessary. You just live with your mom until you get a job—that should be any time a job comes looking for you. Why should you bother to go looking for it? Even your parents can't find work.

> Hard rocks do what they want to do when they want to do it. When a hard rock goes to prison it builds up his reputation. He develops a bravado that's like a long sad joke. But it's all lies and excuses. It's a hustle to keep ahead of the fact that he's going nowhere. . . .

This, then, is the face behind the mask we call "the crime problem."

Having identified the kind of crime that causes public anxiety and the kind of people who commit it, we can now consider some alternative responses. For purpose of analysis, we can divide the alternatives into two types. The first set, which enjoys the greatest currency in the political arena today, consists of short-term proposals. They proceed from our universally acknowledged need to protect ourselves *immediately* from the menace of crime. These kinds of prescriptions are endorsed by many good people in high places, including the Chief Justice of the United States and the Mayor of New York. The short-term proposals rely principally on deterrence and incapacitation as means of controlling the symptoms of our national disease. The second, more long-term proposals seek to attack the root causes of crime. Both of these approaches have great costs as well as benefits that must be carefully understood and weighed before we set our course.

173

9. WILL TOUGHER SENTENCING REDUCE CRIME?

DETERRENCE

Let us first examine the short-run proposals. Deterrence has always been intuitively attractive. The recent spate of prescriptions underscores the popularity of this theory and have taken many forms. The Chief Justice says we must provide "swift and certain consequences" for criminal behavior. The California Attorney General advocates mandatory prison terms for certain kinds of crimes. New York Mayor Edward Koch favors harsher sentences including the death penalty. Former U.S. Attorney Whitney North Seymour, Jr., contends that tougher prosecution is necessary. Each of these proposals is premised on Harvard University Prof. James Q. Wilson's theory that, "if the expected cost of crime goes up without a corresponding increase in the expected benefits, then the would-be criminal—unless he or she is among that small fraction of criminals who are utterly irrational—engages in less crime." To the same effect, Wayne State Prof. Ralph Slovenko wrote in a letter to the editor of *The New York Times* that, since "[p]rofits are tax-free and penalties are minimal," those who violate the law are "criminals by choice."

This "rational man" theory of crime is quite plausible with respect to certain kinds of criminals. I can believe that those who have alternatives to crime can indeed be dissuaded from choosing the lawless path if the price is made high enough. If the Abscam episode accomplished nothing else, it induced some potentially corrupt politicians to forebear from taking bribes— at least where there might be cameras around. In fact, white-collar offenders may be so susceptible to deterrence that punishment is superfluous. The fellow country-club members of a corporate embezzler whose life is ruined in a storm of publicity may not need to actually see him go to jail in order to be deterred.

However, the white-collar criminal is *not* the object of these deterrence proposals. Seymour says his proposals are aimed at "the hoodlums and ruffians who are making life in our cit[ies] a nightmare for many citizens"; in other words, at the "hard rocks." Can *these* kinds of criminals be effectively deterred? Diana Gordon, Executive Vice Pres. of the National Council on Crime and Delinquency, points out that the threat of prison may be a meaningless deterrent to one whose urban environment is itself a prison; and as our 15-year old ghetto resident informs us, "[w]hen a hard rock goes to prison it builds up his reputation."

Common sense is confirmed by experience. New York's highly touted Rockefeller drug law did not produce a decrease in heroin use. In fact, it was actually followed by an increase in property crimes associated with heroin users. Nor is the New York situation unique. Since 1965, the average time served in Federal prison has *risen* from 18 to 30 months. Yet, crime continues to rise unabated.

Even the high priest of deterrence, Prof. Wilson, recognizes the limits of this theory. Although many bandy about his name in support of get-tough proposals, Wilson suggests that the *severity* of punishment has little deterrent effect. Indeed, "the more severe the penalty, the more unlikely that it will be imposed." The benefits of deterrence, according to Wilson, lie only in *certainty* of punishment.

How can we increase that certainty? The *Miranda* rule, the right to seek collateral review, and even the time to prepare for trial have all come under attack in the name of "swift and certain" punishment. These trial and appellate safeguards reflect our fundamental commitment to the presumption of innocence. Before we trade them away, we must know what we are getting in return. From an exhaustive review of the evidence, Silberman concluded that "criminal courts generally *do* an effective job of separating the innocent from the guilty; most of those who should be convicted are convicted, and most of those who should be punished are punished." Today, we prosecute, convict, and incarcerate a larger proportion of those arrested for felonies than we did 50 years ago; yet, the crime rate continues to rise. Clearly, the uncertainty about punishment derives from the great unlikelihood of *arrest.* For every 100 crimes committed, only six persons will be arrested. Thus, sacrificing the constitutional protections of those charged with crime will do little to deter the "hard rocks."

What must we do to achieve certainty of arrest sufficient to have an impact on crime? I asked my good friend, Maurice Cullinane, the former Chief of Police of the District of Columbia, about this. He presided over a force with far more policemen per capita than any other in the country, and that is aside from the several thousand park, Capitol, and other Federal police visible all over Washington. Chief Cullinane told me that, in order to deter street crime to any significant degree, he would have to amass an enormous concentration of patrolmen in one particular area. Only then might the physical presence of a policeman on virtually every block possibly keep crime under control. Of course, crime suppressed in one neighborhood would burgeon in other, unguarded parts of the city. Before we can endorse certainty of arrest as an effective deterrent, we must consider whether we could tolerate the kind of police state it might require.

We need to know much more about the precise costs of an effective program of

deterrence before we can dismiss the recent proposals. At the present time, however, the case for deterrence has not been convincingly made. After a comprehensive review of the literature, a panel of the National Academy of Sciences concluded:

> Despite the intensity of the research effort, the empirical evidence is still not sufficient for providing a rigorous confirmation of the existence of a deterrent effect. . . . Policy makers in the criminal justice system are done a disservice if they are left with the impression that the empirical evidence, which they themselves are frequently unable to evaluate, strongly supports the deterrence hypothesis.

INCAPACITATION

A more realistic rationale put forth for short-term proposals, in my opinion, is incapacitation. This politely named theory has become the new aim of corrections. No one who has been in an American prison can seriously adhere to the ideal of rehabilitation, and more and more of us have come to suspect the futility of deterrence. The new theory of incapacitation essentially translates as lock the bastards up. At least then they will pose no threat to us while incarcerated. Incapacitation takes many forms: preventive detention, isolation of "career criminals," and stricter parole release requirements.

This notion has something to be said for it. We *must* do something to protect ourselves immediately so that we may "live to fight another day." Thus, the swift and tough route is appealing—get the attackers off the street forthwith; put them away fast and long so that the threat they pose to our daily lives can be neutralized.

A thorough commitment to this policy might indeed make our streets somewhat safer, but at what price? Consider first the cost in dollars. Today, even without an avowed commitment to incapacitation, we already imprison a larger proportion of our citizens than any other industrialized nation in the world, except Russia and South Africa. This dubious honor has cost us dearly. A soon-to-be published survey by the Department of Justice's National Institute of Justice reports that the 1972–78 period saw a 54% increase in the population of state prisons. The survey predicts that the demand for prison space will continue to outstrip capacity. It has been conservatively estimated that we need $8–10,000,000,000 immediately for construction just to close the gap that exists *now*.

Embarking on a national policy of incapacitation would require much more than closing the gap. One study has estimated that, in New York, a 264% increase in state imprisonment would be required to reduce serious crime by only 10%! Diana Gordon has worked out the financial requirements for this kind of incapacitation program. In New York alone, it would cost about $3,000,000,000 just to construct the additional cells necessary and probably another $1,000,000,000 each year to operate them. The public must be made aware of the extraordinary financial costs of a genuine incapacitation policy.

In addition, there are significant nonmonetary costs. Incapacitation rests on the assumption that convicted offenders would continue to commit crimes if not kept in prison, but can we determine in advance which offenders would in fact repeat and which would not? We simply do not know enough about the "hard rocks" to decide who to warehouse, and for how long. It has been estimated that, to be sure of identifying one potential criminal, we would have to include as many as eight people who would not offend. Thus, to obtain the benefits of incapacitation, we might have to incarcerate a substantial number of people who would have led a blameless life if released. A policy of sentencing individuals based on crimes not yet committed would therefore raise serious doubts about our dedication to the presumption of innocence. The thought of having to choose between immediate safety and sacred constitutional values is frightening.

Nor can there be any comfort that the grave moral and financial costs of incapacitation will only be temporary. Even as we put one generation of offenders behind bars, another set of "hard rocks" will emerge from the hopeless subculture of our ghettos, ready to follow the model set by their fathers and brothers. Unless we intend to keep *every* criminal and potential criminal in prison *forever*, we must acknowledge the futility of expecting them to behave when they get out. As journalist Tom Wicker recently observed, "to send them to the overcrowded, underfunded, inadequately staffed and policed prisons of America would negate [the] purpose; because more, and more frightening, criminals come out of these schools of crime and violence than go into them." Merely providing inmates with educational and counseling services would do little good "when they return to a society largely unwilling to hire them." We should not fool ourselves that the "hard rocks" will emerge from the cesspools of American prisons willing or able to conduct law-abiding lives.

Incapacitation, then, must be recognized as an extraordinarily costly and risky policy. To meaningfully affect crime, it might require a garrison state. This is not to deny that our "clear and present danger" must be addressed immediately. Still, reason and good faith require us to consider alternatives to a program of endlessly warehousing succeeding generations of human beings.

ATTACKING THE ROOT CAUSES OF CRIME

A more long-term response to crime is to attack its root causes. This approach also offers no decisive balance of costs and benefits. The unique advantage of a successful attack on the roots of crime would be the promise of *enduring* social tranquility. If we can first break the cycle of suffering which breeds crime, we could turn it to our advantage. We would achieve more than "damage control." Our nation could begin to tap the resources of those we now fear. Instead of a police or garrison state, ours would then be a social order rooted in the will and hearts of our people. We would achieve criminal justice by pursuing social justice.

However, like the short-term solutions, this path would involve substantial risks and uncertainties. The root causes of crime are, of course, far more complex and insidious than simple poverty. After all, the vast majority of the poor commit no crime. Our existing knowledge suggests that the roots of street crime lie in poverty *plus*— plus prejudice, plus poor housing, plus inadequate education, plus insufficient food and medical care, and, perhaps most importantly, plus a bad family environment or no family at all.

Accepting the full implications of what we know about street crime might require us to provide every family with the means to create the kind of home all human beings need. It might require us to afford the job opportunities that pose for some the only meaningful alternatives to violence. It would assure all children a constructive education, a decent place to live, and proper pre- and post-natal nutrition. It

would seek to provide those children of inadequate family environments with proper day care or foster care. More fundamentally, it would seek to eradicate racism and prejudice.

Such an attack on the roots of crime would obviously be an extremely long and expensive process. Before we can determine which programs offer the greatest promise, we must face what we know about the crime and build on previous efforts to attack its root causes.

More importantly, a genuine commitment to attacking the roots of crime might force us to reconsider our entire social and economic structure. Like the short-term approach, this might conflict with other deeply held values. Can we break the cycle at crime's roots without invading the social sphere of the ghetto? Would this require the state to impose its values on the young? If we really want a lasting solution to crime, can we afford not to?

In short, any approach we take to crime presents attractive benefits and frightening risks. None of our choices offers a cheap or easy solution. Analysis takes us this far. As I have repeatedly emphasized, we can not choose which difficult path to take without facing the realities of street crime. Obviously, we can not deter those whom we do not understand. Nor can we make a rational assessment of incapacitation without knowing how many we will have to incapacitate and for how long. Finally, of course, we can not evaluate the long-term approach without some idea of its specific strategies and their various costs.

A constructive and fruitful debate about the best means of solving the nightmare of street crime is long overdue. The public's fear of crime cries out for a response and our leaders have made it a national priority, but we can never hope to achieve a just and lasting solution to crime without first facing the realities that underlie it. Emerson said, "God offers to every mind its choice between truth and repose." Truth will not come easy. It will take patience and the strength to put aside emotional reactions. If we do not strive for truth, this nation and all it stands for is bound to enjoy only a brief, false, and dangerous repose.

POSTSCRIPT

WILL TOUGHER SENTENCING REDUCE CRIME?

It may be said of crime—as Mark Twain said of the weather—that everyone talks about it but nobody does anything about it. Perhaps that is because the easy solutions only sound easy. If we are to "lock 'em all up," where are we going to put them? The public applauds tough talk but seems unwilling to pay for new prison space. On the other hand, getting at the so-called "root causes" of crime—which supposedly include poverty and discrimination—is no easier. This approach assumes that these phenomonena *are* the basic causes of crime. Yet violent crime was much lower during the poverty-ridden, racist decade of the 1930's than it was during the affluent and enlightened 1960's. Unfortunately, crime is a problem that will not yield to slogans, whether those slogans are liberal or conservative in origin.

Aryeh Neier, executive director of the American Civil Liberties Union, has proposed what he calls a "radical solution" to the crime problem. In his book *Crime and Punishment* (Stein and Day, 1976), he suggests that jail space could be freed up by not incarcerating people for "victimless crimes" such as marijuana smoking, curfew violations, or public drunkenness. Neier claims that much police time is taken up with prosecuting these offenders. Charles E. Silberman, in *Criminal Violence, Criminal Justice* (Random House, 1978), seeks to clear up a variety of public misunderstandings about crime; one of his themes is that police action cannot do much to control crime if the community's morale and spirit of self-control have disintegrated—a point with which both Bazelon and Wilson might agree. Also deserving close attention by all sides in the "law and order" debate are Yong Hyo Cho's; *Public Policy and Urban Crime* (Ballinger, 1974) and Stuart's *The Prevention of Crime* (Behavioral Publications, 1973; Both books contain a wealth of factual information as well as assessments of proposed solutions.

No matter which solutions are attempted, Judge Bazelon and Professor Wilson have helped to set the terms of the debate: Bazelon finds the roots of crime in social injustice and Wilson suggests that people commit crimes because they know they can get away with committing them. Bazelon focuses on the irrational and compulsive nature of criminality, while Wilson sees a deliberate, calculating streak in the minds of criminals. Each is adept at finding the weakness in the other's proposed solution. If together they fail to inspire fresh answers to the crime problem, they at least show us that the old answers, whether grounded upon "toughness" or "compassion," need considerable re-thinking.

ISSUE 10

IS CAPITAL PUNISHMENT JUSTIFIED?

YES: Walter Berns, from *For Capital Punishment: Crime and the Morality of the Death Penalty* (New York, 1979)

NO: Donal E.J. MacNamara, from "The Case Against Capital Punishment," *Social Action* (April 1961)

ISSUE SUMMARY

YES: Professor Walter Berns is convinced that the death penalty has a place in modern society and that it serves a need now, as it did when the Constitution was framed.

NO: Criminologist Donal MacNamara presents a ten-point argument against capital punishment, raising ethical and practical questions concerning the death penalty.

Although capital punishment (the death penalty) is ancient, both the definition of capital crimes and the legal methods of putting convicted persons to death have changed. In eighteenth-century Massachusetts, there were fifteen capital crimes, including blasphemy and the worship of false gods. Slave states often imposed the death sentence upon blacks for crimes that, when committed by whites, were punished by only two or three years' imprisonment. It has been estimated that in this century approximately ten percent of all legal executions have been for the crime of rape, one percent for all other crimes (robbery, burglary, attempted murder, etc.), and nearly ninety percent for the commission of murder.

Long before the Supreme Court severely limited the use of the death penalty, executions in the United States were becoming increasingly rare. In the decade of the 1930s there were 1,667; the total for the 1950s was 717. In the 1960s, the numbers fell even more dramatically. For example, seven persons were executed in 1965, one in 1966, and two in 1967. Put another way, in the 1930s and 1940s, there was one execution for every sixty or seventy homicides committed in states that had the death penalty; in the first half of the 1960s, there was an execution for every two hundred homicides; and by 1966 and 1967, there were only three executions for approximately twenty thousand homicides.

Then came the case of *Furman v. Georgia* (1972), which many thought—mistakenly—"abolished" capital punishment in America. Actually, only two members of the *Furman* majority thought that capital punishment *per se* violates the Eighth Amendment's prohibition against "cruel and unusual punishment." The other three members of the majority took the view that capital punishment is unconstitutional only when applied in an arbitrary or a racially discriminatory manner, as they believed it was in this case. There were four dissenters in the *Furman* case, who were prepared to uphold capital punishment both in general and in this particular instance. Not suprisingly, then, with a slight change of Court personnel—and with a different case before the Court—a few years later, the majority vote went the other way.

In the latter case, *Gregg v. Georgia* (1976), the majority upheld capital punishment under certain circumstances. In his majority opinion in the case, Justice Potter Stewart noted that the law in question (a new Georgia capital-punishment statute) went to some lengths to avoid arbitrary procedures in capital cases. For example, courts were not given complete discretion in handing out death sentences to convicted murderers but had to consult a series of guidelines spelling out "aggravating circumstances," such as whether the murder had been committed by someone already convicted of murder, whether it endangered the lives of bystanders, and whether it was committed in the course of a major felony. These guidelines, Stewart said, together with other safeguards against arbitrariness included in the new statute, preserved it against Eighth Amendment challenges.

Although the Court has upheld the constitutionality of the death penalty, it can always be abolished by legislatures. Most Western deomocracies have abolished it by that means. It seems unlikely, however, that this will happen in the states of America. If anything, the opposite is occurring. Almost immediately after the *Furman* decision of 1972, state legislatures began enacting new death penalty statutes designed to meet the objections raised in the case. By the time of the *Gregg* decision, thirty-five new death penalty statutes had been enacted.

In the readings that follow, Donal E.J. MacNamara sums up virtually every widely used argument against the death penalty, while Walter Berns focuses his defense upon the moral right of retribution and its compatibility with the American Constitution.

YES

Walter Berns

CRIME AND THE MORALITY
OF THE DEATH PENALTY

It must be one of the oldest jokes in circulation. In the dark of a wild night a ship strikes a rock and sinks, but one of its sailors clings desperately to a piece of wreckage and is eventually cast up exhausted on an unknown and deserted beach. In the morning, he struggles to his feet and, rubbing his salt-encrusted eyes, looks around to learn where he is. The only human thing he sees is a gallows. "Thank God," he exclaims, "civilization." There cannot be many of us who have not heard this story or, when we first heard it, laughed at it. The sailor's reaction was, we think, absurd. Yet, however old the story, the fact is that the gallows has not been abolished in the United States even yet, and we count ourselves among the civilized peoples of the world. Moreover, the attempt to have it abolished by the U.S. Supreme Court may only have succeeded in strengthening its structure . . . .

Perhaps the Court began to doubt its premise that a "maturing society" is an ever more gentle society; the evidence on this is surely not reassuring. The steady moderating of the criminal law has not been accompanied by a parallel moderating of the ways of criminals or by a steadily evolving decency in the conditions under which men around the world must live their lives. . . .

An institution that lacks strength or purpose will readily be what its most committed constituents want it to be. Those who maintain our criminal justice institutions do not speak of deferring to public opinion but of the need to "rehabilitate criminals"—another pious sentiment. The effect, however, is the same. They impose punishments only as a last resort and with the greatest reluctance, as if they were embarrassed or ashamed, and they avoid executing even our Charles Mansons. It would appear that Albert Camus was right when he said that "our civilization has lost the only values that, in a certain way, can justify [the death] penalty." It is beyond doubt that our intellectuals are of this opinion. The idea that the presence of a gallows could indicate the presence of a civilized people is, as I indicated at the outset, a joke. I certainly thought so the first time I heard the story; it was only a few years ago that I began to

From *For Capital Punishment: Crime and the Morality of the Death Penalty*, pages 3, 5, 7, 8-9, 31-40, 153-155, 188-189 by Walter Berns. Copyright ©1979 by Walter Berns. Reprinted by permission of Basic Books, Inc.

suspect that that sailor may have been right. What led me to change my mind was the phenomenon of Simon Wiesenthal.

Like most Americans, my business did not require me to think about criminals or, more precisely, the punishment of criminals. In a vague way, I was aware that there was some disagreement concerning the purpose of punishment—deterrence, rehabilitation, or retribution—but I had no reason then to decide which was right or to what extent they may all have been right. I did know that retribution was held in ill repute among criminologists. Then I began to reflect on the work of Simon Wiesenthal, who, from a tiny, one-man office in Vienna, has devoted himself since 1945 exclusively to the task of hunting down the Nazis who survived the war and escaped into the world. Why did he hunt them, and what did he hope to accomplish by finding them? And why did I respect him for devoting his life to this singular task? He says that his conscience forces him "to bring the guilty ones to trial." And if they are convicted, then what? Punish them, of course. But why? To rehabilitate them? The very idea is absurd. To incapacitate them? But they represent no present danger. To deter others from doing what they did? That is a hope too extravagant to be indulged. The answer—to me and, I suspect, everyone else who agrees that they should be punished—was clear: *to pay them back.* And how do you pay back SS Obersturm-führer Franz Stangl, SS Untersturm-führer Wilhelm Rosenbaum, SS Ober-sturmbannführer Adolf Eichmann, or someday—who knows?—Reichsleiter Martin Bormann? As the world knows, Eichmann was executed, and I suspect that most of the decent, *civilized* world

agrees that this was the only way he could be paid back. . . .

The argument . . . does not turn on the answer to the utilitarian question of whether the death penalty is a deter-rent. . . . The evidence on this is unclear and, besides, as it is usually understood, deterrence is irrelevant. The real issue is whether justice permits or even requires the death penalty. I am aware that it is a terrible punishment, but there are terrible crimes and terrible criminals. . . .

Anger is expressed or manifested on those occasions when someone has acted in a manner that is thought to be unjust, and one of its bases is the opinion that men are responsible, and should be held responsible, for what they do. Thus, anger is accompanied not only by the pain caused by him who is the object of anger, but by the pleasure arising from the expectation of exacting revenge on someone who is thought to deserve it. We can become very angry with an inanimate object (the door we run into and then kick in return) only foolishly attributing re-sponsibility to it, and we cannot do that for long, which is why we do not think of returning later to revenge ourselves on the door. For the same reason, we cannot be more than momentarily angry with an animate creature other than man; only a fool or worse would dream of taking revenge on a dog. And, finally, we tend to pity rather than to be angry with men who—because they are insane, for example—are not responsible for their acts. Anger, then, is a very human passion not only because only a human being can be angry, but also because it acknowl-edges the humanity of its objects: it holds them accountable for what they do. It is an expression of that element of the soul that is connected with the view that there is responsibility in the world; and in holding particular men responsible, it pays them that respect which is due them as men. Anger recognizes that only men have the capacity to be moral beings and, in so doing, acknowledges the dignity of human beings. Anger is somehow connected with justice, and it is this that modern penology has not understood; it tends, on the whole, to regard anger as merely a selfish passion. . . .

Criminals are properly the objects of anger, and the perpetrators of terrible crimes—for example, Lee Harvey Oswald and James Earl Ray—are properly the objects of great anger. They have done more than inflict an injury on an isolated individual; they have violated the foundations of trust and friendship, the necessary elements of a moral community, the only community worth living in. A moral community, unlike a hive of bees or a hill of ants, is one whose members are expected freely to obey the laws and, unlike a tyranny, are trusted to obey the laws. The criminal has violated that trust, and in so doing has injured not merely his immediate victim but the community as such. He has called into question the very possibility of that community by suggesting that men cannot be trusted freely to respect the property, the person, and the dignity of those with whom they are associated. If, then, men are not angry when someone else is robbed, raped, or murdered, the implication is that there is no moral community because those men do not care for anyone other than themselves. Anger is an expression of that caring, and society needs men who care for each other, who share their pleasures and their pains, and do so for the sake of the others. It is the passion that can cause us to act for

reasons having nothing to do with selfish or mean calculation; indeed, when educated, it can become a generous passion, the passion that protects the community or country by demanding punishment for its enemies. It is the stuff from which heroes are made. . . .

THE CONSTITUTIONAL ARGUMENT

We Americans have debated the morality and necessity of the death penalty throughout almost the entire period of our experience as a nation, and, until 1976 when the Supreme Court ruled in favor of its constitutionality, it had been debated among us in constitutional terms, which is not true elsewhere. The Eighth Amendment clearly and expressly forbids the imposition of "cruel and unusual punishments," a prohibition that applies now to the states as well as to the national government; it was argued that the death penalty was such a punishment.

It is, of course, incontestable that the death penalty was not regarded as cruel and unusual by the men who wrote and ratified the amendment. They may have forbidden cruel and unusual punishments but they acknowledged the legitimacy of capital punishment when, in the Fifth Amendment, they provided that no person "shall be held to answer for a capital . . . crime, unless on a presentment or indictment of a Grand Jury," and when in the same amendment they provided that no one shall, for the same offense, "be twice put in jeopardy of life or limb," and when, in the Fifth as well as in the Fourteenth Amendment, they forbade, not the taking of life, but the taking of life "without due process of law." We also know that the same Congress which proposed the Eighth Amendment also provided for the death penalty for murder and treason, and George Washington, despite powerful entreaties, could not be persuaded to commute the death sentence imposed on Major John Andre, the British officer and spy involved in Benedict Arnold's treachery. So the death penalty can be held to be cruel and unusual in the constitutional sense only if it has somehow become so in the passage of time. . . .

In 1958 the Supreme Court . . . said that the meaning of cruel and unusual depends on "the evolving standards of decency that mark the progress of a maturing society." Surely, it is argued, hanging or electrocution or gassing is, in our day, regarded as equally cruel as expatriation, if not more cruel. Is it not relevant that the American people have insisted that executions be carried out by more humane methods, that they not be carried out in public, and that the penalty be imposed for fewer and fewer crimes; and is it not significant that juries have shown a tendency to refuse to convict for capital crimes? In these ways the people are merely demonstrating what has been true for centuries, namely, that when given the opportunity to act, the average man (as opposed to judges and vindictive politicians) will refuse to be a party to legal murder. . . . The fact of the matter, or so it is alleged, is that American juries have shown an increasing tendency to avoid imposing the death penalty except on certain offenders who are distinguished not by their criminality but by their race or class. Justice Douglas emphasized this in his opinion in the 1972 capital punishment cases. "One searches our chronicles in vain for the execution of any members of the affluent strata of this society," he said. "The Leopolds and Loebs are given prison terms, not sen-

tenced to death.". . . Death sentences are imposed not out of a hatred of the crimes committed, it is said, but out of a hatred of blacks. Of the 3,859 persons executed in the United States in the period 1930-1967, 2,066, or 54 percent, were black. More than half of the prisoners now under sentence of death are black. In short, the death penalty, we have been told, "may have served" to keep blacks, especially southern blacks, "in a position of subjugation and subservience." That in itself is unconstitutional.

In the 1972 cases only two of the nine justices of the Supreme Court argued that the death penalty as such is a violation of the Eighth Amendment, regardless of the manner of its imposition. Justice Brennan was persuaded by what he saw as the public's growing reluctance to impose it that the rejection of the death penalty "could hardly be more complete without becoming absolute." Yet, on the basis of his own evidence it is clear that the American people have not been persuaded by the arguments against the death penalty and that they continue to support it for *some* criminals—so long as it is carried out privately and as painlessly as possible. At the very time he was writing there were more than 600 persons on whom Americans had imposed the sentence of death. He drew the conclusion that the American people had decided that capital punishment does not comport with human dignity, and is therefore unconstitutional, but the facts do not support this conclusion. This may explain why his colleague, Justice Marshall, felt obliged to take up the argument.

Marshall acknowledged that the public opinion polls show that, on the whole, capital punishment is supported by a majority of the American people, but he

185

denied the validity—or the "utility"—of ascertaining opinion on this subject by simply polling the people. The polls ask the wrong question. It is not a question of whether the public accepts the death penalty, but whether the public when "fully informed as to the purposes of the penalty and its liabilities would find [it] shocking, unjust, and unacceptable."

> In other words, the question with which we must deal is not whether a substantial proportion of American citizens would today, if polled, opine that capital punishment is barbarously cruel, but whether they would find it to be so in the light of all information presently available.

This information, he said, "would almost surely convince the average citizen that the death penalty was unwise." He conceded that this citizen might nevertheless support it as a way of exacting retribution, but, in his view, the Eighth Amendment forbids "punishment for the sake of retribution"; besides, he said, no one has ever seriously defended capital punishment on retributive grounds. It has been defended only with "deterrent or similar theories." From here he reached his conclusion that "the great mass of citizens" would decide that the death penalty is not merely unwise but also "immoral and therefore unconstitutional." They would do so if they knew what he knew, and what he knew was that retribution is illegitimate and unconstitutional and that the death penalty is excessive and unnecessary, being no more capable than life imprisonment of deterring the crimes for which it is imposed. He conceded that the evidence on the deterrence issue is not "convincing beyond all doubt, but it is persuasive."

Thus, the death penalty *is* cruel and unusual punishment because the American people *ought* to think so. Shortly after this decision thirty-five states enacted new statutes authorizing the death penalty for certain crimes.

This public support for capital punishment is a puzzling fact, especially in our time. It is a policy that has almost no articulate supporters in the intellectual community. The subject has been vigorously debated and intensively investigated by state after state and country after country—California and Connecticut, Texas and Wisconsin; Britain and Canada, Ceylon and "Europe"; even the United Nations; and, of course, various committees of the U.S. Congress. Among those willing to testify and publish their views, the abolitionists outweigh the "retentionists" both in number and, with significant exceptions, in the kind of authority that is recognized in the worlds of science and letters. Yet the Harris poll reports 59 percent of the general population to be in favor of capital punishment, and that proportion is increasing—at this time, at least. . . .

It is sometimes argued that the opinion polls are deceptive insofar as the question is posed abstractly—and can only be posed abstractly—and that the responses of these publics would be different if they had to decide whether particular persons should be executed. This is entirely possible, or even probable; nevertheless, there is no gainsaying the fact that juries, for whom the issue is very concrete indeed, continue to impose death sentences on a significant number of criminals. Ordinary men and women seem to be unpersuaded by the social science argument against deterrence, or they regard it as irrelevant; they seem to be oblivious to the possibility that innocent people might be executed; they know nothing about the natural public law disagreement between Beccaria and Kant; they surely do not share the opinion that executions are contrary to God's commands; indeed, they seem to display the passions of many a biblical character in their insistence that, quite apart from all these considerations, murderers should be paid back. In fact, the essential difference between the public and the abolitionists is almost never discussed in our time; it has to do with retribution: the public insists on it without using the word and the abolitionists condemn it whenever they mention it.

The abolitionists condemn it because it springs from revenge, they say, and revenge is the ugliest passion in the human soul. They condemn it because it justifies punishment for the sake of punishment alone, and they are opposed to punishment that serves no purpose beyond inflicting pain on its victims. Strictly speaking, they are opposed to punishment. They may, like Beccaria, sometimes speak of life imprisonment as the alternative to executions, but they are not in fact advocates of life imprisonment and will not accept it. . . .

They condemn retribution because they see it, rightly or wrongly, as the only basis on which the death penalty can be supported. To kill an offender is not only unnecessary but precludes the possibility of reforming him, and reformation, they say, is the only civilized response to the criminal. Even murderers—indeed, especially murderers—are capable of being redeemed or of repenting their crimes. . . .

The goal of the abolitionists is not merely the elimination of capital punishment but the reform or rehabilitation of the criminal, even, if he is a murderer. The public that favors capital punishment is of the opinion that the murderer deserves to be punished, and does not deserve to be treated, even if by treatment he could be rehabilitated. . . .

When abolitionists speak of the barbarity of capital punishment and when Supreme Court justices denounce expatriation in almost identical language, they ought to be reminded that men whose moral sensitivity they would not question have supported both punishments. Lincoln, for example, albeit with a befitting reluctance, authorized the execution of 267 persons during his presidency, and ordered the "Copperhead" Clement L. Vallandigham banished; and it was Shakespeare's sensitivity to the moral issue that required him to have Macbeth killed. They should also be given some pause by the knowledge that the man who originated the opposition to both capital and exilic punishment, Cesare Beccaria, was a man who argued that there is no morality outside the positive law and that it is reasonable to love one's property more than one's country. There is nothing exalted in these opinions, and there is nothing exalted in the versions of them that appear in today's judicial opinions. Capital punishment was said by Justice Brennan to be a denial of human dignity, but in order to reach this conclusion he had to reduce human dignity to the point where it became something possessed by "the vilest criminal." Expatriation is said by the Court to be unconstitutional because it deprives a man of his right to have rights, which is his citizenship, and no one, no matter what he does, can be dispossessed of the right to have rights.

(Why not a right to the right to have rights?) Any notion of what Justice Frankfurter in dissent referred to as "the communion of our citizens," of a community that can be violated by murderers or traitors, is wholly absent from these opinions; so too is any notion that it is one function of the law to protect that community.

But, contrary to abolitionist hopes and expectations, the Court did not invalidate the death penalty. It upheld it. It upheld it on retributive grounds. In doing so, it recognized, at least implicity, that the American people are entitled *as a people* to demand that criminals be paid back, and that the worst of them be made to pay back with their lives. In doing this, it gave them the means by which they might strengthen the law that makes them a people, and not a mere aggregation of selfish individuals.

NO

Donal E.J. MacNamara

THE CASE AGAINST
CAPITAL PUNISHMENT

The infliction of the death penalty is becoming less frequent and the actual execution of the sentence of death even more rare, both in the United States and in foreign countries. Not only is this trend apparent in those nations and states which have formally repudiated the *lex talionis* and have eliminated capital punishment from their penal codes but it is almost equally clear in many of the jurisdictions which still retain the ultimate sanction for from one to fourteen crimes. This diminished frequency is a reflection of the popular distaste for executions and of the recognition by many criminologically and psychiatrically oriented judges, juries, prosecutors, and commuting and pardoning authorities that capital punishment is as ineffective as a special capital crimes deterrent as it is ethically and morally undesirable.

The case against the death penalty is supported by many arguments—with the order of their importance or precedence dependent upon the orientation of the proponent or the composition of the audience to whom the argument is being addressed. The late Harold Laski, in opening his series of lectures to one of my graduate seminars in political theory, suggested that a lecturer or writer was under obligation to his audience to define both the articulate and inarticulate basic premises upon which his theoretical structure, and its practical application to the matters under discussion, rested. This writer, then, is a practicing criminologist with both administrative and operational experience in police and prison work over a period of more than two decades; he was brought up in a Catholic household, went to parochial schools for twelve years, and then took degrees from two non-sectarian institutions. He is a "convert" to abolition, for during his active police and prison career he not only accepted the death penalty pragmatically as existent, necessary, and therefore desirable but participated in one or another formal capacity in a number of executions.

The case against capital punishment is ten-fold:

From "The Case Against Capital Punishment," *Social Action*, April, 1961. Reprinted by permission of The Office for Church in Society, United Church of Christ.

10. IS CAPITAL PUNISHMENT JUSTIFIED?

1. *Capital punishment is criminologically unsound.* The death penalty is the antithesis of the rehabilitative, non-punitive, non-vindictive orientation of twentieth century penology. It brutalizes the entire administration of criminal justice. No criminologist of stature in America or abroad gives it support. And those "arm-chair" and so-called "utilitarian" criminologists who plead its necessity (never its desirability or morality) do so in terms of Darwinian natural selection and/or as a eugenics-oriented, castration-sterilization race purification technique, an economical and efficient method of disposing of society's jetsam. Those who advance these arguments are probably not aware that they are rationalizing a residual lust for punishment or propagating an immoral, virtually paganistic, philosophy.

2. *Capital punishment is morally and ethically unacceptable.* The law of God is "Thou shalt not kill," and every system of ethics and code of morals echoes this injunction. It is well recognized that this Commandment (and the laws of man based upon it) permit the killing of another human being "in the lawful defense of the slayer, or of his or her husband, wife, parent, child, brother, sister, master or servant, or of any other person in his presence or company" when there is "imminent danger" and in "actual resistance" to an assault or other criminal act. It is equally well recognized that society, organized as a sovereign state, has the right to take human life in defending itself in a just war against either internal or external unjust aggression. But the individual citizen has no right in law or morals to slay as punishment for an act, no matter how vile, already committed; nor has he legal or moral justification to kill when—his resistance to an attempted criminal act having proved successful short of fatal force—the imminent danger is eliminated and the criminal attack or attempt discontinued.

Individuals in groups or societies are subject to the same moral and ethical codes which govern their conduct as individuals. The state, through its police agents, may take human life when such ultimate measure of force is necessary to protect its citizenry from the imminent danger of criminal action and in actual resistance to felonious attempts (including attempts forcibly to avoid arrest or escape custody). Once, however, the prisoner has been apprehended and either voluntarily submits to custody, or is effectively safeguarded against escape (maximum security confinement), the right of the state to take his life as punishment, retribution, revenge, or retaliation for previously committed offenses (no matter how numerous or heinous) or as an "example" to deter others, or as an economical expedient, does not exist in moral law.

I argue this despite the fact that it is a position which is contrary to that expounded by a number of eminent theologians, notably Thomas Aquinas. Writing in times long past and quite different, and expressing themselves in terms of conditions, logic and experiences of those times, such theologians have defended the right of the state to take human life as a punishment "when the common good requires it." Moreover, they have held that, under certain conditions, the state is morally bound to take human life and that not to take it would be sinful. Although I am philosophically opposed to war whether as an extension of diplomacy or an instrument of national policy, I recognize the right of a nation, through its armed forces and in accord with the rules of civilized warfare, to take human life in defense of its sovereignty, its national territory, and its citizens. Such recognition is in no way inconsistent with my views [against] the death penalty, for the Geneva Convention makes it clear that the killing of one's enemy (no matter how many of one's troops he has slaughtered in battle) after he has laid down his arms, surrendered, or been taken prisoner, will not be countenanced by civilized nations.

3. Capital punishment has demonstrably failed to accomplish its stated objectives. The proponents of the death penalty base their support largely on two basic propositions: (1) that the death penalty has a uniquely deterrent effect on those who contemplate committing capital crimes; and (2) that the provision of the death penalty as the mandatory or alternative penalty for stated offenses in the statute books removes for all time the danger of future similar offenses by those whose criminal acts have made them subject to its rigors.

Neither of these propositions will stand logical or statistical analysis. Proposition 1 is dependent upon acceptance of the repudiated "pleasure-pain" principle of past-century penology. This theory presupposes a "rational man" weighing the prospective profit or pleasure to be derived from the commission of some future crime against the almost certain pain or loss he will suffer in retribution should he be apprehended and convicted. That many persons who commit crimes are not "rational" at the time the crime is committed is beyond dispute. Avoiding the area of psychiatric controversy for the moment, let it be sufficient to report that Dr. Shaw Grigsby of the University of Florida in his recent studies at the Raiford (Florida) State Penitentiary found that

more than seventy-five percent of the males and more than ninety percent of the females then in confinement were under the influence of alcohol at the time they committed the offenses for which they were serving sentence; and that Dr. Marvin Wolfgang's studies of the patterns in criminal homicide in Philadelphia in large measure lend support to Dr Grigsby's findings.

While perhaps the theological doctrine of "sufficient reflection and full consent of the will" as necessary prerequisites to mortal sin is somewhat mitigated by the mandate to "avoid the occasions of sin" in the determination of moral responsibility, we are here discussing rationality in terms of weighing alternatives of possible prospective deterrence rather than adjudicated post-mortem responsibility. Proposition 1 further presupposes knowledge by the prospective offender of the penalty provided in the penal code for the offense he is about to commit—a knowledge not always found even among lawyers. It further assumes a non-self-destructive orientation of the offender and, most importantly, a certainty in his mind that he will be identified, apprehended, indicted, convicted, sentenced to the maximum penalty, and that the ultimate sanction will indeed be executed. When one notes that of 125 persons indicted for first degree murder in the District of Columbia during the period 1953–1959, only one (a Negro) was executed despite the mandatory provision of the law; and further that, despite the fact that more than three million major felonies were known to the police in 1960, the total prison population (federal and state) at the 1961 prison census (including substantially all the convicted felons of 1960 and many from prior years) stood at a miniscule 190.000.

191

the rational criminal might very well elect to "play the odds."

The second part of the proposition assumes that all or a high proportion of those who commit crimes for which the death penalty is prescribed will in fact be executed—an assumption, rebutted above, which was false even in the heyday of capital punishment when more than two hundred offenses were punishable on the gallows. It shows no awareness that the mere existence of the death penalty may in itself contribute to the commission of the very crimes it is designed to deter, or to the difficulty of securing convictions in capital cases. The murderer who has killed once (or committed one of the more than thirty other capital crimes) and whose life is already forfeit if he is caught would find little deterrent weight in the prospect of execution for a second or third capital crime— particularly if his victim were to be a police officer attempting to take him into custody for the original capital offense. The suicidal, guilt-haunted psychotic might well kill (or confess falsely to a killing) to provoke the state into imposing upon him the punishment which in his tortured mind he merits but is unable to inflict upon himself.

Prosecutors and criminal trial lawyers have frequently testified as to the difficulty of impanelling juries in capital cases and the even greater difficulty of securing convictions on evidence which in non-capital cases would leave little room for reasonable doubt. Appeals courts scan with more analytical eye the transcripts in capital cases, and error is located and deemed prejudicial which in non-capital cases would be overlooked. The Chessman case is, from this viewpoint, a monument to the determination on the part of American justice that no man shall be executed while there is the slightest doubt either as to his guilt or as to the legality of the process by which his guilt was determined. Criminologists have pointed out repeatedly that the execution of the small number of convicts (fewer than fifty each year in the United States) has a disproportionately brutalizing effect on those of us who survive. Respect for the sanctity and inviolability of human life decreases each time human life is taken. When taken formally in the circus-like atmosphere which unfortunately characterizes twentieth century trials and executions (both here and abroad), emotions, passions, impulses and hostilities are activated which may lead to the threshold of murder many who might never have incurred the mark of Cain.

4. *Capital punishment in the United States has been and is prejudicially and inconsistently applied.* The logic of the retentionist position would be strengthened if the proponents of capital punishment could demonstrate that an "even-handed justice" exacted the supreme penalty without regard to race or nationality, age or sex, social or economic condition; that all or nearly all who committed capital crimes were indeed executed; or, at least, that those pitiful few upon whom the sentence of death is carried out each year are in fact the most dangerous, the most vicious, the most incorrigible of all who could have been executed. But the record shows otherwise.

Accurate death penalty statistics for the United States are available for the thirty-year period, 1930-1959. Analysis of the more than three thousand cases in which the death penalty was exacted discloses that more than half were Negroes, that a very significant proportion were defended by court-appointed lawyers, and that few of them were professional killers. Whether a man died for his offense depended, not on the gravity of his crime, not on the number of such crimes or the number of his victims, not on his present or prospective danger to society, but on such adventitious factors as the jurisdiction in which the crime was committed, the color of his skin, his financial position, whether he was male or female (we seldom execute females), and indeed oftentimes on what were the character and characteristics of his victim (apart from the justifiability of the instant homicidal act).

It may be exceedingly difficult for a rich man to enter the Kingdom of Heaven but case after case bears witness that it is virtually impossible for him to enter the execution chamber. And it is equally impossible in several states to execute a white man for a capital crime against a Negro. Professional murderers (and the directors of the criminal syndicates which employ them) are seldom caught. When they are arrested either they are defended successfully by eminent and expensive trial counsel; or they eliminate or intimidate witnesses against them. Failing such advantages, they wisely bargain for a plea of guilty to some lesser degree of homicide and escape the death chamber. The homicidal maniac, who has massacred perhaps a dozen, even under our archaic M'Naghten Rule, is safely outside the pale of criminal responsibility and escapes not only the death penalty but often even its alternatives.

5. *The innocent have been executed.* There is no system of criminal jurisprudence which has on the whole provided as many safeguards against the conviction and possible execution of an innocent man as the Anglo-American. Those of us who oppose the death penalty do not raise this argument to condemn our courts or our judiciary, but only to underline the fallibility of human judgment and human procedures. We oppose capital punishment for the guilty; no one save a monster or deluded rationalist (e.g., the Captain in Herman Melville's *Billy Budd*) would justify the execution of the innocent. We cannot however close our minds or our hearts to the greater tragedy, the more monstrous injustice, the ineradicable shame involved when the legal processes of the state, knowingly or unknowingly, have been used to take the life of an innocent man.

The American Bar Foundation, or some similar research-oriented legal society, might well address itself to an objective analysis of the factors which led to the convictions of the many men whose sentences for capital crimes have in the past few decades been set aside by the appellate courts (or by the executive authority after the courts had exhausted their processes), and who later were exonerated either by trial courts or by the consensus of informed opinion. Especial attention should be directed to the fortunately much smaller number of cases (e.g., the Evans-Christie case in England and the Brandon case in New Jersey) in which innocent men were actually executed. Perhaps, too, a reanalysis would be profitable of the sixty-five cases cited by Professor Edwin Borchard in his *Convicting the Innocent,* the thirty-six cases mentioned by U.S. Circuit Court of Appeals Judge, Jerome Frank in *Courts on Trial,* and the smaller number of miscarriages of justice outlined by Erle Stanley Gardner in *Court of Last Resort.*

6. *There are effective alternative penalties.* One gets the impression all too frequently, both from retentionist spokesmen and, occasionally, from the

statements of enthusiastic but ill-informed abolitionists, that the only alternative to capital punishment is no punishment; that, if the death penalty does not deter, then surely no lesser societal response to the violation of its laws and injury to its citizens will prove effective.

The record in abolition jurisdictions, some without the death penalty, both in the United States and abroad, in which imprisonment for indeterminate or stated terms has been substituted for the penalty of death, is a clear demonstration that alternative penalties are of equal or greater protective value to society than is capital punishment.

In every instance in which a valid statistical comparison is possible between jurisdictions scientifically equated as to population and economic and social conditions, the nations and states that have abolished capital punishment have a smaller capital crimes rate than the comparable jurisdictions that have retained the death penalty. Further, the capital crimes rate in those jurisdictions which, while retaining the death penalty, use it seldom or not at all is in most instances lower than the capital crimes rates in the retentionist jurisdictions which execute most frequently.

And, finally, comparing the before, during, and after capital crimes rates in those jurisdictions (nine in the United States) which abolished capital punishment and then restored it to their penal codes, we find a consistently downward trend in capital crimes unaffected by either abolition or restoration. Startling comparisons are available. The United State Navy has executed no one in more than 120 years; yet it has maintained a level of discipline, effectiveness, and morale certainly in no sense inferior to that of the United States Army which has inflicted the death penalty on more than 150 soldiers in just the last three decades.

Delaware, the most recent state to abolish the death penalty, experienced a remarkable drop in its capital crimes rate during the first full year of abolition. No criminologist would argue that abolition will necessarily reduce capital crimes; nor will he attempt to demonstrate a causal connection between absence of the death penalty and low capital crime rates. In point of fact, homicide is the one major felony which shows a consistent downward trend in both capital punishment and abolition jurisdictions—indicating to the student of human behavior that the crime of murder, particularly, is largely an irrational reaction to a concrescence of circumstances, adventitiously related, wholly independent of and neither positively nor negatively correlatable with the legal sanction provided in the jurisdiction in which the crime actually took place. Dr. Marvin Wolfgang has pointed out with some logic that our decreasing murder rate is probably in no small part due to improved communications (ambulance gets to the scene faster), improved first aid to the victim, and the antibiotics, blood banks, and similar advances in medicine which save many an assault victim from becoming a corpse—and of course his assailant from being tagged a murderer. The consistent upward trend in assaultive crimes gives support to Dr. Wolfgang's thesis.

7. *Police and prison officers are safer in non-death penalty states.* The studies of Donald Campion, S.J., associate editor of *America,* and others indicate (albeit with restricted samplings) that the life of a police officer or a prison guard is slightly safer in the non-death penalty states, although the difference is so slight as to

be statistically insignificant. Prison wardens overwhelmingly support abolition but large segments of the police profession support the retention of the death penalty both as a general crime deterrent (which it demonstrably is not) and as a specific safeguard to members of their own profession. Significantly, few of the police officers who serve in non-death penalty states are active in the fight to restore capital punishment and most of those who oppose abolition in their own jurisdictions have never performed police duties in an abolition state. It is a criminological axiom that it is the certainty, not the severity, of punishment that deters. Improvements in the selection, training, discipline, supervision, and operating techniques of our police will insure a higher percentage of apprehensions and convictions of criminals and, even without the death penalty, will provide a greater general crime deterrent and far more safety both for the general public and for police officers than either enjoys at present.

8. *Paroled and pardoned murderers are no threat to the public.* Studies in New Jersey and California, and less extensive studies of paroled and pardoned murderers in other jurisdictions, indicate that those whose death sentences have been commuted, or who have been paroled from life or long-term sentences, or who have received executive pardons after conviction of capital crimes are by far the least likely to recidivate. Not only do they not again commit homicide, but they commit other crimes or violate their parole contracts to a much lesser extent than do paroled burglars, robbers, and the generality of the non-capital crimes convicts on parole. My own study of nearly 150 murderers showed that not a single one had killed again and only two

had committed any other crime subsequent to release. Ohio's Governor Michael DiSalle has pointed out (as Warden Lewis Lawes and other penologists have in the past) that murderers are by and large the best and safest prisoners; and he has demonstrated his confidence by employing eight convicted murderers from the Ohio State Penitentiary in and about the Executive Mansion in Columbus in daily contact with members of his family.

9. *The death penalty is more costly than its alternatives.* It seems somewhat immoral to discuss the taking of even a murderer's life in terms of dollars and cents; but often the argument is raised that capital punishment is the cheapest way of "handling" society's outcasts and that the "good" members of the community should not be taxed to support killers for life (often coupled with the euthanasian argument that "they are better off dead"). The application of elementary cost accounting procedures to the determination of the differential in costs peculiar to capital cases will effectively demonstrate that not only is it not "cheaper to hang them"; but that, on the contrary, it would be cheaper for the taxpayers to maintain our prospective executees in the comparative luxury of first-rate hotels, with all the perquisites of non-criminal guests, than to pay for having them executed. The tangible costs of the death penalty in terms of long-drawn-out jury selection, extended trials and retrials, appeals, extra security, maintenance of expensive, seldom-used death-houses, support of the felon's family, etc., are heavy.

10. *Capital punishment stands in the way of penal reform.* Man has used the death penalty and other forms of retributive punishment throughout the centuries

to control and govern the conduct of his fellows and to force conformity and compliance to laws and codes, taboos and customs. The record of every civilization makes abundantly clear that punishment, no matter how severe or sadistic, has had little effect on crime rates. No new approach to the criminal is possible so long as the death penalty, and the discredited penology it represents, pervades our criminal justice system. Until it is stricken from the statute books, a truly rehabilitative approach to the small percentage of our fellowmen who cannot or will not adjust to society's dictates is impossible of attainment. That there is a strong positive correlation between advocacy of the death penalty and a generally punitive orientation cannot be gainsaid. Analysis of the votes for corporal punishment bills, votes against substitution of alternatives for mandatory features in the few mandatory death penalty jurisdictions, votes against study commissions and against limited period moratoria, and comparison with votes for bills increasing the penalties for rape, narcotics offenses, and other felonies discloses a pattern of simple retributive punitiveness, characterizing many of our legislators and the retentionist witnesses before legislative committees.

Many church assemblies of America and individual churchmen of every denomination have underscored the moral and ethical nonacceptability of capital punishment. Church members have the responsibility to support the campaign to erase this stain on American society. Capital punishment is brutal, sordid, and savage. It violates the law of God and is contrary to the humane and liberal respect for human life characteristic of modern democratic states. It is unsound criminologically and unnecessary for the protection of the state or its citizens. It makes miscarriages of justice irredeemable; it makes the barbaric *lex talionis* the watchword and inhibits the reform of our prison systems. It encourages disrespect for our laws, our courts, our institutions; and, in the words of Sheldon Glueck, "bedevils the administration of justice and is the stumbling block in the path of general reform in the treatment of crime and criminals."

POSTSCRIPT

IS CAPITAL PUNISHMENT JUSTIFIED?

Opinion on the death penalty has always been sharply divided in the United States. While Massachusetts in 1785 defined nine capital crimes (that is, crimes punishable by death) and North Carolina as late as 1837 had more than twenty, other states rejected the death sentence entirely at an early date. American sentiment has been so divided that at least eleven states have abolished the death penalty only to restore it some years later.

In the readings in this issue, MacNamara catalogues the most popular arguments for the removal of the death penalty, attempting to rebut each in turn. Berns uses a different tactic. He narrows in on one of the more controversial justifications for punishment—retribution, "paying back" the criminal—and tries to show that it speaks to something decent and humane in our nature. Neither of these closely reasoned arguments is likely to be upset by any more statistical or historical data. Facts, even "inconvenient" ones, can usually be incorporated into a wide variety of viewpoints. Nevertheless, the debate can only be enriched by empirical study, and the student will find a trove of it in William J. Bowers' *Executions in America* (Lexington Books, 1974). The movement that led to the abolition of the death penalty in Great Britain prompted the publication of several books, the most stimulating of which is Arthur Koestler's and C.H. Rolph's *Hanged by the Neck* (Penguin, 1961). Probably the most reflective, and almost certainly the most engrossing, literature on the subject is to be found in the many books dealing with the executions of Sacco and Vanzetti (plays and films have also dealt with their case), the Rosenbergs, and Caryl Chessman. In each of these cases, deep feelings favoring and opposing their execution were aroused by political issues and questions regarding their guilt, as well as by divided sentiments on the exercise of capital punishment. Almost certainly, popular attitudes toward the death sentence in these cases were never entirely separable from other circumstances.

Apart from the constitutional issues, the debate is more narrowly drawn than in earlier times. Although the death penalty is sometimes urged as punishment for such acts as treason or skyjacking, it is principally considered in connection with the crime of murder. There is little dispute over the proposition that the manner of execution should be the least painful (no one is drawn and quartered in civilized society), although there is no unanimity of opinion about whether death by electrocution, gas, or hanging best meets that test. Some states, such as Texas and New Jersey, have adopted the method of fatal injections, though the experience with its use in Texas has raised doubts about its painlessness. It may well be that the firing squad, perhaps the most "violent" means of execution permitted in the United States, could also be the quickest and most painless. However, how or how often to impose capital punishment is not the question society must examine, but whether we should take a life for a life.

ISSUE 11

IS AFFIRMATIVE ACTION REVERSE DISCRIMINATION?

YES: Glenn C. Loury, from "Beyond Civil Rights," *The New Republic* (October 7, 1985)

NO: Herman Schwartz, from "In Defense of Affirmative Action," *Dissent* (Fall 1984)

ISSUE SUMMARY

YES: Harvard professor Glenn Loury contends that insistence on "ill-suited" civil rights strategies makes it impossible for blacks to achieve full equality in American society.
NO: Law professor Herman Schwartz argues that we must somehow undo the cruel consequences of racism that still plague our society and its victims.

"We didn't land on Plymouth Rock, my brothers and sisters—Plymouth Rock landed on *us!*" Malcolm X's observation is well borne out by the facts of American history. Snatched from their native land, transported thousands of miles—in a nightmare of disease and death—and sold into slavery, blacks were reduced to the legal status of farm animals. Even after emancipation, blacks were segregated from whites by law in some states and by social practice almost everywhere. American *apartheid* continued for another century.

In 1954 the Supreme Court declared state-compelled segregation in schools unconstitutional, and it followed up that decision with others which struck down other forms of official segregation. Still, many forms of "private" discrimination survived, and in most southern states blacks were either discouraged or prohibited from exercising their right to vote.

Not until the 1960s was compulsory segregation finally and effectively challenged. Between 1964 and 1968 Congress passed the most sweeping civil rights legislation since the end of the Civil War. It banned discrimination in employment, public accommodations (hotels, motels, restaurants, etc.), and housing; it also guaranteed voting rights for blacks, and even authorized federal officials to take over the job of voter registration in areas suspected of disenfranchising blacks. Today, several agencies in the federal government exercise sweeping powers to enforce these civil rights measures. The result is that blatant discrimination against blacks has all but disappeared in America.

But is that enough? Equality of condition between blacks and whites seems as elusive as ever. The black unemployment rate is double that of whites (black teenage unemployment is three times that of white teenagers). The percentage of black families living in poverty is nearly four times that of whites. On average, blacks don't live as long as whites, more of their children die in infancy, more of their mothers die in childbirth. Only a tiny percentage of them ever make it into medical school or law school, and that percentage seems to be declining.

Advocates of "affirmative action" have focused upon these *de facto* differences to bolster their argument that it is no longer enough just to stop discriminating. The damage done by three centuries of racism now has to be remedied, they argue, and effective remediation requires a policy of "affirmative action." At the heart of affirmative action is the use of "numerical goals." Opponents call them "racial quotas." Whatever the name, what they imply is the setting-aside of a certain number of jobs or positions earmarked for blacks or other historically oppressed groups. It doesn't have to be a strict percentage, but it does require some degree of "race-consciousness" in the selection process.

Opponents charge that "affirmative action" really amounts to "reverse discrimination," that it penalizes innocent people simply because they are white, that it often results in unqualified appointments, and that it ends up harming blacks instead of helping them. Supporters of "affirmative action" counter that it is a necessary remedy to undo the long-term effects of racism.

What has the Supreme Court had to say about affirmative action? Many things. In *Regents of the University of California* v. *Bakke* (1978), a 5-4 majority ruled that a white applicant to a medical school had been wrongly excluded due to the school's affirmative action policy; yet the majority also agreed that "race-conscious" policies may be used in admitting candidates—as long as they do not turn into fixed "quotas." In *United Steelworkers* v. *Weber* (1979), the Court upheld an agreement between an aluminum plant and a union to establish a quota for blacks in admitting applicants to a special training program. In *Fullilove* v. *Klutznick* (1980), the Court upheld the constitutionality of a federal public works program requiring that ten percent of federal funds be set aside for contracts with minority construction firms.

The above decisions gave Supreme Court endorsement to the principle of "race-conscious" remedies. But in *Memphis Firefighters* v. *Stotts* (1984) and *Wygant* v. *Jackson Board of Education* (1986) the Court seemed to retreat from that view. In *Stotts* it ruled that federal courts may not order the firing of white employees who have more seniority than blacks simply for the purpose of saving the jobs of newly hired blacks during the period of layoffs. In *Wygant* it ruled that a Michigan school board's policy of laying off white teachers before minority-group teachers was unconstitutional.

But in July of 1986 the Court twice again endorsed affirmative action policies. In *Local 93* v. *City of Cleveland* it held that local courts can approve settlements that involve the preferential hiring of blacks, and in *Local 28* v. *Equal Employment Opportunity Commission* it approved a lower court order requiring a union local to hire a fixed quota of blacks by 1987. Putting it all on a scorecard: as of this writing, the Court has handed down seven decisions concerning the use of "race-conscious" remedies, five in favor and two against.

In the following selections, Professors Glenn C. Loury and Herman Schwartz debate the merits of affirmative action. Loury, who rose from a Chicago ghetto to Harvard's prestigious Kennedy School, argues that affirmative action demoralizes blacks. Schwartz, a law professor, maintains that it is an essential tool for undoing the effects of racism.

YES   Glenn C. Loury

BEYOND CIVIL RIGHTS

There is today a great deal of serious discussion among black Americans concerning the problems confronting them. Many, if not most, people now concede that not all problems of blacks are due to discrimination, and that they cannot be remedied through civil rights strategies or racial politics. I would go even further: using civil rights strategies to address problems to which they are ill-suited thwarts more direct and effective action. Indeed, the broad application of these strategies to every case of differential achievement between blacks and whites threatens to make it impossible for blacks to achieve full equality in American society.

The civil rights approach has two essential aspects: first, the cause of a particular socioeconomic disparity is identified as a racial discrimination; and second, advocates seek such remedies for the disparity as the courts and administrative agencies provide under the law.

There are fundamental limitations on this approach deriving from our liberal political heritage. What can this strategy do about those important contractual relationships that profoundly affect one's social and economic status but in which racial discrimination is routinely practiced? Choice of marital partner is an obvious example. People discriminate here by race with a vengeance. A black woman does not have an opportunity equal to that of white woman to become the wife of a given white man. Since white men are on the whole better off financially than black men, this racial inequality of opportunity has substantial monetary costs to black women. Yet surely it is to be hoped that the choice of husband or wife will always be beyond the reach of the law.

The example is not facetious. All sorts of voluntary associations—neighborhoods, friends, business partnerships—are the result of choices often influenced by racial criteria, but which lie beyond the reach of civil rights laws. A fair housing law cannot prevent a disgruntled white resident from moving away if his neighborhood becomes predominantly or even partly black. Busing for desegregation cannot prevent unhappy parents from sending their children to private schools. Withdrawal of university support for student clubs with discriminatory selection rules cannot prevent student cliques from forming along racial lines. And a vast majority of Americans would have it no other way.

As a result, the nondiscrimination mandate has not been allowed to interfere much with personal, private, and intimately social intercourse. Yet such exclusive social connections along group lines have important economic consequences. An extensive literature in economics and sociology documents the crucial importance of family and community background in determining a child's later success in life. Lacking the right "networks," blacks with the same innate abilities as whites wind up less successful. And the elimination of racial discrimination in the economic sphere—but not in patterns of social attachment—will probably not be enough to make up the difference. There are thus elemental limits on what one can hope to achieve through the application of civil rights strategies to what must of necessity be a restricted domain of personal interactions.

The civil rights strategy has generally been restricted to the domain of impersonal, public, and economic transactions such as jobs, credit, and housing. Even in these areas, the efficacy of this strategy can be questioned. The lagging economic condition of blacks is due in significant part to the nature of social life *within* poor black communities. After two decades of civil rights efforts, more than three-fourths of children in some inner-city ghettos are born out of wedlock; black high school dropout rates hover near 50 percent in Chicago and Detroit; two-fifths of murder victims in the country are blacks killed by other blacks; fewer black women graduate

from college than give birth while in high school; more than two in five black children are dependent on public assistance. White America's lack of respect for blacks' civil rights cannot be blamed for all these sorry facts. This is not to deny that, in some basic sense, most of these difficulties are related to our history of racial oppression, but only to say that these problems have taken on a life of their own, and cannot be effectively reversed by civil rights policies.

Higher education is a case in point. In the not too distant past, blacks, Asians, and women faced severe obstacles to attending or teaching at American colleges and universities, especially at the most prestigious institutions. Even after black scholars studied at the great institutions, their only possibilities for employment were at the historically black colleges, where they faced large teaching loads and burdensome administrative duties. Their accomplishments were often acknowledged by their white peers only grudgingly, if at all.

Today opportunities for advanced education and academic careers for blacks abound. Major universities throughout the country are constantly searching for qualified black candidates to hire as professors, or to admit to study. Most state colleges and universities near black population centers have made a concerted effort to reach those in the inner city. Almost all institutions of higher learning admit blacks with lower grades or test scores than white students. There are special programs funded by private foundations to help blacks prepare for advanced study in medicine, economics, engineering, public policy, law, and other fields.

Yet, with all these opportunities (and despite improvement in some areas), the number of blacks advancing in the academic world is distressingly low. The percentage of college students who are black, after rising throughout the 1970s, has actually begun to decline. And though the proportion of doctorates granted to blacks has risen slightly over the last decade, a majority of black doctorates are still earned in the field of education. Despite constant pressure to hire black professors and strenuous efforts to recruit them, the percentage of blacks on elite university faculties has remained constant or fallen in the past decade.

Meanwhile, other groups traditionally excluded are making impressive gains. Asian-Americans, though less than two percent of the population, make up 6.6 percent of U.S. scientists with doctorates; they constitute 7.5 percent of the students at Yale, and nine percent at Stanford. The proportion of doctorates going to women has risen from less than one-seventh to nearly one-third in the last decade. Less than two percent of Harvard professors at all ranks are black, but more than 25 percent are women.

Now, it is entirely possible that blacks experience discrimination at these institutions. But as anyone who has spent time in an elite university community knows, these institutions are not racist in character, nor do they deny opportunities to blacks with outstanding qualifications. The case can be made that just the opposite is true—that these institutions are so anxious to raise the numbers of blacks in their ranks that they overlook deficiencies when making admissions or appointment decisions involving blacks.

One obvious reason for skepticism about discrimination as the cause of the problem here is the relatively poor academic performance of black high school and college students. Black performance on standardized college admissions tests, though improving, still lags far behind whites. In 1982 there were only 205 blacks in the entire country who scored above 700 on the math component of the SAT. And, as Robert Klitgaard shows convincingly in his book *Choosing Elites*, post-admissions college performance by black students is less than that of whites, even when controlling for differences in high school grades and SAT scores. These differences in academic performance are not just limited to poor blacks, or to high school students. On the SAT exam, blacks from families with incomes in excess of $50,000 per year still scored 60 to 80 points below comparable whites. On the 1982 Graduate Record Exam, the gap between black and white students' average scores on the mathematics component of this test was 171 points. According to Klitgaard, black students entering law school in the late 1970s had median scores on the LSAT at the eighth percentile of all students' scores.

Such substantial differences in educational results are clearly a matter of great concern. Arguably, the government should be actively seeking to attenuate them. But it seems equally clear that this is not a civil rights matter that can be reversed by seeking out and changing someone's discriminatory behavior. Moreover, it it possible that great harm will be done if the problem is defined and pursued in those terms.

Take the controversy over the racial quotas at the Boston Latin School, the pride and joy of the city's public school system. It was founded before Harvard, in 1635, and it has been recognized ever since as a center of academic excellence. Boston Latin maintains its very high standards through a grueling program of study, including Latin, Greek, calculus, history, science, and the arts. Three hours of homework per night are typical. College admissions personnel acknowledge the excellence of this program; 95 percent of the class of 1985 will go to college.

The institution admits its students on the basis of their marks in primary school and performance on the Secondary School Admissions Test. In 1974, when Boston's public schools became subject to court-ordered desegregation, Judge Arthur Garrity considered closing Boston Latin, because the student population at the time was more than 90 percent white. In the end, a racial admissions quota was employed, requiring that 35 percent of the entering classes be black and Hispanic. Of the 2,245 students last year, over half were female, 57 percent white, 23 percent black, 14 percent Asian, and six percent Hispanic.

Historically the school has maintained standards through a policy of academic "survival of the fittest." Those who were unable to make it through the academic rigors simply transferred to another school. Thus, there has always been a high rate of attrition; it is now the range of 30 percent to 40 percent. But today, unlike the pre-desegregation era, most of those who do not succeed at Boston Latin are minority students. Indeed, though approximately 35 percent of each entering class is black and Hispanic, only 16 percent of last year's senior class was. That is, for each non-Asian minority student who graduates from Latin, there is one who did not. The failure rate for whites is about half that. Some advocates of minority student interest have complained of discrimination, saying in effect that the school is not doing enough to assist those in academic difficulty. Yet surely one reason for the poor performance of the black and Hispanic students is Judge Garrity's admissions quota. To be considered for admission, whites must score at the 70th percentile or higher on the admissions exam, while blacks and Hispanics need only score above the 50th percentile.

Recently Thomas Atkins, former general counsel of the NAACP, who has been representing the black plaintiffs in the Boston school desegregation lawsuit, which has been going on for ten years, proposed that the quota at Boston Latin be raised to roughly 50 percent black, 20 percent Hispanic and Asian, and 30 percent white —a reflection of the racial composition of the rest of Boston's public schools. Unless there were a significant increase in the size of the school, this could only be accomplished by doubling the number of blacks admitted while cutting white enrollment in half. This in turn, under plausible distributional assumptions, would require that the current difference of 20 points in the minimum test scores required of black and white students accepted be approximately doubled. Since the additional black students admitted would be less prepared than those admitted under the current quota, one could expect an even higher failure rate among minorities were this plan to be accepted. The likely consequence would be that more than three-fourths of those leaving Boston Latin without a degree would be blacks and Hispanics. It is also plausible to infer that such an action would profoundly alter, if not destroy, the academic climate in the school.

This is not simply an inappropriate use of civil rights methods, though it is surely that. It is an almost wanton moral surrender. By what logic of pedagogy can these students' difficulties be attributed to racism, in view of the fact that the school system has been run by court order for over a decade? By what calculus of fairness can those claiming to be fighting for justice argue that outstanding white students, many from poor homes themselves (80 percent of Latin graduates require financial aid in college), should be denied the opportunity for this special education so that minority students who are not prepared for it may nonetheless enroll? Is there so little faith in the aptitude of the minority young people that the highest standards should not be held out for them? It would seem that the real problem here—a dearth of academically outstanding black high school students in Boston—is not amendable to rectification by court order.

Another example from the field of education illustrates the "opportunity costs" of the civil rights strategy. In 1977 the Ann Arbor public school system was sued by public interest lawyers on behalf of a group of black parents with children in the primary grades. The school system was accused of denying equal educational opportunity to these children. The problem was that the black students were not learning how to read at an acceptable rate, though the white youngsters were. The suit alleged that by failing to take into account in the teaching of reading to these children the fact that they spoke an identifiable, distinct dialect of the English language—Black English—the black students were denied equal educational opportunity. The lawsuit was successful.

As a result, in 1979 the court ordered that reading teachers in Ann Arbor be given special "sensitivity" training so that, while teaching standard English to these children, they might take into account the youngsters' culturally distinct patterns of speech. Ann Arbor's public school system has dutifully complied. A recent discussion of this case with local educators revealed that, as of six years after the initial court order, the disparity in reading achievement between blacks and whites in Ann Arbor persists at a level comparable to the one before the lawsuit was brought. It was their opinion that, though of enormous symbolic importance, the entire process had produced little in the way of positive educational impact on the students.

This is not intended as a condemnation of those who brought the suit, nor do I offer here any opinion on whether promotion of Black English is a good idea. What is of interest is the process by which the problem was defined, and out of which a remedy was sought. In effect, the parents of these children were approached by lawyers and educators active in civil rights, and urged to help their children learn to read by bringing this action. Literally thousands of hours went into conceiving and trying this case. Yet, in the end only a hollow, symbolic victory was won.

But it is quite possible that this line of attack on the problem caused other more viable strategies not to be pursued. For example, a campaign to tutor the first and second graders might have made an impact, giving them special attention and extra hours of study through the voluntary participation of those in Ann Arbor possessing the relevant skills. With roughly 35,000 students at the University of Michigan's Ann Arbor campus (a fair number of whom are black), it would have required that only a fraction of one percent of them spare an afternoon or evening once a week for there to be sufficient numbers to provide the needed services. There were at most only a few hundred poor black students in the primary grades experiencing reading difficulties. And, more than providing this needed aid for specific kids, such an undertaking would have helped to cultivate a more healthy relationship between the university and the town. It could have contributed to building a tradition of direct services that would be of more general value. But none of this happened, in part because the civil rights approach was almost reflexively embraced by the advocating parties concerned.

The danger to blacks of too broad a reliance on civil rights strategies can be subtle. It has become quite clear that affirmative action creates uncertain perceptions about the qualifications of those minorities who benefit from it. In an employment situation, for example, if it is known that different selection criteria are used for different races, and that the quality of performance on the job depends on how one did on the criteria of selection, then in the absence of other information, it is rational to expect lower performance from persons of the race that was preferentially favored in selection. Using race as a criterion of selection in employment, in other words, creates objective incentives for customers, co-workers, and others to take race into account after the employment decision has been made.

The broad use of race preference to treat all instances of "underrepresentation" also introduces uncertainty among the beneficiaries themselves. It undermines the ability of people confidently to assert, if only to themselves, that they are as good as their achievements would seem to suggest. It therefore undermines the extent to which the personal success of any one black can become the basis of guiding the behavior of other blacks. Fewer individuals in a group subject to such preferences return to their communities of origin to say, "I made it on my own, through hard work, self-application, and native ability, and so can you!" Moreover, it puts even the "best and brightest" of the favored group in the position of being supplicants of benevolent whites.

And this is not the end of the story. In order to defend such programs in the political arena—especially at the elite institutions—it becomes necessary to argue that almost no blacks could reach these heights without special favors. When there is internal disagreement among black intellectuals, for example, about the merits of affirmative action, critics of the policy are often attacked as being disingenuous, since (it is said) they clearly owe their own prominence to the very policy they criticize. The specific circumstances of the individual do not matter in this, for it is presumed that *all* blacks, whether directly or indirectly, are indebted to civil rights activity for their achievements. The consequence is a kind of "socialization" of the individual's success. The individual's effort to claim achievement for himself (and thus to secure the autonomy and legitmacy needed to deviate from group consensus, should that seem appropriate) is perceived as a kind of betrayal. There is nothing wrong, of course, with acknowledging the debt all blacks owe to those who fought and beat Jim Crow. There is everything wrong with a group's most accomplished persons feeling that the celebration of their personal attainment represents betrayal of their fellows.

In his recent, highly esteemed comparative history of slavery, *Slavery and Social Death*, sociologist Orlando Patterson defines slavery as the "permanent, violent domination of natally alienated and generally dishonored persons." Today's policy debates frequently focus on (or perhaps more accurately, appropriate) the American slave experience, especially the violent character of the institution, its brutalization of the Africans, and its destructive effects on social life among the slaves. Less attention is paid nowadays to the *dishonored* condition of the slave, and by extension, of the freedman. For Patterson this dishonoring was crucial. He sees as a common feature of slavery wherever it has occurred the parasitic phenomenon whereby masters derive honor and standing from their power over slaves, and the slaves suffer an extreme marginality by virtue of having no social existence except that mediated by their masters. Patterson rejects the "property in people" definition of slavery, arguing that relations of respect and standing among persons are also crucial. But if this is so, it follows that emancipation—the ending of the master's property claim—is not of itself sufficient to convert a slave (or his descendant) into a genuinely equal citizen. There remains the intractable problem of overcoming the historically generated "lack of honor" of the freedman.

This problem, in my judgment, remains with us. Its eventual resolution is made less likely by blacks' broad, permanent reliance on racial preferences as remedies for academic or occupational under-performance. A central theme in Afro-American political and intellectual history is the demand for respect—the struggle to gain inclusion within the civic community, to become coequal participants in the national enterprise. This is, of course, a problem that all immigrant groups also faced, and that most have overcome. But here, unlike some other areas of social life, it seems that the black population's slave origins, subsequent racist exclusion, and continued dependence on special favors from the majority uniquely exacerbates the problem.

Blacks continue to seek the respect of their fellow Americans. And yet it becomes increasingly clear that, to do so, black Americans cannot substitute judical and legislative decree for what is to be won through the outstanding achievements of individual black persons. That is, neither the pity, nor the guilt, nor the coerced acquiescence in one's demands—all of which have been amply available to blacks over the last two decades—is sufficient. *For what ultimately is being sought is the freely conveyed respect of one's peers.* Assigning prestigious positions so as to secure a proper racial balance—this as a permanent, broadly practiced policy—seems fundamentally inconsistent with the attainment of this goal. It is a truth worth noting that not everything of value can be redistributed.

If in the psychological calculus by which people determine their satisfaction such status considerations of honor, dignity, and respect are important, then this observation places basic limits on the extent to which public policy can bring about genuine equality. This is especially so with respect to the policy of racially preferential treatment, because its use to "equalize" can actually destroy the good that is being sought on behalf of those initially unequal. It would seem that, where the high regard of others is being sought, there is no substitute for what is to be won through the unaided accomplishments of individual persons.

NO

Herman Schwartz

IN DEFENSE OF AFFIRMATIVE ACTION

The Reagan administration's assault on the rights of minorities and women has focused on the existing policy of affirmative action. This strategy may be shrewd politics but it is meanspirited morally and insupportable legally. . . .

Affirmative action has been defined as "a public or private program designed to equalize hiring and admission opportunities for historically disadvantaged groups by taking into consideration those very characteristics which have been used to deny them equal treatment." The controversy swirls primarily around the use of numerical goals and timetables for hiring or promotion, for university admissions, and for other benefits. It is fueled by the powerful strain of individualism that runs through American history and belief.

It is a hard issue, about which reasonable people can differ. Insofar as affirmative action is designed to compensate the disadvantaged for past racism, sexism, and other discrimination, many understandably believe that today's society should not have to pay for their ancestors' sins. But somehow we must undo the cruel consequences of the racism and sexism that still plague us, both for the sake of the victims and to end the enormous human waste that costs society so much. Civil Rights Commission Chairman Pendleton has conceded that discrimination is not only still with us but is, as he put it, "rampant." As recently as January 1984, the dean of faculty at Amherst College wrote in the *New York Times*:

> In my contacts with a considerable range of academic institutions, I have become aware of pervasive residues of racism and sexism, even among those whose intentions and conscious beliefs are entirely nondiscriminatory. Indeed, I believe most of us are afflicted with such residues. Beyond the wrongs of the past are the wrongs of the present. Most discriminatory habits in academia are nonactionable; affirmative action goals are our only instrument for focusing sustained attention.

The plight of black America not only remains grave, but in many respects, it is getting worse. The black unemployment rate—21 percent in early 1983—is

From, "Affirmative Action," by Herman Schwartz in *Minority Report: What Has Happened to Blacks, Hispanics, American Indians, and Other Minorities in the Eighties*, edited by Leslie Dunbar. Copyright © 1984. Reprinted by permission of Pantheon Books, a division of Random House, Inc.

11. IS AFFIRMATIVE ACTION REVERSE DISCRIMINATION?

double that for whites and the gap continues to increase. For black 20- to 24-year-old males, the rate—an awful 30 percent—is almost triple that for whites; for black teenagers the rate approaches 50 percent. More than half of all black children under three years of age live in homes below the poverty line. The gap between white and black family income, which pior to the '70s had narrowed a bit, has steadily edged wider, so that black-family income is now only 55 percent of that of whites. Only 3 percent of the nation's lawyers and doctors are black and only 4 percent of its managers, but over 50 percent of its maids and garbage collectors. Black life expectancy is about six years less than that of whites; the black infant mortality rate is nearly double.

Although the situation for women, of all races, is not as bad, the average earnings of women still, at most, are only two-thirds of those of their male counterparts. And the economic condition of black women, who now head 41 percent of the 6.4 million black families, is particularly bad; a recent Wellesley study found that black women are not only suffering in the labor market, but they receive substantially less public assistance and child support than white women. The economic condition of female household heads of any race is just as deplorable: 90 percent of the 4 million single-parent homes are headed by women, and more than half are below the poverty line. Bureau of Labor Statistics data reveal that in 1983 women actually earned *less* than two-thirds of their male counterparts' salaries, and black women earned only 84 percent of the white female incomes. In his 1984 State of the Union address, President Reagan claimed dramatic gains for women during the 1983 recovery. A *Washington Post* analysis the next day charitably de-

scribed his claims as "overstated," noting that the Bureau of Labor Statistics reports (on which the president relied) showed that "there was no breakthrough. The new jobs which the president cited included many in sales and office work, where women have always found work" and are paid little.

We must close these gaps so that we do not remain two nations, divided by race and gender. Although no one strategy can overcome the results of centuries of inequity, the use of goals and timetables in hiring and other benefit distribution programs has helped to make modest improvements. Studies in 1983 show, for example, that from 1974 to 1980 minority employment with employers subject to federal affirmative action requirements rose 20 percent, almost twice the increase elsewhere. Employment of women by covered contractors rose 15 percent, but only 2 percent among others. The number of black police officers nationwide rose from 24,000 in 1970 to 43,500 in 1980; that kind of increase in Detroit produced a sharp decline in citizen hostility toward the police and a concomitant increase in police efficiency. There were also large jumps in minority and female employment among firefighters, and sheet metal and electrical workers.

Few other remedies work as well or as quickly. As the New York City Corporation Counsel told the Supreme Court in the *Fullilove* case about the construction industry (before Mayor Edward Koch decided that affirmative action was an "abomination"), "less drastic means of attempting to eradicate and remedy discrimination have been attempted repeatedly and continuously over the past decade and a half. They have all failed."

208

What, then, is the basis for the assault on affirmative action?

Apart from the obvious political expediency and ideological reflex of this administration's unvarying conclusion that the "haves" deserve government help and the "have-nots" don't, President Reagan and his allies present two related arguments: (1) hiring and other distributional decisions should be made solely on the basis of individual merit; (2) racial preferences are always evil and will take us back to *Plessy* vs. *Ferguson* and worse.

Quoting Dr. Martin Luther King Jr., Thurgood Marshall, and Roy Wilkins to support the claim that anything other than total race neutrality is "discriminatory," Assistant Attorney General Reynolds warns that race consciousness will "creat[e] . . . a racial spoils system in America," "stifle the creative spirit," erect artificial barriers, and divide the society. It is, he says, unconstitutional, unlawful, and immoral.

Midge Decter, writing in the *Wall Street Journal* a few years ago, sympathized with black and female beneficiaries of affirmative action programs for the "self-doubts" and loss of "self-regard" that she is sure they suffer, "spiritually speaking," for their "unearned special privileges."

Whenever we take race into account to hand out benefits, declares Linda Chavez, the new executive director of the Reagan Civil Rights Commission, we "discriminate," "destroy[ing] the sense of self."

The legal position was stated by Morris Abram, in explaining why the reshaped Commission hastened to do Reagan's bidding at its very first meeting by withdrawing prior Commission approval of goals and timetables:

I do not need any further study of a principle that comes from the basic bedrock of the Constitution, in which the words say that *every* person in the land shall be entitled to the equal protection of the law. Equal means equal. Equal does not mean you have separate lists of blacks and whites for promotion, any more than you have separate accommodations for blacks and whites for eating. Nothing will ultimately divide a society more than this kind of preference and this kind of reverse discrimination.

In short, any form of race preference is equivalent to racism.

All of this represents a nadir of "Newspeak," all too appropriate for this administration in Orwell's year. For it has not only persistently fought to curtail minority and women's rights in many contexts, but it has used "separate lists" based on color, sex, and ethnic origin whenever politically or otherwise useful.

For example, does anyone believe that blacks like Civil Rights Commission Chairman Clarence Pendleton or Equal Employment Opportunities Commission Chairman Clarence Thomas were picked because of the color of their *eyes*? Or that Linda Chavez Gersten was made the new executive director for reasons having nothing to do with the fact that her maiden and professional surname is Chavez?

Perhaps the most prominent recent example of affirmative action is President Reagan's selection of Sandra Day O'Connor for the Supreme Court. Obviously, she was on a "separate list," because on any unitary list this obscure lower-court state judge, with no federal experience and no national reputation, would never have come to mind as a plausible choice for the highest court. (Incidentally, despite Ms. Decter's, Mr. Reynolds's and Ms. Chavez's concern about the loss of "self-regard" suffered by beneficiaries of such preferences, "spiritually speaking" Justice O'Connor seems to be bearing her loss and spiritual pain quite easily.) And, like so many other beneficiaries of affirmative action given an opportunity that would otherwise be unavailable, she may perform well.

This is not to say that Reagan should not have chosen a woman. The appointment ended decades of shameful discrimination against women lawyers, discrimination still practiced by Reagan where the lower courts are concerned, since he has appointed very few female federal judges apart from Justice O'Connor—of 123 judgeships, Reagan has appointed no women to the courts of appeals and only 10 to the district benches. Of these judgeships, 86 percent went to white males. But the choice of Sandra O'Connor can be explained and justified only by the use of affirmative action and a separate list, not by some notion of neutral "individual merit" on a single list.

But is affirmative action constitutional and legal? Is its legal status, as Mr. Abram claims, so clear by virtue of principles drawn from the "basic bedrock of the Constitution" that no "further study" is necessary?

Yes, but not in the direction that he and this administration want to go. Affirmative action is indisputably constitutional. Not once but many times the Supreme Court has upheld the legality of considering race to remedy the wrongs of prejudice and discrimination. In 1977, for example, in *United Jewish Organizations* vs. *Carey,* the Supreme Court upheld a New York statute that "deliberately increased the nonwhite majorities in certain districts in order to enhance the opportunity for election of nonwhite representatives from those districts," even if it disadvantaged certain white Jewish communities. Three members of the Court including Justice Rehnquist explained that "no racial slur or stigma with respect to whites or any

other race" was involved. In the *Bakke* case, five members of the Court upheld the constitutionality of a state's favorable consideration of race as a factor in university admissions, four members would have sustained a fixed 16 percent quota. In *United Steelworkers of America* vs. *Weber,* a 5:2 majority held that private employers could set up a quota system with separate lists for selecting trainees for a newly created craft program. In *Fullilove* vs. *Klutznick,* six members of the Court led by Chief Justice Burger unequivocally upheld a congressional set-aside of 10 percent for minority contractors on federal public works programs.

All members of the present Court except for Justice O'Connor have passed on affirmative action in one or more of these four cases, and each has upheld it at one time or another. Although the decisions have been based on varying grounds, with many differing opinions, the legal consequence is clear: affirmative action is lawful under both the Constitution and the statutes. To nail the point home, the Court in January 1984 not once but *twice* rejected the Justice Department's effort to get it to reconsider the issue where affirmative action hiring plans are adopted by governmental bodies (the Detroit Police Department and the New York State Corrections system), an issue left open in *Weber,* which had involved a private employer.

The same result obtains on the lower-court levels. Despite the persistent efforts of Reagan's Justice Department, all the courts of appeals have unanimously and repeatedly continued to sustain hiring quotas.

Nor is this anything new. Mr. Reynolds told an audience of prelaw students in January 1984 that the Fourteenth Amendment was intended to bar taking race into account for any purpose at all, and to ensure race neutrality. "That was why we fought the Civil War," he once told the *New York Times.* If so, he knows something that the members of the 1865–66 Congress, who adopted that amendment and fought the war, did not.

Less than a month after Congress approved the Fourteenth Amendment in 1866 the very same Congress enacted eight laws exclusively for the freedman, granting preferential benefits regarding land, education, banking facilities, hospitals, and more. No comparable programs existed or were established for whites. And that Congress knew what it was doing. The racial preferences involved in those programs were vigorously debated with a vocal minority led by President Andrew Johnson, who argued that the preferences wrongly discriminated against whites.

All these governmental actions reflect the obvious point that, as Justice Harry Blackmun has said, "in order to get beyond racism, we must first take account of race. There is no other way." Warren Burger, our very conservative chief justice, had made the point even clearer in the prophetic commentary on this administration's efforts to get the courts to ignore race when trying to remedy the ravages of past discrimination. Striking down in 1971 a North Carolina statute that barred considerations of race in school assignments, the chief justice said:

> The statute exploits an apparently neutral form to control school assignments' plans by directing that they be "color blind"; *that requirement, against the background of segregation, would render illusory the promise of Brown.* Just as the race of students must be considered in determining whether a constitutional violation has occurred so also must race be considered in formulating a rem-

edy . . . *[color blindness] would deprive school authorities of the one tool [race consideration] absolutely essential to fulfillment of their constitutional obligation to eliminate existing dual school systems.* [Emphasis added.] . . .

But what of the morality of affirmative action? Does it amount to discrimination? Is it true, as Brian Weber's lawyer argued before the Supreme Court, that "you can't avoid discrimination by discriminating"? Will racially influenced hiring take us back to *Plessy* vs. *Ferguson,* as Pendleton and Reynolds assert? Were Martin Luther King, Jr., Thurgood Marshall, Roy Wilkins, and other black leaders against it?

Hardly. Indeed, it is hard to contain one's outrage at this perversion of what Dr. King, Justice Marshall, and others have said, at this manipulation of their often sorrow-laden eloquence, in order to deny a handful of jobs, school admissions, and other necessities for a decent life to a few disadvantaged blacks out of the many who still suffer from discrimination and would have few opportunities otherwise.

No one can honestly equate a remedial preference for a disadvantaged (and qualified) minority member with the brutality inflicted on blacks and other minorities by Jim Crow laws and practices. The preference may take away some benefits from some white men, but none of them is being beaten, lynched, denied the right to use a bathroom, a place to sleep or eat, being forced to take the dirtiest jobs or denied any work at all, forced to attend dilapidated and mind-killing schools, subjected to brutally unequal justice, or stigmatized as an inferior being.

Setting aside, after proof of discrimination, a few places a year for qualified minorities out of hundreds and perhaps thousands of employees, as in the Kaiser plant in the *Weber* case, or 16 medical-school places out of 100 as in *Bakke*, or 10 percent of federal public work contracts as in *Fullilove*, or even 50 percent of new hires for a few years as in some employment cases—this has nothing in common with the racism that was inflicted on helpless minorities, and it is a shameful insult to the memory of the tragic victims to lump together the two.

This administration claims that it does favor "affirmative action" of a kind: "employers should seek out and train minorities," Linda Chavez told a *Washington Post* interviewer. Apart from the preference involved in setting aside money for "seeking out" and "training" minorities (would this include preference in training programs like the *Weber* plan, whose legality Mr. Reynolds said was "wrongly decided"?), the proposed remedy is ineffectual—it just doesn't work. As the "old" Civil Rights Commission had reported, "By the end of the 1960s, enforcement officials realized that discernible indicators of progress were needed." Consequently,

"goals and timetables" came into use. . . .

There are indeed problems with affirmative action, but not of the kind or magnitude that Messrs. Reynolds and Abram claim: problems about whether these programs work, whether they impose heavy burdens, how these burdens can be lightened, and the like. They are not the basis for charges that affirmative action is equivalent to racism and for perverting the words of Dr. King and others.

"Equal is equal" proclaims Morris Abram, and that's certainly true. But it is just as true that equal treatment of unequals perpetuates and aggravates inequality. And gross inequality is what we still have today. As William Coleman, secretary of transportation in the Ford administration, put it,

> For black Americans, racial equality is a tradition without a past. Perhaps, one day America will be color-blind. It takes an extraordinary ignorance of actual life in America today to believe that day has come. . . . [For blacks], there is another American "tradition"—one of slavery, segregation, bigotry, and injustice.

POSTSCRIPT

IS AFFIRMATIVE ACTION
REVERSE DISCRIMINATION?

Much of the argument between Loury and Schwartz turns on the question of "color-blindness." To what extent should our laws be "colorblind"? During the 1950s and early 1960s, civil rights leaders were virtually unanimous on this point. "I have a dream," said Martin Luther King, that white and black people "will not be judged by the color of their skin but on the content of their character." This was the consensus view in 1963, but today Schwartz seems to be suggesting that the statement needs to be qualified. In order to *bring about* color-blindness, it may be necessary to become temporarilty color-conscious. But for how long? And is there a danger that this temporary color-consciousness may become a permanent policy?

Robert M. O'Neil, in *Discriminating Against Discrimination* (Indiana, 1975), studied preferential admissions to universities and supported preferential treatment without racial quotas. Those critical of this distinction hold that preferential treatment necessarily implies racial quotas, or at least race-consciousness. Another area that requires officials to focus upon race is that of busing, a policy of which Lina A. Graglia's *Disaster by Decree* (Cornell, 1976) is highly critical. The focus of Allan P. Sindler's *Bakke, DeFunis, and Minority Admissions* (Longman, 1978) is on affirmative action in higher education.

Whatever the Supreme Court says today or in the future, it will not be easy to lay to rest the issue of affirmative action. There are few issues on which opposing sides are more intransigent. It appears as if there is no satisfactory "solution," and, at the moment, no compromise that can satisfy the passionate convictions on both sides. Those who are sick of the whole controversy may be tempted to fall back on the cliche that "time will heal all wounds" and the corresponding hope that the controversy will someday be resolved to everyone's satisfaction. They should consider, however, that the time required may be many decades. Thomas N. Dayment estimates that the differences between black and white earnings will require half a century to decrease substantially (see "Racial Equity or Racial Equality," *Demography*, Vol. 17, 1980, pp. 379-393).

Whatever the Supreme Court says today or in the future, it will not be easy to lay to rest the issue of affirmative action. There are few issues on which opposing sides are more intransigent. It appears as if there is no satisfactory "solution," and, at the moment, no compromise that can satisfy the passionate convictions on both sides. Those who are sick of the whole controversy and wish it would go away may be tempted to fall back on the cliche that "time" will settle it. They should be reminded of Martin Luther King's sober observation that "time is neutral. It can be used either destructively or constructively."

ISSUE 12

SHOULD WORKERS BE PAID ACCORDING TO "COMPARABLE WORTH"?

YES: Ronnie Steinberg and Lois Haignere, from "Now Is the Time for Pay Equity," *Consumer Research* (October 1984)

NO: Geoffrey Cowley, from "Comparable Worth: Another Terrible Idea," *Washington Monthly* (January 1984)

ISSUE SUMMARY

YES: Feminist writers Ronnie Steinberg and Lois Haignere argue that, since certain tasks traditionally assigned to females are low-paying, we must redesign pay scales in general, according to their "comparable worth."
NO: Geoffrey Cowley, a newspaper columnist, claims that it is impossible to calculate "comparable worth," and that the effort to do so will create a confusing bureaucratic tangle and even worse inequities.

Congresswoman Patricia Schroeder of Colorado calls it "the civil rights issue of the 1980s." Clarence Pendleton, chairman of the Civil Rights Commission, calls it "the looniest idea since Looney Tunes." The issue, the idea, is "comparable worth." Its supporters see it as a way to correct a serious problem of equity in America—a large gap between average wages paid men and those paid women. According to a study by the Rand Corporation, women's pay overall is about 64 percent of men's pay.

But the opponents of "comparable worth" charge that it is a misguided concept that could destroy the free market and lead to much worse inequities than exist at present. The concept has been rejected by most members of the federal Civil Rights Commission, by the Equal Employment Opportunity Commission, and by a federal Appeals Court in San Francisco, which overturned an earlier District Court decision based upon it. Yet it is supported by the Democratic Party, the National Organization for Women, some labor unions, and many leading national figures, such as Senator Gary Hart of Colorado.

What is "comparable worth"? It is sometimes also called "pay equity," but that term is somewhat ambiguous. To understand the ambiguity is to understand what "comparable worth" is—and is not.

"Pay equity" in the sense of "equal pay for identical jobs" has been around for a long time. The Equal Pay Act of 1963 requires it, and Section

VII of the Civil Right Act of 1964 bans discrimination in hiring by race or sex. In this sense, there is nothing particularly controversial about "pay equity." Most people agree that it would be unfair for an employer to hire, say, two typists, one male and one female, and then pay the male a higher salary for no other reason than that he is a male.

But the kind of "pay equity" advocated by Congresswoman Schroeder and others is somewhat different than "equal pay for identical jobs." The principle is "equal pay for *comparable* jobs." Suppose the employer were to hire a female typist and a male plumber. Neither has a college education, but both have undergone extensive training. Both perform jobs that have unpleasant features: the plumber's work is dirty but the secretary's is tedious (she must also, unlike the plumber, keep herself neat); the plumber has to lift heavy pipes but the secretary must strain herself to take dictation and get the mail out on time. Both work eight-hour shifts and come home tired. Yet the plumber makes twice the salary of the typist.

The reason for the difference, say the advocates of "comparable worth," is that a typist is a traditional "woman's job" and is thus "undervalued" by employers. The solution should be to break down all jobs into the various attributes that make them up—e.g., the skill and effort involved, the years of preparation required, the working conditions—and give each attribute a quantitative value. The sum total of those values should provide us with a quantitative measure of those jobs' "worth." Employees should then receive pay in accordance with those numbers. If, for example, it were found that typists and plumbers were indeed doing "comparable" work, then the typist's salary should be increased, or the plumber's cut, or a little of both, until they even out.

A number of objections have been made to the concept of "comparable worth." One of the major objections is aimed at the central assumption behind the concept, the assumption that people get paid different amounts for doing different jobs because of sexist "undervaluation" of work that is usually done by women. The critics say that it is the law of supply and demand, not sexism, that leads to such pay differentials. In the case of the plumber versus the typist, the fact is that there is now a big market for plumbers (in part because everyone wants to go to college). Therefore, if you want a plumber, you have to pay. If a business cuts its plumber's salary, its typist will soon discover that the toilet doesn't work. Of course, "equity" can be reached without cutting the plumber's salary but by increasing that of the typist. Then the problem becomes how the business is to absorb the new loss of revenue. The U.S. Chamber of Commerce estimates that "comparable worth" policies could end up costing U.S. business $320 billion.

Still, businesses have had to absorb many revenue losses in this century. It cost them when they had to conform to child labor laws, to accept union demands, to install antipollution devices, and so on. Ours has never been a perfect "market economy." The question is whether, both from an economic and ethical standpoint, "comparable worth" would work in America. Dissolving jobs into quantifiable "units" and making them the basis of equity claims would be a radical departure from the *status quo*. Would it bring us a new day of sexual equality? Or a nightmare of bureaucratism? Would it bring us closer to justice in the workplace? Or would it bring us even more bias and subjectivity? In the following selections, feminist writers Ronnie Steinberg and Lois Haignere debate these questions with columnist Geoffrey Cowley.

YES

Ronnie Steinberg
and Lois Haignere

NOW IS THE TIME FOR PAY EQUITY

In 1870, Miss Virginia Penny advised her readers that "in the different departments of woman's labor, both physical and mental, there exists a want of harmony of labor done and the compensation." Writing on *How Women Make Money: Married or Single*, she offered a comparable-worth comparison: "a gilder [typically male] in a book bindery gets $6 a week . . . which is equal to ten cents an hour. A girl, at most mechanical employments, receives for her sixty hours' labor, $3 a week . . . [or] five cents an hour."

The "want of harmony" remains. Over a century later, in 1981, the National Research Council of the National Academy of Sciences (NRC/NAS) concluded: "Not only do women do different work than men, but the work women do is paid less, and the more an occupation is dominated by women the less it pays."

The policy of equal pay for work of comparable worth has evolved to rectify the wage discrimination that is a by-product of occupational segregation. This policy broadens the earlier policy of equal pay for equal work, which prohibited wage discrimination if women and men were doing the same or essentially similar work. Dubbed "comparable worth" for short, equal pay for comparable worth means that different and dissimilar jobs of equivalent worth to the employer should be paid the same wages.

Conceptually, the goal of equal pay for work of comparable worth, or pay equity, concerns the issue of whether work done primarily by women and minorities is systematically undervalued because the work has been and continues to be done primarily by women and minorities. By systematic undervaluation, we mean that the wages paid to women and men engaged in historically female or minority work are artificially depressed relative to what those wages would be if the jobs had been and were being performed by white males. Operationally, pay equity involves correcting the practice of paying women and minorities less than white men for work that requires equivalent skills, responsibilities, stresses, personal contacts and working conditions.

From, "Now Is the Time for Pay Equity," by Ronnie Steinberg and Lois Haignere, exerpted from *Gender at Work: Perspectives on Occupational Segregation and Comparable Worth*. Copyright © 1984. Reprinted by permission of The Women's Research and Education Institute, Washington, DC.

Comparable-worth studies examine potential wage discrimination in such predominantly female jobs as garment worker, launderer, food service worker, institutional caretaker, retail salesworker and entry-level clerk typist. Minorities are disproportionately represented in these jobs as well.

In 1981, three very different events contributed to the development of comparable-worth policy.

In June 1981, the Supreme Court ruled in *County of Washington v. Gunther* that wage discrimination claims brought under Title VII are not restricted to claims for equal pay for substantially equal work. One month later, the public employees of San Jose, California, struck to obtain contract language accepting the principle of comparable worth and providing approximately $1.5 million to begin adjusting wages in underpaid, female-dominated jobs. Finally, the NRC/NAS issued *Women, Work and Wages: Equal Pay for Jobs of Equal Value*, which concluded:

> on the basis of a review of the evidence, our judgment is that there is substantial discrimination in pay, [and] . . . in our judgment job evaluation plans provide measures of job worth that, under certain circumstances, may be used to discover and reduce wage discrimination.

And further that:

> women are systematically underpaid . . . [and]the strategy of "comparable worth" . . . merits consideration as an alternative policy of intervention in the pay-setting process.

The concentration of women and minorities in jobs not commonly done by white men can contribute to the wage gap in one of two ways. First, women and minorities may be systematically channeled into jobs that require less skill, ef-fort and responsibility than jobs filled by white males. One study completed by NRC/NAS staff found that job content differences such as degree of complexity and supervisory duties did explain some small percentage of the difference in earnings. Affirmative action policies are in place to eliminate this source of the wage gap through incentives and sanctions that increase the mobility of women and minorities into higher-paying jobs.

Second, women and minorities may be segregated into jobs that require the equivalent amount of skill, effort and responsibility as white male jobs, but are paid less for that equivalent work. Put somewhat differently, their jobs are systematically undervalued *because* the work is performed predominantly by women and minorities. This type of wage discrimination is the focus of comparable worth. Comparable worth, then, is only concerned with eliminating those differences in wage rates that cannot be accounted for by productivity-related job content characteristics.

The technique of job evaluation has been used to assess whether or not pay equity exists in a firm. But in order to use this approach for comparable worth, it is necessary to use one relatively bias-free evaluation system to classify all jobs. A job evaluation system that is free of bias must:

• *describe job content* (i.e., behaviors, tasks, functions) accurately, comprehensively and consistently; and
• *assign to each specific content factor a standard of worth* that can be systematically applied without bias across all jobs in the specified work force.

The first of these two processes is called *job content analysis* and the second is called *job evaluation.*

ACCURATE DESCRIPTIONS

The general purpose of job content analysis is to gather thorough and accurate descriptions of the range of tasks, behaviors or functions associated with a job. Accurate job descriptions are not only a function of asking the "right" questions about job content in a well-designed questionnaire, however. Equally important are (1) selecting a sample of job titles representative of the range of work performed in the work organization, (2) selecting a large enough sample of incumbents within a job title to ensure that the information collected is representative of the range and variety of the work actually performed in the job and (3) carrying out some procedure for averaging across specific positions within a job title.

In order to obtain job content information, such broad job characteristics as skill, effort, responsibility and working conditions may be examined. Alternatively, the characteristics of a job may be defined more specifically to include such items as job-related experience, formal training time required, frequency of review of work, total number of personnel an employee is responsible for, impact on and responsibility for budget, physical stress, time spent working under deadlines, time spent in processing information and so on. Information typically is gathered through questionnaires (completed by job incumbents, supervisors, job analysts or some combination of these) and/or observation by a job analyst of a group of employees performing their jobs.

The purpose of job evaluation is to specify standards of worth by applying a single set of job-content criteria to *all* job titles in a work organization. Typically, jobs are assigned points in terms of the weighting of these criteria. Most important for the discussion here is that, based on the point value, wages are established for a job in relation to the wages paid for all jobs in that organization.

Comparable-worth studies have been and are being carried out across the country, primarily in the public sector. Completed studies consistently report that female-dominated job titles receive between five and 20 percent lower pay than male jobs with the same number of factor points.

In 1974, Washington State commissioned a comparable-worth study, the results of which showed that state employees in traditionally female jobs received about 20 percent less on average than state employees in traditionally male jobs of comparable value. In 1975, an update of this study extended it to 85 more jobs (additional updates were done in 1979 and 1980).

A Connecticut study completed in February 1980 found that, for jobs of equivalent worth, individuals in "women's" jobs earn from 81 to 92 percent of the salary of individuals in "men's" jobs. In Idaho, in 1975, the implementation of a revised classification plan, which was formulated without an explicit concern with comparable worth, resulted in larger salary increases for predominantly female classifications than for traditionally male classifications. A 1981 Michigan Department of Labor study found that the "actual maximum pay rates for female-dominated jobs were lower than would be predicted."

Those attempting to discredit comparable-worth reforms frequently level two criticisms at job evaluation techniques. The first is that comparing different jobs is like comparing apples and oranges. The second is that job evaluation techniques are inadequate for estimating wages because they seemingly do not take market factors and supply and demand into account.

We note that, in fact, apples and oranges can and have been compared by any number of empirical standards. For example, they can be systematically assessed in terms of number of calories, vitamin content or mineral content. A nutritionist could then establish equivalencies among fruits for a person needing to follow a special diet.

Similarly, jobs that are not identical are comprised of tasks and characteristics that can be empirically described. Jobs may then be ranked from high to low based on their characteristics, and equivalences established according to a consistently applied set of standards. This can be translated into a wage rate. In fact, this is just what employers have been doing for decades in order to justify their existing wage structures. The *Dictionary of Occupational Titles*, published by the U.S. Department of Labor, is a ranking of jobs from most important and valuable to least important and valuable according to three general categories. This ranking has been offered to and used by thousands of firms as an aid to setting salaries.

The second general criticism of the use of job evaluation for assessment of comparable worth is it fails to pay attention to the market, that is, to supply and demand as the true basis by which wages are set. This criticism reveals a serious misunderstanding of how job evaluation is done.

The evaluations do incorporate market considerations in the weighting of job content factors. Resulting wages are based on the productive contribution of jobs to the firm. The point factors assigned to jobs in *a priori* approaches have been developed by management consultants on the basis of what the market pays for a given job content characteristic. These general point

values are further grounded in the particular labor market by taking a set of so-called benchmark jobs with the same number of points and averaging across the specific wages paid for each job in other geographically proximate firms.

Moreover, while there is considerable overlap in wage rates across firms, the overall wage structure within a firm will differ from that of other firms, depending on such market factors as types of jobs, unionization and characteristics of the industry. Comparable-worth studies must take these firm-based market differences into account in developing a discrimination-free wage structure. For these reasons, the standards used in determining worth must be derived partly from market wages and, perhaps more important, must be firm-based.

A related concern of comparable-worth critics is that a job evaluation-based wage structure will wreak havoc on the economic system. This is surprising, given that well over two-thirds of all employees work in firms where there now exists some form of job evaluation underlying the wage structure.

Interference with the free market is very common in our society. Sometimes we interfere for economic reasons to protect employers. We bail out Lockheed or protect the auto industry from the import of Japanese cars. Sometimes we interfere to protect employees, as with child labor and other wage and hour laws. We also have laws that prohibit paying women, blacks and other protected classes less than white males just because they will accept lower wages.

As proponents of comparable worth build up a body of scientific evidence, establish legal precedents and introduce pay equity adjustments into contracts, they negate the arguments of critics of comparable worth. Criticisms are best addressed when the policy is effectively implemented and without deleterious consequences. Moreover, as more firms adopt comparable worth, the resultant salary adjustments will permeate the wage structure of local markets. Through the process of pressure, innovation, education, imitation and adjustment, the wages paid for work done primarily by women will catch up with the other profound changes in women's place in the labor market.

These concrete actions transform a highly charged and controversial political demand into what no doubt eventually will become a routine and institutionalized feature of equal employment.

NO

Geoffrey Cowley

COMPARABLE WORTH: ANOTHER TERRIBLE IDEA

[In November of 1983,] a federal judge in Tacoma, Washington, made national news by ruling that the state had discriminated against women. Sex discrimination lawsuits are hardly new to American life, but the issue in Washington was not whether the state was willing to hire women, or whether it offered equal pay for equal work. Rather, it was whether the 15,000 state workers holding traditionally female jobs—nurses and secretaries, for example—should be paid the same as those holding "comparable," male-dominated jobs in different trades, like plumbing or carpentry. In deciding against the state of Washington, Judge Jack Tanner declared that Title VII of the 1964 Civil Rights Act "was designed to bar not only overt employment discrimination, but also practices that are fair in form but discriminatory in operation," among which he counted the state's failure to grant equal pay for work of comparable worth. Tanner found the state guilty of "pervasive and intentional" discrimination, and promptly awarded the plaintiffs a projected $1 billion in back pay and wages.*

No one missed the opportunity to hail the ruling as a major turning point in the battle against sexism. "The state of Washington was the defendant in this case," said a local spokesman for the American Federation of State, County, and Municipal Employees, the union that brought the suit, "but all of society was on trial. This ruling gives us great cause for hope, because it will provide a model for other suits across the country." Dan Evans, the Republican ex-governor recently elected to fill Henry Jackson's Senate seat, proposed that Congress create a commission to "study how the federal government . . . can root out gender bias" within its own workforce. And Gary Hart, who along with Walter Mondale, John Glenn, and Alan Cranston has jumped on the comparable worth bandwagon, was so overcome with enthusiasm that he hopped a plane to Seattle to hold a press conference where he called Tanner's decision "a national example of how women's organizations and unions can use existing laws to destroy wage discrimination."

Support for the notion of comparable worth has come to be expected of anyone who claims to care about the equality of women in our society. Proponents of the doctrine rightly argue that "equal pay for equal work" is only a partial solution to the problem women face in the workforce. The average working woman earns only 62 cents for every dollar a man earns. Women's groups correctly point out that the real problem isn't that female professionals are paid less than their male counterparts; if half of all lawyers were women who received the same salaries as their male colleagues, a wide income gap

*This decision was overturned by a federal Appeals Court in September of 1985—Eds.

From, "Comparable Worth: Another Terrible Idea," by Geoffrey Cowley, *The Washington Monthly*, January 1984. Copyright © 1984. Reprinted by permission of the Washington Monthly Co., Inc.

would still exist. The real problem they say, is that secretaries and other women who toil in traditionally "female occupations" are making considerably less than men who possess the same, or lower, levels of skill, intelligence, and responsibility.

The egalitarian appeal of the comparable worth principle is obvious: why *shouldn't* a female secretary with an M.A. in English literature and responsibility for managing the office's accounts get paid the same as a Teamsters truck driver who hauls frozen chickens? But when it comes to larger problems of inequality faced by both women and society at large, comparable worth is a principle that will ultimately prove not merely inadequate, but destructive. Its greatest asset is that it affords politicians a way to demonstrate their solidarity in the battle for sexual equality, while leaving all the necessary little details that the "comparable worth" standard implies—like deciding who is worth what, and exactly how one goes about comparing the job of a deputy assistant to the administrator to that of a cleaning woman—to somebody else. And it isn't hard to figure out who that "someone else" is going to be. When Tanner's decision was handed down, lawyers and consultants everywhere no doubt experienced something akin to the thrill felt by Cortez when he first gazed upon the shimmering Aztec temples of Tenochtitlan.

TAKE A NUMBER, PLEASE

The state of Washington first began to toy with the idea of comparable worth back in 1973, when then-Governor Dan Evans hired the Seattle consulting firm of Norman D. Willis & Associates to figure out whether the state was paying women as much as it was paying men at "a comparable level" of skill and responsibility.

The study found a 20 percent wage gap. For example, laundry workers, who were mostly women, were estimated to be worth the same as low-level truck drivers, who were mostly men, but the laundry workers were making 41 percent less than the truck drivers.

Perhaps you're wondering how to figure out how much a laundry worker is worth. After all, such questions have perplexed philosophers and theologians for centuries. (They have even been known to give personal-injury lawyers some difficulty.) The answer is to develop "point-factor job evaluation systems" to do the job for you.

Each system works on a slightly different conception of "worth," of course, but all share a cheerfully mathematical view of qualities that you would think would be hard to quantify. Let's take a closer look at the Willis scale, which Judge Tanner relied on in making his decision. It assumes that the worth of any job, from circus clown to key-punch operator, varies in relation to the "knowledge and skills," "mental demands," "accountability," and "working conditions" it entails. Each of these components is further broken down into two or three subcomponents, and points are awarded on the basis of each one. Under "accountability," for instance, you can win points for your "freedom to take action" as well as for the nature and size of your "impact." Admittedly, the guidelines the instruction manual for the system offers are somewhat informal; for example, on "impact," the consultants instruct, "The simplest way to look at Size is to say the job most clearly impacts on something BIG, or on something LITTLE, or on something IN-BETWEEN."

The "knowledge and skills" component breaks down into "managerial," "interpersonal," and "technical" dimensions, each of which carries its own rating. To top out on the "managerial" scale, you have to manage "subfunctions that have significantly different natures, or where the end results of the subordinate subfunctions tend to be conflicting or competitive with each other and require special harmonizing." Got that? In English, "you have to know how to do different things and how to play your assistants against one another." There are two kinds of "mental demands"— "judgment" and "problem solving"—and three kinds of "working conditions"—"uncomfortable," strenuous," and "hazardous."

To calculate all these factors, Willis assembled a group of people from within the state civil service. These civil servants reviewed job descriptions, interviewed their fellow workers and then, after much solemn mutual consultation, assigned each job a score. Thus a clerk-typist became a "152," or, to be more precise, a "C1N 106 C2-f 23 C1N 23 L1A 0." Broken down, this meant a clerk-typist scored 106 on "knowledge and skills," 23 on "mental demands," 23 on "accountability," and 0 on "working conditions." (A score of 0 on "working conditions" is the Willis method's understated way of saying either that the employee has nothing to complain about or that he or she is working in embarrassingly plush surroundings. Because there are no negative points on the Willis scale, access to excessive perks does not lower anybody's score.) Broken down still further, the clerk-typist rating on "knowledge and skills" is level C on a "technical" scale from A to G, level 1 on "managerial skills" scale of one to three, and level N on an "interpersonal skills" scale that is too complicated to explain without the aid of an astrolabe and a mood ring.

With the help of Willis's team of metaphysicians, Washington state calculated the worth of every civil service job

category on the payroll. These were unveiled in 1974, revealing the awkward 20 percent gap between what women were earning and what their male "comparability" counterparts were earning. True to a long-standing tradition of how to respond to consultants bearing bad tidings, Evans ordered a second, more detailed Willis study. This study, published in 1976, estimated that the wage gap between "comparable" men and women could be closed by paying the women $38 million more a year (What? Lower the wages for the men instead, you say? You must be kidding.) The $38 million gap struck the legislature as a problem warranting still further study. By July 1982 AFSCME had run out of patience, and filed suit.

The decision that resulted will be a serious blow to the finances of Washington state. The state will now have to cough up not $38 million, as the second Willis study showed, but an estimated $1 billion over the next 28 months. When Winn Newman, the lawyer who argued AFSCME's case, was asked about this he answered, "Congress didn't put a price tag on ending discrimination when it passed the Civil Rights Act. It didn't say to employers, 'Stop underpaying women and minorities when you think it's convenient.' The only ones saying we can't *afford* to stop discrimination are bigots—bigots and people with an interest in perpetuating it."

Surprisingly, the decision was disowned by none other than Norman Willis, who, despite the hubris of his worth-measuring enterprise, recoils at the thought that his or anybody else's scorecard should become law. Even some of those who support the decision seem hard-pressed to find a sound legal basis for Tanner's reasoning. When I asked Gary Hart about this, for example, he said, "I don't think it's appropriate for legislators to run around commenting on judicial rulings," even though that's exactly what he had come to Seattle to do.

MOVE OVER, MAX PLANCK

Hart and Newman have their hearts in the right place; we *do* want to pay people what they deserve, rather than what society's petty prejudices dictate. But if the courts are going to define "discrimination" so broadly that it applies to people who do different things and earn different salaries, they can't just go around measuring it on any scale they like—there will have to be state and federal laws saying there shall always be, say, three kinds of occupational adversity, as opposed to two or 20, and just two kinds of mental demands. Otherwise, employers will start defining worth any way they please. Truck drivers could end up being paid entirely on the basis of their familiarity with *Finnegans Wake*.

Getting the nation to unite behind the Willis or the Hay or the Jones system of worth detection will be tricky, for we all have direct, and conflicting, interests in how the scale is calibrated. A ditchdigger could argue that the Willis system favors mental over physical exertion, a typist that it doesn't adequately register boredom. And anyone could claim, rightfully, that it gives more weight to meaningless job requirements—for instance, why should a probation officer need a master's degree—than it does to individual initiative and resourcefulness.

But even if we agree on a scale, we'll have to accept the possibility that it will produce widely different results when applied in different environments. Unless we take the next step, which is to treat the whole economy as a single firm and determine the proper salary for every position in it, we'll have no way of knowing that secretaries are keeping up with each other, let alone staying ahead of the nation's janitors.

Imagine the nightmarish society that might result. A waitress down at Uncle Bob's House of Ribs might sue her boss because her sister-in-law was getting twice as much (and better tips) waiting tables at the diner across the street. Executives would knock back martinis after coming home on the five-forty-eight and torment themselves about their prospects for ever making F1Y 380 E4-k 122 E1D 160 L1A 0. Children would have new ways to taunt one another in the sandbox:

"My daddy's a 634!"

"Oh yeah? Well, *my* daddy's a 723, and he says if he can harmonize subordinate subfunctions three more times this week we can go to Bermuda!"

AFSCME isn't proposing anything as ambitious as a planned economy, of course; it is simply claiming that individual employers have an obligation to rise above the sexism inherent in the marketplace. Once employers have done away with the wage gap between men's and women's professions, a spokesman for the union says, the problem will have been solved and everything will return to normal.

But will it? Many civil servants in Washington state who hold jobs as "worthy" as other, higher paying jobs are men. But unless they can prove that they're being discriminated against for performing "women's work"—legally defined as any job where women comprise more than 70 percent of the workforce—they won't get the raise that the nurses and the secretaries will get. It isn't hard to imagine the next step: a lawsuit by the men, arguing that they deserve "comparable worth" raises, too.

Then there are the inevitable adjustments that will have to be made to keep the worth scale up-to-date. Maintaining a standard as vague as "worth" could make quantum mechanics look simple. It's fairly easy for the Equal Employment Opportunity Commission to spot a disparity in the wages an employer pays men and women to perform "equal work"; all it takes is a glance at the payroll. But checking out a comparable-worth complaint would be quite another matter. In order to determine whether a Lockheed audit-machine operator II was legally entitled to the same pay as a senior stem-dryer maintainer, the EEOC would have to haul in a committee to perform a company-wide worth analysis.

The courts, too, would have to evaluate the working of an entire industry every time they heard a discrimination suit. Major civil rights battles would turn on such questions as whether error-free typing is a greater corporate asset than leak-free plumbing, or whether sitting at a VDT places greater strain on Betty's eyes than pipefitting places on Jack's back. And does Doris, the floor manager at Sears, "most clearly impact on something "IN-BE-TWEEN" as opposed to "something LITTLE"?

If the administrative and judicial aspects of comparable worth are messy, the economics could be even messier. In the marketplace, people are paid in part according to the availability of labor. At Weyerhaeuser, for example, where a Willis comparable worth survey rated the job of personnel manager at 916 and that of pulp mill superintendent at 760, pulp mill superintendents make more money than personnel managers—because good ones are harder to find. Under a comparable worth standard, Weyerhaeuser could end up with two choices: pay the pulp mill su-

perintendents less, thereby making good ones even harder to find, or give the deskbound manager a big raise.

Comparable worth also creates problems for labor-management relations. Subjected to the worth standard, many existing collective-bargaining agreements could be shown to have disparate impacts on men and women in different jobs. And if the unions that negotiated those agreements didn't move fast enough to pin the blame on the employers, as AFSCME did in its claim against Washington state, they could face massive lawsuits from their own members. (In fact, the AFSCME local that brought the suit against Washington pays its own employees not on the basis of comparable worth but by the same allegedly sexist pay scales used by the state.)

WORTHIER THAN THOU

Advocates of the worth standard insist that this is all beside the point; as Newman says, you can't put a price tag on discrimination. But if anyone's putting a price tag on justice, it's the worth proponents themselves. Just take a look at the Willis scale. A beginning licensed practical nurse scores 158 comparable worth points, while an "Information Specialist III"—an experienced PR flack—scores 324. Or look at a janitor, who scores 101, while an "Advisory Sanitarian II"—someone who doesn't actually clean anything himself, but makes sure local hospitals and nursing homes do—scores 395. Why on earth should our society value people who issue press releases or fill out reports all day long more than people who save lives and do the dirty work?

This is the most pernicious aspect of comparable worth—it would do nothing to endanger the larger inefficiencies and inequalities that are built into the present hierarchy. In fact, it would solidify them by giving them the force of law. Whereas today we overpay lawyers regardless of their need, skill, and general value to society, because we are irrationally adversarial, credential-loving snobs who hope someday to behave more sensibly, in a world governed by comparable worth we would do so because it is the law. The purpose of comparable worth is not to balance the earnings of lawyers and secretaries who make equal contributions to the common good, but to make fine distinctions about the "worth" of jobs already accorded roughly the same status within society.

The comparable worth scale reflects the same credentialism that corrupts the society it is designed to mirror. Why is an advisory sanitarian any worthier than a janitor? Because it is suggested that advisory sanitarians have "an M.A. in public health, environmental health, or a closely allied field," and you must be registered as a sanitarian—an affiliation whose only advantage might be that its monthly four-color newsletter, *Sanitarians Today*, advertises cheap charters to Luxembourg. AFSCME doesn't have any problem with unequal arrangements that result from society's obsession with credentialism; to the contrary, one official of the union was quoted a couple of years ago as complaining, "When a person whose job requires a college education makes less than what is basically a common laborer, there's something wrong." Advocates of comparable worth don't want to achieve equality or a system of rewards based on true merit. They want a merit-blind system of inequality.

Willis insists that his scale doesn't pretend to measure a person's contribution to the social good. Instead, it is a "bias-free instrument." But what does this bias-free instrument measure? It measures the biases of society. That's the problem. When a lawyer calls in his secretary to ask her to type up a brief on comparable worth, he isn't demonstrating to her his willingness to flatten the income curve; he's demonstrating to her the inevitability of her inferior status. Even if she's the best secretary in the world, and he the worst lawyer, comparable worth dictates that the lawyer will always be worth more than the secretary.

There are far better ways to fight sexual discrimination in the workplace. Where sexism obviously exists in hiring decisions, an antidiscrimination lawsuit is just one way to apply pressure. Another is to combat the deep-seated cultural prejudices that funnel women into jobs like that of secretary and nurse to begin with. And a final remedy is to fight the rigid rules that exist to keep women—and men—who occupy the lower status rungs in their place. Nurses and midwives, for instance, should have more freedom to perform essential medical services. And legal secretaries ought to have the authority to prepare wills and other documents that they now draw up for their bosses.

Obviously, the problem of sexual discrimination runs deep in our society. At least for a while, there will still be bosses who look upon their underpaid—and more intelligent—secretaries with condescension and perhaps lust. But comparable worth, appealing as the idea might sound, won't help end that inequality. Instead, it will enshrine it, while fine-tuning lesser inequalities through the use of questionably "scientific" means to measure what is ultimately unmeasurable.

POSTSCRIPT

SHOULD WORKERS BE PAID ACCORDING TO "COMPARABLE WORTH"?

In response to the oft-repeated objection that "comparable worth" seeks to compare "apples and oranges," Steinberg and Haignere contend that apples and oranges *can* be compared. They can be "systematically assessed in terms of the number of calories, vitamin content or mineral content." But is it the sum of these that really accounts for the essence of "appleness" and "orangeness"? The question would have intrigued the metaphysicians of the Middle Ages, but it also has practical consequences. If a job is more than the sum of its individual "characteristics," then it is hard to see how it can be compared to any other job.

Elaine Johansen's *Comparable Worth: The Myth and the Movement* (Westview, 1984) traces the historical roots of the "comparable worth" issue, particularly in its application to public-sector employment. Carol A. Whitehurst's *Women in America: The Oppressed Majority* (Goodyear, 1977) has a chapter on "Women in the Economy" which lays the groundwork for "comparable worth" claims by arguing that our "cultural assumptions" about women's abilities have helped to ghettoize the workplace. Phyllis Schlafly, on the other hand, thinks that advancement of working women is already ensured by laws, regulations, court decisions, and an improved atmosphere in the business world. See her *The Power of Positive Woman* (Arlington House, 1977).

Even though a federal Appeals Court has rejected a major suit based on the principle of "comparable worth," the principle is far from being defeated, at least in the area of government employment. The governor of the state of Washington has said that his state would bargain with its employees to establish "a program of pay equity." A number of other states, including New York, Connecticut, and Minnesota, have agreed to set up similar programs. If they make good on their promises, we'll soon have, in effect, a series of pilot studies of "comparable worth." Then, perhaps, we can better see who is right and who is wrong in this controversy.

ISSUE 13

DOES OUR WELFARE SYSTEM HURT THE POOR?

YES: Charles Murray, from *Losing Ground: American Social Policy, 1950-1980* (New York, 1984)

NO: Sar A. Levitan, from "The Evolving Welfare System," *Society,* January-February 1986

ISSUE SUMMARY

YES: Political scientist Charles Murray maintains that the best welfare policy, at least for able-bodied working-age people, is no welfare support by the government.
NO: Economics professor Sar A. Levitan believes that the welfare system has been a rational, necessary and workable instrument for dealing with poverty.

Programs of mass assistance began in the Great Depression days of the New Deal. For fifty years they grew in number and scope. By the 1970s, the welfare state seemed here to stay.

Yet the election of Ronald Reagan demonstrated at least an ambivalence on the part of millions of Americans who were disappointed that ever-larger expenditures of welfare funds appeared to have little effect in reducing welfare rolls. President Reagan succeeded in securing sharp cuts in the rate growth of such welfare programs as food stamps and Aid to Families of Dependent Children. Reagan insisted on a distinction between excessive welfare programs and support for the "truly needy." He promised to maintain a "safety net" to ensure that those who genuinely required governmental assistance would be able to secure it.

Numerous instances were cited by his critics of cases where needy families were deprived of essential resources. By rigorously enforcing laws enacted before he came into office, Reagan sought to reduce the rolls of those receiving disability benefits. Appeals earned reinstatement for many who had been cut from the rolls, and Congress acted in late 1984 to make it more difficult for the government to remove recipients.

Critics of the welfare state cited the growth of public assistance programs even in good times. The vast increase in single-parent families headed by a woman, the uncounted number of illegal and illiterate immigrants, the disturbing proportion of unschooled and unemployed teenagers, and the greater likelihood of all of these conditions among American blacks, all suggested that welfare did not work, that is, it did not succeed in creating work or encouraging unemployed people to seek work.

Relying less upon welfare and more upon the stimulation of business activity, President Reagan argued that increasing prosperity would result in more job opportunities for the poor: "A rising tide will lift all boats." The problem, as has been pointed out, is that a rising tide will not raise shipwrecks at the bottom of the sea. People too long unemployed become unemployable, lacking not only the skills but the wills.

Can poverty be eradicated, or at least sharply reduced? Or must the poor always be with us? When America enjoyed a revival of business beginning in 1983, unemployment fell and many Americans found themselves better off, but the proportion below the poverty level remained high.

Political scientist Charles Murray argues that the welfare program has produced the unintended consequences of encouraging unemployment and increasing poverty. Murray's solution is radical, but his analysis raises questions to which defenders of the welfare system must respond. In contrast, economist Sar Levitan concedes that poverty cannot be eradicated by a welfare system, but must be accompanied by a sustained commitment of social resources. At the same time, he insists, the system works well in meeting the basic needs of the destitute, disabled and aged.

YES
Charles Murray

THE WELFARE SYSTEM
DOESN'T WORK

. . . If social policy may be construed, as I suggest . . . , as transfers from the haves to the have-nots, the proper first question is, "What is the justification for any transfers at all?" Why should one person give *anything* to a stranger whose only claim to his help is a common citizenship?

Suppose that I am not opposed to the notion of government transfers, but neither do I think that equality of outcome is always a good in itself. I attach considerable value to the principle that people get what they deserve. In other words, "I" am a fairly typical citizen with a middle-of-the-road, pragmatic political philosophy.

I am asked to consider the case of a man who has worked steadily for many years and, in his fifties, is thrown out of his job because the factory closes. Why should I transfer money to him—provide him with unemployment checks and, perhaps, permanent welfare support? The answer is not difficult. I may rationalize it any number of ways, but at bottom I consent to transfer money to him because I want to. The worker has plugged along as best he could, contributed his bit to the community, and now faces personal disaster. He is one of my fellows in a very meaningful way—"There but for the grace of God . . ."—and I am happy to see a portion of my income used to help him out. (I would not be happy to see so much of my income transferred that I am unable to meet my obligations to myself and my family, however.)

A second man, healthy and in the prime of life, refuses to work. I offer him a job, and he still refuses to work. I am called upon to answer the question again: Why should I transfer money to him? Why should I not let him starve, considering it a form of suicide?

It is a question to ponder without escape hatches. I may not assume that the man can be made to change his ways with the right therapeutic intervention. I may not assume that he has some mental or environmental handicap that relieves him of responsibility. He is a man of ordinary capacities who wishes to live off my work rather than work for himself. Why should I consent?

Suppose that I decide not to let him starve in the streets, for reasons having to do with the sanctity of life (I would prevent a suicide as well). The decision does not take me very far in setting up an ideal policy. At once, I run into choices when I compare his situation (we will call him the drone) with that of the laid-off worker.

Suppose that I have only enough resources either (a) to keep both alive at a bare subsistence level or (b) to support the laid-off worker at a decent standard of living and the drone at a near-starvation level. What would be the just policy? Would it be right, would it be fair, to make the worker live more miserably so that I might be more generous to the drone?

We may put the question more provocatively: Suppose that scarce resources were not a problem—that we could afford to support both at a decent standard of living. Should we do so? Is it morally appropriate to give the same level of support to the two men? Would it be right to offer the same respect to the two men? The same discretionary choice in how to use the help that was provided?

These are not rhetorical questions nor are they questions about expedient policy. They ask about the justice and humanity of the alternatives. I submit that it is not humane to the laid-off worker to treat him the same as the drone. It is not just to accord the drone the respect that the laid-off worker has earned.

The point is that, in principle, most of us provide some kinds of assistance gladly, for intuitively obvious reasons. We provide other kinds of assistance for reasons that, when it comes down to it, are extremely hard to defend on either moral or practical grounds. An ethically ideal social policy—an *intuitively* satisfying one—would discriminate among recipients. It would attach a pat on the back to some

transfers and give others begrudgingly.

We have yet to tackle the question of whether the point has anything to do with recipients in the workaday world. Who is to say that the drone has no justification for refusing to work (he was trained as a cook and we offer him a job sweeping floors)? Who is to say whether the laid-off worker is blameless for the loss of his job (his sloppy workmanship contributed to the factory's loss of business to the Japanese)? Who is to say that the income of the taxpaying donor is commensurate with his value to society—that he"deserves" his income any more than the drone deserves the gift of a part of it? But such questions define the operational barriers to establishing a social policy that discriminates among recipients according to their deserts. They do not touch on the legitimacy of the principle.

ROBBING PETER TO PAY PAUL: TRANSFERS FROM POOR TO POOR

When we think of transfers, we usually think in terms of economic transfers from richer to poorer. In reality, social policy can obligate one citizen to turn over a variety of "goods" as a donation on behalf of some other person; access to parking spaces reserved for the handicapped is a simple example.

Sometimes these noneconomic transfers, like the economic ones, are arranged so that the better-off give up something to the worse-off, and the argument about whether the transfer is appropriate follows the lines of the issues I have just raised. But in a surprising number of instances the transfers are mandated by the better-off, while the price must be paid by donors who are just as poor as the recipient.

Now suppose that the same hypothetical "I" considers the case of two students in an inner-city high school. Both come from poor families. Both have suffered equal deprivations and social injustices. They have the same intelligence and human potential. For whatever reasons—let us assume pure accident—the two students behave differently in school. One student (the good student) studies hard and pays attention in class. The other student (the mischievous student) does not study and instead creates disturbances, albeit good-natured disturbances, in the classroom.

I observe a situation in which the teacher expels the mischievous student from the classroom more or less at will. The result is that he becomes further alienated from school, drops out, and eventually ends up on welfare or worse. I know that the cause of this sequence of events (his behavior in class) was no worse than the behavior of millions of middle-class students who suffer nothing like the same penalty. They too are kicked out of class when they act up, but for a variety of reasons they stay in school and eventually do well. Further yet, I know that the behavior of the teacher toward the student is biased and unfairly harsh because the student is an inner-city black and the teacher is a suburban white who neither understands nor sympathizes with such students.

On all counts, then, I observe that the mischievous student expelled from the classroom is a victim who deserves a system that does not unfairly penalize him. I therefore protect him against the bias and arbitrariness of the teacher. The teacher cannot expel the student from class unless the student's behavior meets certain criteria far beyond the ordinary talking and laughing out of turn that used to get him in trouble.

The result, let us say, is that the student continues to act as before, but remains in the classroom. Other students also respond to the reality of the greater latitude they now have. The amount of teaching is reduced, and so is the ability of students to concentrate on their work even if they want to.

I know, however, that some benefits are obtained. The mischievous student who formerly dropped out of school does not. He obtains his diploma, and with it some advantages in the form of greater education (he learned something, although not much, while he stayed in school) and a credential to use when applying for a job.

This benefit has been obtained at a price. The price is not money—let us say it costs no more to run the school under the new policy than under the old. No transfers have been exacted from the white middle class. The transfer instead is wholly from the good student to the mischievous one. For I find that the quality of education obtained by the good student deteriorated badly, both because the teacher had less time and energy for teaching and because the classroom environment was no longer suitable for studying. One poor and disadvantaged student has been compelled (he had no choice in the matter) to give up part of his education so that the other student could stay in the classroom.

What is my rationale for enforcing this transfer? In what sense did the good student have an excess of educational opportunity that he could legitimately be asked to sacrifice? . . .

Such transfers from poor to poor are at the heart of the inequities of social policy. Saying that we meant well does not quite cover our transgressions. Even during the period of the most active reform we could not help being aware, if only at the back of our minds, of certain moral problems. When poor delinquents arrested for felonies were left on probation, as the elite wisdom prescribed they should be, the persons put most at risk were poor people who lived in their neighborhoods. They, not the elite, gave up the greater part of the good called "safety" so that the disadvantaged delinquent youth should not experience the injustice of punishment. When job-training programs were set up to function at the level of the least competent, it was the most competent trainees who had to sacrifice their opportunities to reach potentials. When social policy reinforced the ethic that certain jobs are too demeaning to ask people to do, it was those who preferred such jobs to welfare whose basis for self-respect was stripped from them. . . .

I begin with the proposition that it is within our resources to do enormous good for some people quickly. We have available to us a program that would convert a large proportion of the younger generation of hardcore unemployed into steady workers making a living wage. The same program would drastically reduce births to single teenage girls. It would reverse the trendline in the breakup of poor families. It would measurably increase the upward socioeconomic mobility of poor families. These improvements would affect some millions of persons.

All these are results that have eluded the efforts of the social programs installed since 1965, yet, from everything we know, there is no real question about whether they would occur under the program I propose. A wide variety of persuasive evidence from our own culture and around the world, from experimental data and longitudinal studies, from theory and practice, suggests that the program would achieve such results.

The proposed program . . . consists of scrapping the entire federal welfare and income-support structure of working-aged persons, including AFDC, Medicaid, Food Stamps, Unemployment Insurance, Worker's Compensation, subsidized housing, disability insurance, and the rest. It would leave the working-aged person with no recourse whatsoever except the job market, family members, friends, and public or private locally funded services. It is the Alexandrian solution: cut the knot, for there is no way to untie it.

It is difficult to examine such a proposal dispassionately. Those who dislike paying for welfare are for it without thinking. Others reflexively imagine bread lines and people starving in the streets. But as a means of gaining fresh perspective on the problem of effective reform, let us consider what this hypothetical society might look like.

A large majority of the population is unaffected. A surprising number of the huge American middle and working classes go from birth to grave without using any social welfare benefits until they receive their first Social Security check. Another portion of the population is technically affected but the change in income is so small or so sporadic that it makes no difference in quality of life. A third group comprises persons who have to make new arrangements and behave in different ways. Sons and daughters who fail to find work continue to live with their parents or relatives or friends. Teenaged mothers have to rely on support from their parents or the father of the child and perhaps work as well. People laid off from work have to use their own savings or borrow from others to make do until the next job is found. All these changes involve great disruption in expectations and accustomed roles. . . .

Adolescents who were not job-ready find they are job-ready after all. It turns out that they can work for low wages and accept the discipline of the workplace if the alternative is grim enough. After a few years, many—not all, but many—find that they have acquired salable skills, or that they are at the right place at the right time, or otherwise find that the original entry-level job has gradually been transformed into a secure job paying a decent wage. A few—not a lot, but a few—find that the process leads to affluence.

Perhaps the most rightful, deserved benefit goes to the much larger population of low-income families who have been doing things right all along and have been punished for it: the young man who has taken responsibility for his wife and child even though his friends with the same choice have called him a fool; the single mother who has worked full time and forfeited her right to welfare for very little extra money; the parents who have set an example for their children even as the rules of the game have taught their children that the example is outmoded. For these millions of people, the instantaneous result is that no one makes fun of them any longer. The longer-term result will be that they regain the status that is properly theirs. They will not only be the bedrock upon which the community is founded (which they always have been), they will be recognized as such. The process whereby they regain their position is not magical, but a matter of logic. When it becomes highly dysfunctional for a person to be dependent, status will accrue to being independent, and in fairly short order. Noneconomic rewards will once again reinforce the economic rewards of being a good parent and provider.

The prospective advantages are real and extremely plausible. In fact, if a government program of the traditional sort (one that would "do" something rather than simply get out of the way) could *as plaus-*

ibly promise these advantages, its passage would be a foregone conclusion. Congress, yearning for programs that are not retreads of failures, would be prepared to spend billions. Negative side-effects (as long as they were the traditionally acceptable negative side-effects) would be brushed aside as trivial in return for the benefits. For let me be quite clear: I am not suggesting that we dismantle income support for the working-aged to balance the budget or punish welfare cheats. I am hypothesizing, with the advantage of powerful collateral evidence, that the lives of large numbers of poor people would be radically changed for the better.

There is, however, a fourth segment of the population yet to be considered, those who are pauperized by the withdrawal of government supports and unable to make alternate arrangements: the teenaged mother who has no one to turn to; the incapacitated or the inept who are thrown out of the house; those to whom economic conditions have brought long periods in which there is no work to be had; those with illnesses not covered by insurance. What of these situations?

The first resort is the network of local services. Poor communities in our hypothetical society are still dotted with storefront health clinics, emergency relief agencies, employment services, legal services. They depend for support on local taxes or local philanthropy, and the local taxpayers and philanthropists tend to scrutinize them rather closely. But, by the same token, they also receive considerably more resources than they formerly did. The dismantling of the federal services has poured tens of billions of dollars back into the private economy. Some of that money no doubt has been spent on Mercedes and summer homes on the Cape. But some has been spent on capital investments that generate new jobs. And some has been spent on increased local services to the poor, voluntarily or as decreed by the municipality. In many cities, the coverage provided by this network of agencies is more generous, more humane, more wisely distributed, and more effective in its results than the services formerly subsidized by the federal government.

But we must expect that a large number of people will fall between the cracks. How might we go about trying to retain the advantages of a zero-level welfare system and still address the residual needs? As we think about the nature of the population still in need, it becomes apparent that their basic problem in the vast majority of the cases is the lack of a job, and this problem is temporary. What they need is something to tide them over while finding a new place in the economy. So our first step is to re-install the Unemployment Insurance program in more or less its previous form. Properly administered, unemployment insurance makes sense. Even if it is restored with all the defects of current practice, the negative effects of Unemployment Insurance *alone* are relatively minor. Our objective is not to wipe out chicanery or to construct a theoretically unblemished system, but to meet legitimate human needs without doing more harm than good. Unemployment Insurance is one of the least harmful ways of contributing to such ends. Thus the system has been amended to take care of the victims of short-term swings in the economy.

Who is left? We are now down to the hardest of the hard core of the welfare-dependent. They have no jobs. They have been unable to find jobs (or have not tried to find jobs) for a longer period of time than the unemployment benefits cover. They have no families who will help. They

have no friends who will help. For some reason, they cannot get help from local services or private charities except for the soup kitchen and a bed in the Salvation Army hall.

What will be the size of this population? We have never tried a zero-level federal welfare system under conditions of late-twentieth-century national wealth, so we cannot do more than speculate. But we may speculate. Let us ask of whom the population might consist and how they might fare.

For any category of "needy" we may name, we find ourselves driven to one of two lines of thought. Either the person is in a category that is going to be at the top of the list of services that localities vote for themselves, and at the top of the list of private services, or the person is in a category where help really is not all that essential or desirable. The burden of the conclusion is not that every single person will be taken care of, but that the extent of resources to deal with needs is likely to be very great—not based on wishful thinking, but on extrapolations from reality.

To illustrate, let us consider the plight of the stereotypical welfare mother—never married, no skills, small children, no steady help from a man. It is safe to say that, now as in the 1950s, there is no one who has less sympathy from the white middle class, which is to be the source of most of the money for the private and local services we envision. Yet this same white middle class is a soft touch for people trying to make it on their own, and a soft touch for "deserving" needy mothers—AFDC was one of the most widely popular of the New Deal welfare measures, intended as it was for widows with small children. Thus we may envision two quite different scenarios.

In one scenario, the woman is presenting the local or private service with this proposition: "Help me find a job and day-care for my children, and I will take care of the rest." In effect, she puts herself into the same category as the widow and the deserted wife—identifies herself as one of the most obviously deserving of the deserving poor. Welfare mothers who want to get into the labor force are likely to find a wide range of help. In the other scenario, she asks for an outright and indefinite cash grant—in effect, a private or local version of AFDC—so that she can stay with the children and not hold a job. In the latter case, it is very easy to imagine situations in which she will not be able to find a local service or a private philanthropy to provide the help she seeks. The question we must now ask is: What's so bad about that? If children were always better off being with their mother all day and if, by the act of giving birth, a mother acquired the inalienable right to be with the child, then her situation would be unjust to her and injurious to her children. Neither assertion can be defended, however—especially not in the 1980s, when more mothers of all classes work away from the home than ever before, and even more especially not in view of the empirical record for the children growing up under the current welfare system. Why should the mother be exempted by the system from the pressures that must affect everyone else's decision to work? . . .

Billions for equal opportunity, not one cent for equal outcome—such is the slogan to inscribe on the banner of whatever cause my proposals constitute. Their common theme is to make it possible to get as far as one can go on one's merit, hardly a new ideal in American thought. . . .

NO
Sar A. Levitan

THE WELFARE SYSTEM CAN WORK

Half a century has elapsed since the United States embarked on the development of its welfare system. Driven by the devastating impacts of the Great Depression, the architects of the New Deal designed a structure that would provide a measure of economic security to all Americans. In doing so, they followed in the footsteps of other industrialized nations.

Broadly defined, the American welfare system as it evolved over the years is the product of a sustained drive for greater economic security by all income groups; it is not merely a vehicle for providing assistance to the poor. Through social insurance programs, tax expenditures, and human capital investments, government aid reaches far into the ranks of middle- and upper-income America. Federal social welfare policies not only seek to prevent extreme deprivation among the most disadvantaged, but also attempt to cushion the impact of economic misfortune and uncertainty on more advantaged and affluent members of society. The resulting safety net has been remarkably successful in shielding diverse segments of the population from the full brunt of the vagaries and hardships implicit in a free market economy.

Despite these achievements the system has failed to gain universal acceptance. In recent years, attacks on the welfare system have grown more strident and shrill. Critics have sought to link rising incidences of crime, drug abuse, divorce, and other social ills with federal social welfare interventions. Some have even claimed that the welfare system is the direct cause of an alleged unraveling of the American social fabric and moral fiber.

As a result of these assaults, the terms *welfare, mess,* and *crisis* have become virtually inseparable in contemporary public discourse. Criticisms of the welfare system have emanated from diverse sources. Liberals have found fault with the absence of federal standards for a comprehensive system of income support and constraints on the more aggressive use of government powers to improve the quality of life. Conservatives contend that the welfare system has grown too large and unwieldy, frequently undermining the very objectives that it is designed to achieve. Under attack from all sides, the image of the welfare system as irrational, unmanageable, and in need of immediate and wholesale reform has come to dominate popular wisdom in the mid-1980s.

The notion of a welfare crisis is enhanced by tendencies to define the American welfare system narrowly as providing cash and in-kind assistance only to the poor. Without a perceived stake in the system, the middle class majority responds quickly to suggestions that welfare is a mess—too costly, mismanaged, unfair, and in many cases undeserved. When the welfare system is defined more realistically to include the host of entitlements and protections against economic insecurity available to the nonpoor, perceptions of crisis and prescriptions for sweeping retrenchment lose much of their appeal.

A balanced and objective analysis would reveal that reports of a welfare crisis are greatly exaggerated. Removed from the distortions of budget battles and political ideologies, the record of federal social welfare interventions suggests that the system is a rational and necessary response to emerging societal needs and has functioned relatively well under the pressures of competing interests and conflicting demands.

PURSUING ECONOMIC SECURITY

Viewed in the context of societal goals first articulated half a century ago, the welfare system has nearly achieved its fundamental objectives. Most of the destitute have been assured at least a meager stipend to meet basic needs, and the percentage of Americans living in poverty declined dramatically during the three decades following World War II. Social security and medicare have removed the greatest threats to solvency in old age.

Workers forced into idleness have gained temporary support through unemployment compensation programs, and disabled workers are protected by insurance which provides medical care and basic income. Tax expenditures and federally sponsored financial institutions have enabled unprecedented numbers to purchase their own homes. Favorable tax policies have spurred the growth of private health insurance and government regulations have guaranteed employees that their private pensions would be available upon retirement. Substantial public investments in education, training, and employment have enabled millions to enter or remain in the mainstream of the United States economy, thereby reaffirming the promise of opportunity that lies at the heart of American society. . . .

The persistence of poverty despite rising affluence during the 1960s prompted expansion of cash support under the Aid to Families with Dependent Children (AFDC) program for the nonaged poor. This included liberalization of eligibility requirements and enhanced benefits that rose more rapidly than average earnings. The federal government also accepted responsibility for expanded direct aid to impoverished aged, blind, and disabled persons through the establishment of the Supplemental Security Income (SSI) program in 1972. Substantial additional help for the needy, including the working poor, was authorized with the creation of the food stamp program in 1972 and its expansion during the recession in 1974. The working poor were also helped by wider coverage of the minimum wage and unemployment insurance laws during the Carter administration.

In-kind assistance has also been offered to low-income Americans when necessary to compensate for market inadequacies, and to insure that public funds would be devoted to the fulfillment of basic human needs. Low-income housing programs were initiated when it became evident that income support alone would not serve as a short-term remedy for an inadequate private housing stock. Health care coverage under medicaid represented further acknowledgment that cash stipends could not guarantee access to essential services in an efficient manner when individual needs are not directly related to income. In some cases it was easier to persuade Congress to provide in-kind help rather than cash assistance. For example, food stamps gained political support both as a response to the cry of hunger and malnutrition as well as a boost to the United States farm economy.

Because assistance to the poor is commonly viewed as unearned, it attracts the greatest political attention and controversy. Yet means-tested aid constitutes only a sixth of the total transfer payments provided through the broader welfare system and less than a tenth of total federal outlays go to the poor. The federal share of the AFDC budget, commonly associated with welfare, accounts for only about 2 percent of federal income transfers, and total outlays for the program (including state and local contributions) represent 0.5 percent of personal incomes in the United States. An analysis of in-kind benefits within the welfare system would yield similar results with large portions of aid (including indirect subsidies) for housing, health care, and other supportive services directed to the nonpoor.

As a matter of policy as well as politics, the American welfare system has never identified income maintenance as an appropriate long-term response to economic misfortune and deprivation. The initiatives of the Great Society were founded upon the premise that only a two-pronged assault on poverty could lead to greater economic security for the poor: income support to meet immediate basic needs coupled with attempts to expand economic opportunities and to change institutions in order to promote long-term self-sufficiency. Guided by this philosophy, the Great Society sought to stimulate public investments in education and training, seeking to open doors to permanent employment for the disadvantaged. During the late 1960s and 1970s, federal support for educational programs (ranging from primary and secondary schools to vocational and postsecondary education) and job training initiatives increased substantially. All segments of American society shared in the fruits of these investments, although they have not been sufficient to provide alternatives to long-term dependency for a minority of the nation's poor. . . .

The broad layer of additional security provided by the welfare system and related federal initiatives has contributed to greater economic stability since World War II, even though periodic recessions persist. The American public's resistance to major retrenchments attests to the broad support for these reforms and virtually guarantees that an extensive welfare system serving as a buffer against economic uncertainty is here to stay. Indeed, some measure of protection against economic misfortune and aid to the poor are rational and necessary responses to rising societal affluence. Just as private insurance to reduce financial risk becomes more affordable and attractive as personal income increases, government policies to spread or socialize the risks of a free market system become more prudent and popular with growing national wealth. The potential for humanitarian aid to relieve deprivation and for longer-term investments to help the disadvantaged become contributing members of society also increases with rising national income. In the absence of federal interventions through the welfare system, the gap between rich and poor would tend to widen in an advanced economy, generating unacceptable income disparities and straining the fabric of an open, free, and democratic society. . . .

What of the alleged failures of the modern welfare system? Federal interventions in the complex realm of social policy have brought their share of frustrations and excesses. Yet the more important issues are the extent to which social welfare policies and programs have been revised to reflect the lessons of the past, and the standards by which progress in the welfare system is measured. A balanced and reasonable assessment suggests that we have learned from our mistakes—some inevitable, others the result of overly ambitious efforts—during two decades of frequently bold innovation, and that past gains have been generally encouraging in light of the ambitious and competing goals set out for the modern welfare system.

The designers of the emerging welfare system, from the New Deal to the founding of the Great Society, tended to underestimate the deep-seated problems associated with poverty. The authors of the Social Security Act in 1935 assumed that needs-tested public assistance would wither away as younger workers became fully covered by social insurance—an expectation that was shattered by changing demographics and steadily expanding welfare rolls and benefits during the postwar period. Similarly, a central premise of President Johnson's War on Poverty was that investments in education and training, civil rights protections, and community organizations representing the have-nots

could dramatically lift this generation's poor out of deprivation and ensure their children a decent life. Cycles of poverty and dependency have proved considerably more intractable. It became increasingly clear that there are no easy answers or quick solutions to discrimination, economic deprivation, and other social ills. As some of the experiments turned out to be counterproductive as well as politically divisive, the ensuing disillusionment sorely taxed the nation's will to sustain the welfare system in pursuit of steady but incremental gains.

Because many social problems have proved more pervasive and persistent than originally believed, the welfare system has been forced to rely upon more varied and costly strategies for their long-term amelioration. Such comprehensive, long-term approaches frequently involved offering preferential treatment to targeted groups at the cost of legitimate aspirations of the more fortunate. It has proven extremely difficult politically to defend these actions. Social programs requiring high initial investments and yielding delayed or cumulative benefits have often been abandoned, being victims of public resentment and insufficient commitments of funds over too brief a period of time. Every solution to deep-seated social ills has created new problems. Even when government interventions have achieved their intended results, the process of change in some instances has generated unwanted side effects and posed new problems for policymakers. One clear lesson provided by the experience of the past two decades is that the search for remedies to complex social problems is inherently difficult, particularly when the process involves helping the have-nots to compete effectively with those who have made it. In a democratic society, those who have gained privileged status generally have the clout to abort such changes.

The experience of recent decades suggests that the federal government must proceed on several fronts simultaneously if it is to be successful in efforts to alleviate poverty. For example, unless suitable employment and economic development programs are also initiated, the training of low-income workers is unlikely to have a significant impact on overall poverty levels or welfare caseloads when provided amid high unemployment or in declining economic regions. In contrast, although income transfers address the immediate needs of the poor, they do not result in lasting improvements in earning capacity and self-sufficiency unless complemented by public efforts to enhance the skills of recipients and to alter the institutions that trap them in poverty. The interdependence of these antipoverty strategies can create the appearance of failure when individual initiatives are viewed in isolation, particularly when concomitant interventions necessary for their success are not undertaken. At the same time, the benefits of comprehensive approaches are cumulative and can far exceed the potential of isolated efforts.

One of the clearest lessons arising out of America's experience with the modern welfare system is that poverty cannot be eliminated solely through reliance upon income transfers. Income maintenance is an essential component of any antipoverty effort, but a strategy relying upon transfers alone can neither enhance self-sufficiency nor avoid conflicts in labor markets. . . .

The Reagan administration's rhetorical crusade to focus federal aid on those with greatest need has not been unfounded. Despite the difficulty of judging the appropriate balance between targeting and universality, a strong case could be made

by 1980 that too large a share of scarce federal resources were being diverted into benefits for the nonneedy. Unfortunately, the administration's response to this imbalance has proven to be narrow, inequitable, and devoid of vision. Eligibility for programs aiding the poor has been restricted to the most needy as a means of slashing federal outlays. No broader effort to shift resources from universal entitlements or subsidies for the affluent to means-tested programs serving low-income Americans has been undertaken. Only this year, with opportunities for significant budget savings from means-tested programs seemingly exhausted, has President Reagan challenged the flow of aid to middle- and upper-income households through the broader welfare system.

The Reagan administration has similarly clouded the perennial debate over the appropriate sharing of social responsibilities among federal, state, and local governments as well as the private sector. The Reagan program, under the banner of New Federalism, has aggressively sought to shift responsibility for the administration and financing of social welfare initiatives to the states. The Reagan administration has also relied heavily upon the conviction that social welfare efforts, whenever feasible, should be left to private voluntary efforts. This perspective, founded on ideology rather than empirical evidence, has been useful in buttressing attempts to reduce federal expenditures but precludes a balanced and reasoned assessment of appropriate public and private roles in the modern welfare system.

Taking the principle of subsidiarity (i.e., the belief that the federal government should not undertake functions that can be performed by a lower level of government or private groups) to the extreme, opponents of federal intervention seek to

13. DOES OUR WELFARE SYSTEM HURT THE POOR?

obscure the reasons much of the responsibility for the welfare system has fallen upon the federal government. Contrary to idealized notions of community responsibility, state and local governments in prior decades consistently failed to marshal the will and the resources to alleviate poverty and expand economic opportunity for the most disadvantaged. By definition, the poorest states and localities faced the most severe problems while having the least capacity to redress them. Competition among states and localities also has discouraged responses to pressing social needs prior to federal intervention, as these smaller jurisdictions have attempted to attract new businesses and industries by holding down tax rates and public expenditures. Because the federal government relies upon more equitable financing structures and a broader revenue base than state or local jurisdictions, its capacity to support large-scale income maintenance and human resource programs is far greater. For all these reasons, any effective welfare system must include a central federal role in setting national priorities, providing direction for equitable policies and program development, and generating the resources necessary to meet social welfare goals. . . .

The need for a strong federal role in the welfare system is clear, and yet public understanding of this federal responsibility has been undermined by the virulent antigovernment ideology of the New Right and nourished by President Reagan. The most pressing question for the future of the welfare system may rest upon the nation's ability to regain confidence in government responsibility for the welfare of the citizenry and belief in the legitimacy of collective action to meet societal needs. . . .

POSTSCRIPT

DOES OUR WELFARE SYSTEM HURT THE POOR?

The welfare issue appeals too easily to our emotions. Liberals will cite touching instances of poor families being denied adequate assistance. Conservatives will counter with examples of welfare cheats and waste. Liberals are castigated as "bleeding hearts" and conservatives as "hard hearted."

Is the problem insoluble? Levitan and Murray agree that appropriate policies can reduce poverty and that there are no easy solutions. In all other respects, they could not be farther apart. Where Levitan insists that the welfare system works and is here to stay, Murray concludes that the system fails and should be abandoned.

What's wrong with the welfare system, many liberals argue, is that we have been undermining it. This is the view of Robert Lekachman, *Greed Is Not Enough: Reaganomics* (Pantheon, 1982); Frances Fox Piven and Richard A. Cloward, *The New Class War: Reagan's Attack on the Welfare State and Its Consequences* (Pantheon, 1982); and Michael Harrington, *The New American Poverty* (Holt, Rinehart, 1984).

The conservative critics maintain that what's wrong is the welfare system itself. An influential statement of this position will be found in George Gilder, *Wealth and Poverty* (Basic Books, 1981). It is also supported by "The Future of the Welfare State," the subject of the Fall 1982 issue of *The Public Interest*. A moving study that provides factual ammunition for both sides is Ken Auletta, *The Underclass* (Random House, 1983).

One of the tough questions which Americans may eventually have to ask themselves is whether there may have grown up in America a permanent class of dependent people, who lack both the skills and aspirations to support themselves. There are many more who have not lost the desire to work, only the opportunity. The challenge is to provide the opportunity—and somehow stimulate the will to work.

ISSUE 14

SHOULD PORNOGRAPHY BE PROTECTED AS FREE SPEECH?

YES: Hendrik Hertzberg, from "A "Stacked" Commission," *The New Republic,* July 14, 1986

NO: James C. Dobson, from *Final Report, Attorney General's Commission on Pornography,* Washington, D.C., June 1986

ISSUE SUMMARY

YES: Hendrik Hertzberg, editor of the *New Republic,* is concerned that the 1986 report of the Attorney General's Commission on Pornography may lead to the suppression of free speech.
NO: Dr. James Dobson, one of the members of the Commission, supports the Commission's conclusion that violent and degrading pornography is harmful and should be prosecuted under existing law.

In the 1950s, movie producer Otto Preminger defied Hollywood censors by producing a movie which used the word "virgin." Television was less venturesome. Actress Faye Emerson was dropped from a show for wearing a gown which displayed too much cleavage.

Times have changed. Situations involving premarital and extramarital sex are the common coin of television entertainment, and movies involving nudity and simulated intercourse appear on cable TV; for gamier tastes, hardcore videotapes can be purchased or rented at local video outlets. Then there is New York City's 42st Street and its counterpart in other cities, where the most bizarre kinds of sexual acts may be viewed in theaters and "peep shows."

The Supreme Court, too, has changed its standards on pornography. In the landmark case of *Roth* v. *United States* (1957), a Court majority opinion by Justice William Brennan flatly stated that obscenity is not protected by the First Amendment.

In the *Roth* case, Justice Brennan's majority opinion distinguished between sex and obscenity. There is nothing necessarily wrong with sexual material, Brennan said; otherwise we would have to ban parts of the Bible and Shakespeare. Obscene material is something else again. It is material "which deals with sex in a manner appealing to prurient interest." What is meant by "prurient"? Brennan tried some dictionary definitions like "lewd," "lascivious," and "itching," but he must have realized that those definitions require further definition.

Brennan tried two other tests of obscenity. One was "whether to the average person, applying contemporary community standards, the dominant theme of the material taken as a whole appeals to prurient interest." Another was whether the sexually explicit material is "utterly without redeeming social value." Whether or not Brennan noticed it at the time, the two tests are quite ambiguous. The "dominant theme" test allows a community to ban material according to its view of the material "taken as a whole." The "utterly" test would seem to prevent the community from prohibiting material unless the material is lacking—utterly lacking—in any "social value." Even the randiest material might have *some* social value.

In the 1960s the Court began turning to this latter test, the "utterly" test, in deciding whether the authorities could prosecute pornography cases. Its decisions made it difficult for federal and state authorities to sustain convictions in pornography cases, with the result that the authorities pulled back, tolerating what they would have cracked down on a few years earlier.

The Court's decisions produced a backlash. Conservative activists blamed the Supreme Court for the increasingly explicit movies and "adult" bookstores that cropped up in the late 1960s. The criticisms began to bear fruit when Richard Nixon was elected president. Nixon appointed four new members of the Court, and they helped to shift its balance. In a new landmark decision, *Miller* v. *California* (1973) the Court took a tougher line on pornography. The Court now said that it is not necessary for the authorities to demonstrate that sexual material is "utterly without redeeming value" in order to punish those who sell or display it; all the authorities have to do is to show that the "dominant theme" of the material is designed to appeal to "prurient interest." The roots of this go back to the 1957 *Roth* decision, which Justice Brennan now disowned.

Significantly, *Miller* left the definition of "prurience" in the hands of local communities, the reason being that what is "prurient" to a community in Georgia might not be so to people in Manhattan. Although the Court has qualified its decision since 1973 (it does not leave unlimited discretion in the hands of local communities), the *Miller* standard is still the ruling doctrine of the Court.

Is pornography harmful? Opinions differ. In 1967 a presidential commission was created to investigate the issue. In 1970 it submitted its report, which concluded that there is no empirical evidence linking pornography to anti-social behavior such as rape. It recommended that pornography be decriminalized. (President Nixon disavowed the report.) Fifteen years later, Attorney General Edwin Meese appointed another commission to investigate the same topic, and in 1986 it came to the opposite conclusion. On some questions the Commission was not unanimous, but its members did agree that (a) violent pornography is harmful and should not be decriminalized, and (b) pornography involving children should be prosecuted more vigorously.

Critics of the report attacked not only the Commission's conclusions but its methods and its makeup. They claimed that the Commission was "stacked" with members whose conclusions had been formed long before the Commission even met. These are among the points made by *New Republic* editor Hendrik Hertzberg, who favors the decriminalization of pornography. Opposing him is James C. Dobson, a member of the Commission, who contends that pornography does not deserve First Amendment protection.

YES   Hendrik Hertzberg

A "STACKED" COMMISSION

. . . In the conservative dialectic that defines the Reagan counterrevolu-
tion, the report of the Meese commission—known officially as the Attorney
General's Commission on Pornography—is designed to be the antithesis of
its ancestor, the notorious 1970 report of the federal Commission on Obscenity
and Pornography. The two reports and the two commissions are indeed antithetical, and not only in the ways Meese intended. If the old commission
was the federal equivalent of *Playboy*, the new one is the equivalent of
Hustler—low-budget, weak on fact-checking, unsubtle, and fascinated by the
perverse.

The 1970 commission had a budget of $2 million, a staff of 22, and two
years to complete its mission. That mission, as defined by Congress, was to
analyze the obscenity laws, to study the effects on the public of the traffic in
obscenity and pornography, and, if necessary, to recommend ways "to regulate effectively the flow of such traffic." The 1970 commission sponsored a
wide range of original research by reputable scholars, psychologists, and universities. Its chairman, William B. Lockhart, appointed by President Johnson,
was the dean of the University of Minnesota Law School.

The 1986 commission, by contrast, had a budget of $400,000 (the equivalent
in 1970 dollars of around $150,000), a staff of nine, and one year to com-
plete its mission. That mission, as defined by Ed Meese, was to study the impact of pornography and to recommend "more effective ways in which the
spread of pornography could be contained." The 1986 commission sponsored
no original research, and its consultants were mostly policemen and antiporn
activists. Its Meese-appointed chairman, Henry Hudson, is a Virginia county
prosecutor who conducted an avid campaign against adult bookstores, and who
once told the *Washington Post*, "I live to put people in jail." While serving
as chairman, Hudson was angling for a job—for which he has since been
nominated—as a U.S. Attorney.

From, "Big Boobs," by Hendrick Hertzberg, *The New Republic,* July 14, 1986. Reprinted by permission of The New Republic, Copyright © 1986, The New Republic, Inc.

By all accounts the 1970 commission approached its duties with an open mind. Two or three of its 18 members had taken public positions on pornography, but the rest had not. When it produced its recommendations, they included calls for "a massive sex education effort" aimed at "providing accurate and reliable sex information through legitimate sources," for the prohibition of public displays and the sale to minors of "sexually explicit pictorial materials," and—most surprisingly—for the outright repeal of federal, state, and local laws against "the sale, exhibition, or distribution of sexual materials to consenting adults." The Nixon administration indignantly disavowed the commission, and few of its recommendations were enacted. Not a single state repealed its obscenity laws. But those laws, already spottily enforced, fell increasingly into disuse as police departments turned their attention to more pressing threats to public safety.

The 1986 commission has been stacked to prevent unwelcome surprises. Of its 11 members, six have well-established public records of supporting government action against sexy books and films. One of the commissioners, for example, is a Franciscan priest who has condemned Dr. Ruth Westheimer, the chirpy radio sex adviser, for advocating orgasms in premarital sex. Another is a religious broadcaster whose best-selling book, *Dare to Discipline*—a title that would not be out of place in the bondage section of an adult bookstore—advocates corporal punishment of children. A third is a University of Michigan law professor who has argued in law review articles that pornography is not constitutionally protected. The Meese commission lacked the financial and staff resources of its predecessor, but since its conclusions were preordained, it didn't really need them.

The Meese report will recommend a long list of stern measures. They include changing obscenity laws to make any second offense a felony rather than a misdemeanor, with a mandatory one-year jail term; prosecuting the producers of porn films under the prostitution laws (because the actors are paid for their work); changing the forfeiture laws to permit the government to confiscate the assets of any business found in violation of the federal obscenity laws (allowing, for example, the seizure of a whole convenience store for the sale of a single dirty magazine); and a big enforcement push, including the appointment of a "high-level" Justice Department task force on obscenity cases. Where the pornography in question is too mild to bring the obscenity laws into play, the report somewhat cautiously recommends "private action"—picketing, boycotts, and the like.

Under the federal sunshine laws, the Meese commission has conducted virtually all of its business in public—not only the hearings it staged in Washington, Chicago, Houston, Los Angeles, Miami, and New York but also the working sessions it held in tandem with the hearings. Given the appeal of the subject, the show played to curiously empty houses. Not a single major newspaper assigned a reporter to cover the story on a regular basis. The only reporters who turned up for every meeting, and who assiduously collected the chaotic pastiche of hastily written drafts and documents that will make up the final report, were two representatives of what might be called the trade press. Philip Nobile and Eric Nadler of *Forum*, a kind of journal of sexual opinion put out by the Penthouse empire, will publish their researches next month in a book, *The United States of America vs. Sex: How the Meese Commission Lied about Por-*

nography, which combines solid reporting with lively and intelligent polemics. It is thanks to an advance reading of their manuscript and collection of documents that I have some idea of how the commission went about its work.

It was quite a show. The commissioners heard 208 witnesses, including 68 policemen, 30 "victims," and 14 representatives of antipornography organizations. They were subjected to slide shows that were—in the words of the two ultimately dissenting commissioners, Ellen Levine, editor of *Woman's Day,* and Judith Becker, a Columbia University psychiatrist— "skewed to the very violent and extremely degrading," including, in one case, a picture of a man having sex with a chicken. They made field trips to "adult bookstores." They listened as a retired FBI agent assured them that the pornography industry was dominated by organized crime. They engaged in many a zany, aimless conversation, including one discussion of necrophilia during which a commissioner wondered aloud, "Is it legal to have sex with a corpse if you're married to it?"

The "victims" who testified before the commission included former prostitutes, former abused wives and children, former junkies, and people who complained that a relative had spent the family savings on dirty books. All blamed their troubles on pornography, though the causal connections were never clear. One of the most curious victims was a wispy, neatly dressed man of 38 who appeared, Bible in hand, at the commission's Miami hearing.

"I am a victim of pornography," the witness began. "At age 12, I was a typically normal, healthy boy. My life was filled with normal activities and hobbies. All that changed the following summer when I went to visit relatives, a married couple, who decided to teach me about sex. . . . I saw a *Playboy* magazine for the first time in my life.

"All the trouble began a few months later, back at my mother's home. The house we rented had a shed out back, and that's where I found a hidden deck of cards. All 52 cards depicted hard-core pornography—penetration, fellatio, and cunnilingus. These porno cards highly aroused me and gave me a desire I never had before."

The witness then detailed his subsequent record of wrongdoing, all of it, according to him, ascribable to the fatal deck of cards. From shoplifting, he descended to masturbation, anal intercourse with another teenage boy, peeping on his mother, "oral and finger stimulation on my parents' dogs," reading sex magazines ('I used to read Hugh Hefner's *Playboy* philosophy, and I am sure through his help I bought the program of the '60s, hook, line, and sinker"), taking drugs, and—the ultimate degradation—"watching R-rated movies on HBO and Showtime cable."

In conclusion, the witness solemnly told the by now stupefied commissioners, "If it weren't for my faith in God, and the forgiveness of Jesus Christ, I would now possibly be a pervert, an alcoholic, or dead. I am a victim of pornography."

Even the most ardently antiporn commissioners were embarrassed by this sort of testimony—much of which, Chairman Hudson admitted during one of the working sessions, was written and structured by the commission staff.

At the beginning of March, that staff, under the guidance of its executive director, a 34-year-old federal prosecutor from Kentucky named Alan Sears, presented the commissioners with a proposed draft of the final report. It quickly became apparent that this elephantine draft—whose 1,200 pages included 200 pages of lurid, unsubstantiated "victim" testimony—owed more than a little to the porno-card school of discourse. One of the commissioners, Frederick Shauer, the Michigan law school professor, protested.

In a letter to his colleagues, Shauer set forth his complaints. He pointed out that the ex-FBI agent who had testified on the connection between pornography and organized crime was a convicted shoplifter with (in the words of the judge who tried him) "a great propensity to lie." He noted that one publication cited in the draft was included only "because it was astoundingly gross, bizarre, and disgusting," and added: "But that does not make it legally obscene, and it does not make us any less of a laughingstock for including it." He called the section on constitutional law "so one-sided and oversimplified that I cannot imagine signing anything that looks remotely like this." On the "victim" testimony, he wrote; "If this section is included as is, we will have confirmed all the worst fears about the information on which we relied, and all of the worst fears about our biases." Finally, he announced his intention to write an entirely new draft himself, taking into account the views of the other commissioners. Six weeks later, he had done just that.

Whether Edwin Meese realizes it or not, he owes Frederick Shauer a great deal, for Shauer has saved him from issuing a report that it would have been superfluous to ridicule. The Shauer draft, 211 pages long, immediately became the basis for the text of the [Commission's report.] Though the draft has its share of howlers, on the whole it is reasonable and civilized in tone. It is written in a calm, even stately style. It contains little in the way of hysteria. To the limited extent that it takes note of the views of those who disagree, it treats

those views with civility. Yet it preserves the basic conclusion Meese had programmed the commission to reach.

The conclusion, as best I can make it out through the fog of professorial qualifications and unacknowledged internal contradictions, is that pornography is "harmful," and that therefore the police powers of the state should be mobilized to suppress it. More precisely, according to the report, certain kinds of violent and "degrading" pornography seem to cause certain ill-defined varieties of "harm"—though not nearly as much harm, the report admits in two separate places, as either "weaponry magazines" that focus on "guns, martial arts, and related topics" or "slasher" movies of the *Friday the 13th* variety.

The process by which this conclusion is reached relies on a spectacularly tenuous chain of causation. For example, in certain laboratory studies, male college students were shown certain movies—exactly what movies the body of the report does not say, though it seems that in one case they included Lina Wertmuller's highly acclaimed *Swept Away*—and then were taken to mock rape trials. Afterward, they were asked to fill out questionnaires. According to the results of the questionnaires, the students who saw the movies seemed to show less sympathy for the complainants in the rape case than did students who had not been shown movies. From this it is concluded that pornography causes—well, maybe not sex crimes, exactly, maybe not even a disposition to "unlawful" sexual aggressiveness, but *something*. (And never mind that Edward Donnerstein, the University of Wisconsin psychologist whose findings the commission relies on, has repudiated its interpretation of his work.)

This is as intellectually rigorous as the report gets where the question of "harm"

14. SHOULD PORNOGRAPHY BE PROTECTED AS FREE SPEECH?

is concerned. Mostly it turns with relief to more capacious definitions. "An environment, physical, cultural, moral, or aesthetic, can be harmed," it argues, "and so can a community, organization, or group be harmed independent of identifiable harms to members of that community." Broad enough? Apparently not, for in the very next sentence we are assured that "the idea of harm is broader than that."

Another bit of slippery reasoning in the report concerns the report's division of pornography into four "classes." In this scheme, Class I, violent pornography, and Class II, "degrading" pornography, are definitely "harmful," while Class III, non-violent and nondegrading materials (such as depictions of ordinary vaginal intercourse), is probably harmless, and Class IV, simple nudity, is definitely harmless. This definition would seem to put the vast bulk of commercially available erotica, including magazines like *Playboy* and *Penthouse,* in Classes III and IV. But in drafting this section, Shauer broadened the definition of Class II. Taking a leaf from Andrea Dworkin, the renegade feminist antipornography crusader, Shauer incorporated into the "degrading" category "material that, although not violent, depicts people, usually women, as existing solely for the sexual satisfaction of others, usually men, or that depicts people, usually women, in decidedly subordinate roles in their sexual relations with others." By this sleight of hand, Class III suddenly became "quite small in terms of currently available materials," while erotica of the *Playboy-Penthouse* variety just as suddenly became "degrading"—and therefore, in the commission's view, subject to suppression. . . .

. . . Posturing against porn may not yet be quite the political equivalent of herpes—it will still be required of Republicans in places where the religious right is strong—but the issue has now lost much of its punch. As for the president, he may be expected to make a Saturday morning speech in order to please his friend Meese and to placate the constituency Meese represents. But the old trouper—who has a history of tolerance for sexual unconventionality among his Hollywood chums, his staffers, and his wife's social circle, who has a daughter whose recent novel includes the normal quota of steamy sex scenes and a son working for *Playboy,* and who himself divorced one actress and then married another after remarking that he was tired of not knowing the names of the starlets he was waking up next to—will probably refrain from expending much of his popularity on an issue that was never especially congenial for him and is now a proven political loser as well.

Still, even if the report fails to touch off the hoped-for national crusade, it is bound to play an important part in a decentralized but wider effort to constrict personal liberty and freedom of expression. Most of the fuss over dirty books occurs at the local level, in small cities and towns. Typically, an ambitious or perfervid prosecutor decides that obscenity busts are the road to political advancement or social salubrity, or an ad hoc group of self-righteous citizens tries to make its own narrow preferences mandatory for a whole community, particularly for its schools, libraries, and convenience stores. When such people succeed, the result is censorship of a small but tangible kind. They will get plenty of encouragement from the Meese report.

Experience shows that these vigilante actions are almost never aimed at violent or even "hard core" pornography. The targets are usually books that treat sex realistically, or, in the case of convenience stores, popular men's magazines. And the commission has shown the way.

Last February Alan Sears wrote to a number of large companies informing each of them that the commission had "received testimony alleging that your company is involved in the sale or distribution of pornography." He invited them to explain themselves, adding ominously, "Failure to respond will necessarily be accepted as an indication of no objection." Attached to the letter addressed to the Southland Corporation, which operates the 7-Eleven chain of convenience stores, was a photocopy of a page that read in part, "The general public usually associates pornography with sleazy porno bookstores and theaters. However, many of the major players in the game of pornography are well-known household names. Few people realize that 7-Eleven convenience stores are the leading retailers of porn magazines in America." There was no indication of where the page came from. (In fact, it was from the testimony of Donald Wildmon, executive director of a religious right organization called the National Federation of Decency.) A few weeks later, Southland removed *Playboy* and *Penthouse* from its stores.

No doubt the Constitution will survive. Yet the fact remains that in some areas convenience stores are the only places magazines are sold. *Playboy* and *Penthouse* publish not only erotica but also what might be called politica. Nobody buys these magazines for the articles, despite what husbands caught with them tell their wives. Still, the articles are sometimes read. *Playboy* and *Penthouse* are sources of faintly heretical ideas as well as sexy pictures. Their removal from their largest sales outlet by what amounts to government intimidation does not improve the political health of the country.

Furthermore, there's no logical reason why the commission's slippery-slope syllogism should be limited to porn. The syllogism goes like this: (a) stores have the right not to carry any publication they don't want to carry; (b) private citizens have the right to boycott or protest in front of any store that carries a publication they don't like; (c) government approval or encouragement of such private efforts doesn't violate the First Amendment. The issue here is a technique of suppression. Some would argue that it is freedom of political speech that is protected by the Constitution. Yet once it is established that indirect government pressure on magazine distributors is okay, there is no guarantee that such pressure won't be applied to publications that the reigning ideologues don't like for political reasons. "Private action" isn't so private when government commissions explicitly encourage it.

The Meese report also will encourage the kind of local crusaders for decency who are forever trying to ban supposedly dirty books from schools and libraries. One doesn't need to exaggerate the likely impact of this sort of thing to understand that it will be real enough for the schoolteachers and librarians forced to choose between their consciences and their jobs. Finally, the commission will probably succeed in its goal of encouraging local prosecutors to do their worst. Given the commission's loose definition of harmful pornography and the advent of the Rehnquist Supreme Court, their worst might ultimately turn out to be quite bad.

Despite its many assertions to the contrary, the Meese commission has simply failed to demonstrate that pornography constitutes a meaningful threat to the public interest. At a minimum, the commission is guilty of what Levine and Becker, in their dissent, call "unacceptable efforts" to "tease the current data into proof of a causal link." But even if some such showing could be made, it would not follow that freedom of speech and of the press ought therefore to be abridged. The First Amendment contains no requirement that the speech it protects be harmless. On the contrary, speech that somebody thinks is harmful is the only kind that needs protecting.

The commission's report will be widely read, because even a government book about sex is still a book about sex. And it's especially irresistible if it's as fat, as obsessed with kink, and as full of inadvertent humor as this one. A final, apposite example of the last: After a long section on the problem of "underprosecution," the commissioners conclude, "We urge that many of the specific recommendations we suggest be taken seriously."

How wonderfully lame. The logically required corollary, of course, would be this: "We urge that some of the recommendations we suggest not be taken seriously."

Though insufficiently inclusive, this seems wise.

NO

James C. Dobson

PORNOGRAPHY HARMS SOCIETY

Now that the work of the Attorney General's Commission on Pornography has come to an end, I look back on this fourteen-month project as one of the most difficult . . . and gratifying . . . responsibilities of my life. On the down side, the task of sifting through huge volumes of offensive and legally obscene materials has not been a pleasant experience. Under other circumstances one would not willingly devote a year of his life to depictions of rape, incest, masturbation, mutilation, defecation, urination, child molestation, and sadomasochistic activity. Nor have the lengthy and difficult deliberations in Commission meetings been without stress. But on the other hand, there is a distinct satisfaction in knowing that we gave ourselves unreservedly to this governmental assignment and, I believe, served our country well.

I now understand how mountain climbers must feel when they finally stand atop the highest peak. They overcome insurmountable obstacles to reach the rim of the world and announce proudly to one another, "we made it!" In a similar context, I feel a sense of accomplishment as the Commission releases its final report to the President, the Attorney General and the people. For a brief moment in Scottsdale last month, it appeared that our differing philosophies would strand us on the lower slopes. And of course, we were monitored daily by the ACLU, the pornographers, and the press, who huddled together and murmured with one voice, "they are doomed!" But now as we sign the final document and fling it about to the public, it does not seem pretentious to indulge ourselves in the satisfaction of having accomplished our goals. By George, I think we made it!

Let me indicate now, from the viewpoint of this one commissioner, what the final report *is* and *is not*. First, it is not the work of a biased Commission which merely rubber stamped the conservative agenda of the Reagan administration. A quick analysis of our proceedings will reveal the painstaking process by which our conclusions were reached. If the deck were stacked, as some have suggested, we would not have invested such long, arduous hours in debate and compromise. Serving on the Commission were three attorneys, two psychologists, one psychiatrist, one social worker, one city council member, one

From, Attorney General's Commission on Pornography, *Final Report*, Washington, DC, US Government Printing Office, June 1986, pages 71-87.

Catholic priest, one federal judge, and one magazine editor. Some were Christians, some Jewish, and some atheists. Some were Democrats and some Republicans. All were independent, conscientious citizens who took their responsibility very seriously. Our diversity was also evident on strategic issues about which society itself is divided. Our voting on these more troublesome matters often split 6-5, being decided by a swing member or two. Some whitewash! So the characterization of this seven-man, four-woman panel as an ultra-conservative hit squad is simply poppycock. Read the transcripts. You will see.

Second, the final report does not do violence to the First Amendment to the Constitution. The *Miller* standard,* by which the Supreme Court clearly reaffirmed the illegality of obscene matter in 1973, was not assaulted during any of our deliberations. No suggestion was made that the Court had been too lenient . . . or that a constitutional Amendment should lower the threshold of obscenity . . . or that the Justices should reconsider their position. No. The *Miller* standard was accepted and even defended as the law of the land. What *was* recommended, to the consternation of pornographers, was that government should begin enforcing the obscenity laws that are already on the books . . . criminal laws that have stood constitutional muster! Considering the unwillingness of our elected representatives to deal with this issue, that would be novel, indeed.

Third, the hearings on which this report was based were not manipulated to produce an anti-pornography slant. *Every* qualified libertarian and First Amendment

advocate properly requesting the right to testify was granted a place on the agenda, limited only by the constraints of time. A few individuals and organizations on *both* sides of the issue were unable to testify because the demand far exceeded available opportunities. However, objective procedures were established to deal fairly with those wishing to be heard, and complaints alleging bias were, I believe, unfounded. In fact, several organizations were asked to speak on behalf of sexually explicit materials but either declined or failed to appear. It *is* true that more witnesses testified against pornography than those who favored it, but that was a function of the disproportionate requests that were received by the executive director. Furthermore, I think it also reflects a disproportionate number of American citizens who oppose the proliferation of obscenity.

Looking now at the other side of the coin, let me express what the final report is and what I believe its impact is likely to be. First, the Commission expressed an unmistakable condemnation of sexually explicit material that is violent in nature. We were unanimous in that position throughout our deliberations. There is no place in this culture for material deemed legally obscene by the courts which depicts the dismemberment, burning, whipping, hanging, torturing, or raping of women. The time has come to eradicate such materials and prosecute those who produce it. There was no disagreement on that point.

Second, we were also unanimous in our condemnation of sexually explicit materials which depict women in situations that are humiliating, demeaning, and subjugating. I can still recall photographs of nude young women being penetrated by broom handles, smeared with feces, urinated upon, covered in blood or kneeling

*Dobson refers to the case of *Miller v. California* (1973), which was discussed in the Introduction to this Issue.—Eds.

submissively in the act of fellatio. Most American citizens have no idea that such gruesome scenes are common in the world of obscene publications today. When asked to describe pornography currently on the market, they think in terms of airbrushed centerfolds in the popular "men's magazines." But steady customers of pornography have long since grown tired of simple heterosexual nudity. Indeed, a visit to an adult bookstore quickly reveals the absence of so-called "normal" sexuality. The offerings today feature beribboned 18- to 20-year-old women whose genitalia have been shaved to make them look like little girls, and men giving enemas or whippings to one another, and metal bars to hold a woman's legs apart, and 3-foot rubber penises, and photographs of women sipping ejaculate from champagne glasses. In one shop which our staff visited on Times Square, there were 46 films for sale which depicted women having intercourse or performing oral sex with different animals . . . pigs, dogs, donkeys, and horses. This is the world of pornography today, and I believe the public would rise up in wrath to condemn it if they knew of its prominence.

Finally, our Commission was unanimously opposed to child pornography in any form. Though categorically illegal since 1983, a thriving cottage industry still exists in this country. Fathers, step-fathers, uncles, teachers, and neighbors find ways to secure photographs of the children in their care. They then sell or trade the pictures to fellow pedophiles. I will never forget a particular set of photographs shown to us at our first hearing in Washington, D.C. It focused on a cute, nine-year-old boy who had fallen into the hands of a molester. In the first picture, the blond lad was fully clothed and smiling at the camera. But in the second, he was nude,

dead, and had a butcher knife protruding from his chest. I served for 14 years as a member of a medical school faculty and thought I had seen it all. But my knees buckled and tears came to my eyes as these and hundreds of other photographs of children were presented . . . showing pitiful boys and girls with their rectums enlarged to accommodate adult males and their vaginas penetrated with pencils, toothbrushes, and guns. Perhaps the reader can understand my anger and disbelief when a representative for the American Civil Liberties Union testified a few minutes later. He advocated the free exchange of pornography, *all* pornography, in the marketplace. He was promptly asked about material depicting children such as those we had seen. This man said, with a straight face, that it is the ACLU's position that child pornography should not be produced, but once it is in existence, there should be no restriction on its sale and distribution. In other words, the photographic record of a child's molestation and abuse should be a legal source of profit for those who wish to reproduce, sell, print, and distribute it for the world to see. And that, he said, was the intent of the First Amendment to the Constitution!

Speaking personally, I now passionately support the control of sexually explicit material that is legally obscene, whether it relates to children or adults. Though the Commission has dealt at some length in its report with specific "harms" associated with pornography, I would like to list the dangers here from my own point of view. Our critics have alleged that the Commission wishes to usher in a new era of sexual repression . . . that we favor governmental interference in America's bedrooms and even in our thoughts. That is nonsense. On the other hand, I have seen enough evidence in the past year to

255

convince me of the devastation inflicted on victims of pornography. It is on their behalf that we must intervene. Here, then, are the harms as I perceive them.

(1) Depictions of violence against women are related to violence against women everywhere. Though social research on this subject has been difficult to conduct, the totality of evidence supports the linkage between illustration and imitation. Furthermore, pornography perpetrates the so-called "rape myth" whereby women are consistently depicted as wanting to be assaulted even when they deny it. They are shown as terrified victims in the beginnings of rape scenes, but conclude by begging for more. Men who want to believe that women crave violent sex can find plenty of pornographic evidence to support their predilections.

(2) For a certain percentage of men, the use of pornographic material is addictive and progressive. Like the addiction to drugs, alcohol, or food, those who are hooked on sex become obsessed by their need. It fills their world, night and day. And too often, their families are destroyed in the process.

(3) Pornography is degrading to women. How could any of us, having heard Andrea Dworkin's moving testimony, turn a deaf ear to her protest? The pornographic depictions she described are an affront to an entire gender, and I would take that case to any jury in the land. Remember that men are the purchasers of pornography. Many witnesses testified that women are typically repulsed by visual depictions of the type therein described. It is provided primarily for the lustful pleasure of men and boys who use it to generate excitation. And it is my belief, though evidence is not easily obtained, that a small but dangerous minority will then choose to act aggressively against the nearest available females. Pornography is the theory; rape is the practice.

(4) It appears extremely naive to assume that the river of obscenity which has inundated the American landscape has not invaded the world of children. This seven-billion-dollar industry pervades every dimension of our lives. There are more stores selling pornographic videos than there are McDonald hamburger stands. More than 800,000 phone calls are made each day to dial-a-porn companies in New York (180,000,000 in 1984), many placed by boys and girls still in elementary school. Furthermore, recent clinical observations by Dr. Victor Cline and others have indicated that a growing number of children are finding their parents' sexually explicit videos and magazines, and are experimenting with what they have learned on younger children. The problem is spreading rapidly. Obviously, obscenity cannot be permitted to flow freely through the veins of society without reaching the eyes and ears of our children. Latchkey kids by the millions are watching porn on Cable TV and reading their parents' adult magazines. For 50 cents, they can purchase their own pornographic tabloids from vendor machines on the street. Or they can hear shocking vulgarities for free on their heavy metal radio stations. At an age when elementary school children should be reading Tom Sawyer and viewing traditional entertainment in the spirit of Walt Disney, they are learning perverted facts which neither their minds nor bodies are equipped to handle. It is my belief, accordingly, that the behavior of an entire generation of teenagers is being adversely affected by the current emphasis on premarital sexuality and general eroticism seen nightly on televison, in the movies, and in the other sources of pornography I have mentioned. It is not surprising that

the incidence of unwed pregnancy and abortions has skyrocketed since 1970. Teens are merely doing what they've been taught, that they should get into bed, early and often. And to a large degree, pornography has done this to them.

(5) Organized crime controls more than 85 percent of all commercially produced pornography in America. The sale and distribution of these materials produces huge profits for the crime lords who also sell illegal drugs to our kids and engage in murder, fraud, bribery, and every vice known to man. Are we to conclude that the 7 billion (or more) tax-free dollars that they receive each year from the pornography industry is not harmful to society? Is malignant melanoma harmful to the human body?

(6) Pornography is often used by pedophiles to soften children's defenses against sexual exploitation. They are shown nude pictures of adults, for example, and are told, "See. This is what mommies and daddies do." They are then stripped of innocence and subjected to brutalities that they will remember for a lifetime.

(7) Outlets for obscenity are magnets for sex-related crimes. When a thriving adult bookstore moves into a neighborhood, an array of "support-services" typically develops around it. Prostitution, narcotics, and street crime proliferate. From this perspective, it is interesting that law enforcement officials often claim they do not investigate or attempt to control the flow of obscenity because they lack the resources to combat it. In reality, their resources will extend farther if they first enforce the laws relating to pornography. The consequent reduction in crime makes this a cost-effective use of taxpayer's funds.

The City of Cincinnati, Ohio, has demonstrated how a community can rid

itself of obscenity without inordinate expenditures of personnel and money.

(8) So-called adult bookstores are often centers of disease and homosexual activity. Again, the average citizen is not aware that the primary source of revenue in adult bookstores is derived from video and film booths. Patrons enter these 3-by-3 foot cubicles and deposit a coin in the slot. They are then treated to about 90 seconds of a pornographic movie. If they want to see more, they must continue to pump coins (usually quarters) in the machine. The booths I witnessed on New York's Times Square were even more graphic. Upon depositing the coin, a screen was raised, revealing two or more women and men who performed live sex acts upon one another on a small stage. Everything that is possible for heterosexuals, homosexuals, or lesbians to do was demonstrated a few feet from the viewers. The booths from which these videos or live performers are viewed become filthy beyond description as the day progresses. Police investigators testified before our Commission that the stench is unbearable and that the floor becomes sticky with semen, urine, and saliva. Holes in the walls between the booths are often provided to permit male homosexuals to service one another. Given the current concern over sexually transmitted diseases and especially Acquired Immune Deficiency Syndrome (AIDS), it is incredible that health departments have not attempted to regulate such businesses. States that will not allow restaurant owners or hairdressers or counselors or acupuncturists to operate without licenses have permitted these wretched cesspools to escape governmental scrutiny. To every public health officer in the country I would ask, "Why?"

(9) Finally, pornography is a source of significant harm to the institution of the

family and to society at large. Can anything which devastates vulnerable little children, as we have seen, be considered innocuous to the parents who produced them? Raising healthy children is the primary occupation of families, and anything which invades the childhoods and twists the minds of boys and girls must be seen as abhorrent to the mothers and fathers who gave them birth. Furthermore, what is at stake here is the future of the family itself. We are sexual creatures, and the physical attraction between males and females provides the basis for every dimension of marriage and parenthood. Thus, *anything* that interjects itself into that relationship must be embraced with great caution. Until we *know* that pornography is not addictive and progressive . . . until we are *certain* that the passion of fantasy does not destroy the passion of reality . . . until we are *sure* that obsessive use of obscene materials will not lead to perversions and conflict between husbands and wives . . . then we dare not adorn them with the crown of respectability. Society has an absolute obligation to protect itself from material which crosses the line established objectively by its legislators and court system. That is not sexual repression. That is self-preservation.

If not limited by time and space, I could describe dozens of other harms associated with exposure to pornography. Presumably, members of Congress were also cognizant of these dangers when they drafted legislation to control sexually explicit material. The President and his predecessors would not have signed those bills into criminal laws if they had not agreed. The Supreme Court must have shared the same concerns when it ruled that obscenity is not protected by the First Amendment—reaffirming the validity and constitutionality of current laws. How can

it be, then, that these carefully crafted laws are not being enforced? Good question! The refusal of federal and local officials to check the rising tide of obscenity is a disgrace and an outrage. It is said that the production and distribution of pornography is the only unregulated industry remaining today . . . the last vestige of "free enterprise" in America. Indeed, the *salient* finding emerging from 12 months of testimony before our Commission reflected this utter paralysis of government in response to the pornographic plague. As citizens of a democratic society, we have surrendered our right to protect ourselves in return for protection by the State. Thus, our governmental representatives have a constitutional mandate to shield us from harm and criminal activity . . . including that associated with obscenity. It is time that our leaders were held accountable for their obvious malfeasance. Attorney General Meese, who has courageously supported other unpopular causes, has been reluctant to tackle this one. He is reportedly awaiting the final report from the Commission before mobilizing the Department of Justice. We will see what happens now. . . .

. . . [It] is my hope that the effort we invested will provide the basis for a new public policy. But that will occur only if American citizens demand action from their government. Nothing short of a public outcry will motivate our slumbering representatives to defend community standards of decency. It is that public statement that the pornographers fear most, and for very good reason. The people possess the power in this wonderful democracy to override apathetic judges, disinterested police chiefs, unmotivated U.S. Attorneys, and unwilling federal officials. I pray that they will do so. If they do not, then we have labored in vain. . . .

POSTSCRIPT

SHOULD PORNOGRAPHY BE PROTECTED AS FREE SPEECH?

Much of the argument over pornography seems to turn on the question of causality. Does viewing certain kinds of material tend to cause antisocial behavior? Dobson and the other majority members of the Attorney General's Commission say yes; their critics say no, or at least deny that there is sufficient evidence to say yes. The problem of causality in the social sciences is notoriously complicated. But do we always have to produce evidence of harmful effects before banning an activity? Gambling, prostitution, school segregation, guns, and drugs all belong in a shadowy area of the law—they are either illegal or heavily regulated—though we lack indisputable evidence of their bad effects on society. Civil libertarians reply that society may regulate public behavior to a greater extent than it may inhibit free expression.

One of the categories of pornography studied by the Attorney General's Commission was "nonviolent but degrading" pornography. Can the two categories be separated? Feminist writer Susan Brownmiller, in her book *Against Our Will: Men, Women, and Rape* (Simon and Schuster, 1975), argues that they cannot. Political scientist Harry Clor also argues, in *Obscenity and Public Morality* (University of Chicago, 1969), that degradation is the Siamese twin of violence. Both Brownmiller and Clor think that certain kinds of pornography should be banned, while attorney Charles Rembar (*The End of Obscenity*, Random House, 1968) who has argued for the defense in several obscenity cases, considers that unwise and unconstitutional.

There is, of course, no real "end of obscenity," nor any end of debate over it. Every age seems to redefine it according to contemporary standards. Neither the *Roth* decision of 1957, nor the *Miller* decision of 1973, nor the Pornography Commission Report of 1986, has settled the question of what precisely pornography *is*. Perhaps that is why we can all appreciate the artlessness of the late Supreme Court Justice Potter Stewart, who said he couldn't define pornography but "I know it when I see it."

ISSUE 15

SHOULD ABORTION BE OUTLAWED?

YES: Ronald Reagan, from "Abortion and the Conscience of the Nation,"
Human Life Review (Spring 1983)

NO: Beverly Wildung Harrison, from *Our Right to Choose: Toward a New
Ethic of Abortion* (Beacon Press, 1983)

ISSUE SUMMARY

YES: President Ronald Reagan argues that abortion involves the killing of
innocent human beings and is not essentially different from infanticide.
NO: Ethics Professor Beverly Wildung Harrison contends that the right to
abort must be included among the rights essential to women's freedom.

At one time, laws forbade even the publication of information regarding
contraception and abortion, and it was not until 1965 that the Supreme
Court declared that the law could not prohibit the dispensing of
contraceptive devices to married men and women. In 1973 the Supreme
Court made its landmark rulings on abortion, which have shaped the
subsequent political debates. The Court ruled that during the first trimester
of pregnancy, women have a constitutionally protected right to secure an
abortion and that during the second trimester of pregnancy (that is, the
fourth through sixth months), only restrictions reasonably related to a
woman's health could be imposed upon her right to secure an abortion.
Only during the final three months of pregnancy, the Court ruled, may the
state prohibit abortion—but even then abortions must be allowed if the
physician believes the procedure is indicated to preserve the mother's life
or health. This includes psychological as well as physical well-being.
The Court's rulings aroused a storm of controversy that has not abated,
and it is not likely to die down within the foreseeable future. Although
illegal abortions were widely performed before state laws forbidding
abortions had been invalidated, the number of abortions increased rapidly
in the years after the Court's 1973 decisions. It has been estimated that

260

over one and a half million abortions have been performed in each of the past several years. If current trends continue, four out of every ten females will become pregnant between the ages of fourteen and twenty. Barring changes in the law, half of these pregnancies will be terminated by abortion.

Can a statute declare the existence of a scientific fact? The opponents of abortion believe that it is a fact that life begins at conception and that the law may therefore restate and enforce this concept. They argue that the human fetus is a live human being, and they note all the familiar signs of life displayed by the fetus: a beating heart, brain waves, thumb-sucking, and so on. The defenders of abortion maintain that human life does not begin before the development of specifically human charac-teristics and possibly not until the birth of a child. As Justice Harry Blackmun put it in 1973: "There has always been strong support for the view that life does not begin until live birth."

Distinctions can be made regarding the right to abortion when pregnancy is caused by rape or results from incest, when the health of either the pregnant woman or the fetus may be adversely affected, when the pregnant woman is unmarried and either unwilling or unable to marry the father of the baby, or when economic circumstances create pressures to limit the size of the family. Most of the people who feel most strongly about the right of abortion do not make most of these distinctions and either favor or oppose the right without qualifications. While public opinion polls show the majority of people favor the right of abortion where rape, incest, or the life of the mother are involved, different polls reach contradictory conclusions regarding public sentiment about the general right of abortion.

The opponents of abortion have launched a counterattack against the Supreme Court's decisions. Federal funding for Medicaid abortions has been cut off, and federal courts have affirmed the right of Congress not to pay for abortions. Critics of the law have charged that it simply discriminates against poor women because it does not inhibit the ability of women who are able to pay for an abortion to obtain one. Broader efforts to outlaw abortion have taken the forms of a proposed Human Rights Amendment and a Human Rights Bill. Different versions of a constitutional amendment have been proposed: One would outlaw abortions throughout the nation; the other, a less sweeping proposal, would allow states freedom to enact their own anti-abortion laws if they wanted to. The Human Life Bill would get into particulars. Since the Court in the Roe case said that it could not say precisely when human life begins, the Bill would be aimed at guiding the Court by saying that life begins with conception. Thus far, for a variety of reasons—from filibusters in the Senate to the difficulty of meeting the two-thirds requirement for the passage of a constitutional amendment—neither the amendment nor the bill have emerged from Congress.

In the following selections, President Reagan, who supported both the constitutional amendment and the Human Life Bill, states his reasons for opposing abortion, while ethics professor Beverly Wildung Harrison states her case for supporting the freedom of women to have an abortion.

YES

Ronald W. Reagan

ABORTION AND THE
CONSCIENCE OF THE NATION

The 10th anniversary of the Supreme Court decision in *Roe v. Wade* is a good time for us to pause and reflect. Our nationwide policy of abortion-on-demand through all nine months of pregnancy was neither voted for by our people nor enacted by our legislators—not a single State had such unrestricted abortion before the Supreme Court decreed it to be national policy in 1973. But the consequences of this judicial decision are now obvious: since 1973, more than 15 million unborn children have had their lives snuffed out by legalized abortions. That is over ten times the number of Americans lost in all our nation's wars.

Make no mistake, abortion-on-demand is not a right granted by the Constitution. No serious scholar, including one disposed to agree with the Court's result, has argued that the framers of the Constitution intended to create such a right. Shortly after the *Roe v. Wade* decision, Professor John Hart Ely, now Dean of Stanford Law School, wrote that the opinion "is not constitutional law and gives almost no sense of an obligation to try to be." Nowhere do the plain words of the Constitution even hint at a "right" so sweeping as to permit abortion up to the time the child is ready to be born. Yet that is what the Court ruled.

As an act of "raw judicial power" (to use Justice White's biting phrase), the decision by the seven-man majority in *Roe v. Wade* has so far been made to stick. But the Court's decision has by no means settled the debate. Instead, *Roe v. Wade* has become a continuing prod to the conscience of the nation.

Abortion concerns not just the unborn child, it concerns every one of us. The English poet, John Donne, wrote: ". . . any man's death diminishes me, because I am involved in mankind; and therefore never send to know for whom the bell tolls; it tolls for thee."

We cannot diminish the value of one category of human life—the unborn—without diminishing the value of all human life. We saw tragic proof of this truism last year when the Indiana courts allowed the starvation death of "Baby Doe" in Bloomington because the child had Down's Syndrome.

Many of our fellow citizens grieve over the loss of life that has followed *Roe v. Wade*. Margaret Heckler, soon after being nominated to head the largest department of our government, Health and Human Services, told an audience that she believed abortion to be the greatest moral crisis facing our country today. And the revered Mother Teresa, who works in the streets of Calcutta ministering to dying people in her world-famous mission of mercy, has said that "the greatest misery of our time is the generalized abortion of children."

Over the first two years of my Administration I have closely followed and assisted efforts in Congress to reverse the tide of abortion—efforts of Congressmen, Senators and citizens responding to an urgent moral crisis. Regrettably, I have also seen the massive efforts of those who, under the banner of "freedom of choice," have so far blocked every effort to reverse nationwide abortion-on-demand.

Despite the formidable obstacles before us, we must not lose heart. This is not the first time our country has been divided by a Supreme Court decision that denied the value of certain human lives. The *Dred Scott* decision of 1857 was not overturned in a day, or a year, or even a decade. At first, only a minority of Americans recognized and deplored the moral crisis brought about by denying the full humanity of our black brothers and sisters; but that minority persisted in their vision and finally prevailed. They did it by appealing to the hearts and minds of their countrymen, to the truth of human dignity under God. From their example, we know that respect for the sacred value of human life is too deeply engrained in the hearts of our

people to remain forever suppressed. But the great majority of the American people have not yet made their voices heard, and we cannot expect them to—any more than the public voice arose against slavery—until the issue is clearly framed and presented.

What, then, is the real issue? I have often said that when we talk about abortion, we are talking about two lives—the life of the mother and the life of the unborn child. Why else do we call a pregnant woman a mother? I have also said that anyone who doesn't feel sure whether we are talking about a second human life should clearly give life the benefit of a doubt. If you don't know whether a body is alive or dead, you would never bury it. I think this consideration itself should be enough for all of us to insist on protecting the unborn.

The case against abortion does not rest here, however, for medical practice confirms at every step the correctness of these moral sensibilities. Modern medicine treats the unborn child as a patient. Medical pioneers have made great breakthroughs in treating the unborn—for genetic problems, vitamin deficiencies, irregular heart rhythms, and other medical conditions. Who can forget George Will's moving account of the little boy who underwent brain surgery six times during the nine weeks before he was born? Who is the *patient* if not that tiny unborn human being who can feel pain when he or she is approached by doctors who come to kill rather than to cure?

The real question today is not when human life begins, but, *What is the value of human life?* The abortionist who reassembles the arms and legs of a tiny baby to make sure all its parts have been torn from its mother's body can hardly doubt whether it is a human being. The real question for him and for all of us is whether that tiny

15. SHOULD ABORTION BE OUTLAWED?

human life has a God-given right to be protected by the law—the same right we have.

What more dramatic confirmation could we have of the real issue than the Baby Doe case in Bloomington, Indiana? The death of that tiny infant tore at the hearts of all Americans because the child was undeniably a live human being—one lying helpless before the eyes of the doctors and the eyes of the nation. The real issue for the courts was *not* whether Baby Doe was a human being. The real issue was whether to protect the life of a human being who had Down's Syndrome, who would probably be mentally handicapped, but who needed a routine surgical procedure to unblock his esophagus and allow him to eat. A doctor testified to the presiding judge that, even with his physical problem corrected, Baby Doe would have a "non-existent" possibility for "a minimally adequate quality of life"—in other words, that retardation was the equivalent of a crime deserving the death penalty. The judge let Baby Doe starve and die, and the Indiana Supreme Court sanctioned his decision.

Federal law does not allow Federally-assisted hospitals to decide that Down's Syndrome infants are not worth treating, much less to decide to starve them to death. Accordingly, I have directed the Departments of Justice and HHS to apply civil rights regulations to protect handicapped newborns. All hospitals receiving Federal funds must post notices which will clearly state that failure to feed handicapped babies is prohibited by Federal law. The basic issue is whether to value and protect the lives of the handicapped, whether to recognize the sanctity of human life. This is the same basic issue that underlies the question of abortion.

The 1981 Senate hearings on the beginning of human life brought out the basic issue more clearly than ever before. The many medical and scientific witnesses who testified disagreed on many things, but not on the *scientific* evidence that the unborn child is alive, is a distinct individual, or is a member of the human species. They did disagree over the *value* question, whether to give value to a human life at its early and most vulnerable stages of existence.

Regrettably, we live at a time when some persons do *not* value all human life. They want to pick and choose which individuals have value. Some have said that only those individuals with "consciousness of self" are human beings. One such writer has followed this deadly logic and concluded that "shocking as it may seem, a newly born infant is not a human being."

A Nobel Prize winning scientist has suggested that if a handicapped child "were not declared fully human until three days after birth, then all parents could be allowed the choice." In other words, "quality control" to see if newly born human beings are up to snuff.

Obviously, some influential people want to deny that every human life has intrinsic, sacred worth. They insist that a member of the human race must have certain qualities before they accord him or her status as a "human being."

Events have borne out the editorial in a California medical journal which explained three years before *Roe v. Wade* that the social acceptance of abortion is a "defiance of the long-held Western ethic of intrinsic and equal value for every human life regardless of its stage, condition, or status."

Every legislator, every doctor, and every citizen needs to recognize that the real issue is whether to affirm and protect the sanctity of all human life, or to embrace a social ethic where some human lives are valued and others are not. As a nation, we must choose between the sanctity of life

264

ethic and the quality of life ethic.

I have no trouble identifying the answer our nation has always given to this basic question, and the answer that I hope and pray it will give in the future. America was founded by men and women who shared a vision of the value of each and every individual. They stated this vision clearly from the very start in the Declaration of Independence, using words that every schoolboy and schoolgirl can recite:

> We hold these truths to be self-evident, that all men are created equal, that they are endowed by their Creator with certain unalienable rights, that among these are life, liberty, and the pursuit of happiness.

We fought a terrible war to guarantee that one category of mankind—black people in America—could not be denied the inalienable rights with which their Creator endowed them. The great champion of the sanctity of all human life in that day, Abraham Lincoln, gave us his assessment of the Declaration's purpose. Speaking of the framers of that noble document, he said:

> This was their majestic interpretation of the economy of the Universe. This was their lofty, and wise, and noble understanding of the justice of the Creator to His creatures. Yes, gentlemen, to all His creatures, to the whole great family of man. In their enlightened belief, nothing stamped with the divine image and likeness was sent into the world to be trodden on... They grasped not only the whole race of men then living, but they reached forward and seized upon the farthest posterity. They erected a beacon to guide their children and their children's children, and the countless myriads who should inhabit the earth in other ages.

He warned also of the danger we would face if we closed our eyes to the value of life in any category of human beings:

> I should like to know if taking this old Declaration of Independence, which declares that all men are equal upon principle and making exceptions to it where will it stop. If one man says it does not mean a Negro, why not another say it does not mean some other man?

When Congressman John A. Bingham of Ohio drafted the Fourteenth Amendment to guarantee the rights of life, liberty, and property to all human beings, he explained that *all* are "entitled to the protection of American law, because its divine spirit of equality declares that all men are created equal." He said the rights guaranteed by the amendment would therefore apply to "any human being." Justice William Brennan, writing in another case decided only the year before *Roe v. Wade*, referred to our society as one that "strongly affirms the sanctity of life."

Another William Brennan—not the Justice—has reminded us of the terrible consequences that can follow when a nation rejects the sanctity of life ethic:

> The cultural environment for a human holocaust is present whenever any society can be misled into defining individuals as less than human and therefore devoid of value and respect.

As a nation today, we have *not* rejected the sanctity of human life. The American people have not had an opportunity to express their view on the sanctity of human life in the unborn. I am convinced that Americans do not want to play God with the value of human life. It is not for us to decide who is worthy to live and who is not. Even the Supreme Court's opinion in *Roe v. Wade* did not explicitly reject the traditional American idea of intrinsic worth and value in all human life; it simply dodged this issue. . . .

We must all educate ourselves to the reality of the horrors taking place. Doctors today know that unborn children can feel a touch within the womb and that they respond to pain. But how many Americans are aware that abortion techniques are allowed today, in all 50 states, that burn the skin of a baby with a salt solution, in an agonizing death that can last for hours?

Another example: two years ago, the *Philadelphia Inquirer* ran a Sunday special supplement on "The Dreaded Complication." The "dreaded complication" referred to in the article—the complication feared by doctors who perform abortions—is the *survival* of the child despite all the painful attacks during the abortion procedure. Some unborn children *do survive the late-term abortions* the Supreme Court has made legal. Is there any question that these victims of abortion deserve our attention and protection? Is there any question that those who *don't* survive were living human beings before they were killed?

Late-term abortions, especially when the baby survives, but is then killed by starvation, neglect, or suffocation, show once again the link between abortion and infanticide. The time to stop both is now. As my Administration acts to stop infanticide, we will be fully aware of the real issue that underlies the death of babies before and soon after birth.

Our society has, fortunately, become sensitive to the rights and special needs of the handicapped, but I am shocked that physical or mental handicaps of newborns are still used to justify their extinction. This Administration has a Surgeon General, Dr. C. Everett Koop, who has done perhaps more than any other American for handicapped children, by pioneering surgical techniques to help them, by speaking out on the value of their lives, and by working with them in the context of loving families. You will not find his former patients advocating the so-called quality of life ethic.

I know that when the true issue of infanticide is placed before the American people, with all the facts openly aired, we will have no trouble deciding that a mentally or physically handicapped baby has the same intrinsic worth and right to life as the rest of us. As the New Jersey Supreme Court said two decades ago, in a decision upholding the sanctity of human life, "a child need not be perfect to have a worthwhile life."

Whether we are talking about pain suffered by unborn children, or about late-term abortions, or about infanticide, we inevitably focus on the humanity of the unborn child. Each of these issues is a potential rallying point for the sanctity of life ethic. Once we as a nation rally around any one of these issues to affirm the sanctity of life, we will see the importance of affirming this principle across the board.

Malcolm Muggeridge, the English writer, goes right to the heart of the matter: "Either life is always and in all circumstances sacred, or intrinsically of no account; it is inconceivable that it should be in some cases the one, and in some the other." The sanctity of innocent human life is a principle that Congress should proclaim at every opportunity.

It is possible that the Supreme Court itself may overturn its abortion rulings. We need only recall that in *Brown v. Board of Education* the Court reversed its own earlier "separate-but-equal" decision. I believe if the Supreme Court took another look at *Roe v. Wade,* and considered the real issue between the sanctity of life ethic and quality of life ethic, it would change its mind once again.

As we continue to work to overturn *Roe v. Wade,* we must also continue to lay the groundwork for a society in which abortion is not the accepted answer to unwanted pregnancy. Pro-life people have already taken heroic steps, often at great personal sacrifice, to provide for unwed mothers. I recently spoke about a young pregnant woman named Victoria, who said, "In this society we save whales, we save timber wolves and bald eagles and Coke bottles. Yet, everyone wanted me to throw away my baby." She has been helped by Sav-a-Life, a group in Dallas, which provides a way for unwed mothers to preserve the human life within them when they might otherwise be tempted to resort to abortion. I think also of House of His Creation in Coastesville, Pennsylvania, where a loving couple has taken in almost 200 young women in the past ten years. They have seen, as a fact of life, that the girls are *not* better off having abortions than saving their babies. I am also reminded of the remarkable Rossow family of Ellington, Connecticut, who have opened their hearts and their home to nine handicapped adopted and foster children.

The Adolescent Family Life Program, adopted by Congress at the request of Senator Jeremiah Denton, has opened new opportunities for unwed mothers to give their children life. We should not rest until our entire society echoes the tone of John Powell in the dedication of his book, *Abortion: The Silent Holocaust,* a dedication to every woman carrying an unwanted child: "Please believe that you are not alone. There are many of us that truly love you, who want to stand at your side, and help in any way we can." And we can echo the always-practical woman of faith, Mother Teresa, when she says, "If you don't want the little child, that unborn child, give him to me." We have so many families in America seeking to adopt children that the slogan "*every* child a *wanted* child" is now the emptiest of all reasons to tolerate abortion.

I have often said we need to join in prayer to bring protection to the unborn. Prayer and action are needed to uphold the sanctity of human life. I believe it will not be possible to accomplish our work, the work of saving lives, "without being a soul of prayer." The famous British Member of Parliament, William Wilberforce, prayed with his small group of influential friends, the "Clapham Sect," for *decades* to see an end to slavery in the British empire. Wilberforce led that struggle to Parliament, unflaggingly, because he believed in the sanctity of human life. He saw the fulfillment of his impossible dream when Parliament outlawed slavery just before his death.

Let his faith and perseverance be our guide. We will never recognize the true value of our own lives until we affirm the value in the life of others, a value of which Malcolm Muggeridge says: ". . . however low it flickers or fiercely burns, it is still a Divine flame which no man dare presume to put out, be his motives ever so humane and enlightened."

Abraham Lincoln recognized that we could not survive as a free land when some men could decide that others were not fit to be free and should therefore be slaves. Likewise, we cannot survive as a free nation when some men decide that others are not fit to live and should be abandoned to abortion or infanticide. . . .

NO

Beverly Wildung Harrison

OUR RIGHT TO CHOOSE

THE WIDER MORAL FRAMEWORK FOR THE ACT OF ABORTION

... I argue that a society which would deny the conditions of procreative choice to women, or which treats women merely or chiefly as reproductive means to some purported end of that society's own self-perpetuation, is one that mandates women's inferior status as less than full, rational beings, denying women full claim to intrinsic value in the process. Likewise, a society that incorporates a perdurable structure of coercion, even violence, against women as morally appropriate to its functioning, but claims that it upholds the sanctity of or respect for human life is deluded. ...

It is little wonder, then, that feminist efforts to articulate a moral argument about bodily integrity and its relevance to procreation are met with almost incredulous disbelief, derision, or trivialization in the ethical literature on abortion. To be sure, when fetal life is adjudged full, existent human life, appeals to body-right will not have automatic, overriding force because where two existent human beings are involved there will be a conflict of rights. (Such conflicts occur all the time in our social world.) But this recognition of *possible* conflict of rights is not usually what is assumed in discussions of the morality of abortion. Rather, appeals women make to their right to bodily self-control and self-direction are treated, at best, as nonmoral, morally irrelevant, or ethically confused and, at worst, as selfish, whimsical, or positive evidence of the immorality of women who choose to have or to defend legal abortions.

I claim that the fact of women's biological fertility and capacity for childbearing in no way overrides our moral claim to the "right" of bodily integrity, because this moral claim is inherent to human well-being. Furthermore, if the full implications of women's history were comprehended, including the morally onerous attitudes and violent practices toward women, then reproductive self-determination would be understood to reinforce the substantive social justice claim about bodily integrity. Reproductive choice for women is requisite to any adequate notion of what constitutes a good society. Transformed social conditions of reproduction are absolutely critical to all women's wellbeing. No society that coerces women at the level of reproduction may lay claim to moral adequacy.

I agree strongly with those who have argued that the notion of "rights" is intrinsically social; it pertains to conditions of relationship between existent beings. I would insist one ought not to impute the existence of "rights" in a social relation unless all parties fall within some justifiable definition of "existents" vis-à-vis our human relations. In discussing the moral meaning of fetal life, we cannot afford to overlook the social character of "rights." When anyone invokes the claim that a fetus has "a right to life," we are justified in being wary, unless or until a plausible account is given of the criteria grounding the contention that a fetus is properly a full member of the class of human beings.

I have also stressed a more utilitarian or "concrete consequentialist" argument for procreative choice that correlates with but is logically discrete from the foregoing one: namely that given women's overall, continuing, disadvantaged socioeconomic situation, together with the de facto reality of childbearing, women should have procreative choice. Women most frequently must provide the life energy, physical and emotional support, and, increasingly, the economic wherewithal for infant survival, growth, and development. Under such circumstances, optimal conditions of procreative choice for women are mandatory.

I have constructed my case to put both good society or rights arguments and utilitarian teleological arguments in the forefront, not only because of my own methodological convictions but, even more important, because so much con-

temporary philosophical and religioethical analysis approaches the morality of abortion with such a weak sense of the relevance of these considerations. No moralist would be considered reputable if he or she argued the morality of economic life either by abdicating reflection on the meaning of a good society or by ignoring the concrete effects of economic policy and practice on people's lives. But, indeed, it *is* acceptable to discuss the morality of abortion without examining the implications of our moral judgments on what a "good society" should be and without taking into account the actual condition of women in society. Hence my ongoing contention is that, given the present climate of opinion among ethicists, it is necessary to insist that the positive principle of justice and the issue of social welfare, or social utility, are both at stake in procreative choice, or noncoercion in childbearing.

If one approaches the question of the morality of abortion without an acute sense of the viability of all these moral claims, then the question of the moral valuation of fetal life inevitably appears to be the only relevant question and the moral problematic of abortion seems to pose a fairly simple moral quandary. If, however, one recognizes the moral dubiousness of a society that treats women as less than full persons with an appropriate and serious moral claim to well-being, self-respect, self-direction and noncoercion in childbearing, and if one also recognizes the disadvantaged state of most women's lives, one's approach to the morality of abortion must shift. Even if one holds, as I do *not*, that fetal life is, from conception or at the point when the genetic code is implanted, essentially a *full, existent* human life, it is necessary to comprehend that we are dealing with a genuine moral dilemma, a conflict of "rights," not a moral chimera in which the "innocent party"—the fetal "person"—is, *by definition,* the "wronged" party in the moral equation.

To address the question "When does human life begin?" or to ask more precisely "What is the moral status of fetal life?" is something we are bound to do, given our modern scientific understanding of embryological development. Yet the questions are a far more intricate matter than they may appear at face value. Biological science itself is a complex, cultural construct, and biological scientists themselves differ over the moral implications of their paradigm. None of us nontechnical interpreters of these scientific data proceed untouched by our own operating cultural and social understandings. In fact, beneath the diverse judgments moralists make about the meaning of fetal life lie differing philosophies of nature and of science, including quite disparate views of biological theory, as well as conflicting methodological assumptions about how scientific "fact" and moral valuation interrelate. . . .

Even though there are reasonable grounds for positing the existence of a genetically developed individuated human body form from sometime after the midpoint of pregnancy onward, it does not follow that we should consider a fetus to be "a person" from this earliest possible point of species differentiation. Many have argued that the term *person* should be reserved to designate those who *actually belong* to the moral community by virtue of criteria derived from our understanding of living human beings. In a notable defense of this position, philosopher Mary Anne Warren has proposed the following criteria for "personhood":

> I suggest that the traits which are most central to the concept of personhood, or humanity in the moral sense, are, very roughly, the following:

1. consciousness (of objects and events external and/or internal to the being), and in particular the capacity to feel pain;
2. reasoning (the developed capacity to solve new and relatively complex problems);
3. self-motivated activity (activity which is relatively independent of either genetic or direct external control);
4. the capacity to communicate, by whatever means, messages of an indefinite variety of types, that is, not just with an indefinite number of possible contents, but on indefinitely many possible topics;
5. the presence of self-concepts, and self-awareness, either individual or social, or both.

Warren does not suppose that any of these criteria are indisputable, but what she does maintain, correctly I believe, is that a fetus possesses *none* of the criteria that come to mind when we think normatively of a "person." . . .

In the debate over the morality of abortion, those who correlate "personhood" with any level of gestational maturation seem to me to obscure, or to fail to appreciate, the integrity of arguments formulated by pro-choice supporters about the importance of "quality of life" questions regarding procreation or birth. Whether or not we wish to acknowledge it, the constitutive foundations of personality are bound up not with biological maturation of the human species life form but with the quality of our social relations. For centuries, even millennia, we human beings have permitted ourselves the luxury of imagining that our personal life follows inexorably from our existence as a natural or species life form, ignoring the now growing evidence that it is our human social relations, the quality of our interaction with each other, that conditions all that we become after birth. Ours is a world in which there is "a crisis of the personal"— that is, a loss of the very conditions that make it possible for individuals who share human species being to live, grow, and thrive as genuinely personal beings having deeply centered personal relations to others. A biologically reductionist understanding of our species, which fully conflates the biologically human and the "person," threatens to intensify this crisis in our human moral relations. Ironically, the "fetishizing of fetuses" in the abortion debate may well exacerbate our already overdeveloped tendency to consider ourselves "normatively human" quite apart from the world of social relations our moral action creates. The birth of an infant, understood from the standpoint of organic embryological development, is an event. Birth is an inexorable watershed in organic process, however, because the care and nurturance of a newborn inaugurates an infinitely complex series of actions. . . .

With respect to the abortion controversy, it is worth remembering that *any* definition of "a human life" or "person" that neglects the moral reality required to nurture and sustain life after birth is very dangerous to our self-understanding. A "pro-life" movement that invites us to "respect" fetal rights from conception or genetic implantation onward actually undermines us by tempting us to imagine that personal rights inhere in natural processes, apart from any genuine covenant of caring, including the human resolve to create viable conditions of life for all who are born among us. Human rights are qualities that ought to inhere in our social relations. Any use of the concept that neglects this fact invites us to take with less than full seriousness the sort of claim we ought to be making when we say that human beings have "a right to life." Early fetal life does *not* yet possess

even the minimal organic requirements for participation in the sphere of human rights. And like Mary Anne Warren, I do not believe that even the highly developed fetus can yet be said to have "an intrinsic right to life." Even so, I recognize that it is morally wise to extend such respect, de facto, to fetuses in late stages of gestation. But to do so is also and simultaneously to insist that rights are moral relations, born of our freedom as mature, other-regarding persons. In extending "a right to life" to fetuses in late stages of development, we are attesting that it is a good use of our freedom as agents, from a moral point of view, to do so.

To argue that *we* may appropriately predicate to fetuses, in the late stages of gestation, "a right to life" does not mean, however, that the life of the pregnant woman should be overridden in decisions about late-stage pregnancies. Rather, it means that abortions, at least in the second half of gestation, are not to be undertaken without serious justifications. My own belief is that the physical and emotional well-being of the pregnant woman, as a valuable existent person, still outweighs the incremental value of the fetus her life sustains. Of course, it is true that in the later stages of pregnancy, abortions are matters of high risk for pregnant women. But doctors, who under most existing laws have discretion as to whether an abortion is advisable at this stage, are themselves not likely to be "frivolous" about the decisions that confront them given the danger of late abortions. . . .

[A]bortions will continue to be available whether or not they are legal. Ironically, then, those persons insisting that a human life begins at conception or at an early stage of genetic human development may help to create a situation in which abortions, though they will not cease, will occur at a later stage of gestation. . . .

Persons of authentic theological sensibility must continue to insist that every child who is born among us deserves to be embraced in a covenant of love and affirmation that includes not merely the love of a mother, or a father, but the active concern and respect of the wider community. We must never imagine that the conditions for such deeply humane covenant exist. I noted at the outset that if women did not have to deliberate the questions relating to our procreative power in an atmosphere of taboo, we would be able to turn our attention to the positive moral task I have commended: what it means for us to use our procreative power responsibly. In the present condemnatory atmosphere, such moral reasoning will go largely undeveloped.

Even so, the deepest reappropriation of the theological theme of the covenant that women can make requires our perception of procreation as a moral act, one we must enter into with maximum awareness of what it means to bear a child. We are still a long way from a historical situation in which women really will have the conditions that make such a genuine covenant and choice an easy matter. Safe surgical abortion has created only the negative conditions for procreative choice. We often now live in situations where it is easier to say no than to say yes to this prospective

covenant. The current circumstances in which women choose abortions are often dominated by desperation. And yet it is now possible to begin to anticipate what it would mean to incorporate this covenantal image into the total process of species reproduction. When such a covenant of life is embodied in the birth of every child, an incredible reduction in human suffering will have been accomplished.

Any of us who have experienced human joy in the knowledge of our birth at some level have heard God's call to life through the "yes" of our parents. Without that yes, life is immeasurably impoverished. In fact, it is necessary to put the point more strongly. Those who are born in the absence of such an act of human covenant by already living persons (of course, not merely by our biological parents) frequently do not really live at all. Our acknowledgment of each other in relation is not an optional addition to life, an afterthought; it is constitutive of life itself. For a vital human life to be born, a woman must say yes in a strong and active way and enter positively into a life-bearing, demanding, and, at times, extremely painful process. Freedom to say yes, which, of course, also means the freedom to say no, is constitutive of the sacred covenant of life itself. Failure to see this is also failure to see how good, how strong and real, embodied existence is in this world we are making together. . . .

POSTSCRIPT

SHOULD ABORTION BE OUTLAWED?

One of the intriguing and troubling issues raised by the abortion controversy is whether the logic of abortion leads to infanticide and euthanasia. President Reagan thinks it does, and cites as an example the case of "Baby Doe," a newborn child in Indiana suffering from Down's syndrome, who was allowed to die of hunger and thirst because his parents would not permit a routine operation to unblock his esophagus. (Since then, other related cases have been publicized, notably a "Baby Jane" case in New York.) It is not clear where Professor Harrison stands on the right to life for those who are already-born. On the one hand, her "quality of life" approach and her belief that rights come not from nature but from society might lead to the kind of results that Reagan fears. On the other hand, Harrison carefully distinguishes between biological human beings who have already entered the world (and are thus entitled to all the rights of human beings in society) and those who are still *in utero*. This would seem to ensure the protection of the already-born.

These and other puzzles have to be wrestled with if we are to discuss the abortion topic intelligently. Among the more thoughtful books on the topic is John Noonan's, *A Private Choice* (The Free Press, 1979) and James T. Burtchaell's *Rachel Weeping and Other Essays* (Andrews and McMeel, 1981) which make the case against abortion, and Lawrence Lader's *Abortion II: Making the Revolution* (Beacon Press, 1973) and Rosalind Petchesky's *Abortion and Woman's Choice* (Longman's, 1984), which are pro-choice on the abortion issue.

If dispassionate debate on the abortion issue is possible at all, it is possible only if we investigate some key issues: Is legalized abortion producing a general insensitivity to human life in our society? Do abortions cause pain to fetuses? Is there a scientific basis for defining the beginnings of human life? If so, can it serve as the basis for legislation prohibiting abortion? If a ban on abortions were reinstated, would it be enforceable? Would such a ban produce an unacceptable level of evasion and noncompliance, much as Prohibition did in the 1920s? Perhaps no one can answer these questions with certainty, but no responsible advocate—pro-life or pro-choice—can ignore them.

ISSUE 16

SHOULD WE HAVE A "WALL OF SEPARATION" BETWEEN CHURCH AND STATE?

YES: James E. Wood, Jr., from "Religious Pluralism and American Society," *Journal of Church and State,* Autumn 1985

NO: George Goldberg, *Reconsecrating America* (Grand Rapids, MI, 1984)

ISSUE SUMMARY

YES: Professor James E. Wood, Jr., maintains that religious pluralism is the historical source of and best argument for church-state separation.
NO: Lawyer George Goldberg holds that government may not prefer one religion over another but should accommodate the needs of different faiths.

The United States has more members (well in excess of 100 million) of more churches (more than 300,000) than any other country in the world. More than ninety-five percent of all Americans profess a belief in God. Recently, the growth of so-called "cult" religions and the increasing visibility of "born-again" Christians remind us that religion remains a powerful force in American society.

It was because religion loomed so large when the United States was founded that the first clauses of the First Amendment to the Constitution deal with the relationship between the nation and religion. The Supreme Court now interprets these clauses to be binding upon the states as well as the national government.

The actual words are: "Congress shall make no law respecting an establishment of religion, or prohibiting the free exercise thereof." With some notable exceptions (involving such issues as textbooks and blood transfusions), the "free exercise" clause does not pose many constitutional controversies. The "establishment" clause does.

For the past forty years, the United States Supreme Court has been examining and resolving these controversies. Sometimes it has appeared as if the Supreme Court supports the view of those who invoke Thomas Jefferson's famous metaphor about the necessary "wall of separation" between church and state. This appears to be the case in what has proven to be the most controversial church-state issue, the right of children and teachers to start their school day with a prayer.

In the case of *Engel* v. *Vitale* (1962), this twenty-two word prayer, recited daily in a number of public schools throughout the state of New York, became the center of a national controversy:

> Almighty God, we acknowledge our dependence upon Thee, and we beg
> Thy blessings upon us, our parents, our teachers and our country.

The prayer, composed by the New York State Board of Regents (the governing body of the school system), was intended to be nondenominational. It was also voluntary, at least in the sense that the children were not required to recite it and could leave the room during the time in which it was recited. Nevertheless, the Court declared it unconstitutional, and in subsequent cases it also outlawed Bible reading and the Lord's Prayer.

Other Supreme Court decisions have defended the right of the state to accommodate differing religious views. The Court has upheld a state's reimbursement of parents for the cost of sending their children to church-related schools on public buses, the loan of state-owned textbooks to parochial school students, and grants to church-related colleges for the construction of religiously-neutral facilities. Public acknowledgement of religion is supported by the long-standing practice of having chaplains in the armed forces, providing tax exemption for churches, and the motto "In God We Trust" on coins.

The Supreme Court has sought to define the constitutional boundaries of state support of religion by forbidding religious instruction in a public school class but permitting "released time" programs, which allow a student to be absent from public school in order to attend a religious class elsewhere.

Neither those who believe in total separation nor those who believe in total cooperation between church and state embrace such distinctions. Those who would build an impregnable wall of separation would forbid direct or indirect aid to religious bodies or the cause of religion. At the other extreme are those who propose a constitutional amendment to declare that the United States is a Christian nation and who would rewrite the laws and textbooks to reflect that conviction.

Neither James E. Wood, Jr., nor George Goldberg advocates such absolutist positions, but Wood's support for stricter separation and Goldberg's plea for increasing accommodation are clearly opposed to one another. Because feelings run so high, discussion of church and state in America is often marked and marred by charges impugning the good faith and morality of one's opponents. The following selections represent thoughtful contributions to a debate that is likely to endure throughout our national history.

YES
James E. Wood, Jr.

RELIGIOUS PLURALISM
AND AMERICAN SOCIETY

At a time when there is a resurgence of the notion of a "Christian" America, accompanied by a widespread antipathy to a view of this nation as a secular state, there is a growing need to recognize the importance of religious pluralism to church-state relations in the United States. While religious pluralism has never been readily welcomed in this nation's history, it has been an integral part and a distinct characteristic of America throughout its history. Moreover, religious pluralism has long been seen as both descriptive of American culture and a normative expression of American society, a clue both to the character and the freedom of religion in America.

I

The extraordinary diversity of religion has been one of the distinct features of this nation throughout its history. From the beginning, religious diversity characterized the colonies. French and Spanish explorations brought the Roman Catholic faith to the New World in the sixteenth century. In the seventeenth century, English colonies were planted in the New World. Unlike the French and Spanish, English colonial authorities did not impose a pattern of religious uniformity in any of the colonies other than in Virginia. A deliberate policy of toleration on the part of the British authorities inevitably encouraged religious diversity through the English colonies, since it offered to religious dissenters of England and the Continent a greater measure of freedom in the New World than they had known in their homelands.

By and large, religious immigrants to the New World belonged mainly to religious groups that shared religious beliefs that were discriminated against in the Old World: Puritans, Baptists, Calvinists, Irish Catholics, Mennonites, Jews, Dunkers, Moravians, Pietists (Puritanic Lutherans), and Scotch-Irish Presbyterians. Within the colonies, religious pluralism was rampant. In Rhode Island, where religious liberty was first made a part of organic law, it was said that "hardly any two Rhode Islanders shared the same beliefs." By 1664, the governor of New Amsterdam reported that eighteen different languages could be heard on the island of Manhattan and the surrounding area. The colonists came from many lands and different cultural and religious backgrounds. An analysis of the census of 1790 indicates that the population of that time was composed of national stocks with English barely 60 percent of the population.

From, "Religious Pluralism and American Society," *Journal of Church and State*, Autumn 1985.

Not only did religious pluralism prevail throughout the colonies, but the vast majority of the population of the colonies was unchurched, described as "the largest proportion of unchurched in Christendom.". . .

Today, let it be remembered that although religious pluralism was not something desired by the American colonies, nor was this religious pluralism generally met by toleration in colonial America, the absence of religious uniformity contributed immeasurably to the guarantees of the institutional separation of church and state and religious freedom in the founding of the American Republic. At the time of this nation's founding, an establishment of religion was both practically and ideologically an impossibility if the ideal of *E Pluribus Unum* were to be realized. At the same time, the exclusion of the authority of government from religious affairs and the assurance of the free exercise of religion were eloquently championed by religious and political leaders alike. As James Madison wrote, "The religion . . . of every man, must be left to the conviction and conscience of every man. . . . We maintain, therefore, that in matters of religion no man's right is abridged by the institution of civil society; and that religion is wholly exempt from its cognizance." A person's religious opinions, it was argued, were not in any way to be related to the exercise of one's civil liberties, a viewpoint that has never been universally shared by all Americans. As Thomas Jefferson stated in the Bill for Establishing Religious Freedom in Virginia, "All men shall be free to profess, and by argument to maintain, their opinions in matters of religion, and that the same shall in no wise diminish, enlarge, or affect their civil capacities." As is well known, this document became the primary source of other state statutes and the First Amendment.

As a result of these developments, scarce consideration was even given to the subject of religion at the constitutional convention in Philadelphia in May 1787. Article VI, "No religious test shall ever be required as a qualification to any office or public trust under the United States," was the only reference to religion in the original document. This itself was a profound acknowledgment of the secular character of the state and an expression of the constitutional assurance that religious identity or opinions should have no bearing upon one's qualifications for holding a position of public trust, a view now being vigorously challenged by those of the New Religious Right who insist upon some quota of "Evangelicals" holding public office. From dissenters, especially the Baptists and the Presbyterians, came the demand in the form of a Bill of Rights to guarantee the separation of church and state and to provide some explicit assurance of the free exercise of religion. Establishment of religion, at least on a national level, was in 1789 clearly prohibited and official acknowledgment was thereby made as to the pluralistic character of the new nation. Ratification of the First Amendment in 1791, in effect, constitutionally confirmed and assured the pluralistic character of the new Republic.

By the middle of the nineteenth century, America's foremost church historian, Philip Schaff, observed that America was already "a motley sampler of all church history." In spite of the constitutional achievement with respect to Article VI and the First Amendment which, in effect, provides an indissoluble link in America between religious freedom and religious pluralism, the nineteenth century is replete with examples of widespread bigotry and intolerance toward Catholics and Jews as well as toward new religions as they were introduced from abroad or within the new nation itself. Religious discrimination against Catholics and Jews was felt in both social and political areas, reenforced in many instances by state laws and state constitutions. . . .

II

In America, religious pluralism is both a constitutional right as well as a historical or social reality. In the American experience, this religious pluralism is to be seen not as an aberration simply to be tolerated, but rather as a right guaranteed all religion as well as irreligion under the law. As John Leland, a prominent Baptist minister, wrote in 1820, "The liberty I contend for is more than toleration. The very idea of toleration is despicable; it supposes that some have a pre-eminence above the rest to grant indulgence; whereas all should be equally free, Jews, Turks [Muslims], Pagans and Christians. Test oaths and established creeds should be avoided as the worst of evils."

With the enactment of the First Amendment, "Congress shall make no law respecting the establishment of religion or prohibiting the free exercise thereof," the entanglement of government in religious affairs was constitutionally prohibited. As president, Thomas Jefferson wrote, "I consider the government of the United States as interdicted by the Constitution from intermeddling with religious institutions. . . . I do not believe it is for the interest of religion to invite the civil magistrates to direct its exercises, its discipline, or its doctrine." A little over a century ago President James A. Garfield declared in his inaugural address (1881), "In my judgment, while it is the duty of Congress to respect to the uttermost the conscientious convictions and religious scruples of every citizen . . . not any ecclesiastical organization can be safely permitted to usurp in the smallest degree the functions and power of the national government." Full religious liberty, it was reasoned, required a secular state in which the people have excluded the authority and jurisdiction of the state from religious affairs; no religious group is to be the object of privilege or discrimination under the law. The most militant atheist, along with the most fervent theist within one of the most socially accepted denominations, is to be assured of full rights of citizenship and equal protection under the law.

So long as one's free exercise of religion does not infringe upon the rights of others or contravene the just civil laws of the state or threaten public health and order, both the rights of religious dissent and the free exercise of that dissent are guaranteed to all citizens. To be sure, these broad principles have not always conformed to historical reality, any more than other civil rights have applied to all citizens without regard to race or sex. "Equal protection under the law," the only words to appear over the main outside entrance to the United States Supreme Court, constitutes a firm commitment of this nation to religious rights as well as to all other civil rights.

Those who are inclined today to malign the United States Supreme Court for its separationist views (as the New Religious Right and leading members of the Reagan administration, among others, are fond of doing), would do well to note the separationist views enunciated by the Supreme Court a century ago. In *Melvin v. Easley* (1860), the Court declared, "Christianity is not established by law, and the genius of our institutions requires that the Church and the State should be kept separate. . . . The State confesses its incompetency to judge spiritual matters between men or between man and his maker . . . spiritual matters are exclusively in the hands of the teachers of religion." Or, as in *Darwin* v. *Beason* (1890), the Court affirmed that "the First Amendment to the Constitution . . . was intended to allow everyone under the jurisdiction of the United States to entertain such notions respecting his relation to his maker and the duties they impose as may be approved by his conscience, and to exhibit his sentiments in such form of worship as he may think proper, nor injurious to the rights of others, and to prohibit legislation for the support of any religious tenets, or the modes of worship of any sect."

Since minority rights are perennially endangered by the will of majorities, marginal religious groups have understandably sought judicial redress rather than legislative remedy in their struggle for their religious rights and equality under the law with mainline religions. As Leo Pfeffer rightly observed, "The smaller the minority, the more likely it is to need constitutional protection; the greater it is, the more likely it is to obtain the protection it needs through legislative exemption rather than judicial intervention." This is amply reflected in the disproportionate number of church-state cases to reach the United States Supreme Court on behalf of religious groups outside of the mainline religious denominations. These include, among others, the Church of Jesus Christ of Latter-day Saints, the Jehovah's Witnesses, the Seventh-day Adventists, the "I Am" movement, the Black Muslims, the Amish, the Hare Krishna movement (ISKON), the Worldwide Church of God, the Unification Church, and the Church of Scientology.

Religious diversity in America needs to be seen today, as in the past, as the natural corollary of religious freedom. Meanwhile, the legitimation of unconventional or new religions may be an appropriate reminder that all faiths were once "new" religions and only gradually were they able to gain social acceptance of a status of influence to the degree that they are no longer perceived to be a threat to the norms of society.

Marginal or new religions have contributed significantly to American understanding of religious pluralism as well as to judicial interpretations of religious liberty, far out of proportion to their numerical membership or institutional strength. No better example of this fact may be cited than the case of Jehovah's Witnesses, who have been responsible for more court cases concerned with religious liberty than any other single group of religious adherents. In a famous Jehovah's Witness case, *West Virginia Board of Education* v. *Barnett* (1943), the Court forthrightly reenforced the constitutional guarantee of religious pluralism: "If there is any fixed star in our constitutional constellation, it is that no official, high or petty, can prescribe what shall be orthodox in politics, nationalism, religion, or other matters of opinion or force citizens to confess by word or act their faith therein. If there are any circumstances which permit any exception, they do not occur to us."

The following year, in *United States* v. *Ballard* (1944), the Supreme Court addressed the claims of the "truth or falsity of religious beliefs or doctrines" of anyone, even though those beliefs "might seem incredible, if not preposterous, to most people." In defending the constitutional rights of even a religious group whose views the society at large may view as "presposterous," the Court noted that in the Constitution, "Man's relation to his God was made no concern of the state. He was granted the right to worship as he pleased and to answer to no man for verity of his religious beliefs."

III

The special place given by this administration to a particular form of sectarian religion, with its presumed hegemony in the life of the nation, poses serious problems for religious pluralism in American society. The renewed assault on the separation of church and state in America threatens not only the secular state and free society concepts that have been distinctive of this nation, but also the equality of all religion and irreligion before the law. This attack on the separation of church and state augurs for the strengthening of ties between church and state and the disregarding of America's religious pluralism.

Ironically, separation of church and state, which was an inevitable consequence of the religious diversity of the thirteen original colonies and was claimed at the time of the founding of the Republic by the churches for themselves so as to ensure their independence from state control, is today being characterized as alien to religious faith and even hostile to religion. Recently in a public address, Secretary of Education William J. Bennett vigorously denounced the separationist views of the United States Supreme Court as representing "almost four decades of misguided court decisions." In responding to the Court's most recent church-state decisions (*Wallace* v. *Jaffree, Grand Rapids School District* v. *Ball*, and *Aguilar* v. *Felton* . . .) invalidating the use of public funds for remedial programs and secular subjects for children in parochial schools and public school sponsorship of a period of silence for prayer and meditation,

Bennett deplored the decisions for showing a "fastidious disdain for religion." The religious intolerance of the Court, Bennett declared, has now given way to "a new aversion to religion." Attorney General Edwin Meese found these same decisions to be "somewhat bizarre."

Since, it is reasoned, the Court's support of "separation of church and state" and "no entanglement of church and state" are rooted in an aversion to religion, those who support these views of the Court are characterized as hostile to religion. As a major spokesperson for the Reagan administration on religion and public education, Bennett has declared that anyone who favors strict separation of church and state is motivated by a militant form of "secularism." Similar charges have been directed at the Supreme Court as a result of its decisions on religion in the public schools and the use of public funds for parochial schools. Almost no attention has been given by this administration to the phenomenon of religious pluralism in American society and its direct bearing on such issues as religion in public education and the use of public funds for parochial schools, as well as a whole range of other issues in church-state relations in the United States.

It is a distortion to suggest that anyone who favors a strict separation of church and state is impelled by "secularism." Such denunciations of America's separationists simply fail to explain the strong resistance to public school-sponsored religious exercises and the allocation of public funds to parochial schools from such organizations as the American Jewish Committee and the American Jewish Congress, the Baptist Joint Committee on Public Affairs, the National Council of Churches, and the Lutheran Council in the U.S.A.; such religious groups as Methodists, Presbyterians, Disciples of Christ, and Quakers; and such prominent religious leaders as the general secretary of the United Church of Christ, the presiding bishop of the Protestant Episcopal Church, and the president of Georgetown University, an eminent Jesuit priest. Far from being rooted in any aversion to religion, the strongest support for the separationist views of the United States Supreme Court have come, by and large, from the vast majority of America's mainline religious denominations.

In light of the American experience, it may well be argued that institutional separation of church and state has contributed significantly to America's religious pluralism, which rests on the notion of the equality of all religious denominations before the law. The refusal of the United States Supreme Court to grant state sponsorship or support of religion may be seen as inextricably intertwined with the free exercise of religion. Religious pluralism is not served by charging the Court with being anti-Catholic whenever public funds or state services are denied all parochial schools, any more than the Court should be charged with being antireligious for its resistance to efforts aimed at Christianizing the public schools and eliminating the secular character guaranteed them in this republic by the First Amendment.

The repudiation of America as a secular state and the effort to identify this nation with God and sectarian religious values does not bode well for religious pluralism in the United States, in which all of the world's religions are represented among its citizens—not to mention the rise of many diverse new expressions of older religious traditions or indigenous faiths from out of the American milieu. The

secular state is one in which church and synagogue, religion and irreligion are equal in the sight of the state and where citizens may neither enjoy any advantages nor suffer any disadvantages because of their religion. It is a state which seeks neither to promote nor to hinder the free exercise of religion, in which neither religion nor irreligion enjoys any official status or support on the part of government.

Religious pluralism has contributed immeasurably to the American experience from the beginning. As in the past, religious pluralism remains one of the most distinctive features of American society and integral to the American tradition of church and state. Twenty-five years ago, America's first Roman Catholic to be elected president of the United States appropriately wrote of religious pluralism and American society as crucial to this nation's understanding of church-state relations. "It is my firm belief," President John F. Kennedy wrote,

> that there should be separation of church and state as we understand it in the United States—that is, that both church and state should be free to operate, without interference from each other in their respective areas of jurisdiction. We live in a liberal, democratic society which embraces wide varities of belief and disbelief. There is no doubt in my mind that the pluralism which has developed under our Constitution, providing as it does a framework within which diverse opinions can exist side by side and by their interaction enrich the whole, is the most ideal system yet devised by man. I cannot conceive of a set of circumstances which would lead me to a different conclusion.

These words are particularly worth remembering a generation later.

NO

George Goldberg

RECONSECRATING AMERICA

The current controversy over church-state relations in America, in particular the issues of prayers in public schools, governmental support of parochial schools, and displays of religious symbols in public places, is unfortunate and unnecessary. A constitutional amendment to resolve these issues would be worse.

The United State Supreme Court, whose decisions beginning in 1940 gave rise to the current controversy, seems at last to be aware of the mistake it made. Recent decisions of the Court have gone a long way to rectifying the problems and defusing the controversy. But the Court, which earned much of the public disapproval it received in recent years, now needs informed public support for its efforts to repair the damage it did in its series of misguided and confusing decisions involving the religion clauses of the First Amendment. Such support has not been forthcoming, neither from public officials issuing resounding calls for a constitutional amendment which would only usher in another generation of conflict over interpretation and application, nor from "strict separationists" demanding, with cool disdain for the desires of the overwhelming majority of Americans and with a sorry ignorance of American history, the complete exclusion of all forms of religious expression from public life.

The great mass of American people has watched the emotional debate with anxiety. They see the admirable and precious interfaith amiability of recent years disturbed by completely unnecessary lawsuits over issues as divisive as they are irrelevant to true religious freedom. To me, a Jew living in a country where almost everybody else is Christian, there is only one religious issue: equal treatment. If the New Testament is read in public schools, I want the Old Testament too. If Catholic parochial schools receive financial aid, I want yeshivas to get their fair share. If public employees get time off for Good Friday, I want them to get time off for Yom Kippur. If a crèche is displayed during the Christmas season on the lawn of the public library, I want to see a menorah nearby.

From, *Reconsecrating America*, by George Goldberg. Copyright © 1984 by George Goldberg. An updated edition will be published in early 1987 by Regnery/Gateway under the title, *The Supreme Court and the Tooth Fairy: The Religious Clauses Upside Down.*

My position is hardly unduly modest. Imagine in almost any other country of the world a member of a religious group representing less than 3 percent of the population *demanding*, and with a fair chance of receiving, equal treatment with the dominant religion. And yet there are Americans—Jews, Unitarians, "humanists," atheists, even some Protestants—who believe I do not demand enough. They do not want equal time with their neighbors, they want absolute veto power over their neighbors' actions. As they do not wish to say prayers in public school, they insist that nobody else be permitted to do so. As they do not send their children to parochial schools, they insist that no public aid be given such schools, although the parents of parochial school children are assessed for public school taxes at the same rate as everyone else. They are offended by any form of religious symbol in a public place and cannot be consoled with the right to erect their own there—especially if they do not have any.

We are a free country and there is no reason, apart from good taste and respect for the sensitives of others, why a person so disposed should not lobby against the provision at public expense of textbooks to parochial schools. But to raise such a personal preference to constitutional status is wrong and dangerous. It invites a change in the Constitution, and we already have the most liberal constitution in the world, with greater protections for minorities than most nations dream of. We would be crazy to tamper with it.

But we cannot expect the vast majority of Americans to be willing to be governed by a document which a small minority is able to manipulate for its own benefit. Moreover, the supposed benefit is nonexistent, except for those who make their living conducting wasteful litigation. Barring Handel's *Messiah* from the public schools will have far less impact on the Christian child who can sing it in church than on the Jewish child who will thereby be "protected" from exposure to an important and enriching part of the culture of the Western world; and if creches and menorahs are given comparable prominence in public displays the prime beneficiary will be the menorah. FCC equal-time rules primarily benefit minority candidates. . . .

CONCLUSION

The essence of religious freedom in a multisectarian society is, as our Founding Fathers perceived, twofold: (1) freedom from governmental compulsion to worship in any particular way, and (2) freedom to worship in one's own particular way. It was in recognition of this dual aspect of religious freedom that the federal government was explicitly forbidden to establish or disestablish any religion or to interfere with anyone's exercise of his faith. . . .

There is little question but that to the Founding Fathers "religion" did essentially have one meaning: the beliefs and practices associated with the worship of God, whether the Christian God, the Jewish God, nature's God, or Divine Providence. With that broad definition, and with the concomitant understanding, which the Founding Fathers also shared, that the only thing prohibited by the establishment clause of the First Amendment was *compulsion* of worship or the *preferential* treatment of one religion over competing religions, there would be little trouble today over interpretation and application of the establishment clause, and little "tension" between it and the free exercise clause.

But the Supreme Court greatly expanded both the definition of "religion" and the scope of the prohibitions of the establishment clause, with the result that an impasse, the classical irresistible force meeting immovable object, was created. As phrased by the Court, "tension inevitably exists between the Free Exercise and the Establishment clauses." But there was nothing inevitable about it.

There are good reasons for expanding the definition of "religion" to include virtually anything anybody deems sacred. The alternative puts the courts in the business of defining and assessing professed religious beliefs, a business for which they are neither equipped nor suited. If Henry David Thoreau occupies a place in a person's life comparable to that occupied by God in the life of a believer (the Supreme Court's phraseology in the conscientious objector cases), there seems no good reason why *Walden* should not enjoy all the protections accorded sacred scripture. But this special status extended to a writing under the free exercise clause will be a cruel joke if *as a consequence* it ends up on the establishment clause index.

Actually, if establishment continued to be defined as compulsion or preferential treatment, religion could be defined as broadly as might be desired. The "tension" only appears when the definition of religion is broadened for free exercise purposes *and* it is held that any governmental aid of religion, no matter how evenhanded, is prohibited by the establishment clause. *Then* it is inevitable that there will be tension between what the free exercise clause *requires* and what the establishment clause *forbids*.

The courts have become, if rather late in the day, fully aware of this dilemma. When in 1973 the Supreme Court struck down a New York plan to reimburse low-income families for parochial school tuition, it admitted that "it may often not be possible to promote the [free exercise clause] without offending the [establishment clause]." Similarly, when in 1980 the United States Court of Appeals for the Second Circuit held that the establishment clause required a public high school to deny the request of students to be allowed to hold prayer meetings on school grounds before the beginning of the school day, it conceded that the denial would violate their free exercise rights.

The preference of the courts for the establishment clause over the free exercise clause has given rise to much comment. It has been observed that free exercise is the goal of *both* of the religion clauses, the prohibition of establishment merely constituting a necessary means by which to realize it. According to this interpretation, whenever tension appears between the clauses, free exercise should prevail. . . .

That brings us to the central questions: (1) What is an establishment of religion? and (2) What is the free exercise thereof? It seems to me, after reading what Jefferson and Madison wrote on the subject, studying the cases, state and federal, and considering the observations of legal scholars of varying predilections, that there really should be no serious disagreement over the meaning of either of the religion clauses of the First Amendment.

The free exercise clause is perhaps the simpler one to understand, so I will consider it first. In essence it means that, consistent with public morals and an orderly society, every person should be allowed, and wherever possible helped, to worship whatever it is he deems sacred in whatever manner he deems appropriate. The qualifying phrase, "consistent with public morals and an orderly society," should and usually has been interpreted to require a showing of significant public harm to justify inhibiting a religious practice. Thus an Indian tribe was permitted to use an hallucinatory drug in its rituals despite its general proscription as a "controlled substance," Old Order Amish were permitted to remove their children from school at fourteen despite a law requiring school attendance until sixteen, and Jehovah's Witness children were permitted to abstain from pledging allegiance to the flag, which their religion held was a graven image, but no exemptions from the general laws were granted to polygamists or to Amish employers who did not wish to pay social security taxes for their employees. . . .

The free exercise clause, then, interpreted broadly and applied with common sense and goodwill, should not give rise to serious problems. Establishment clause cases are inherently more difficult; yet they too could be decided with relative ease with the application of a bit more common sense and goodwill than has been in evidence in judicial decisions striking down nondiscriminatory public assistance programs.

. . . The Supreme Court in 1983 upheld a state statute providing reimbursement of parochial school tuition. But the Court was obliged to accomplish this result by means of a disingenuous acceptance of a farfetched rationale of universality. But why shouldn't a nondiscriminatory program of public support of all schools within a jurisdiction, public, secular private, and church-sponsored, be allowed? In other words, let us consider the extreme case where a state offers its citizens educational vouchers redeemable at any school meeting state accreditation requirements. Such a system has been advocated, notably by Milton and Rose Friedman, and has been opposed with great vehemence by the educational establishment. Should the political processes by which such a program could be adopted or rejected be

short-circuited by a judicial holding that it would be unconstitutional under the establishment clause because aid would be given to parochial schools along with public and secular private schools?

The issue of *compulsion* can be quickly disposed of. No one under a voucher program would be obliged to attend a parochial school. Indeed, the issue of school prayers, usually considered under the rubric of compulsion, would be significantly defused if children could attend any school they desired. If prayers were important, then, a child could be sent to a school which said them; and [an atheist's child] probably could go, with children of similarly minded parents, to a school which didn't.

The issue of *preferential treatment* of one religion over others would seem as easily disposed of. In a scheme of vouchers redeemable at any accredited school, no issue of preference could arise. The argument that such a scheme would primarily benefit the Catholic Church, because most parochial schools are Catholic, completely misconstrues the purpose of the establishment clause. It might as well be argued that maintaining the roads favors Catholics because they use them to go to church more often than Protestants, Jews, or Madalyn Murray O'Hair, or that lowering postal rates for books supports Southern Baptists who mail so many Bibles. As long as equal benefits are available to all religions, a scheme is not rendered unconstitutionally preferential because one or more religious groups choose not to take equal advantage of it.

There would thus appear to be *no* establishment clause reason why an educational voucher system should not be sponsored by a state. (There might be an equal protection clause reason if such a system tended to result in racially segregated schools, but that could be dealt with, as it was in the tuition reimbursement scheme allowed by the Court, by requiring that beneficiary schools agree to adhere to civil rights legislation.) Yet I fear that the Court, even as constituted today, would have difficulty in allowing such a program.

Why? Because of Justice Black's formulation of the establishment clause thirty-seven years ago:

> The "establishment of religion" clause of the First Amendment means at least this: Neither a state nor the Federal Government can set up a church. Neither can pass laws which aid one religion, *aid all religions*, or prefer one religion over another.

The answer to Justice Black is that he was wrong, and that thirty-seven years of adherence by the Supreme Court to a wrong theory is enough. As stated by a leading American legal scholar:

> The historical record shows beyond peradventure that the core idea of "an establishment of religion" comprises the idea of *preference*; and that any act of public authority favorable to religion in general cannot, without manifest falsification of history, be brought under the ban of that phrase.

There remains but one church-state issue to consider: religious activities in public schools—prayers, Bible recitations, hymn singing, Christmas and Hanukkah pageants, grace before milk and cookies. No discussion of church-state relations in America can be complete without a candid discussion of this difficult issue, and it should be noted at the outset that there are men and women of goodwill on both sides, and that reference to the Founding Fathers is of limited assistance since the first public school was founded in 1821 (in Boston) and public schools were not widespread

in the United States until after the Civil War.

The arguments in favor of school religious exercises boil down to a belief that "spiritual" values must be inculcated in our children and that the home and the church are unequal to the job. The principal argument against is that religion in our pluralistic society is essentially divisive and must be kept out of the public schools which have been a major vehicle for creating a cohesive society. . . .

. . . It is fascinating how the same people who on certain occasions profess great sympathy for minorities and poor people turn into Marie Antoinette when confronted with school prayers: let them go to private school, or let their parents teach them religion. How can a person who in the context of aid to dependent children cites statistics of broken homes, rodent-infested apartments crowded beyond imagination, and children roaming the streets untended, in the context of school prayers conjure up warm families sitting around the fireside listening to the paterfamilias (50 percent of minority children in the United States live in fatherless homes) recite verses from the Bible with appropriate commentary?

But middle-class children from two-parent families may not receive much more religious training at home than ghetto children. For the image of the patriarchical family reading the Bible (or anything else) around the hearth is nearly as fanciful in the suburbs as in the central city. Only judges of venerable age and advanced myopia can suppose that there is time and occasion in the modern middle-class home for morning prayers. In the real world the weekday morning is a paradigm of chaos—of father racing about shaving, searching for the one tie he really likes with this suit, gulping a Danish and coffee, grabbing his briefcase, and rushing off to catch the 7:07; of mother trying to feed everyone (maybe even herself), dress herself and the five-year-old, search for the ten-year-old's math paper, assure the thirteen-year-old that she did not hide his sneakers, drive the children to school(s) and/or bus stop(s), and perhaps also get to her job on time (half of American mothers hold jobs outside the home). In this frenetic, frantic atmosphere, the possibility of stopping everything for three minutes to calm the spirit and give thanks to something beyond ourselves . . . is remote.

After-school opportunities for familial contemplation of eternity are even fewer. Extracurricular activities consume most of the children's time before dinner, shopping and cooking and perhaps her job consume all of mother's, and father is lucky if he makes it home for dinner. And then there is the ubiquitous television set by means of which the children will be taught that happiness may be found, may *only* be found, through the acquisition of nonessentials—a toy, a vacation, a car capable of going 120 mph in a country with a 55 mph speed limit. They see grown men and women exploding with joy because they guessed the price of an appliance they do not need and now will be given; they see fairytale children playing blissfully in an enchanted land and are told that their palpable joy derives from chewing a certain brand of gum; they see portrayals of camaraderie, of intimacy and sharing among handsome men and lovely women untouched by sickness or human frailty in a pastoral idyll based solely on the consumption of a certain brand of beer. . . .

That, your Honor, is what children learn at home. Perhaps religious faith is a sham, a chronic disease of the imagination contracted in childhood," the opium of the people. Perhaps Charlie's angels have more to offer than those Billy Graham writes about. But if you think so, why not say so? To pay lip service to the "spiritual needs of our young people" and then tell them that they must seek their fulfillment at home and only at home, is ignorant or dishonest or both.

Sex must be taught in the schools because parents are unequal to the task, but religious instruction is held to be within their competence. Surely the evidence compels the opposite conclusion.

The argument that, like Sergeant Friday in the old *Dragnet* series, schools are only concerned with *facts*, is equally untenable. The selection and presentation of the limitless supply of available observations, theories, and opinions determine the direction and meaning of the educational process. George Washington was born in 1732. So was Haydn. So, no doubt, were many other people, including saints and sadists and blasphemers and traitors. All *facts*, but which will you disinter and teach? Obviously it depends upon your animating principles. The Founding Fathers were animated by a belief in Divine Providence, a faith broad enough to take in theism and even, perhaps, pantheism, along with traditional religions. Some of us are still animated by similar beliefs, others are busy looking out for "Number 1," and still others are totally immersed in the beliefs and rituals of ancient religions. The one thing we should all be able to agree upon is that the courts should not take sides in the ongoing debate.

But *what about prayers*? The Court has now held that prayers may be said at the beginning of legislative and judicial sessions . . . [but] prayers are still banned from all public elementary and high schools in the country.

It should be understood that the ban is

virtually total. For example, in 1982 the Tennessee legislature was considering a bill to allow (not require) public schools to set aside time for—well, for whatever the courts would allow. It had before it a statute drawn up by the Georgia legislature according to which a school could set aside up to three ten-minute periods a day— before school, after school, or during the lunch break—when students who so desired could use an empty classroom for prayers or silent meditation. The attorney general of Tennessee advised the legislature that the statute was unconstitutional. After several tries the legislature finally agreed on one minute of silence at the beginning of the school day and included in the statute a warning that teachers were not to suggest what the students should be thinking about during that minute. Even this statute was submitted to the attorney general for an opinion. He reviewed the cases, noted that "It is well-settled that the Establishment Clause forbids the state from requiring or even condoning perceptible religious exercises in public schools," and said that as long as the teachers did not encourage the students to say prayers during the minute of silence, the statute was constitutional.

Isn't that ridiculous? Any attempt to restrict the availability of obscene, racist novels in public school libraries is immediately attacked as Nazism in the making; public school students are held to have a constitutional right to select their dress and hairstyles and to demonstrate in class against governmental policies of which they disapprove; but *God* has become so terrible a word that all the legal talent in the country must be mustered to exclude it absolutely from the public schools.

It is true that America's religions did not always live together in peace and harmony. The Puritans were not known for their tolerance of dissenters, anti-Catholic agitation once disfigured a large part of our public life, and no one named Goldberg is unaware of the history of anti-Semitism in America. But it is equally true that the tables have turned 180 degrees, and shields have been transformed into swords. . . .

Intolerance is ugly, no matter who practices it. When a minority practices it, it is also foolhardy, for intolerance breeds more intolerance, and minorities naturally suffer the most from an atmosphere of intolerance. With tolerance for the beliefs and practices of others, however foolish they may seem, and enlisting the aid of the courts not to prevent others from doing what they want but only to enforce one's own right to equal time, the issue of prayers in public school can be resolved without amending the Constitution. . . .

POSTSCRIPT

SHOULD WE HAVE A "WALL OF SEPARATION" BETWEEN CHURCH AND STATE?

Few issues in American politics arouse such deep feelings as those relating to moral and religious convictions, and those deep feelings find eloquent expression in these essays.

James E. Wood, Jr., is convinced that the fact that America was settled and populated by people of many faiths constitutes both the historical basis for the First Amendment's religion clauses and the most persuasive reason for keeping the state neutral in all matters of religion. George Goldberg is equally persuaded that state neutrality in theory is anti-religion in practice, because it often effectively denies the practice of religious belief.

Those on opposing sides of this issue freely and frequently invoke the Founding Fathers when making their arguments, finding appropriate quotations to establish—at least to their own satisfaction—the continuity of tradition. However, it should be obvious that many of the specific issues raise points of intersection between church and state that the Framers could not have imagined.

When the Supreme Court invalidated prayers in the public schools, critical reaction was so strong that many school districts simply disregarded the Court's decrees. Thoughtful consideration of this and other issues is best undertaken in the larger context of church-state relations. An exploration from the perspective of liberal Catholicism is John Courtney Murray's, *We Hold These Truths* (Doubleday Image, 1964). Leo Pfeffer, *Creeds in Competition* (Greenwood, 1978, originally published in 1958), proceeds from the Jeffersonian premise of "a wall of separation between government and religion." Will Herberg, *Protestant-Catholic-Jew* (Doubleday, 1955) is a sensitive study of the relationship among America's three major creeds.

The separationist position on current issues will be found in articles in *Church and State*, the publication of Americans United for Separation of Church and State. The accommodationist approach is supported in articles in *National Review* and *Public Interest*. Church-state issues are frequently discussed from a variety of perspectives in *America, Commentary, Commonweal* and *Christianity and Crisis*.

PART IV
AMERICA AND THE WORLD: WHICH POLICIES ARE BEST?

The World War II alliance between the Soviet Union and the United States fell apart within two years of the war's end. By 1947 it was clear that the two countries were adversaries. In the past, that would have been the prelude to a new war. But by the early 1950s, the Soviets acquired nuclear weapons and the means of delivering them. An all-out "hot" war with the Soviets thus became so fearful a prospect that talk of "victory" in it began to sound hollow. In place of "hot" war, then, the issue became the "cold war."

People's attitudes toward the cold war usually correlate with their view of who is responsible for it. Some would fasten the blame upon the United States. This position is a minority position, and is hard to defend. A more widely shared view is that the cold war is a product of mutual misunderstanding and irrational suspicion by both sides. In their view, our policies should be ones which seek accommodation with a country we have never properly understood. Others argue that the cold war is a result of Soviet expansionism. Their solution is to check that expansion at every turn and even roll it back when feasible. Both sides seek to avoid war, but their strategies come from opposite perspectives. Is nuclear war the result of too many weapons—or of too little strength, which tempts aggressors? Is the turmoil in Central America an indigenous revolution—or Soviet-fueled aggression? Should we oppose all human rights violations—or take into account our need for allies, even "authoritarian" ones, in confronting Soviet expansion?

Central America: Should the U.S. Aid the "Contras"?

Can American Military Action Curb International Terrorism?

Should We Continue "Star Wars" Research?

Human Rights: Should We Prefer Authoritarianism to Communism?

ISSUE 17

CENTRAL AMERICA: SHOULD THE US AID THE "CONTRAS"?

YES: John P. East, from US Senate Debate, June 18, 1984

NO: Christopher Dodd, from US Senate Debate, March 29, 1984

ISSUE SUMMARY

YES: The late Senator John East says that without Contra aid the Soviets will be able to impose a military solution in Central America.
NO: Senator Christopher Dodd contends that more American military force in Central America is not the way to deal with the underlying problems of the region.

"I told him," wrote the former secretary of state, "that we should contest the right of Russia to *any* territorial establishment on this continent." The remark sounds contemporary, but it was written nearly a century and a half ago by former Secretary of State (later President) John Quincy Adams. Adams was referring to America's refusal to countenance any more European colonization of Latin America. The oral warning soon took written, official form. In his annual message of 1823 President James Monroe was merely rephrasing his secretary of state when he said that "the American continents" are "henceforth not to be considered subjects for future colonization by any European powers." The Monroe Doctrine, as it was soon called, drew a line around Latin America, declaring it off-limits to European penetration.

The Monroe Doctrine was a reaction to the intrigues of czarist Russia. But by 1917 the Russian Czar and his family were dead, murdered by revolutionaries calling themselves "Bolsheviks." By 1921, after a bloody civil war, the Bolsheviks assumed total control of Russia and some of its vassal-states, which together became the Soviet Union. The Soviets were candidly expansionist, believing that their revolution would eventually triumph throughout the world. Until the end of World War II, the Soviets had all they could do to maximize their leverage over their own and adjacent countries. But by the 1950s, the Soviet Union was already showing interest in "wars of national liberation" in lands far from its borders. It was fear of Soviet subversion in Guatemala in 1954 that led the United States to lend covert support to a successful revolt against the leftist regime of Jacobo Arbenz Guzman. To many Americans, the suspicion that the Soviets were penetrating Latin America seemed fully justified five years later when Fidel Castro, whose revolution in Cuba had been heralded as a purely indigenous event, announced that he was a Marxist-Leninist and aligned himself with the Soviet Union. Two years later the American CIA sponsored an ill-fated invasion of Cuba by anti-Communist exiles; the following year, in 1962, President Kennedy blockaded Cuba after discovering that the Soviets were shipping missiles there. In 1965 President Johnson sent Marines into the Dominican Republic during a period of violent turmoil, partly to protect American lives, but also because Johnson feared that "another Cuba" was in the making.

The present crisis in America's relations with Central America grows from the fear that "another Cuba" has indeed appeared in the region, and that more will emerge very soon unless the United States acts quickly. In 1979 the corrupt but pro-American regime of Anastasio Somoza in Nicaragua was overthrown by a group calling itself the Sandinistas (named after a Nicaraguan patriot). Despite moral and financial support from the Carter administration, the new revolutionary government was openly hostile to the United States, putting anti-American lines into its new Nicaraguan anthem. More ominously, hundreds of Soviet-bloc "advisers" began arriving in Nicaragua, as well as large-scale shipments of arms.

The Reagan administration charged that the new Nicaraguan regime was a Soviet client state serving the purpose of subverting and overthrowing other governments in the region. It sought to counter this perceived threat by a variety of means, including US military support of anti-communist guerrillas in Nicaragua—the so-called "Contras." Critics of Reagan's policy worried that it would lead the US into another Vietnam-type "quagmire," and they succeeded in cutting off all aid to the Contras in 1984. In 1985 the Administration persuaded Congress to provide non-military assistance to the Contras, and in 1986 it managed to obtain $100 million in both military and nonmilitary assistance. Yet the debate is far from over.

In the following selections, the late North Carolina Senator John East makes the case for Contra aid, while Connecticut Senator Christopher Dodd argues against it.

YES
John P. East

MILITARY ASSISTANCE TO CENTRAL AMERICA IS ESSENTIAL

I speak in opposition to this amendment which I think is ill-conceived and would be counterproductive to the very thing which its proponents seek to avoid in Central America—namely, a greater broadening of the conflict.

Former Secretary of State Henry Kissinger has indicated that in order to accomplish the very ends that the supporters of this amendment seek—namely, a more equitable social and economic system—that in order to build that infrastructure, there must be a shield, if you will, a military shield, in view of Soviet-Cuban military intervention in the area, behind which this process can take place. If you eliminate the military option completely, you certainly telegraph to the enemy the idea that they are free to pursue a military solution.

. . . When President Duarte [of El Salvador] was here—at that time, President-elect—he said it is a very complex situation. It is military, it is social, and it is economic. But his point was that if you have one army on one side and one army on the other and one is armed and the other is not armed, the armed army will win and you, in fact, will have a military solution.

If, in fact, we say and we telegraph to the people in this area and to the world that the United States, under no circumstances, would give sufficient latitude to the President to utilize our conventional military capability, I think you bring about what President Duarte was talking about—namely, that there will be a military solution, and it will be imposed by the Soviet Union and Cuba and those military forces it is backing in that area.

I think it is simply impossible in our time to micromanage American foreign policy, let alone defense decisions, from the floor of the U.S. Senate. To do so will greatly imperil the effectiveness of this country to meet the very serious challenge it meets today from the Soviet Union and her surrogates in every continent in the world.

Let me put it another way: If we do fail in Central America, if the Marxists take control of the military solution, who will be held accountable? Yes, the President will be. I say that if we are going to hold him, as Commander in Chief, and his principal spokesman and formulator for American foreign policy responsible, we had better give him enough elbow room to do that which is necessary in order for his policies to succeed.

But if we try to micromanage every move he makes, we cannot hold him responsible. I think our policy will fail, and you will see, yes, a military solution in Central America, and it will be dictated by Moscow, Havana, and Managua. That is what is going on currently.

From, US Senate Debate on amendment to prohibit use of funds authorized for the introduction of US military forces into El Salvador or Nicaragua for combat, June 18, 1984.

Invariably, in a debate of this kind, I often find it interesting that our most honorable and patriotic opponents say there must be a political solution, in citing Vietnam. Of course, as Duarte has pointed out, if you do not have the military shield, you will not have a political solution; you will have a military solution, and it will be imposed by the superior military forces, which in this case, again, would be those forces in the area backed by the Soviet Union and by Cuba.

The current struggle in the world today, going on right now in the underdeveloped world, is of a guerrilla type. It does not candidly lend itself to formal declarations. It does not lend itself to micromanagement from the floor of the U.S. Senate. Guerrilla warfare is the key to military success in our time.

Alexander Solzhenitsyn remarked one time, "You need not worry about nuclear war in your time." Why? "Because," he said, "they are taking you with their bare hands," and they are. They are doing it in every part of the world. Solzhenitsyn said he did not think the West had read the Communist Manifesto. He did not think they had read the works of Lenin.

The point was that you would take the soft underbelly of the world, the underdeveloped continents of Asia, Latin America, and Central America. You would do it militarily. Yes, you would do it through guerrilla warfare. Those are the realities of warfare in our time. They cannot be denied. Solzhenitsyn is correct: We are losing. We lost in Southeast Asia. Cam Ranh Bay, which used to be a military base, is now a Soviet base. Yes, we were told we were looking for a political solution. What did we get? A military solution, Soviet and Vietnamese imposed. Then they moved into Cambodia, and so it continues.

The same scenario is being repeated in Central America. The same problem exists in Africa. It would exist in the Middle East, were it not for the strength of Israel. Syria and the PLO, backed by the Soviet Union, would impose a military solution in Lebanon—indeed, throughout the entire Middle East. Would it make sense to say to the Israelis, for example, "Disarm"? Or, should we say that we would never, ever, under any circumstances, intervene? That simply telegraphs to the Soviet Union and her surrogates that military solutions are possible. It rules out the potential for political solution. It rules out the shield to which Henry Kissinger has referred.

How are you going to build the infrastructure for social and economic justice and social and economic growth and development where the enemy, the opposition, is free to shoot its way to power, as President Duarte put it?

Recently we adopted overwhelmingly, as I recall, an amendment supporting the Monroe Doctrine concept of 1823, which stated that the United States would not accept foreign intervention and military presence in the New World from the Old. This is precisely what we are allowing to happen now in Central America. The Soviet Union and Cuba are intervening in Central America. They are supplying the armed support to Nicaragua, all out of proportion to the needs of Nicaragua to defend itself.

If you tie the hands of the President of the United States publicly in the Senate and the House and say that under no circumstances can he do this without formal declarations or authorizations, and so forth, it simply telegraphs to Managua, to Havana, and to Moscow: "Gentlemen, full steam ahead." And what will we get? A military solution—the very thing that the proponents, the very honorable propo-

295

nents, of this amendment hope to avoid.

Let me end on this thought in terms of the reality of international relations of our time. There is no question about it. It has been spelled out carefully that the Marxist-Leninist solution is through military guerrilla operation to take the soft underdeveloped parts of the world and ultimately, as Marx and Lenin stated it, "You surround the urban industrial continents of Europe, of North America, including ultimately now Japan, and they in time will fall like ripe fruit."

We have to develop the acumen, the astuteness, the alertness, the ability to respond to that military challenge and it is of a guerrilla warfare nature, and hence we must allow the President the latitude, because we will hold him accountable now, will we not? We will not bear the burden, we will not accept responsibility if the military solution is imposed. We will point down Pennsylvania Avenue to the White House and say they failed, he failed.

I leave us with this thought: Has the United States no area in the world where we have self-interest to assert?

We were told during the Vietnam conflict that was distant, far away, and it was none of our concern. We were told in the Middle East that that perhaps is distant and far away and none of our concern. We are told that Africa is distant and far away and none of our concern.

And now, we are in our own hemisphere. We are in Central America. We see the Monroe Doctrine repudiated de facto, and once again it seems to me the thrust of what the proponents of this amendment are saying again is we have no self-interest.

I ask you this: Where do we, as one of the two great superpowers in the world, have a self-interest?

The Soviet Union moves with impunity into Afghanistan. It sends its surrogates, such as Syria, into Central America. It sends its surrogates into Africa in the form of Cuban troops and into Ethiopia, Angola, and Mozambique. It sends the PLO into Central America. It sends the Eastern European forces into Central America. It sends Cuban forces into Central America. In the Far East it takes over again Southeast Asia, uses Cam Ranh Bay, our former base, as its own base of operation. It gives the moral, logistic support to Vietnam to take over Cambodia, to threaten Thailand, and to broaden and expand its power in that whole part of the world.

Apparently, we have no self-interests in either we are told.

Now, here we are right in our own hemisphere and, again, it seems to me it is the old refrain: So we have no self-interests there. It makes no difference.

But it has been pointed out repeatedly if you allow Nicaragua to become the model in Central America, El Salvador will fall, Costa Rica will fall, Honduras will fall, Guatemala will fall, and Belize will fall. The pressure will be on Mexico and it ultimately will have no option except to itself to succumb to what? Yes, a military solution imposed by Moscow, Havana, and Managua.

Now, as has been pointed out repeatedly, between the Rio Grande and the Panama Canal are 100 million people. We have heard this before, but let me say it. I think it is worth repeating. We have learned from past experience that at least 10 percent of the population invariably flees when the Communists take over. All the voting is one way. Where they can vote with their feet, they come here.

Look at the poor pathetic boat people who went out and drifted in the South China Sea, just waiting for any vessel to come along and pick them up. Is it not curious where people have a choice, the leave? They leave the Communist system. We have to build up walls to keep them out. They have to build up walls to keep them in.

Now, I ask this, and in this case they would not even have to get into boats, they would simply walk. If they take over that area between the Rio Grande and the Panama Canal, of 100 million people, 10 million people will move northward across the Rio Grande. How will you stop it? Will you machinegun them down? Of course you will not.

It will create enormous economic and social disruption in our country and it poses an enormous geopolitical threat to the peace and the freedom and the security and the well-being of this country. It jeopardizes not only your freedom and mine in our time, but that of our children and our grandchildren.

This amendment is a part of that whole fabric of thinking that seems to operate on the assumption that nothing is going on in the world today of consequence. I put it this way: We fiddle while Rome burns. We are excused by two facts. We do not know, first, that we fiddle and, second, we do not know that Rome burns. But Rome is burning in Central America and if you do not allow the President of the United States, who has the responsibility as the Commander in Chief under the separation of power, who has the principal responsibility for the conduct of foreign policy and for the protection of this country, the latitude to do what must be done in this area, I think that what you are going to see is all Central America fall under Soviet and Cuban control and domination and the whole Caribbean basin will simply become a dominant sphere of Soviet influence, military influence.

That I find totally unacceptable. Totally unacceptable from whose standpoint?

From not only those people in that part of the world who must fall under this tyranny, but from the standpoint of the security, the freedom, and the well-being of this country.

So, I urge my colleagues to reflect very seriously on this. The stakes are high in Central America. They are in our own hemisphere, and if we will not defend our friends, our democratic friends, such as Duarte, in our own hemisphere, I simply question, gentlemen, who will we help? Who will we defend?

It is an eminiently fair question to ask where would you draw the line—anywhere? Apparently not.

And that would be the great tragedy of our time and World War III has been subtly lost and it has been lost to Moscow. It has been lost to the Marxist-Leninist world vision. And it is over with a whimper.

And I suspect in due course, as Marx and Lenin predicted, the industrial urban continents of North America, Europe, and Japan will eventually have to succumb to the realities of power in their time. Solzhenitsyn has said the world is finite in geography. At some point the balance tips against you.

I do not know if it has occurred or not. He said psychologically it occurred in Vietnam. Perhaps it has. But it will have occurred, as a matter of reality, if we tie the hands of the President of the United States and allow the Soviet Union and Cuba and her surrogates such as in Managua to take over that area.

It is a very heavy question we face; I think the most serious facing this Congress and this country at this point in our history. And I vigorously disassociate myself from this amendment. I vigorously oppose it. And I hope my colleagues would reflect long and hard and repudiate it, vote it down.

297

NO

Christopher J. Dodd

A NEW AMERICAN POLICY
IN CENTRAL AMERICA

I think we all are aware that President Reagan is greatly concerned about recent developments in Central America and in the Caribbean region and how to deal with them. I would add that he is not alone in that. His concerns are shared by 535 Members of Congress, by Republicans and Democrats alike, by the American public as a whole, by our neighbors in this Hemisphere, and, yes, by friend and foe both near and far.

What heightens these concerns for many of us here at home as well as abroad is the serious doubts and reservations that we have about the course being charted by the President and by his administration.

It comes down to an honest difference of opinion, not unlike differences over budget and tax policy, differences over arms control, and production of the MX missile.

There are legitimate differences on these basic, fundamental issues, and there are certainly legitimate differences on the question of what our policy should be with respect to the nations of Central America.

Clearly, the President and his spokesmen see it one way. They see it largely in terms of our Communist adversaries moving into the Western Hemisphere, expanding their influence, and aiding and abetting wars of national liberation in the Central American region.

While they are not unmindful of the internal conditions within that region, their emphasis is on the external factors and forces, meaning Moscow and Havana; meaning Chernenko and Castro.

Their formula for dealing with communism is a strong dose of anticommunism, which immediately translates into the use of military force, the use of military might, and the use of military power.

Unfortunately, this is a hallmark of this administration's approach to the problems of the region. I believe it was one of the reasons we decided to use military force in Grenada. This is why I believe we are involved in a not-so-secret war in Nicaragua. This is why we are building military bases in Hon-

From, US Senate Debate on amendment to reduce funds provided for El Salvador, March 29, 1984.

duras. This is why the President has already provided hundreds of millions of dollars in military assistance to the region. This is why he is requesting hundreds of millions more. This is why, unfortunately, we are urgently training thousands of soldiers in Central America. This is why the Defense Department wants an increase in the number of U.S. military advisors in the region. This is also why many of us are firmly convinced that the President's approach is as unwise as it is dangerous.

This conviction does not arise because we are oblivious to the threat posed by the Soviet Union, by Cuba, or by their allies. It does not arise because we have turned a blind eye to their efforts in Central America. Nor does it arise because we have illusions about the nature of the Communist system, or because we lack the will or the commitment, or the patriotism to confront that system and to confront it, if need be, with military force.

No, our conviction that the President is proceeding unwisely if not dangerously in Central America arises from a different view, a different interpretation of the fundamental facts in the case.

With the specter of growing American involvement in the Central American region, both in terms of men and treasure, it is time to look at the facts, to look at the reality of the region and our relationship to it, warts and all. The sooner we do so, the sooner we divorce the substance and the reality from the fantasy and the fiction, the better our assessment will be of where we have been, where we are now, and where we are going.

As we proceed in this assessment, I think it should come as no surprise to learn that we know little more about Central America in 1984 than we did about Indochina in 1964. I begin with the very basics.

Spanish-speaking Central America houses five relatively small nations: Costa Rica, El Salvador, Guatemala, Honduras, and Nicaragua. Their land mass is slightly larger than the State of California.

The population of the region comprises some 20 million people, about the same as New York State.

For the most part, the people who live in the area are ill-educated, ill-fed, ill-housed, and ill-treated. Illiteracy is widespread. Infant mortality is relatively commonplace. Malnutrition is virtually endemic. Unemployment is often at staggering levels. Respect for human rights is frequently nonexistent.

Together the Central American nations produce goods valued at less than $20 billion annually, roughly what the United States produces in 2 days. For the most part, income distribution continues to be highly skewed, the very few living in isolated splendor and the very many in shantytown squalor.

Politically, with the exception of Costa Rica, the nations of the region have had more than their fair share of demons, devils, and demagogues. Judging from the past, democratic experience is an alien ideology, to be avoided at all costs and discussed only in the presence of the American Ambassador or a visiting Congressman.

From this standpoint, the Somozas or the Romeros or the Lucases of recent vintage represent something of a time-honored tradition in Central America.

While we hope this tradition can be broken, we must also recognize that the odds seem to be against it. What have we done to help improve the odds? What has been our policy toward this region of Central America?

Well, the policies pursued by the United States toward Central America beginning with the enunciation of the Monroe

Doctrine in 1823 have had a certain consistency to them. Our primary purpose has been to protect and defend the basic security interests of the United States.

A secondary purpose has been to extend the blessings of liberty, freedom, and democracy to our southern neighbors. There has never been serious debate as to the order of priority for the two.

In response, what the democratic leaders of Latin America and their followers see is a historical effort by the United States to keep the hemisphere beyond the reach of any outside influence. We safeguarded Latin America and Central America from the Spanish and British in the 19th century and today from the Russians and the Cubans.

As they see efforts, however, it has never been quite clear whether the U.S. goal was to protect their independence and sovereignty or to extend the power and influence of the United States. While the rhetoric of the United States has maintained it was the former, the actions of the United States all too frequently suggested it really was the latter.

As Latins are quick to point out, these actions include a war with Mexico in 1845 to 1848, resulting in the annexation of what was then northern Mexico and what is today the Western and Southwestern part of the United States; repeated military intervention in the Caribbean and Central American region throughout the first part of this century; with marines stationed in Cuba, Haiti, the Dominican Republic, and Nicaragua; open and strong support for a whole host of antidemocratic regimes, including Batista in Cuba, Trujillo in the Dominican Republic, Ubico, Martinez and Somoza; the toppling of the Arbenz government in Guatemala in 1954 by exiled military forces under the direction of the Central Intelligence Agency; the Bay of Pigs invasion in 1961 and the covert operations designed to terminate the Castro government in Cuba; the sending of Marines to the Dominican Republic in 1965; clandestine efforts to prevent the election of Salvador Allende in Chile and subsequent efforts to overthrow his government, finally leading to Allende's demise in 1973; and, within the last several months, repeated threats of military action, paramilitary operations against Nicaragua, plus stepped up U.S. military involvement in the region, culminating in the decision to invade Grenada.

While the United States may strenuously object to such a list of particulars and to the indictment it brings, the Latin response is clear and concise: "Your actions speak louder than your words." That difference between what we practice and what we preach has made U.S. policy ineffective and impaired our credibility, and neither the Green Berets nor a division of Marines nor a squadron of F-16's can get it back.

I submit that the way to reclaim U.S. credibility and effectiveness in Latin America is to close the gap between what we say we stand for and the actions we are prepared to take to prove it. In other words, we must bring into line our ideals and our endeavors.

POSTSCRIPT

CENTRAL AMERICA: SHOULD THE US AID THE "CONTRAS"?

Dodd and East are looking at Central America from very different perspectives, perhaps because they are using different models for understanding what is happening in the region. Dodd is obviously thinking about Vietnam, where the frequently mindless use of American force led to a major debacle. East is using as his model the period of the 1930s, when the failure of the Western democracies to challenge the expansionist policies of Adolf Hitler's Germany led to a different kind of debacle. Which model is correct? Within the next few years we may have an answer.

Liberal-to-radical perspectives on American policy in Central America can be found in Cynthia Arnson's *El Salvador: A Revolution Confronts the United States* (Institute for Policy Studies, 1982) and Marvin Gettleman, et al., eds., *El Salvador: Central America in the Cold War* (Grove Press, 1981). *Bitter Fruit,* by Stephen Schlessinger and Stephen Kinzer (Doubleday, 1982), purports to tell "the untold story of the American coup in Guatamala" in 1954. It is more difficult to find contemporary books that warn of Communist subversion in Latin America. Even the Hoover Institute-sponsored study by Thomas P. Anderson, *Politics in Central America* (Praeger, 1982), ends on an optimistic note: "A year after the revolution, Nicaragua was in the process of rebuilding, and was channelling its energy toward the creation of a new society." Perhaps the best balance—and ballast—for the above is Paul Hollander's *Political Pilgrims* (Harper & Row, 1983), which recalls all the wonderful and wildly misleading appraisals Western intellectuals have given of revolutionary regimes, from Stalin's in the 1920s to Castro's in the 1960s.

Both sides in the congressional debate agree that Soviet expansion in Central America must be countered. The question turns on the means. One side rules out military options while the other considers them imperative. Choosing sides responsibly is not easy, for Central America contains a complex of problems, from the Soviet presence to the much older problems of poverty and injustice.

ISSUE 18

CAN AMERICAN MILITARY ACTION CURB INTERNATIONAL TERRORISM?

YES: Benjamin Netanyahu, from "Terrorism: How the West Can Win," *Time* magazine, April 14, 1986

NO: Conor Cruise O'Brien, from "Thinking About Terrorism," the *Atlantic Monthly,* June 1986

ISSUE SUMMARY

YES: Benjamin Netanyahu, Israeli ambassador to the United Nations, believes that the United States can sharply reduce terrorism by applying political, economic and military pressure.
NO: Conor Cruise O'Brien, former deputy chief of the Irish delegation to the UN, believes that only American moral consistency will achieve the coordinated international action that can curb terrorism.

Terror for most Americans used to be the advertised ingredient in the late-night horror movies about unreal creatures. Now terror and terrorists have become all too real. The hijacking of airliners and a cruise ship, deadly raids on airports, a night club and other public places, and the kidnapping and killing of innocent civilians have brought home to Americans the realization that there is another kind of war, in which the adversary wears no recognizable identification and the battlefield is wherever he chooses to strike.

Shortly after taking office, President Reagan vowed that terrorists would be punished, but that has proved to be an extraordinarily difficult task. When a car bomb planted hours earlier explodes, it destroys any evidence as to who placed it. When terrorists are willing to die in their act of unbridled violence, punishment does not appear to be a deterrence.

Frustrated by a succession of terrorist actions in 1985, some of which resulted in the death of American citizens travelling abroad, President Reagan directed an aerial strike against Libya, because the US believed that Libyan ruler Colonel Muammar Khaddafi had ordered the bombing of a West Berlin nightclub where US servicemen were killed. The President's action was approved by Americans who wanted the government to act, and their support seemed merited by a decline in terrorist acts.

Others criticized the action because they felt that the United States was succumbing to the use of terrorism and it had acted without conclusive proof of what nations or groups were behind the nightclub attack. Would the US strike again against a nation which we believed was harboring or financing terrorists? Were we prepared to destroy the government of such a nation?

America's European allies were critical, and it remained to be seen how the United States would act in the future. Much terrorism is the work of small fanatical bands which sometimes operate, much as criminal gangs do, without the active complicity of a host country. Curtailing international terrorism may require widespread cooperation among nations.

Critics of American foreign policy cite US intervention in Nicaragua on behalf of the insurgent military groups as a form of terrorism. Terrorists are those who will engage in violent and illegal acts on behalf of a deeply-felt political cause. Were not those who engaged in the Boston Tea Party terrorists? Are not "freedom fighters" everywhere terrorists unless and until they triumph and become transformed historically into revolutionary founding fathers?

The equation of terrorists and "freedom fighters" is a particularly dangerous kind of intellectual and moral confusion, according to Israeli ambassador Benjamin Netanyahu. He carefully distinguishes between the two, and urges Western nations to take tough action against terrorists. He contends that the use of force, including military action, "is the only way to make governments stop launching terrorist killers." Irish diplomat Conor Cruise O'Brien takes a different approach to terrorism. He believes that the United States must first adopt a foreign policy that is morally consistent and then seek a limited consensus with the Soviet Union to eradicate international terrorism.

YES   Benjamin Netanyahu

TERRORISM
HOW THE WEST CAN WIN

International terrorism is not a sporadic phenomeon born of social misery and frustration. It is rooted in the political ambitions and designs of expansionist states and the groups that serve them. Without the support of such states, international terrorism would be impossible.

Access to the media is also indispensable. First the terrorists seize our attention by committing a brutal act. Only then does the real performance begin: the communiqués, the parading of dazed hostages before the cameras, the endless interviews in which the terrorists are respectfully asked to explain their demands and conditions. Slowly, imperceptibly, the initial horror recedes, and in its place comes a readiness to accept the terrorist point of view.

We are asked to shed our normal revulsion for murderous acts and accept the notion, endlessly repeated, that "one man's terrorist is another man's freedom fighter." This is precisely what the terrorist would like us to believe. It is completely untrue. At the risk of belaboring the point, I offer a formal definition: Terrorism is the deliberate and systematic murder, maiming and menacing of the innocent to inspire fear for political ends. This distinction lies at the heart of the matter. For without a clear understanding of terrorism, the problem cannot be tackled.

Terrorists habitually describe themselves as "guerrillas," but guerrillas are not terrorists. They are irregular soldiers who wage war on regular *military* forces. Terrorists choose to attack weak and defenseless civilians: old men, women and children—anyone in fact *except* soldiers if terrorists can avoid it.

This indeed is one of terrorism's most pernicious effects: it blurs the distinction between combatants and noncombatants, the central tenet of the laws of war. It is not only that the terrorist breaks down this standard but that we begin to accept his standards. With each fresh attack, the public is conditioned—first by the terrorists, then by their compliant interpreters in the press—to equate innocent hostages with jailed terrorists and to accept the notion that the murder of children is a regrettable but understandable expression of the terrorists' purported grievances.

Excerpted from *Terrorism: How the West Can Win,* edited by Benjamin Netanyahu, published by Farrar, Straus & Giroux. Copyright © 1986 by the Jonathan Institute. Reprinted by permission of the author.

There are those who say that war is war and that any attempt to define ethical limits is futile. But short of the rare and difficult case of total war, such as during World War II, most people would agree that there is a significant difference between waging war on armed combatants and attacking defenseless civilians. None of the resistance movements in Nazi-occupied Europe conducted or even condoned, terrorist attacks against German noncombatants, such as officers' wives or children. Without such distinctions, the concept of war crimes loses any meaning. For if everything is permissible, why not gas innocent people or machine-gun children?

It is here that the terrorist parts company with humanity. He declares a total war on the society he attacks. For him everyone is a legitimate target. A baby is fair game; he may, after all, grow up to be a soldier. So is the baby's mother; she gave birth to this future soldier. No one is spared, ordinary citizens and leaders alike.

Having defined all of society as a field of combat, the terrorist demands that his activity, which would ordinarily be viewed as gangsterism, be treated with the respect given to legitimate warfare. That is why he often takes on all the trappings of a soldier; that is why he issues "communiqués" instead of simple statements and why he insists that his jailed accomplices, who are in fact dangerous criminals, be accorded the status of prisoners of war.

Though terrorism as such is not new in history, or even in this century, today's terrorism differs in its extent and its violence; it now attacks the territory and citizens of nearly all the democracies. It began its rapid growth in the 1960s. It was sparked by the early successes of two groups of terrorists: the P.L.O., which introduced airline hijacking as an international weapon, and European radical factions, which carried out increasingly bold bombings, kidnapings and assassinations throughout the Continent. Terrorist groups, seemingly independent from one another, soon proliferated throughout Europe, Japan, North and South America and the Middle East. But as the evidence piled up, the Arab P.L.O., the Iranian *mujahedin,* the Armenian A.S.A.L.A., the German Baader-Meinhof gang, the Italian Red Brigades, the Japanese Red Army and others were often found to be linked not only to one another but to the Soviet Union and radical Arab regimes. Only after the P.L.O.'s expulsion from Beirut did captured P.L.O. documents reveal the role of its terrorist ministate in Lebanon as a training center and launching ground for what had become a kind of terrorist international. . . .

As the number of attacks has increased tenfold in the past decade alone, a clear pattern has emerged. The targets of terrorism have been, more and more, Britain and Germany, Spain and Portugal, France and Italy, Israel and Japan, and, above all, the U.S. (whose nationals accounted for roughly a third of terrorism's victims since 1968)—in short, the West. A network of professionnal terrorists seeks to weaken and demoralize democratic societies by attacking their citizens, their leaders, their institutions, thereby disrupting their way of life and sapping their political will. And it is a growing threat. Terrorist attacks now kill and injure not one or two but hundreds at a time. Few doubt that other, more lethal, weapons may be employed in the future.

The terrorist's strategy is premised on the ability to deliver future blows, no matter what. The fear and intimidation that terrorism thrives on are totally dependent on this threat. The primary task in fighting terrorism, then, is to weaken and ultimately destroy the terrorist's ability to launch attacks. This is often presented as a difficult or even impossible task. It is asserted that the clandestine nature of terrorism and the openness of Western societies make terrorism against the West nearly impossible to root out. I would argue the exact opposite. Terrorism can be stopped. The minute you weaken its ability to deliver repeated blows, you have broken its back. And it is well within the means of the West to achieve this.

Consider, for example, the classic terrorist act, the taking of hostages. More than any other act of terrorist violence, it reveals two underlying characteristics of terrorism. First, it is an unmistakably *deliberate* assault on the people who are seized, precisely because they are noncombatants. Second, it affords a stage for dramatization and distortion. Hostage taking places a government in a terrible dilemma: if it uses force to release the hostages, it might end up with more people killed than if it gives in. If it yields, the terrorists emerge victorious. Sometimes the terrorists resolve this dilemma by killing a few hostages and threatening to murder the rest if their demands are not met. The government can then argue that since more hostages are about to be killed, it must take action immediately.

But suppose the terrorists have not started killing hostages. Should they not fear a forcible response? The more terrorists believe that military intervention is likely, the less prone they will be to continue their siege. In the hijacking of both the TWA airliner out of Athens [June 1985] and the cruise ship *Achille Lauro* [Fall 1985], a principal reason that the terrorists released their hostages was their belief in imminent intervention—retaliation afterward in the case of the airliner and military rescue of the *Achille Lauro* (both American and Italian forces were poised to storm the ship

on the day the pirates surrendered).

Terrorists have often escaped retaliation because of the sloppiness of the West's thinking about the use of force. America's loss of clarity in the wake of Viet Nam has become a general Western malaise. The rules of engagement have become so rigid that governments often strait-jacket themselves in the face of unambiguous aggression. But a fundamental principle must be recognized: under no circumstances should a government categorically rule out a military response simply because of the risk of civilian casualties. There is a practical and a moral basis for this position. In practical terms, an inflexible rule against risking civilian casualties would make any military action virtually impossible. In moral terms, an absolute prohibition on civilian casualties today condemns to death or injury many future victims. Terrorism, undeterred, will inevitably increase.

Responsible governments seek to minimize civilian casualties. But they do not grant immunity to an aggressor simply because their response might endanger civilians. If this is true in normal combat, it is truer still in the case of terrorism. An absolute prohibition on civilian casualties provides the terrorist with an invincible shield. This is not only true in cases in which he fears retaliation following his attacks (for example, when the terrorist seeks immunity by planting his bases among civilians). It is also true during the taking of hostages, when the terrorist even more brazenly seeks immunity by daring the authorities to risk the lives of innocent victims by taking action.

Terrorists generally do fear military intervention, and that fear has a tremendously inhibiting effect on hostage taking. This is best demonstrated in the case of Israel. No other nation suffered more from this form of attack. In the 1970s Israel experienced a large number of hostage takings, including the hijacking of planes and the seizing of schools, apartments, hotels and buses. In all these cases, the government refused to capitulate to the terrorists' demands. Soldiers overcame the terrorists and liberated the hostages. This was by no means an easy course to follow. The government painfully recognized that its policy made some civilian casualties unavoidable; in 1974 at Ma'alot, 21 schoolchildren were massacred by the P.L.O. before the terrorists were themselves killed.

But the result of this determined refusal to yield was that hostage taking gradually became a rarity inside Israel. This was not because the P.L.O. was unable to stage such incidents but because it finally realized that there would be no surrender and that the terrorists would fail and probably be killed. Contrary to popular myth, cases of suicidal terrorism are rare; overwhelmingly, terrorists want to live, to escape unpunished.

The P.L.O. sought to overcome Israel's resolve by seizing Israeli planes or hostages outside Israel. But these attempts were defeated as well. In the most celebrated example, the case of Entebbe, Israeli troops flew more than 2,000 miles, liberated the hostages and killed their captors. For a decade afterward, not a single Israeli or Israel-bound plane was hijacked, and virtually no attempts were made to seize Israeli hostages abroad.

The refusal to capitulate and the decision to apply force were adopted in several important instances by other governments. The German government forcibly liberated German hostages on the hijacked Lufthansa airplane in Mogadishu in 1977, the Dutch successfully stormed a train hijacked by the South Moluccans (1977), and the British freed the occupied Iranian embassy in London (1980). For some time afterward, these countries experienced no further hostage takings. Far from engendering a cycle of increased violence, the application of military force or the prospect of such application inhibits terrorist violence.

The only sensible policy for attacked governments, then, is a refusal to yield and a readiness to apply force. This is a policy that says to the terrorist, I will not accept your demands. I demand that you release the hostages. If you do not do so peacefully, I am prepared to use force. I am proposing a simple exchange: your life for the lives of the hostages. The only "deal" I am willing to make with you is that if you surrender peacefully, I will not kill you. . . .

Terrorists may at first respond to a government's policy of firmness with an acceleration of violence, but they usually cannot withstand a sustained and resolute policy of resistance and active pursuit. Retaliation and pre-emption against terrorism are thus acts of self-defense. Denying the necessity for such self-defense, and blurring the moral basis for it, is dangerous. It undermines a basic principle on which government authority is based. A government's first obligation is to protect its citizens. Confusion or vacillation fools no one, least of all terrorists.

One point is central: international terrorism as we know it would simply not be possible without the collaboration of governments that have used terrorism to wage hidden war against their adversaries, especially the West. After the *Achille Lauro* piracy, Abul Abbas, its mastermind, skittered from Egypt to Italy to Yugoslavia and Iraq to South Yemen, where he finally found his most suitable haven. Without the collusion or acquiescence of friendly or passive governments, he would have been caught and brought to trial. The support of friendly regimes and the passivity of others are the crucial assumptions under which international terrorism operates.

Just as hostile governments have caused the internationalization of terror, they are also the key to its end. For states are no less susceptible than the terrorists they support to a sober calculation of costs and benefits. The very reason certain regimes rely on terrorists is to be able to wage war without the risks that war entails. As long as they are successful in denying complicity or involvement, they will easily escape retribution.

Once this is understood, the democracies can begin to act effectively in three broad areas against offending states.

POLITICAL PRESSURES

These could range from international condemnation to cutting off diplomatic relations (as the U.S. and Britain did with Libya). Political pressures signal to the terrorist state that the victim not only is unwilling to yield but is prepared to expose the offender to public censure. This could force other states to take a position against the offender, or at least to curb their support of it. Since many states sponsoring terrorism depend on the ability to deny complicity in terrorist crimes, this is not a minor threat. In the severance of diplomatic relations, an added penalty is the shutting down of embassies. Terrorists simply cannot sustain a concerted campaign of attacks in most Western countries without sanctuary or inviolable means of passing funds, arms and intelligence. . . .

ECONOMIC PRESSURE

Most of these countries desperately need Western goods, weapons or credit. There are certain sophisticated products, including advanced weapons, that only the West can supply. If the democracies used but a fraction of their enormous economic clout, they could cause regimes supporting terrorism to rethink some of their activities. . . .

MILITARY ACTION

This cannot be ruled out; nor should we be bashful about discussing it. When we talk about using military force, we must first consider unilateral action, one state's taking action against terrorists or a state that shelters them. Obviously, if a terrorist action occurs on a government's own soil, it will take action to protect its own citizens and foil the terrorists.

But what about a terrorist attack on a country's citizens abroad, in embassies, businesses or airlines? In the case of a hijacking, piracy or other hostage taking, the responsibility of securing the release of the hostages is that of the government on whose soil (or ship or plane) the incident takes place. One would hope such governments would adopt a firm policy against the terrorists, but if a government cannot or will not undertake forcibly to end a hostage crisis, it forfeits a certain measure of jurisdiction. The country whose nationals (or plane or ship) are held hostage has the right to act when the host country refuses to do so. Take the case of Entebbe. Uganda had an obligation to intervene and end the hijacking. When it refused to do so, the right to act passed to Israel and France (most of the passengers were Israeli; the plane was French). Since France was not considering any military move (although it helped in gathering intelligence), Israel had a perfect right to act

This is at odds with a widely held view that national sovereignty is absolute and cannot be violated. But of course it is no absolute. Countries do not have the right to do *anything* within their borders. They risk the intervention of other states if they fail to live up to elementary international obligations.

Sovereignty does not in any way preclude a government from allowing another government to assist in or carry out a rescue operation, as, for example, the Somalis did when they approved the intervention of West Germany's antiterrorist unit in the Mogadishu incident. In most cases, therefore, even weak or hesitant governments have a choice. Bluntly put, they can either do it themselves or let someone else do it.

What about the use of force in circumstances other than hostage taking? Western governments already possess ample intelligence evidence (such as satellite photos of training camps, interception of communications, reports from agents in the field) of continuous support for terrorists from certain governments. Such a record of complicity is more than strong enough to justify punitive action against these criminal states. Plenty of military or strategic targets can be struck to inflict severe damage, while avoiding excessive, if any, civilian casualties. . . .

A policy of firmness will make it clear that individual terrorists will be pursued, caught and punished; that the organizations that launch them will be subject to attack; that the governments that shelter them will face political, economic and, ultimately, military retaliation; that other governments that collude less brazenly will also be held accountable.

What, then, has inhibited the widespread adoption of this policy by the West? I believe it is the persistent effects of three vices. One is greed, or a heedless promotion of economic self-interest, whatever the political or moral consequences. A second is political cowardice, which means sitting it out while your ally is attacked, or responds to an attack, so as not to invoke the wrath of the terrorists. Both factors played a part in the immediate rejection by several governments of the American initiative for sanctions against Libya following the attacks on the Rome and Vienna airports. Neither cowardice nor greed will easily disappear. If, however, the U.S. persists in its firm stance, I believe that it will eventually succeed in pressuring, even shaming, other Western states into compliance.

But there is a third, even more pernicious impediment that needs to be overcome: a confusion that is both moral and intellectual. We in the West believe in the capacity of politics to mitigate, and resolve, all conflict. We automatically tend to endow an adversary with the same assumptions. These could not be more misplaced than in the case of terrorists, who use political language to destroy the concept of politics altogether. And even when we catch a glimpse of this truth, we fail to grasp its essence. For the West is in awe of fanaticism. It is confused before a supposed willingness to die for a cause, believing that such readiness must be based on a cause that is at least partially just. Even a cursory reading of history tells us how dangerous a notion that is. No people were more prepared to sacrifice their lives for a cause than the Hitler Youth. . . .

The West can win the war against terrorism, and fairly rapidly. But it must first win the war against its own inner weakness. That will require courage. First, government leaders must have the political courage to present the truth, however unpleasant, to their people. They must be prepared to make difficult decisions, to take measures that may involve great risks, that may even end in failure and subject them to public criticism.

Second, the soldiers who may actually be called upon to combat terrorists will need to show military courage. It will be up to them to decide whether they can or cannot undertake a particular operation that a government is considering. In the special units of the Israeli army, for example, no one has ever simply been told by the political leadership that he must accept a perilous assignment. The commanders are always asked: Is it possible? Do you think you can do it? And if they ever said it could not be done, or even if they expressed doubts, that would have been the end of the matter.

But there is also a third kind of courage: the civic valor that must be shown by an entire people. All citizens in a democracy threatened by terrorism must see themselves, in a certain sense, as soldiers in a common battle. They must not pressure their government to capitulate or to surrender to terrorism. This is especially true of public pressure on government by families of hostages. Such pressure can only be called a dereliction of civic duty. If we seriously want to win the war against terrorism, we must be prepared to endure sacrifices and even, should there be the loss of loved ones, immeasurable pain.

Terrorism is a phenomenon that tries to evoke one feeling: fear. It is understandable that the one virtue most necessary to defeat terrorism is therefore the antithesis of fear: courage.

Courage, said the Romans, is not the only virtue, but it is the single virtue without which all the others are meaningless. The terrorist challenge must be answered. The choice is between a free society based on law and compassion and a rampant barbarism in the service of brute force and tyranny. Confusion and vacillation facilitated the rise of terrorism. Clarity and courage will ensure its defeat.

NO
Conor Cruise O'Brien

THINKING ABOUT TERRORISM

Terrorism is disturbing not just emotionally and morally but intellectually, as well. On terrorism, more than on other subjects, commentary seems liable to be swayed by wishful thinking, to base itself on unwarranted or flawed assumptions, and to draw from these assumptions irrational inferences, muzzily expressed.

Let me offer one example, typical of many more. The following is the conclusion to a recent *Washington Post* editorial, "Nervous Mideast Moment":

> The United States, however, cannot afford to let its struggle against terrorism be overwhelmed by its differences with Libya. That gives the Qaddafis of the world too much importance and draws attention from the requirement to go to the political sources of terrorism. A principal source, unquestionably, is the unresolved Palestinian question. The State Department's man for the Middle East, Richard Murphy, has been on the road again, cautiously exploring whether it is possible in coming months to bring Israel and Jordan closer to a negotiation. This quest would be essential even if terrorism were not the concern it is. It marks the leading way that American policy must go.

The clear implication is that negotiation between Israel and Jordan can dry up "a principal source of terrorism." Now, nobody who has studied that political context at all, and is not blinded by wishful thinking, could possibly believe that. For the Arab terrorists—and most other Arabs—"the unresolved Palestinian question" and the existence of the State of Israel are one and the same thing. The terrorists could not possibly be appeased, or made to desist, by Jordan's King Hussein's getting back a slice of the West Bank, which is the very most that could come out of a negotiation between Jordan and Israel. The terrorists and their backers would denounce such a deal as treachery and seek to step up their attacks,, directing these against Jordan as well as Israel.

That *Washington Post* editorial, like many others to the same tune, exemplifies a dovish, or sentimental, variety of wishful thinking on the subject of terrorism. There is also a hawkish, or hysterical, variety. Each has its own misleading stereotype (or stereotypes) of the terrorist. Let us look at the stereotypes:

Sentimental stereotype. According to this stereotype, the terrorist is a misguided idealist, an unsublimated social reformer. He has been driven to violence by political or social injustice or both. What is needed is to identify the measures of reform that will cause him to desist. Once these can be identified and undertaken, the terrorist, having ceased to be driven, stops.

Hysterical stereotype. Less stable than the sentimental variety, this can be divided into subvarieties:

(a) The terrorist is some kind of nut—a "disgruntled abnormal" given to "mindless violence." ("Mindless violence" may be applicable to the deeds of isolated, maverick assassins. As applied to the planned activities of armed conspiracies, it is itself a mindless expression.)

(b) The terrorist is nothing more than a thug, a goon, a gangster. His "political" demands are simply a cover for criminal activity.

(c) The terrorist is an agent, or dupe, or cat's-paw of the other superpower. (He might, of course, be a nut or a goon as well as a dupe.)

These stereotypes serve mainly to confuse debate on the subject. There is no point in arbitrarily attributing motives, nice or nasty, to the terrorist. It might be more useful to look at the situations in which terrorists find themselves and at how they act, and may be expected to act, given their situations.

In what follows I shall bear in mind mainly (though not exclusively) the members of the most durable terrorist organizations of the twentieth century: the IRA (including its splinter groups) and the PLO (including its splinter groups).

Terrorists have a grievance, which they share with members of a wider community: the division of Ireland, the division of Palestine, the inroads of secularism into Islam, or whatever. But they also have, from the moment they become terrorists, significant amounts of power, prestige, and access to wealth, and these constitute vested interests in the present, irrespective of the attainment or non-attainment of their declared long-term political objectives.

The sentimentalist thinks of the terrorist as driven to violence by grievance or oppression. It would be more realistic to think of the terrorist as hauling himself up, by means of the grievance or oppression and the violence it legitimizes, to relative power, prestige, and privilege in the community to which he belongs. For an unemployed young man in a slum in Sidon or Strabane, for example, the most promising channel of upward social mobility is his neighborhood branch of the national terrorist organization. There are risks to be run, certainly, but for the adventurous, aggressive characters among the unemployed or the otherwise frustrated, the immediate rewards outweigh the risks. In this situation the terrorist option is a rational one: you don't have to be a nut, a dupe, or an idealist.

I don't mean that the terrorist is necessarily, or even probably, insincere about the national (or religious or other collective) grievance or in his hatred toward those seen as responsible for the grievance. On the contrary, hatred is one of the things that keep him going,, and the gratification of hatred is among the rewards of the terrorist. The terrorist is not just a goon out for the loot. His political motivation is genuine. But there are other rewards in hi way of life as well as the hazy reward of progress toward the political objective. The possession of a known capacity and willingness to kill confers authority and glamour in the here and now, even on rank-and-file members in the urban ghetto or in the village. On the leaders it confers national and even international authority and glamour, and independence from financial worries.

If we accept that the terrorist's way of life procures him immediate rewards of that nature, and that he is probably not insensible to at least some of the rewards in question, it seems to follow that he will probably be reluctant to relinquish those rewards by voluntarily putting himself out of business.

The situation thus outlined has a bearing of a negative nature on the notion that there are "negotiated solutions" to the "problems" that "cause" terrorism.

First of all, a negotiated solution—being by definition an outcome that offers some satisfaction to both parties—will be inherently distasteful to terrorists and their admirers, accustomed as these are to regarding one of the parties (Britain, Israel, or another) as evil incarnate.

Second, to exploit that genuine distaste will be in the interests of the terrorists, in relation to the reward system discussed above. So pride and profit converge into a violent rejection of the "negotiated solution"—which therefore is not a solution to terrorism. . . .

Not only do doves sometimes help terrorists but some hawkish advisers also give inadvertent aid and comfort to the forces they abhor. The combating of terrorism is not helped by bombastic speeches at high levels, stressing what a monstrous evil terrorism is and that its elimination is to be given the highest priority. I'm afraid that the most likely terrorist reaction to such a speech, whether it comes from a President, a Secretary of State, or other important official, is: "You see, they have to pay attention to us now. We are hurting them. Let's give them more of the same." And it all helps with recruitment. A movement that is denounced by a President is in the big time. And some kind of big time is what is most wanted by the aggressive and frustrated, who constitute the pool on which terrorist movements can draw.

What applies to speeches applies a fortiori to unilateral military action against countries harboring terrorists. Whatever short-term advantages may be derived from such attacks, a price will be paid—in increased international sympathy for the "cause" of the terrorists in question, and so in enhanced glamour and elbow room for them, all tending to legitimize and so facilitate future "counterattacks."

Nor does it help to suggest that terrorism is about to be extirpated—because it almost certainly isn't. Today's world—especially the free, or capitalist world—provides highly favorable conditions for terrorist recruitment and activity. The numbers of the frustrated are constantly on the increase, and so is their awareness of the life-style of the better-off and the vulnerability of the better-off. Among the better-off themselves are bored young people looking for the kicks that violence can provide, and thus for causes that legitimize violence, of which there are no shortage. A wide variety of people feel starved for attention, and one surefire way of attracting instantaneous worldwide attention through television is to slaughter a considerable number of human beings, in a spectacular fashion, in the name of a cause.

Although the causes themselves hardly constitute the sole motivation of the terrorists—as terrorists claim they do—they are not irrelevant, either. The cause legitimizes the act of terror in the terrorist's own eyes and in those of others belonging to his nation, faith, or culture. Certain cultures and subcultures, homes of frustrated causes, are destined breeding grounds for terrorism. The Islamic culture is the most notable example. That culture's view of its own rightful position in the world is profoundly at variance with the actual order of the contemporary world. It is God's will that the House of Islam should triumph over the House of War (the non-Moslem world), and not just by spiritual means. "Islam Means Victory" is a slogan of the Iranian fundamentalists in the Gulf War. To strike a blow against the House of War is meritorious; consequently, there is widespread support for activities condemned in the West as terrorist. Israel is one main target for these activities, but the activities would not be likely to cease even if Israel came to an end. The Great Satan in the eyes of Ayatollah Khomeini—and of the millions for whom he speaks—is not Israel but the United States. The defeat of Israel would, in those eyes, be no more than a portent of the impending defeat of the Great Satan. What the West calls terrorism should then be multiplied rather than abandoned.

The wellsprings of terrorism are widespread and deep. The interaction between modern communications systems and archaic fanaticism (and other sources of resentment and ambition) is likely to continue to stimulate terrorist activity. In these conditions, talk about extirpating terrorism—and unilateral exploits backing such talk—are likely to be counterproductive. They present terrorists with a "victory," merely by the fact of being able to continue their activity. Similarly, solemn promises never to negotiate with terrorists can play into the hands of terrorists. Ter-

rorists holding hostages can force a democratic government to negotiate, as happened in the case of the hijacked TWA airliner [June, 1985]. If the democratic government then pretends that no negotiation took place, this helps the credibility of the terrorists, not that of the democratic government.

It is not possible to extirpate terrorism from the face of the globe, but it should be possible to reduce the incidence and effectiveness of terrorism, through coordinated international action. The Reagan Administration's efforts to get better cooperation in this matter from the European allies are justified in principle but flawed in practice. They are justified because the performance of several European countries in relation to international terrorism has often amounted to turning a blind eye, for commercial reasons. The British government, for example, tolerated the conversion of the Libyan Embassy in London into a "Revolutionary People's Bureau," and ignored all reports that the bureau was a center of terrorist activity, until the point was reached at which the revolutionary diplomatists actually opened fire from the embassy windows into St. James's Square, killing a British policewoman. Even after that the policy of playing ball with Qaddafi, as long as there was money to be made out of it, did not altogether disappear, either in Britain or elsewhere in Europe. (Mrs. Thatcher's support for the recent U.S. air strikes against Libyan targets seems to stem from a wish to be seen as the most dependable ally of the United States, rather than from any spontaneous change of heart about the proper way in which to deal with Libya.)

So President Reagan had good reasons for urging the European allies to adopt less complaisant attitudes toward international terrorism. But, unfortunately, the President's remonstrances lack the moral leverage they need to have. They lack such leverage because a very wide international public sees the Reagan Administration itself as engaged in supporting terrorism in Central America, in its backing for the contras in Nicaragau. Public cynicism about American anti-terrorist rhetoric is increased by the strong component of Cold War ideology that the Reagan Administration has been putting into its anti-terrorism, implying that almost all terrorism has its ultimate roots in the Soviet Union. Most of the interested public outside the superpowers tends to see each superpower as calling the terrorists whom it favors "freedom fighters" while reserving the term "terrorists" for the "freedom fighters" favored by the other side. That view of the matter is debatable, but the point, in the present context, is that it is shared by so many people that it inhibits effective international cooperation against international terrorism.

Such cooperation is unlikely to have a strong impact unless both superpowers are prepared to participate in it. Bringing about such cooperation will be difficult but is not inconceivable. Limited superpower consensus has emerged, in the second half of the twentieth century, on at least three occasions: in 1956, against the Anglo-French-Israeli invasion of Egypt; in 1963, against the continued existence of the secessionist "state" of Katanga; and in 1977, against the supply of arms to South Africa.

Can limited superpower consensus be attained for coordinated action against terrorism? I think it can, especially if international terrorist activity grows to the degree that it begins to pose a clear threat to international peace and stability—not just as these are perceived by one superpower but as perceived by both. There is a historical precedent, flawed—like all such

precedents—but suggestive. This is the case of the Barbary pirates, who used to operate in the Mediterranean, out of North African ports. In the seventeenth and eighteenth centuries, rivalries between the European powers provided the Barbary pirates with conditions propitious to their activities, much as global rivalries tend to protect state terrorism today. The Barbary pirates were a general nuisance, but they were a worse nuisance to some powers than to others, and so the enemies of the powers for whom the pirates were making the most trouble were apt to give the pirates a helping hand from time to time. In the first half of the nineteenth century, however, the powers decided, in effect, that the pirates should be treated as a common enemy: the enemy of the human race, *hostes humani generis*. With that change in international approach piracy was brought under control in the Mediterranean.

International terrorism has yet to reach the stage that Mediterranean piracy reached in the nineteenth century. Terrorism is a worse nuisance to one superpower—the United States—than it is to the other. Democratic societies, committed to freedom of information and having governments necessarily sensitive to changing public moods, are far more vulnerable to terrorist blackmail, and offer a far more stimulating environment for terrorist activity, than closed societies like the Soviet Union. (We are often told that there is no terrorist activity in the Soviet Union; in reality we don't know whether there is terrorism or not. But the fact that we don't know and that the Soviet public doesn't know would certainly be advantageous to the Soviet authorities in coping with any terrorists that they may have.)

So the Soviets have no clear and present incentive to join in international activity against terrorism. On the contrary, they have given cautious aid and encouragement to some forms of terrorism (less than right-wing propagandists suggest, but more than the left admits). But it would be wrong to conclude, as most right-wing analysts do, that the Soviets are operating under a doctrinal imperative to destabilize the West. The Soviet authorities—despite their ideological bravado—know well that a destabilized West could be extremely dangerous, and specifically dangerous to the Soviet Union. The superpowers do have an elemental common interest—in survival. That is why limited superpower consensus has been possible in the past, and that is why it remains a possibility for the future with regard to terrorism. Such consensus could take the form of a joint warning that any country harboring terrorists would no longer be allowed to invoke its sovereignty as a protection against international intervention. Once superpower agreement had been reached, that warning could be embodied in a mandatory resolution of the Security Council.

We are very far indeed from that point, though here as elsewhere thought should not treat present actuality as if it were eternal. In the meantime, it appears that the United States has two main alternatives for anti-terrorist policy.

The first alternative, which seems likely to be followed for the remainder of the Reagan Administration, is to go on backing the contras and simultaneously calling for an end to terrorism, with occasional armed spectaculars to lend conviction to such calls. As already indicated, I think this policy is internationally incredible and hopeless, and unnecessarily dangerous, whatever its merits may be in terms of domestic electoral politics.

The second alternative is to provide clear and consistent political and moral leadership in this matter to U.S. allies and the rest of what is called the free world. That would require the United States both to abandon completely its support for the contras in Nicaragua and to accept, without the present reservations, the authority of the World Court. I believe that a President of the United States who had taken these steps would be in a far stronger position than is now the case to give the world a lead in combined action against terrorism and to prepare the way for eventual superpower consensus on this matter. And I think that a President who took such a stand would be bringing new hope on other matters, also, to many people in the world.

POSTSCRIPT

CAN AMERICAN MILITARY ACTION CURB INTERNATIONAL TERRORISM?

Although the United States has had home-grown terrorism (the Weathermen and Symbionese Liberation Army are recent examples), attacks on American citizens and property abroad have dramatically focused American attention on a persistent international phenomenon. It may be noted that Israeli Ambassador Benjamin Netanyahu and Irish diplomat and author Conor Cruise O'Brien have long experienced terrorism in their homelands.

Terrorism is one political issue where nearly all Americans can be found to agree that it is bad. The disagreement comes first in defining it and then in deciding what to do about it.

It is easy enough to say what terrorists do. Terrorists wage unconventional war, hitting, running and hiding. They may engage in arbitrary murder and political assassination, bombings of public places, kidnappings of diplomats, and the hijacking of planes and ships. It may be objected that terrorism is not necessarily bad; the American colonists engaged in illegal and violent acts in rebelling against British rule. Yet Netanyahu shows that a "terrorist" is not a "freedom fighter."

What is the objective of contemporary terrorists? Foreign correspondent Claire Sterling argues in *The Terror Network: The Secret War of International Terrorism* (Holt, Rinehart & Winston, 1981) that an international terrorist conspiracy seeks to undermine Western democracy. An opposing view is held by Edward S. Herman, *The Real Terror Network: Terrorism in Fact and Propaganda* (South End Press, Boston; 1982), who maintains that the real terrorists are authoritarian governments sponsored by the United States.

A broad historical and analytical view can be found in Walter Laqueur, *Terrorism* (Little, Brown, 1977). Harvard historian Franklin L. Ford, in *Political Murder: From Tyrannicide to Terrorism* (Harvard University Press, 1985), examines a form of terrorism we have sadly witnessed in American history. Both books remind us that terrorism is not new and its elimination is not easy.

ISSUE 19

SHOULD WE CONTINUE "STAR WARS" RESEARCH?

YES: Zbigniew Brzezinski, Robert Jastrow and Max M. Kampelman, from "Defense in Space Is Not 'Star Wars,'" *The New York Times Magazine,* January 27, 1985

NO: McGeorge Bundy, George F. Kennan, Robert S. McNamara and Gerard Smith, from "The President's Choice: Star Wars or Arms Control," *Foreign Affairs,* Winter 1984-85

ISSUE SUMMARY

YES: Brzezinski, Jastrow and Kampelman believe that Strategic Defense Initiative can deflect a nuclear attack and thereby enhance the deterrent effect of our security system and reduce the likelihood of nuclear war.
NO: Bundy, Kennan, McNamara and Smith maintain that "Star Wars," holding out a false hope that a defense can be created against nuclear attack, will lead to the development of new weapons rather than arms control.

The cold war between the two superpowers and their allies, which has existed since the end of World War II, has spurred the new technology and the stockpiling of more and more weapons of greater destructive power. As each of the two superpowers succeeded in either deploying a new weapon or surpassing the output of the other in an old one, it was considered necessary for the lagging power to catch up or get ahead.

By the early 1960s, the doctrine of Mutual Assured Destruction (for which the acronym MAD seems fitting) was well entrenched. It argued the importance of deterrence for both sides. As long as the United States and the Soviet Union (and their respective allies) believed that the other side could respond to an attack with a counterattack of equal or superior strengh—what military planners call second strike capability—it was generally accepted that, no matter which side started the war, it would end in mutual assured destruction.

This provided assurance that rational leaders would not undertake a preemptive first strike against the other side. But, the advocates of increasing arms argued, maintenance of deterrence required improved technology and newer weapons so that our side would not fall behind, as well as sheer quantitative increases to keep up with our adversary. Pointing to Soviet superiority in the number of submarine-launched ballistic missiles and the greater firepower of Soviet nuclear warheads, President Reagan requested and received from Congress increased appropriations for military power.

Critics of increased arms expenditures countered that both sides already had stockpiled more than fifty thousand nuclear bombs, which possessed more than one million times the force of the bomb that had been dropped on Hiroshima and more than one hundred times the explosive power necessary to destroy all of the large cities on earth. In the words of one scientist: "The targeters would run out of targets and victims long before they ran out of bombs." What is needed, in the view of critics of American nuclear policy, is a radical reduction of nuclear weapons and the adoption of effective controls that would prevent any of the following possibilities: the proliferation of nations possessing nuclear weapons; the possession of such weapons by terrorists or others who might employ them recklessly; their mistaken or accidental use, which might trigger a nuclear war; or the escalation of a conventional war into a nuclear conflict.

How can we prevent such a disaster? A nuclear freeze? President Reagan has said that a freeze doesn't go far enough, and opponents of his military policy would be the first to agree. Disavow first use? We might be skeptical about whether any nation would respect such a pledge if faced with defeat in so-called conventional war. Nuclear arms reduction? Some analysts point out that nuclear weapons make the superpowers nearly equal, while conventional weapons are "destabilizing" because one side is bound to be superior to the other. Mutual disarmament? Assuming effective enforcement (a major stumbling block in disarmament negotiations) is possible, the problem of how to impose disarmament policy upon nations that are not signatories to such a pact remains. Unilateral disarmament? "Better Red than dead" is an unacceptable policy to nearly all Americans and our allies.

President Reagan proposed the development of a space shield that would deflect a nuclear attack. The proposal, which the President called Strategic Defense Initiative (SDI) was quickly labelled "Star Wars" by his detractors. The proposal raises some obvious questions. Can we develop a practical defense against nuclear attack? Would it deter aggression and contribute to the prospects for peace? President Carter's national security advisor, Zbigniew Brzezinski, physicist Robert Jastrow and lawyer Max M. Kampelman say it can be done.

Or does it hold out an illusory hope and would it lead to the development of new offensive weapons by both the United States and the Soviet Union? That is the critical conclusion of Presidents Kennedy and Johnson's national security advisor, McGeorge Bundy, scholar George F. Kennan, former Secretary of Defense Robert S. McNamara, and former diplomat Gerard Smith.

YES

Zbigniew Brzezinski, Robert Jastrow, and Max M. Kampelman

DEFENSE IN SPACE IS NOT 'STAR WARS'

Faith moves mountains. When it is in eternal religious values, faith is an indispensable strength of the human spirit. When it is directed toward political choices, it is often an excuse for an analytic paralysis.

Regrettably, our national debate over President Reagan's suggestion that the country develop a strategic defense against a Soviet nuclear attack is taking on a theological dimension that has no place in a realistic search for a path out of the world's dilemma. The idea of basing our security on the ability to defend ourselves deserves serious consideration. Certainly, the role of strategic defense was a major issue in the recent dialogue in Geneva between United States Secretary of State George P. Shultz and [then] Soviet Foreign Minister Andrei A. Gromyko on new arms-control negotiations.

For many years, our search for security has been restricted to designing offensive weapons to deter aggression through fear of reprisals. We must not abandon nuclear deterrence until we are convinced that a better means is at hand. But we cannot deny that, for both the Soviet Union and the United States, the costs, insecurities and tensions surrounding this search for newer, more effective and more accurate nuclear missiles produce a profound unease that in itself undermines stability.

The conventional view is that stability in the nuclear age is based on two contradictory pursuits: the acquisition of increasingly efficient nuclear weapons and the negotiation of limits and reductions in such weapons. The United States is diligently pursuing both objectives, but the complexity of arriving at effectual arms-control agreements is becoming apparent as more precise and mobile weapons, with multiple warheads, appear on both sides. Unlike ours, moreover, many Soviet missile silos are reloadable, and thus the number of silos does not indicate the number of missiles, further complicating verification.

We must never ignore the reality that the overwhelming majority of the Soviet strategic forces is composed of primarily first-strike weaponry. And given the large numbers of first-strike Soviet SS-17, -18 and -19 land-based missiles, no responsible American leader can make decisions about security needs without acknowledging that a Soviet first strike can become a practical option.

The Russians could strike us first by firing the reloadable portion of their nuclear arsenal at our missiles, the Strategic Air Command and nuclear submarine bases, and if the surviving American forces (essentially nuclear submarines) were to respond, the Russians could immediately counter by attacking our cities with missiles from nonreloadable silos and, a few hours later, with whatever of their first-strike reloadable weapons had survived our counterattack. They are set up for launching three salvos to our one.

To us, this catastrophic exchange is unthinkable. But, with the strong probability that the American response would be badly crippled at the outset by a Soviet strike, some Russian leader could someday well consider such a potential cost bearable in the light of the resulting "victory." Furthermore, such an analysis might well anticipate that an American President, knowing that a strike against our cities would inevitably follow our response to a Soviet first strike, might choose to avoid such a catastrophe by making important political concessions. No responsible American President can permit this country to have to live under such a threat, not to speak of the hypothetical danger of having to choose either annihilation or submission to nuclear blackmail. Hence the understandable and continual drive for more effective offensive missiles to provide greater deterrence.

The result is that weapons technology is shaping an increasingly precarious American-Soviet strategic relationship. For this reason, we urge serious consideration be given to whether some form of Strategic Defense Initiative (S.D.I.) might not

be stabilizing, enhancing to deterrence and even helpful to arms control. To that end, we address the major issues in strategic defense from three points of view:

(1) The technical: Is a defense against missiles technically and budgetarily feasible?

(2) The strategic: Is a defense against missiles strategically desirable? Does it enhance or diminish the prospects for arms control and a nuclear-weapons build-down?

(3) The political: What are the political implications of strategic defense for our own country and for our relations with our allies? What are the implications for the larger dimensions of our relationship with the Soviet Union? How do we seek the needed domestic consensus on a viable strategy?

A great deal has been written about the state of missile-defense technology. Some experts say the technology sought is unattainable, others that it is merely unattainable in this generation. Yet the promise of the Strategic Defense Initiative is real. Some of the technologies are mature and unexotic. Their deployment around the end of this decade would involve mainly engineering development. Technically, these vital defenses could be in place at this moment were it not for the constraints accepted by the United States in its adherence to the antiballistic missile treaty of 1972.

With development and some additional research, we can now construct and deploy a two-layer or double-screen defense, which can be in place by the early 1990's at a cost we estimate to be somewhere in the neighborhood of $60 billion. A conservative estimate of the effectiveness of each layer would be 70 percent. The combined effectiveness of the two layers would be over 90 percent: Less than one Soviet warhead in 10 would reach its target—more than sufficient to discourage

19. SHOULD WE CONTINUE "STAR WARS" RESEARCH?

Soviet leaders from any thought of achieving a successful first strike.

The first layer in the two-layer defense system—the "boost-phase" defense—would go into effect as a Soviet first-strike missile, or "booster," carrying multiple warheads rises above the atmosphere at the beginning of its trajectory. This boost-phase defense—based on interception and destruction by nonnuclear projectiles—would depend on satellites for the surveillance of the Soviet missile field and the tracking of missiles as they rise from their silos. These operations could only be carried out from space platforms orbiting over the Soviet Union. Because they are weightless in orbit, such platforms could be protected against attack by heavy armor, onboard weapons and maneuverability.

After the booster has burned out and fallen away, the warheads arc through space on their way to the United States. The second layer of the defense—the terminal defense—comes into play as the warheads descend. Interception would be at considerable altitude, above the atmosphere if possible. This second phase requires further engineering, already under way, because interception above the atmosphere makes it difficult to discriminate between real warheads and decoys. In the interim, interception can take place in the atmosphere, where differences in air drag separate warheads from decoys. In either event, destruction of the warheads would take place at sufficiently high altitudes,, above 100,000 feet, so that there would be no ground damage from warheads designed to explode when approached by an intercepting missile.

Of the two layers in the defense, the boost phase is by far the most important. It would prevent the Russians from concentrating their warheads on such high-priority targets as the national-command

authority (the chain of command, beginning with the President, for ordering a nuclear strike), key intercontinental-ballistic missile silos or the Trident submarine pens, because they could not predict which booster and which warheads would escape destruction and get through.

This fact is important. Simply a so-called "point defense" of our missile silos, it has been suggested, would be sufficient to restore much of the credibility of our land-based deterrent, now compromised by 6,000 Soviet ICBM warheads. It is particularly necessary to protect the 550 silos containing our Minuteman III ICBM's, of which 300 have the highly precise Mark 12A warheads. These are the only missiles in the possession of the United States with the combination of yield and accuracy required to destroy hardened Soviet military sites and the 1,500 hardened bunkers that would shelter the Soviet leadership. But their very importance to us illustrates the difficulty of a point defense, because the value of the silos to us means they will be among the highest-priority targets in any Soviet first strike. The Russians can overwhelm any point defense we place around those silos, if they wish to do so, by allocating large numbers of warheads to these critical targets. But if we include a boost-phase defense to destroy their warheads at the time of firing, their objective becomes enormously more difficult to accomplish.

The boost-phase defense has still another advantage. It could effectively contend with the menace of the Soviet SS-18's, monster missiles twice the size of the 97.5-ton MX. Each SS-18 carries 10 warheads, but probably could be loaded with up to 30. The Russians could thus add thousands of ICBM warheads to their arsenal at relatively modest cost. With numbers like that, the costs favor the Rus-

322

sians. But a boost-phase defense can eliminate all a missile's warheads at one time—an effective response to the SS-18 problem.

The likely technology for an early use of the boost-phase defense would use "smart" nonnuclear projectiles that home in on the target, using radar or heat waves, and destroy it on impact. The technology is close at hand and need not wait for the availability of the more devastating but less mature technologies of the laser, the neutral particle beam or the electromagnetic rail gun. The interceptor rocket for this early boost-phase defense could be derived from air-defense interceptors that will soon be available, or the technology of antisatellite missiles (ASAT) launched from F-15 aircraft. These rockets could weigh about 500 pounds, the nonnuclear supersonic projectiles about 10 pounds.

Interceptor rockets would be stored in pods on satellites and fired from space. The tracking information needed to aim the rockets would also be acquired from satellites orbiting over the Soviet missile fields. The so-called "space weapons" of strategic defense are indispensable for the crucial boost-phase defense. To eliminate them would destroy the usefulness of the defense.

We estimate that the cost of establishing such a boost-phase defense by the early 1990's would be roughly $45 billion. That price tag includes 100 satellites, each holding 150 interceptors—sufficient to counter a mass Soviet attack from all their 1,400 silos; plus four geosynchronous satellites and 10 low-altitude satellites dedicated to surveillance and tracking; plus the cost of facilities for ground-control communications and battle management.

The technology used for the terminal defense could be a small, nonnuclear homing interceptor with a heat-seeking sensor, which would be launched by a rocket weighing one to two tons and costing a few million dollars each. Interception would take place above the atmosphere, if possible, to give wider "area" protection to the terrain below. These heat-seeking interceptors can be available for deployment in about five years if a decision is reached to follow that course. One concept for this technology was tested successfully last June by the Defense Department, when an intercepting missile zeroed in on an oncoming warhead at an altitude of 100 miles and destroyed it.

The technology for a terminal defense within the atmosphere would be somewhat different, but would probably also depend on heat-seeking missiles. The cost of this terminal layer of defense would be about $15 billion and include $10 billion for 5,000 interceptors, plus $5 billion for 10 aircraft carrying instruments for tracking of the Soviet warheads.

The estimated $60 billion for this two-layer defense is a ball-park figure, of course. However, even with its uncertainties, it is surely an affordable outlay for protecting our country from a nuclear first strike.

To be sure, the above is not an attractive option to those who place all their eggs in the arms-control basket and underestimate the immense difficulty of attaining an effective and truly verifiable pact. It is also not appealing to those wedded to the idea that it is best to assure survival by simply maintaining the perilous balance of terror between the United States and the Soviet Union. We favor energetically pursuing arms-control negotiations and seeking to achieve credible deterrence, but these options by themselves are unfortunately not as likely to provide a more secure future as the alternative strategy of mutual security combining defense against missiles with retaliatory offense.

19. SHOULD WE CONTINUE "STAR WARS" RESEARCH?

The simplest and most appealing option, quite naturally, is comprehensive arms control. Large reductions in both launchers and warheads, as well as effective restrictions on surreptitious deployment or qualitative improvements, would enhance nuclear stability and produce greater mutual confidence. It would, if properly negotiated and effectively monitored, enhance mutual survival.

How likely is such a future? Some progress in arms control is probably possible, but genuinely effective arms control would require that: (1) there be a restraint imposed on qualitative weapons enhancement; (2) mobile systems, relatively easy to deploy secretly, be subject to some form of direct verification; (3) a method be devised for distinguishing nuclear-armed and nonnuclear cruise missiles, and (4) monitoring arrangements be devised for preventing surreptitious development, testing and deployment of new systems. So far, the Soviet record of compliance with the SALT I and SALT II accords is sufficiently troubling to warrant skepticism regarding the likelihood of implementing any such complex and far-reaching agreement.

Moreover, such an agreement would have to recognize that it is no longer possible to limit space-based systems without imposing a simultaneous limit, along the above lines, on terrestrially deployed systems, which present the greater threat to survival. After all, the space-based defenses include no weapons of mass destruction and no nuclear weapons. And it should be some cause for concern to note the Soviet insistence on prohibiting space-based *defensive systems,* the only method now available to inhibit the first-strike use of land-based Soviet offensive systems.

Finally, a comprehensive and genuine-ly verifiable agreement, limiting both qualitatively and quantitatively the respective strategic forces, on earth and in space, will require a much more felicitous political climate than currently exists. Negotiations may lead to such improvement, but in the setting of intense and profound geopolitical rivalry, how realistic is it to expect in the near future accommodation sufficient to generate the political will essential for a genuine breakthrough in arms-control negotiations? The mere mentions of Afghanistan, Nicaragua, Sakharov and Soviet violations of the humanitarian provisions of the Helsinki Final Act dramatize the depths of the problem. There may be no direct negotiating linkage between these acts of Soviet misconduct and arms control, but their political interaction is evident.

This is why there is currently such an emphasis on maintaining peace via the doctrine of deterrence based on mutual assured destruction, called MAD. But what does this mean in an age when weapons are becoming incredibly precise, mobile and difficult to count? In the absence of a miraculous breakthrough in arms control, the only possible protection within the framework of the deterrence approach is to stockpile more offensive systems. This is in part what we are doing. But how many of such systems will be needed in the likely conditions of the next decade? If Soviet strategic forces continue to grow both quantitatively and qualitatively, our country will have to deploy, at enormous cost, probably no fewer than 1,500 to 2,000 mobile Midgetmen to preserve deterrence. How will they be deployed? Where? And at what cost? And will the Soviet Union and the United States be more or less secure with the deployment of such precise weaponry capable of effective preemption? The Soviet answer is clear: The Russians are busy enhancing the survivability of their leadership and of their key facilities by hardening, dispersal and deception.

This second traditional alternative, mutual assured destruction, cannot be an acceptable, long-run option, although it is a necessary policy in the absence of an alternative, given the dynamics of weapons technology. Thus, a new third option, the Strategy of Mutual Security, must be explored as preferable. The combination of defense against space missiles with retaliatory offense in reserve enhances deterrence.

And it does not compromise stability, even if only the United States were initially to have such a strategic defense. The deployment of the systems described above would not give us absolute protection from Soviet retaliation against a possible first strike by us, a reasonable though misplaced Soviet concern. Furthermore, the Russians know we are not deploying first-strike counterforce systems in sufficient numbers to make a first strike by us feasible. In any case, one can be quite certain that the Russians will also be moving to acquire an enhanced strategic defense, even if they do not accept President Reagan's offer to share ours. Indeed, they are doing so now and have been for some time.

As our strategic space-defense initiative expands incrementally, it should be realistically possible to scale down our offensive forces. Such a transition, first of the United States and eventually of the Soviet Union, into a genuinely defensive posture, with neither side posing a first-strike threat to the other, would not only be stabilizing but it would also be most helpful to the pursuit of more far-reaching arms-control agreements. Strategic defense would compensate for the inevitable difficulties of verification and for the absence of genuine

trust by permitting some risk-taking in such agreements. This is another reason why strategic defense should not be traded in the forthcoming negotiations in return for promises that can be broken at any time.

No significant public policy can be carried out in a democracy without being fully discussed and accepted by the broad polity. Nor can an interested public be expected to resolve disputes among experts as to questions of technical feasibility. The current debate over President Reagan's initiative for a strategic defense program suffers from that conflict among scientists. It is important to clarify this issue.

We can begin a two-tiered strategic defense that would protect command structure as well as our missiles and silos and thus discourage any thoughts by the Soviet military that a first-strike effort would be effective. Some within the scientific community minimize the importance of this technical feasibility and emphasize instead the view that it is scientifically impossible today to provide a strategic defense that will protect our cities. Such a broad defense of populations is today not feasible, but it is prudent for our society to keep in mind the rising tide of technical and scientific advances so rapidly overwhelming the 20th century.

The "impossible" is a concept we should use with great hesitation. It is foolhardy to predict the timing of innovations. We are persuaded that the laws of physics do not in any way prevent the technical requirements of a defensive shield that would protect populations as well as weapons. A total shield should remain our ultimate objective, but there is every reason for us to explore transitional defenses, particularly because the one we have discussed would serve to deter the dangers of a first strike. Defenses against ballistic missiles can be effective without being "perfect," and the technology for this is nearly in hand.

Society must also not forget that ever since the beginning of the scientific age, the organized scientific community has not had a particularly good record of predicting developments that were not part of the common wisdom of the day. In 1926, for example, A.W. Bickerton, a British scientist, said it was scientifically impossible to send a rocket to the moon. In the weapons field, United States Adm. William D. Leahy told President Harry S. Truman in 1945: "That [atomic] bomb will never go off, and I speak as an expert in explosives." And Dr. Vannevar Bush, who directed the Government's World War II science effort, said after the war that he rejected the talk "about a 3,000-mile rocket shot from one continent to the other carrying an atomic bomb . . . and we can leave that out of our thinking." In the strategic area, as late as 1965, the capable Secretary of Defense Robert S. McNamara wrote: "There is no indication that the Soviets are seeking to develop a strategic force as large as our own."

Our debate and our discussion, furthermore, must not ignore what the Russians, who have always understood the need for defenses, are doing in space. They have spent more on strategic defensive forces since the antiballistic missile (ABM) treaty was signed in 1972 than on strategic offensive forces. Their antisatellite program began nearly two decades ago. The Soviet military is now working aggressively on a nationwide missile-defense system; and it now appears ready to deploy a system capable of defending the country not only against aircraft, but also many types of ballistic missiles. Clearly, the Soviet work in strategic defense has taken place in spite of ABM treaty provisions. The large radar installation in central Siberia expressly violates that treaty with us. Yet the planning for it must have begun many years ago.

The recent Geneva meeting must be considered a major productive result of President Reagan's March 1983 speech announcing that we would begin developing a strategic defense initiative. We are reminded that in 1967 President Lyndon B. Johnson proposed to Prime Minister Aleksei N. Kosygin a ban on ABM's, which was flatly rejected. In 1969, President Nixon proposed to the Congress that our country begin such an ABM program, because the Russians showed little desire to join us in prohibiting such weapons. Shortly after Congress approved that program, the Russians embraced the idea of an ABM treaty. Had our Government not announced its S.D.I. program, we might still be in the cold storage of the Soviet freeze precipitated by their walking out of the Geneva negotiations.

Arms control has been said to be at a dead end, and the stalemate has reflected an impasse in thought and in conception. Our present policy requires both us and the Soviet Union to rely on a theory of mutual annihilation based on a strategic balance of offensive weapons. The American approach has been to depend on deterrence alone and not on defending ourselves from Soviet offensive weapons, while the Russians have made it clear by their actions that they intend to defend themselves against our missiles. In any event, what is clear is that mankind must find ways of lifting itself out of this balance of terror. Mutual assured destruction must be replaced by mutual assured survival. Our safety cannot depend on our having no defense against missiles. The proper role of government is to protect the country from aggression, not merely avenge it. It is astounding that a President should be faulted for seeking a formula and an approach that will protect us from the continual threats and terrors coming from the volatile vagaries of adventurism and miscalculation.

Even if a perfect defense of our population should be impossible to achieve—and none of us can be certain of that—the leaders of our Government have a responsibility to seek defense alternatives designed to complicate and frustrate aggression by our adversaries. The very injection of doubt into their calculations strengthens the prospect of hesitation and deterrence. It may not be possible to destroy the world's ballistic missiles, but if we can return them to the status of a retaliatory deterrent rather than a pre-emptive strike we will have reduced the need for the existing large arsenal and thereby the threat of war.

The argument has been made that the S.D.I. is politically harmful because our North Atlantic Treaty Organization allies have not received the initiative with any enthusiasm. Their skepticism is an understandable initial reaction. First of all, our allies were taken by surprise by the President's March proposal of a Strategic Defense Initiative. At times, secret discussions are necessary, but doubtless allied cooperation will be forthcoming in direct proportion to timely and honest consultation. Furthermore, European political leaders feel under great pressure from an activist peace movement that emphasizes traditional arms-control negotiations as a major objective. A new approach, which the Russians criticize as hostile, is, therefore, looked upon as troubling, regardless of its merit.

As to the substance of the initiative, coupling our national security interest with that of our allies is a foundation of NATO defense. Any tendency toward decoupling produces great concern on their part.

Western European leaders look upon all security proposals with that criterion in mind. Should America technically succeed in providing a shield against missiles, Europeans wonder whether they would then not be left in an exposed position, facing a superior Soviet conventional military force.

The concerns may be understandable, but will diminish with time and discussion. First of all, President Reagan's call for strategic defense brought the Russians back to the Geneva negotiating table. More important, however, it will become increasingly evident to our friends, as some of the confusion about the technology dissipates, that the ability of the United States to protect its missiles immeasurably strengthens our power to deter and thereby serves to protect our allies. Indeed, such a system is expected to be at least as effective against the SS-20's aimed at western Europe as it is against ICBM's. Finally, a development pulling the world away from the precipice of nuclear terror goes far to help create an encouraging atmosphere for dialogue and agreement, a vital prerequisite for peace.

In light of the above, we reach two basic conclusions:

(1) Developing a stabilizing, limited two-tier strategic defense capability is desirable and called for by the likely strategic conditions immediately ahead. Such a deployment would be helpful both in the military and in the political dimensions. It is a proper response to the challenge posed by political uncertainties and the dynamics of weapons development. The two-layered defense described here can be deployed by the early 1990's. Americans will rest easier when that limited defense is in place, for it will mean that the prospect of a Soviet first strike is almost nil.

(2) A three- or four-layer defense, us-

327

ing such advanced technologies as the laser now under investigation in the research phase of the Strategic Defense Initiative, may become a reality by the end of the century. If this research shows an advanced system to be practical, its deployment may well boost the efficiency of our defense to a level so close to perfection as to signal a final end to the era of nuclear ballistic missiles. A research program offering such enormous potential gains in our security must be pursued, in spite of the fact that a successful outcome cannot be assured at this juncture.

The current debate is necessary. There are many questions, technical and political, ahead of us. For the debate to be constructive, however, we must overcome the tendency to politicize it on a partisan basis. Our objectives should be to find a way out of the current maze of world terror. The President's initiative toward that end is a major contribution to arms control and stability. The aim of making nuclear weapons impotent and obsolete should be encouraged and not savaged.

NO
McGeorge Bundy
George F. Kennan
Robert S. McNamara
Gerard Smith

THE PRESIDENT'S CHOICE: STAR WARS OR ARMS CONTROL

The reelection of Ronald Reagan makes the future of his Strategic Defense Initiative the most important question of nuclear arms competition and arms control on the national agenda since 1972. The President is strongly committed to this program, and senior officials, including Secretary of Defense Caspar W. Weinberger, have made it clear that he plans to intensify this effort in his second term. Sharing the gravest reservations about this undertaking, and believing that unless it is radically constrained during the next four years it will bring vast new costs and dangers to our country and to mankind, we think it urgent to offer an assessment of the nature and hazards of this initiative, to call for the closest vigilance by Congress and the public, and even to invite the victorious President to reconsider. While we write only after obtaining the best technical advice we could find, our central concerns are political. We believe the President's initiative to be a classic case of good intentions that will have bad results because they do not respect reality.

[The Strategic Defense Initiative] was launched by the President on March 23, 1983, in a surprising and quite personal passage at the end of a speech in praise of his other military programs. In that passage he called on our scientists to find means of rendering nuclear weapons "impotent and obsolete." In the briefings that surrounded the speech, Administration spokesmen made it clear that the primary objective was the development of ways and means of destroying hostile missiles—meaning in the main Soviet missiles—by a series of attacks all along their flight path, from their boost phase after launch to their entry into the atmosphere above the United States. Because of the central position the Administration itself gave to this objective, the program promptly

From, "The President's Choice: Star Wars or Arms Control," by McGeorge Bundy, Robert S. McNamara and Gerard Smith, *Foreign Affairs*, Winter 1984-85. Copyright © 1984 by the Council on Foreign Relations, Inc. Reprinted by permission.

acquired the name Star Wars, and the President's Science Advisor, George Keyworth, has admitted that this name is now indelible. We find it more accurately descriptive than the official "Strategic Defense Initiative."[1]

What is centrally and fundamentally wrong with the President's objective is that it cannot be achieved. The overwhelming consensus of the nation's technical community is that in fact there is no prospect whatever that science and technology can, at any time in the next several decades, make nuclear weapons "impotent and obsolete." The program developed over the last 18 months, ambitious as it is, offers no prospect for a leak-proof defense against strategic ballistic missiles alone, and it entirely excludes from its range any effort to limit the effectiveness of other systems—bomber aircraft, cruise missiles, and smuggled warheads. . . .

The notion that nuclear weapons, or even ballistic missiles alone, can be rendered impotent by science and technology is an illusion. It reflects not only technological hubris in the face of the very nature of nuclear weapons, but also a complete misreading of the relation between threat and response in the nuclear decisions of the superpowers.

The first and greatest obstacle is quite simply that these weapons are destructive to a degree that makes them entirely different from any other weapon in history. The President frequently observes that over the centuries every new weapon has produced some countervailing weapon, and up to Hiroshima he is right. But conventional weapons can be neutralized by a relatively low rate of kill, provided that the rate is sustained over time. The classic modern

example is defense against nonnuclear bombing. If you lose one bomber in every ten sorties, your force will soon be destroyed. A pilot assigned to fly 30 missions will face a 95-percent prospect of being shot down. A ten-percent rate of kill is highly effective.

With nuclear weapons the calculation is totally different. Both Mr. Reagan's dream and his historical argument completely neglect the decisive fact that a very few nuclear weapons, exploding on or near population centers, would be hideously too many. At today's levels of superpower deployment—about 10,000 strategic warheads on each side—even a 95-percent kill rate would be insufficient to save either society from disintegration in the event of general nuclear war. Not one of Mr. Reagan's technical advisers claims that any such level of protection is attainable. They know better. In the words of the of the officer in charge of the program, Lieutenant General James Abrahamson, "a perfect defense is not a realistic thing." In response to searching questions from Senator Sam Nunn of Georgia, the senior technical official of the Defense Department, Under Secretary Richard DeLauer, made it plain that he could not foresee any level of defense that would make our own offensive systems unnecessary.

Among all the dozens of spokesmen for the Administration, there is not one with any significant technical qualifications who has been willing to question Dr. DeLauer's explicit statement that "There's no way an enemy can't overwhelm your defenses if he wants to badly enough." The only senior official who continues to share the President's dream and assert his belief that it can come true is Caspar Weinberger, whose zealous professions of confidence are not accompanied by technical support.

The terrible power of nuclear weapons

has a second meaning that decisively undermines the possibility of an effective Star Wars defense of populations. Not only is their destructive power so great that only a kill rate closely approaching 100 percent can give protection, but precisely because the weapons are so terrible neither of the two superpowers can tolerate the notion of "impotence" in the face of the arsenal of the opponent. Thus any prospect of a significantly improved American defense is absolutely certain to stimulate the most energetic Soviet efforts to ensure the continued ability of Soviet warheads to get through. Ever since Hiroshima it has been a cardinal principle of Soviet policy that the Soviet Union must have a match for any American nuclear capability. It is fanciful in the extreme to suppose that the prospect of any new American deployment which could undermine the effectiveness of Soviet missile forces will not be met by a most determined and sustained response.

This inevitable Soviet reaction is studiously neglected by Secretary Weinberger when he argues in defense of Star Wars that today's skeptics are as wrong as those who said we could never get to the moon. The effort to get to the moon was not complicated by the presence of an adversary. A platoon of hostile moon-men with axes could have made it a disaster. No one should understand the irrelevance of his analogy better than Mr. Weinberger himself. As secretary of defense he is bound to be familiar with the intensity of our own American efforts to ensure that our own nuclear weapons, whether on missiles or aircraft, will always be able to get through to Soviet targets in adequate numbers.

The technical analyses so far available are necessarily incomplete, primarily because of the very large distance between the President's proposal and any clearly

defined system of defense. There is some truth in Mr. Weinberger's repeated assertion that one cannot fully refute a proposal that as yet has no real content. But already important and enduring obstacles have been identified. Two are systemic and ineradicable. First, a Star Wars defense must work perfectly the very first time, since it can never be tested in advance as a full system. Second, it must be triggered almost instantly, because the crucial boost phase of Soviet missiles lasts less than five minutes from the moment of launch. In that five minutes (which new launch technology can probably reduce to about 60 seconds), there must be detection, decision, aim, attack and kill. It is hard to imagine a scheme further removed from the kind of tested reliability and clear presidential control that we have hitherto required of systems involving nuclear danger.

There are other more general difficulties with the President's dream. Any remotely leak-proof defense against strategic missiles will require extensive deployments of many parts of the system in space, both for detection of any Soviet launch and, in most schemes, for transmission of the attack on the missile in its boost phase. Yet no one has been able to offer any hope that it will ever be easier and cheaper to deploy and defend large systems in space than for someone else to destroy them. The balance of technical judgment is that the advantage in any unconstrained contest in space will be with the side that aims to attack the other side's satellites. In and of itself this advantage constitutes a compelling argument against space-based defense.

Finally, as we have already noted, the President's program offers no promise of effective defense against anything but ballistic missiles. Even if we assume, against all the evidence, that a leak-proof defense could be achieved against these particular weapons, there would remain the difficulty of defense against cruise missiles, against bomber aircraft, and against the clandestine introduction of warheads. It is important to remember here that very small risks of these catastrophic events will be enough to force upon us the continuing need for our own deterrent weapons. We think it is interesting that among the strong supporters of the Star Wars scheme are some of the same people who were concerned about the danger of the strategic threat of the Soviet Backfire bomber only a few years ago. Is it likely that in the light of these other threats they will find even the best possible defense against missiles a reason for declaring our own nuclear weapons obsolete?

Inadvertent but persuasive proof of this failing has been given by the President's science advisor. Last February, in a speech in Washington, Mr. Keyworth recognized that the Soviet response to a truly successful Star Wars program would be to "shift their strategic resources to other weapons systems," and he made no effort to suggest that such a shift could be prevented or countered, saying: "*Let* the Soviets move to alternate weapons systems, to submarines, cruise missiles, advanced technology aircraft. Even the critics of the President's defense initiative agree that *those* weapons systems are far more stable deterrents than are ICBMs [land-based missiles]." Mr. Keyworth, in short, is willing to accept all these other means of warhead delivery, and he appears to be entirely unaware that by this acceptance he is conceding that even if Star Wars should succeed far beyond what any present technical consensus can allow us to believe, it would fail by the President's own standard.

The inescapable reality is that there is literally no hope that Star Wars can make nuclear weapons obsolete. Perhaps the first and most important political task for those who wish to save the country from the expensive and dangerous pursuit of a mirage is to make this basic proposition clear. As long as the American people believe that Star Wars offers real hope of reaching the President's asserted goal, it will have a level of political support unrelated to reality. The American people, properly and sensibly, would like nothing better than to make nuclear weapons "impotent and obsolete," but the last thing they want or need is to pay an astronomic bill for a vastly intensified nuclear competition sold to them under a false label. Yet that is what Star Wars will bring us, as a closer look will show.

The second line of defense for the Star Wars program, and the one which represents the real hopes and convictions of both military men and civilians at the levels below the optimistic President and his enthusiastic secretary of defense, is not that it will ever be able to defend *all our people,* but rather that it will allow us to defend *some of our weapons and other military assets,* and so, somehow, restrain the arms race.

This objective is very different from the one the President has held out to the country, but it is equally unattainable. The Star Wars program is bound to exacerbate the competition between the superpowers in three major ways. It will destroy the Anti-Ballistic Missile (ABM) Treaty, our most important arms control agreement; it will directly stimulate both offensive and defensive systems on the Soviet side; and as long as it continues it will darken the prospect for significant improvement in the currently frigid relations between Moscow and Washington. It will thus sharpen the very anxieties the President wants to reduce. . . .

. . . Our government, of course, does not intend a first strike, but we are building systems which do have what is called in our own jargon a prompt hard-target kill capability, and the primary purpose of these systems is to put Soviet missiles at risk of quick destruction. Soviet leaders are bound to see such weapons as a first-strike threat. This is precisely the view that our own planners take of Soviet missiles with a similar capability. . . . [T]he Soviet response to Star Wars is certain to be an intensification of both its offensive and defensive strategic efforts.

Perhaps the easiest way to understand this political reality is to consider our own reaction to any similar Soviet announcement of intent. The very thought that the Soviet Union might plan to deploy effective strategic defenses would certainly produce a most energetic American response, and the first and most important element of that response would be a determination to ensure that a sufficient number of our own missiles would always get through. . . .

There is simply no escape from the reality that Star Wars offers not the promise of greater safety, but the certainty of a large-scale expansion of both offensive and defensive systems on both sides. We are not here examining the dismayed reaction of our allies in Europe, but it is precisely this prospect that they foresee, in addition to the special worries created by their recognition that the Star Wars program as it stands has nothing in it for them. Star Wars, in sum, is a prescription not for ending or limiting the threat of nuclear weapons, but for a competition unlimited in expense, duration and danger. . . .

We have one final deep and strong belief. We think that if there is to be a real step away from nuclear danger in the next four years, it will have to begin at the level of high politics, with a kind of communication between Moscow and Washington that we have not seen for more than a decade. One of the most unfortunate aspects of the Star Wars initiative is that it was launched without any attempt to discuss it seriously, in advance, with the Soviet government. It represented an explicit expression of the President's belief that we should abandon the shared view of nuclear defense that underlies not only the ABM Treaty but all our later negotiations on strategic weapons. To make a public announcement of a change of this magnitude without any effort to discuss it with the Soviets was to ensure increased Soviet suspicion. This error, too, we have made in earlier decades. If we are now to have renewed hope of arms control, we must sharply elevate our attention to the whole process of communication with Moscow.

Such newly serious communication should begin with frank and explicit recognition by both sides that the problem of nuclear danger is in its basic reality a *common* problem, not just for the two of us, but for all the world—and one that we shall never resolve if we cannot transcend negotiating procedures that give a veto to those in each country who insist on the relentlessly competitive maintenance and enlargement of what are already, on both sides, exorbitantly excessive forces.

If it can ever be understood and accepted, as a starting point for negotiation, that our community of interest in the problem of nuclear danger is greater than all our various competitive concerns put together, there can truly be a renewal of hope, and a new prospect of a shared decision to change course together. Alone among the presidents of the last 12 years, Ronald

Reagan has the political strength to lead our country in this new direction if he so decides. The renewal of hope cannot be left to await another president without an appeal to the President and his more sober advisers to take a fresh hard look at Star Wars, and then to seek arms control instead.

POSTSCRIPT

SHOULD WE CONTINUE "STAR WARS" RESEARCH?

The Strategic Defense Initiative (SDI) was proposed by President Reagan as a military system that would destroy hostile missiles, thus rendering nuclear weapons impotent. Supporters say it can be done; detractors say it is unworkable.

Beyond these judgments are different approaches to nuclear peace. Mutual Assured Destruction created a balance of terror and kept the peace. But the cost of escalating armaments has been high and the risk of accidental nuclear war has been real. SDI is intended as a strategic breakthrough, sharply reducing the potency of nuclear weapons.

Critics deny its feasibility, warn that it could be used offensively, and predict that SDI will only heat up the arms race. The rational alternative, they insist, is arms control, with substantial reduction of nuclear weapons.

The literature on nuclear warfare has proliferated almost as much as nuclear weapons have. The Harvard Nuclear Study Group, *Living with Nuclear Weapons* (Harvard University Press, 1983), argues that disarmament does not eliminate the causes of war or even the means to wage it. American nuclear policy is vigorously defended in Norman Podhoretz's *The Present Danger* (Simon and Schuster, 1980) and General Maxwell D. Taylor's *Precarious Security* (Norton, 1976). Jonathan Schell's earlier work, *The Fate of the Earth* (Knopf, 1982), contained a plea for world government, which he has abandoned in *The Abolition* (Knopf, 1984). The organization Ground Zero has published *Nuclear War: What's in It for You?* (Pocket Books, 1982). *Foreign Affairs* devoted its Winter 1981-1982 issue to the topic of nuclear weapons in the 1980s. *The Bulletin of the Atomic Scientists* has published numerous articles critical of the arms race, while *Conservative Digest* has printed defenses of American policy.

Other divisive issues have high stakes, but on the resolution of this issue may depend the survival of civilization. The question remains: What policy regarding nuclear weapons is most likely to assure that survival?

ISSUE 20

HUMAN RIGHTS: SHOULD WE PREFER AUTHORITARIANISM TO COMMUNISM?

YES: Jeane Kirkpatrick, from "Human Rights and American Foreign Policy: A Symposium," *Commentary* (November 1981)

NO: Alan Tonelson, from "Human Rights: The Bias We Need," *Foreign Policy,* Winter 1982–1983

ISSUE SUMMARY

YES: Jeane Kirkpatrick, former ambassador to the United Nations, suggests that by failing to distinguish between "authoritarian" and "totalitarian" forms of government, by concentrating on human rights violations by "friendly" regimes, we are injuring our own interests and failing to protect human rights.

NO: Alan Tonelson, associate editor of *The Wilson Quarterly,* says that we should reverse Kirkpatrick's priorities: we should put public pressure on "friendly" authoritarian regimes and work behind the scenes to stop human rights violations by Communist regimes.

The concept of "human rights" is, at least potentially, an explosive idea. Though its philosophical underpinnings can be traced back to early Christianity and Roman Stoicism, it first appeared as a full-blown political program during the Age of Revolution in the late eighteenth century. Our Declaration of Independence begins with its famous trinity of "unalienable" human rights, goes on to list all the infractions of these rights by King George III and Parliament, and concludes that Americans have the right and even the duty to overthrow such an oppressive government. The French Revolution, which turned out to be far more violent and far-reaching, began with a similar theme: "The Rights of Man and of Citizens."

The doctrine of human rights has its critics, and by no means are they all people who favor repression or autocracy. Edmund Burke, the great British statesman and political thinker of the eighteenth century, was an outspoken supporter of conciliation with America, but he bitterly opposed the French Revolution for trying to re-make society from a blueprint of "the rights of man." Liberty and self-government, Burke said, are gradually built up over centuries on the basis of precedent and tradition. He maintained that the attempt to force change overnight on the basis of abstract, "metaphysical" principles will only result in fanaticism and chaos. Burke's chief opponent was Thomas Paine, whose writings helped to inspire the

American Revolution. Paine defended the French Revolution and criticized Burke's emphasis on precedent, writing: "Government by precedent, without any regard to the principle of the precedent, is one of the vilest systems that can be set up."

Echoes of the Burke-Paine debate can still be heard in some of the more recent controversies over what role "human rights" should play in American foreign policy. When Jimmy Carter came into office, he contended that an "inordinate fear of Communism" had sometimes blinded American administrations to right-wing repression. Carter declared that henceforth he would oppose human rights violations by *any* country, whether ruled by the "right" or the "left." Andrew Young, Carter's UN ambassador, carried the logic of universalism to its conclusion by denouncing racism everywhere, including Sweden and Queens, New York.

If Young's approach seemed to contain the spirit of Thomas Paine's famous credo ("My country is the world, and my religion is to do good"), Jeane Kirkpatrick, formerly Ronald Reagan's UN ambassador, sounds more like Edmund Burke. In an article she wrote in *Commentary* two years before the Reagan administration came into office, she reminded her readers of the long maturation period needed before liberal and democratic regimes can appear. "Decades, if not centuries, are normally required for people to acquire the necessary disciplines and habits," she wrote. Kirkpatrick criticized the Carter approach for trying to force autocratic but friendly regimes to suddenly become "moderate," contending it would destabilize them, making them vulnerable to revolution. Since our own political system is the result of a revolution, many Americans might ask why we need to worry if a revolution does break out. Her answer—an opinion generally shared by Reagan's policymakers—rests upon the implication of a term that did not exist in Edmund Burke's day. The term is "totalitarianism."

Although the terms are sometimes used interchangeably, Reagan officials insist that "totalitarian" regimes are radically different from "authoritarian" ones. Adapting a school of thought that goes back to the 1940s and 1950s to their own policy ends, Reagan's policymakers suggest at least three differences between the two terms: First, totalitarianism is far more lethal to human freedom than is authoritarianism. Totalitarian regimes kill more people, and with less provocation. Second, it is possible to find authoritarian regimes friendly to the United States, but totalitarian regimes are almost invariably hostile. Third, history demonstrates that authoritarian regimes can be liberalized gradually, while totalitarian regimes remain unchanged. Kirkpatrick concludes that Carter helped destabilize the governments of Iran and Nicaragua by his constant criticism of their "human rights records," paving the way for the present totalitarian regimes in those countries.

The Kirkpatrick philosophy has many critics, among them Alan Tonelson, who argues that Kirkpatrick has got it all backwards: what we should really be doing, he contends, is to direct public pressure to where it will do the most good: to "friendly" authoritarian regimes who depend upon us.

YES   Jeane Kirkpatrick

THE LESSER EVIL OVER
THE GREATER EVIL

The human-rights debate of recent years to which this symposium is directed is not really about which should play the most important role in U.S. foreign policy: human rights or the national interest. It is rather a debate about *which* policies promote human rights, *which* regimes threaten them most gravely, *which* policies actually serve the national interest and how the U.S. national interest should be conceived anyway. Some of us believe that because they seek by violent, repressive means total control over the societies they govern, establish great armies, and pursue aggressive and expansionist foreign policies, Marxist-Leninist states constitute the gravest threat to human rights in the contemporary world. Others, including the human-rights establishment of the Carter period, believe that because authoritarian regimes such as those found in Chile, Argentina, and Uruguay tolerate social injustice and sometimes use violence arbitrarily, they perpetrate the gravest offenses against human rights. Involved here are different assessments of practices (which type of regime in fact imprisons, enslaves, tortures, kills most people?); different assessments of the future (which type of regime is most susceptible of liberalization and democratization?); different views of the U.S. national interest (is the establishment of new Marxist-Leninist regimes compatible with our national interest?); different views about the relation of U.S. strength to human rights (is freedom safer if we are strong, or does that matter?); and perhaps most basic of all, different views about the relations between state and society.

All of these questions must be considered if we are to confront seriously *Commentary's* questions. The first of these questions is the easiest: not only should human rights play a central role in U.S. foreign policy, no U.S. foreign policy can possibly succeed that does not accord them a central role. The nature of politics and the character of the United States alike guarantee that this should be the case.

Politics is a purposive human activity which involves the use of power in the name of some collectivity, some "we," and some vision of the collective good. The collective may be a nation, class, tribe, family, or church. The vision of the public good may be modest or grand, monstrous or divine, elaborate or simple, explicitly articulated or simply "understood." It may call for the restoration of the glory of France; the establishment of a Jewish homeland; the construction of a racially pure one-thousand-year Reich; the achievement of a classless society from which power has been eliminated. The point is that governments act with reference to a vision of the public good characteristic of a people. If they are to command popular assent, important public policies must be congruent with the core identity of a people. In democracies the need for moral justification of political action is especially compelling—nowhere more so than in the United States. The fact that Americans do not share a common history, race, language, [or] religion gives added centrality to American values, beliefs, and goals, making them the key element of our national identity. The American people are defined by the American creed. The vision of the public good which defines us is and always has been a commitment to individual freedom and a conviction that government exists, above all, for the purpose of protecting individual rights. ("To protect these rights," says the Declaration of Independence, "governments are instituted among men.") Government, in the American view, has no purpose greater than that of protecting and extending the rights of its citizens. For this reason, the definitive justification of government policy in the U.S. is to protect the rights—liberty, property, personal security—of citizens. Defending these rights or extending them to other peoples is the only legitimate purpose of American foreign policy.

From the War of Independence through the final withdrawal from Vietnam, American Presidents have justified our policies, especially in time of danger and sacrifice (when greatest justification is required), by reference to our national commitment to the preservation and/or extension of freedom—and the democratic institutions through which that freedom is guaranteed. Obviously, then, there is no conflict between a concern for human rights and the American national interest as traditionally conceived. Our national interest flows from our identity, and our identity features a commitment to the rights of persons. (Conventional debate about whether foreign policy should be based on "power" or morality is in fact a disagreement about moral ends and political means.)

It is true that the explicit moral emphasis on presidential pronouncements on U.S. foreign policy had declined in the decade preceding Jimmy Carter's candidacy, partly because of the diminishing national consensus about whether protecting human rights required (or even permitted) containing Communism even through war, and partly because of concern that moral appeals would excite popular passions and complicate the task of limiting the war in Vietnam. It is also true that Jimmy Carter shared this reticence and only reluctantly—and in response to pressure from Senator Henry Jackson—incorporated the human-rights theme into his presidential campaign.

Almost immediately, however, it became clear that the human-rights policies expounded and implemented by Jimmy Carter were different in their conception and their consequences from those of his predecessors. The cultural revolution that had swept through American cities, campuses, and news rooms, challenging basic beliefs and transforming institutional practices, had as its principal target the morality of the American experience and the legitimacy of American national interests. It was, after all, a period when the leading columnist of a distinguished newspaper wrote: "The United States is the most dangerous and destructive power in the world." It was a time when the president of a leading university asserted: "In twenty-six years since waging a world war against the forces of tyranny, fascism, and genocide in Europe we have become a nation more tyrannical, more fascistic, and more capable of genocide than was ever conceived or thought possible two decades ago. We conquered Hitler but we have come to embrace Hitlerism." It was the period when a nationally known cleric said: "The reason for the paroxysm in the nation's conscience is simply that Calley is all of us. He is every single citizen in our graceless land."

If the United States is "the most destructive power in the world," if we are "capable of genocide," if we are a "graceless land," then the defense of our national interest could not be integrally linked to the defense of human rights or any other morally worthy cause.

The cultural revolution set the scene for two redefinitions: first, a redefinition of human rights, which now became something very different from the freedoms and protections embodied in U.S. constitutional practices; and second, a redefinition of the national interest which dissociated morality and U.S. power.

As long as the United States was perceived as a virtuous society, policies which enhanced its power were also seen as virtuous. Morality and American power were indissolubly linked in the traditional conception. But with the U.S. defined as an essentially immoral society, pursuit of U.S. power was perceived as immoral and pursuit of morality as indifferent to U.S. power. Morality now required transforming our deeply flawed society, not enhancing its power.

In the human-rights policies of the Carter administration, the effects of the cultural revolution were reinforced, first, by a secular translation of the Christian imperative to cast first the beam from one's own eye, and, second, by a determinist, quasi-Marxist theory of historical development. The result was a conception of human rights so broad, ambiguous, and utopian that it could serve as the grounds for condemning almost any society; a conception of national interest to which U.S. power was, at best, irrelevant; and a tendency to suppose history was on the side of our opponents. (Of course, the Carter administration did not invent these orientations, it simply reflected the views of the new liberalism that was both the carrier and the consequence of the cultural revolution.)

Human rights in the Carter version had no specific content, except a general demand that societies provide all the freedoms associated with constitutional democracy, all the economic security promised by socialism, and all the self-fulfillment featured in Abraham Maslow's psychology. And it assumed that governments were responsible for providing these. Any society which did not feature democracy, "social justice," and self-fulfillment—that is, any society at all—could be measured against these standards and found wanting. And where all are "guilty," no one is especially so.

The judicial protections associated with the rule of law and the political freedom associated with democracy had no specia priority in the Carter doctrine of human rights. To the contrary, the powerful inarticulate predisposition of the new liberalism favored equality over liberty, and economic over political rights; socialism over capitalism, and Communist dictatorship over traditional military regimes. These preferences, foreshadowed in Carter's Notre Dame speech, found forthright expression in the administration's human-rights policy. UN Ambassador Andrew Young asserted, for example: "For most of the world, civil and political rights . . . come as luxuries that are far away in the future," and he called on the U.S. to recognize that there are various equally valid concepts of human rights in the world. The Soviets, he added, "have developed a completely different concept of human rights. For them, human rights are essentially not civil and political but economic. . . ." President Carter, for his part, tried hard to erase the impression that *his* advocacy of human rights implied an anti-Soviet bias. "I have never had an inclination to single out the Soviet Union as the only place where human rights are being abridged," he told a press conference on February 23, 1977. "I've tried to make sure that the world knows that we're not singling out the Soviet Union for criticism." In Carter's conception of the political universe, strong opposition to Marxist-Leninist totalitarianism would have been inappropriate because of our shared "goals." On April 12, 1978, he informed President Ceausescu of Romania that "our goals are also the same, to have a just system of economics and politics, to let the people of the world share in growth, in peace, in personal freedom.

It should not be supposed that under Carter no distinction was made between totalitarian and authoritarian regimes—for while the Carter administration was reluc-

tant to criticize Communist states for their human-rights violations (incredibly, not until April 21, 1978 did Carter officials denounce Cambodia for its massive human-rights violations), no similar reticence was displayed in criticizing authoritarian recipients of U.S. aid. On the basis of annual reports required by a 1976 law, the Carter administration moved quickly to withhold economic credits and military assistance from Chile, Argentina, Paraguay, Brazil, Nicaragua, and El Salvador, and accompanied these decisions with a policy of deliberate slights and insults that helped delegitimize these governments at the same time it rendered them less open to U.S. influence.

President Carter's 1977 decision to support the mandatory UN arms embargo against South Africa; Secretary Vance's call, before a meeting of the Organization of American States in June 1979, for the departure of Nicaragua's President Somoza; the decision in 1979 to withhold U.S. support from the Shah of Iran; and President Carter's decision, in June 1979, not to lift economic sanctions against the Muzorewa government in Zimbabwe Rhodesia expressed the same predilection for the selective application of an "absolute" commitment to human rights.

Why were South American military regimes judged so much more harshly than African ones? Why were friendly autocrats treated less indulgently than hostile ones? Why were authoritarian regimes treated more harshly than totalitarian ones? Part of the reason was the the curious focus on those countries that received some form of U.S. assistance, as though our interest in human rights were limited to the requirements of the 1976 Foreign Assistance Act; and part of the reason was the exclusive concern with violations of human rights by governments. By definition, guerrilla murders did not qualify as violations of human rights, while a government's efforts to eliminate terrorism qualified as repression. This curious focus not only permitted Carter policy-makers to condemn government "repression" while ignoring guerrilla violence, it encouraged consideration of human-rights violations independently of their context.

Universal in its rhetoric, unflagging in its pursuit of perceived violations—"I've worked day and night to make sure that a concern for human rights is woven through everything our government does, both at home and abroad" (Jimmy Carter, December 15, 1977)—the Carter human-rights policy alienated non-democratic but friendly nations, enabled anti-Western opposition groups to come to power in Iran, and totalitarians in Nicaragua, and reduced American influence throughout the world.

The Carter administration made an operational (if inarticulate) distinction between authoritarianism and totalitarianism and preferred the latter. The reason for its preference lay, I believe, not only in the affinity of contemporary liberalism for other secular egalitarian development-oriented ideologies (such as Communism) but also in the progressive disappearance from modern liberalism of the distinction between state and society. The assumption that governments *can* create good societies, affluent economies, just distributions of wealth, abundant opportunity, and all the other prerequisites of the good life creates the demand that they should do so, and provokes harsh criticism of governments which fail to provide these goods. The fact that primitive technology, widespread poverty, gross discrepancies of wealth, rigid class and caste structures, and low social and economic mobility are characteristic of most societies which also

feature authoritarian governments is ground enough for the modern liberal to hold the existing governments morally responsible for having *caused* these hardships.

The same indifference to the distinction between state and society also renders the new liberals insensitive to the pitfalls and consequences of extending the jurisdiction and the coercive power of government over all institutions and aspects of life in society. It is, of course, precisely this extension of government's plans and power over society, culture, and personality that makes life in totalitarian societies unbearable to so many. Authoritarian governments are frequently corrupt, inefficient, arbitrary, and brutal, but they make limited claims on the lives, property, and loyalties of their citizens. Families, churches, businesses, independent schools and labor unions, fraternal lodges, and other institutions compete with government for loyalties and resources, and so limit its power.

Authoritarian governments—traditional and modern—have many faults and one significant virtue: their power is limited and where the power of government is limited, the damage it can do is limited also. So is its duration in office. Authoritarian systems do not destroy all alternative power bases in a society. The persistence of dispersed economic and social power renders those regimes less repressive than a totalitarian system and provides the bases for their eventual transformation. Totalitarian regimes, to the contrary, in claiming a monopoly of power over all institutions, eliminate competitive, alternative elites. This is the reason history provides not one but numerous examples of the evolution of authoritarian regimes into democracies (not only Spain and Portugal, but Venezuela, Peru, Ecuador, Bangladesh, among others) and *no* example of the democratic transformation of totalitarian regimes.

Authoritarian governments have significant moral and political faults, all the worst of which spring from the possession of arbitrary power. But compared to totalitarian governments, their arbitrary power is limited. Only democracies do a reliable job of protecting the rights of all their citizens. That is why their survival must be the first priority of those committed to the protection of human rights.

The restoration of the subjective conviction that American power is a necessary precondition for the survival of liberal democracy in the modern world is the most important development in U.S. foreign policy in the past decade. During the Vietnam epoch that subjective link between American power and the survival of liberal democratic societies was lost. Its restoration marks the beginning of a new era.

The first implication of that fact is that human-rights policies should be and, one trusts, will be, scrutinized not only for their effect on the total strategic position of the United States and its democratic allies— not because power is taking precedence over morality, but because the power of the U.S. and its allies is a necessary condition for the national independence, self-determination, self-government, and freedom of other nations. The human-rights policy of the Reagan administration has not been fully articulated, but the myriad concrete decisions made so far suggest that it will manifest the following characteristics:

First, clarity about our own commitment to due process, rule of law, democratic government and all its associated freedoms.

Second, aggressive statements in information programs and official pronouncements of the case for constitutional democracy. As the party of freedom we should make the case for freedom by precept as well as by example.

Third, careful assessment of all relevant aspects of any situation in another country in which we may be tempted to intervene, symbolically, economically, or otherwise. In Poland as in El Salvador we should be careful neither to overestimate our power to shape events according to our own preference, nor to underestimate the potential negative consequences of our acts.

Finally, a steady preference for the lesser over the greater evil.

Such policies will not make a perfect world, but at least they will not make the lives of actual people more difficult or perilous, less free than they already are. Conceivably, they might leave some people in some places more secure and less oppressed than they are today.

NO

Alan Tonelson

HUMAN RIGHTS: THE BIAS WE NEED

Once simply the passion of scattered humanitarian activists, the protection of human rights worldwide has become a full-blown dimension of American foreign policy, complete with its own State Department bureau. And the stakes involved in formulating U.S. human rights policies have grown correspondingly large.

A human rights policy, after all, can profoundly affect national security. Arms control negotiations, for example, have been delayed and complicated both by the imposition of martial law in Poland and by recent Soviet campaigns to stamp out the dissident movement. The need to preserve U.S. interests in politically unstable developing countries has turned human rights into a dispute between Washington and several strategically and economically important countries. Further, human rights is increasingly the standard by which Americans judge the legitimacy of their country's avowed interests, particularly toward the Soviet bloc and the Third World.

Thus a human rights policy that does not enhance national security is unjustifiable. But a policy that is not supported by the American people is unsustainable. The last several U.S. administrations can point to policies that have satisfied both criteria. Yet despite—or perhaps because of—the mounting salience of human rights issues, such successes have been few and far between, either under the Nixon and Ford administrations, which generally tried to lock human rights out of American foreign policy; the Carter administration, which aspired to respond evenhandedly to human rights violations by friend and foe alike; or the Reagan administration, which has generally adopted a double standard that favors friendly "authoritarian" regimes of the right over hostile "totalitarian" regimes of the left.

Inept or inconsistent implementation frequently sabotaged each of these three strategies. But their built-in flaws are too deep for even the shrewdest execution to overcome. An alternative course, however, does exist. The criteria for a successful human rights policy can only be met by reserving America's harshest criticisms and sanctions for those authoritarian regimes that President Reagan has favored, while responding to repression by totalitarian governments with a mixture of quiet diplomacy and economic incentives. The obstacles to success will be formidable. It will require a break from traditional ways of thinking about human rights policy goals. It will require a precision of rhetoric American policy makers have rarely displayed. And it will require the recognition that an effective human rights policy may be expensive, at least in the short run.

At the same time, this tilt can establish the balance of power and commitments journalist Walter Lippmann identified as the hallmark of a successful foreign policy. It can turn human rights violators closely tied to the United States into stabler and more reliable allies. It can win the United States good will and long-term influence with the populations of regimes that resist American pressure. It can moderate the foreign policies and internal repression of governments with which the United States currently has little leverage. And it can furnish the moral foundation a human rights policy needs, while avoiding the arrogance to which Americans have often succumbed....

In a world ideal except for human rights violations, the United States would respond to all comparable abuses with equal vigor, regardless of the violator's political leanings. Even in the real world, compelling reasons militate for evenhandedness. Still-sketchy polling data indicate that a majority of Americans do not favor preferential treatment for pro-Western autocrats. The principle of evenhandedness also commands the support of most political and opinion leaders....

Yet the Carter administration's experience indicates that a popular and effective policy of evenhanded actions is a pipe dream. Despite the charges of bias and inconsistency leveled at the Carter human rights record, nothing stands out as strikingly as its scattershot, almost random nature. The contention that U.S. officials picked on friendly authoritarian regimes such as Iran's or Nicaragua's has no foundation. So evident was the concentration on the Soviet bloc in 1977 that Soviet dissident Valery Chalidze reminded the administration in print that human rights violations were not confined to communist countries. After 1977 only the frequency of such public statements declined....

THE POLITICS OF HUMAN RIGHTS

If double and even triple standards are inevitable, then a human rights minded administration must choose a pattern of preferential treatment that enhances national security and attracts widespread support. Reagan has tried to apply just such a bias to human rights diplomacy. He and his top aides have drawn principally on two now well-known analyses of the politics of human rights by U.S. Ambassador to the U.N. Jeane Kirkpatrick and Ernest Lefever....

Kirkpatrick and Lefever urge basing American policy on the clear differences between dictators they classify as "traditional authoritarians" and "revolutionary totalitarians." As Kirkpatrick explains, authoritarian regimes are "less repressive" than their totalitarian counterparts. Their leaders, she has written, "leave in place existing allocations of wealth, power, status, and other resources which ... maintain masses in poverty." They leave untouched "habitual rhythms of work and leisure, habitual places of residence, habitual patterns of family and personal relations." Adds Lefever, authoritarian regimes "often allow opposition parties to operate and a restrained press to publish. . . ."

Further, in Kirkpatrick's words, "right wing autocracies do sometimes evolve into democracies," given enough time and certain economic, social, and political conditions. She also characterizes authoritarian regimes as "more compatible with U.S. interests."

Totalitarian rulers, however, "become the arbiters of orthodoxy in every sphere. . . . The ruling party even usurps the place of God," argues Lefever. Philosopher Michael Novak, who served as U.S. representative to the 37th and 38th sessions of the U.N. Human Rights Commission for the Reagan administration, adds another dimension. The distinguishing crime of totalitarianism "is not the total physical barbarity or total range of State control . . . but the total ideological claim, against which there is no appeal."

Finally, writes Kirkpatrick, virtually all totalitarian regimes existing today are hostile to American interests, and the contamination of most national liberation movements with Marxists practically assures that newcomers to their ranks will be equally anti-American. The challenge of Soviet-inspired subversion all but guarantees that strong pressure on pro-Western authoritarians will lead to disaster for the United States. As Lefever states, the choice between the lesser of two evils is "inescapable." . . .

[T]his distinction has not aged well enough to guide U.S. foreign policy. Virtually all dictatorships today display both totalitarian and authoritarian features. Reagan's sketch of the archetypical authoritarian ruler, content to amass personal wealth and the trappings of power while leaving traditional patterns of life and

limited freedoms intact has simply been mocked by former Ugandan President Idi Amin, Latin American tyrants who nearly exterminated their Indian populations, and the Salvadoran officers who crushed a 1932 revolt by killing some 30,000 peasants.

Even short of killing, authoritarian regimes' harassment of ordinary citizens often approaches totalitarian levels. Although some authoritarian governments—such as the shah's monarchy and the Somoza regime—have sanctioned political parties, many others, notably in the southern cone of South America, have banned all organized political activities for varying lengths of time. Authoritarian governments in countries such as El Salvador, the Philippines, and South Korea have systematically denied the right to form labor unions and have assaulted universities with a vengeance. According to Kurt Gottfried of the American Physical Society, the southern cone governments "have all but destroyed science, intellectual life, and educational systems."

Moreover, all-embracing claims of total political power appear with surprising frequency in the statements and constitutions of authoritarian governments. Brazil's labor code, for example, was modeled on Benito Mussolini's *Carta del Lavoro* and dates from the 1930s, when dictator Getulio Vargas tried to create an *Estado Nôvo* inspired by interwar European fascism. South Korea's National Security Law of 1961 refers specifically to "anti-State organizations" and mandates felony punishment for "any person who has organized an association or group for the purpose of . . . disturbing the State."

Indeed, many scholars contend that a sophisticated structure they call "bureaucratic authoritarianism" has replaced the individual *caudillo* in several Latin Ameri can countries. This structure, they assert, strives "to destroy permanently a perceived threat to the existing structure of socio-economic privilege by eliminating the political participation of the numerical majority."

Totalitarian regimes persistently defy their stereotypes as well. While communism does indeed claim jurisdiction over all aspects of life, tens of millions throughout the communist world cling to family loyalties, to their livelihoods, to their faiths, and even to their vices, despite determined indoctrination programs. On occasions they have risen in revolt against their rulers. Since Stalin's death, limited degrees of free expression have been tolerated in Eastern Europe and even in the USSR. And as the Reagan administration has asserted, even China is moving "slowly toward a more culturally diverse and open society." . . .

The totalitarian-authoritarian dichotomy fails on theoretical grounds as well. The "history of this century provides no grounds for expecting that radical totalitarian regimes will transform themselves," Kirkpatrick has written. Right-wing autocracies, however, sometimes do evolve into democracies—although the process can take "decades, if not centuries." Yet a clever double standard is at work here. The world's oldest totalitarian regime has been in existence only 65 years. The rest of the totalitarian communist world did not come into being until after World War II. Clearly these countries cannot be written off already. For they too deserve the hundreds of years that it took Britain and other West European countries to democratize and that Kirkpatrick has granted to existing authoritarian regimes.

This fundamental misjudgment contributes greatly to the untenable belief that the status quo in most strife-torn authoritarian countries can—and should—be

preserved. Kirkpatrick, for instance, disparages the view that insurgency "is evidence of widespread popular discontent." Yet she refers repeatedly to the chronic "lack of consensus on legitimacy" throughout Latin America, to the "vulnerable," "dependent" economies of the region, and to rising popular expectations—the same historical forces whose prominence in Carter administration rhetoric she derided.

Finally, the correlation between totalitarian governments and anti-American policies is far from perfect. On several occasions, totalitarian governments have supported U.S. interests by design and by coincidence—witness Angola's overall cooperation in the talks seeking independence for Namibia and its excellent relationship with Gulf Oil Corporation, and Yugoslavia's successful rearguard action to contain Soviet and Cuban influence at the 1979 Nonaligned Movement meeting in Havana.

Meanwhile, the friendship of many authoritarian regimes may be questioned. The shah was a leader of the Organization of Petroleum Exporting Countries' so-called price hawks throughout the 1970s. Argentina ignored Carter's embargo and sold the Soviet Union 7.6 million tons of grain in 1980; Moscow has become Argentina's largest trading partner.

A REASONABLE GUIDELINE

One dichotomy exists, however, that can serve as an intelligent, politically sustainable guide for a human rights policy: the difference between countries with which the United States boasts extensive economic and political relations and countries with which it does not. And this distinction points to a policy that purposely and openly focuses its public actions on countries closely tied with the United States and that relies on behind-the-scenes persuasion and incentives for good behavior to achieve human rights goals in countries not so linked.

U.S. leverage with closely related countries makes them logical targets of a human rights diplomacy seeking to ease repression abroad. Even critical rhetoric will probably have more effect on countries that consider themselves U.S. allies than on countries that the United States has treated as neutrals or adversaries.

Critics of the Carter human rights policy have raised numerous objections to such a tilt. Several analysts have attacked basing U.S. policy on the different kinds of relationships established by Washington with foreign countries as unfair or incomprehensible. Thus, Kirkpatrick describes as "curious" Carter's focus on U.S. aid recipients. And in February 1982 the Reagan administration argued that keying actions to leverage would not "fairly represent the distribution of human rights abuses in the world." But differences in leverage are precisely what make the goal of basing U.S. actions on the geographic distribution and the severity of repression unattainable. Lefever proposed a far better guideline: U.S. responsibilities should be "commensurate with our capacity to influence external events."

Some also claim that public criticisms of and sanctions against pro-Western governments frequently backfire. In 1977 and 1978, they note, several Latin American countries renounced varying amounts of U.S. aid following disapproving American actions.

Yet the United States has successfully and publicly twisted the arms of pro-Western dictatorships in the past. From 1948 to 1965 both Democratic and Republican administrations regularly used their enormous influence in South Korea

to curb the worst excesses of Presidents Syngman Rhee and Park Chung Hee. During the Carter years American diplomacy helped achieve many important successes. Starting in early 1977, thousands of political prisoners were released throughout Latin America and Iran. Most striking, a series of strong public warnings helped deter incumbent Joaquin Balaguer and his generals from overturning the election of Antonio Guzman as president of the Dominican Republic. ...

Recent administrations have insisted that friendly relations with autocracies did not constitute endorsement of human rights violations. Yet foreign populations frequently receive just the opposite message from U.S. actions. In Nicaragua, members of Somoza's National Guard often dressed in U.S. fatigues and drove American-made vehicles with U.S. Army markings, and a U.S. ambassador's portrait long adorned Nicaraguan currency. The hostility of Iran's Moslem government and the hostage crisis attest to the Iranian people's bitter resentment of U.S. support for the shah. And South Korean and Philippine dissidents increasingly blame Washington for human rights violations by their governments.

Suspending or curtailing aid or commerce during a period of serious political upheaval or even after crackdowns on dissent by an apparently stable government may win the United States influence or at least good will with opposition groups should they prevail. Moreover, such action runs little risk of permanently antagonizing incumbents, whose political views would make entering the Soviet orbit extremely difficult and who would remain heavily dependent on U.S. resources. Dissociation should be seen as a form of preventive medicine. As Lefever has said, "We should have started many years before to have moved away from the kind of identification we had with the shah and the army and so on."

BEHIND THE SCENES PRESSURE

In countries where the United States has little leverage, dissociation does not come into play. Washington is not linked in any way with repression in these countries. The best hope for reducing abuses in such countries lies in conducting quiet diplomacy and inducing offending governments to improve by offering them carrots. U.S. economic relations with countries such as Vietnam, Cuba, North Korea, and Cambodia are either minuscule or nonexistent. Resource flows to avowedly leftist but noncommunist nations such as Tanzania, Guyana, and Mozambique are somewhat larger. But most seem able to limp along without U.S. help. Trade with America runs as high as 20 per cent of imports or exports with only Guyana, for example.

The Soviet bloc presents a perplexing combination of risks and opportunities. Like other industrialized Western countries, the United States provides members of the Soviet bloc with important margins of capital and high technology goods. The Soviet Union itself appears to possess enough valuable raw materials to sustain even joint Western pressures for the foreseeable future. Other Warsaw Pact economies, however, are much more vulnerable and already drain Moscow's resources. Yet the great volume of Western loans to and trade with the East has exposed major banks and entire countries to serious injury should economic war break out. In addition, as the Siberian gas pipeline controversy demonstrates, American policy today is tripping over an obstacle frequently cited by opponents of sanctions against friendly regimes—the alternate supplier problem.

Still, the calculus of Soviet and Western economic power and political resolve can change and should be reviewed continually. For now, the best results will most likely come from exploiting the acute desire of the Warsaw Pact countries for Western resources and by pressing for human rights improvements behind the scenes.

Problems of history and politics also dim the prospects of using sticks to beat open societies where the United States has little clout. These countries are instinctively suspicious of all U.S. words and actions. They recognize no American right to judge their domestic policies, and they are not inclined to follow American lead. The problem is not how to use leverage, but how to get it; not what to say, but how to gain a hearing. Haig defended quiet diplomacy toward "historic friends" that abuse human rights by arguing that progress is impossible in "the glare of public bludgeoning" or in an atmosphere of "paranoia." Yet this reasoning makes even more sense for countries in which the paranoia and the suspicion already exist.

Preferential treatment for these countries may also enhance U.S. national security by drawing communist and left-leaning countries in the Third World away from the Soviet orbit. Past failures to achieve rapprochement with Cuba and Vietnam demonstrate the difficulties involved. But a policy that writes such countries off must be very comforting to the Kremlin. Implacable hostility to postrevolutionary regimes in Cuba in 1960 and in Vietnam during the late 1940s at the least handed Moscow two effortless political victories.

Within the context of quiet diplomacy, U.S. leaders should take every opportunity when communicating with those countries to affirm the value of the freedoms Americans enjoy. But only a foolish consistency would prevent the United States from expressing its displeasure in votes over distantly related countries' human rights violations taken in the U.N., where Washington has few special powers—none in the General Assembly—by dint of its size and strength; where Washington generally casts just one vote and can easily slough off the primary blame for condemnatory resolutions; and where no action short of the unusual step of imposing sanctions can materially harm a human rights violator. As a rule, however, publicly threatening and reprimanding individual, distantly related countries can only push them back into shells of suspicion and hostility.

POSTSCRIPT

HUMAN RIGHTS: SHOULD WE PREFER AUTHORITARIANISM TO COMMUNISM?

One of the basic issues that divides Kirkpatrick and Tonelson is the question of which way, if at all, America should "tilt" in its policy toward human rights violations. As we have seen from the debate, there seem to be three positions: the Kirkpatrick position, the Carter position, and the Tonelson position. Each may have its peculiar weakness. To its critics the Kirkpatrick position seems hypocritical: She criticizes the Communists for human rights violations while ignoring those of our allies. The Carter position may have a different problem: If, indeed, it was even-handed (which Kirkpatrick denies) it was also ineffective. It deeply angered both the authoritarian right and the Communist left, yet produced few results. Tonelson's advice is to "tilt" the opposite way, to publicly twist the arms of the countries that depend upon us, such as South Korea, while using a softer approach toward Communist countries. Are there any weaknesses in that approach? Is there a danger that it may be viewed as a craven and perverse policy ("America kicks its weak friends and bows to its strong enemies") that is bound to alienate some of our most loyal allies? The question, while rhetorical, can certainly be answered, and Tonelson no doubt has a solution.

A useful general work on the theory and practice of human rights internationally is Vernon Van Dyke's *Human Rights, the United States, and the World Community* (Oxford, 1970). Valery Chaldize, one of the founders of the Moscow Human Rights Committee (who, while on a speaking tour of the United States, was told not to return to his country), recounts his own experiences and tells what goes on in "corrective labor" camps and "psychiatric" wards of the USSR in *To Defend These Rights* (Random House, 1974). On the subject of repression in "friendly" autocracies, Jacobo Timermann writes of his imprisonment and torture in Argentina in *Prisoner Without a Name, Cell Without a Number* (Knopf, 1981).

The fragility of America's "friendship" with Argentina was dramatically demonstrated in the spring of 1982, after Argentina invaded the Falkland Islands. Following an unsuccessful attempt to mediate, the United States sided with Great Britain. Not long afterward, American television viewers were startled to see film of Argentina's foreign minister embracing Fidel Castro. The crisis was embarrassing to the Reagan administration but was not fatal to the Kirkpatrick doctrine, for once the crisis ended the administration moved quickly to repair the damage. The work was made easier by a palace revolt, which replaced the government whose rhetoric was beginning to sound distinctly "anti-Gringo."

CONTRIBUTORS
TO THIS VOLUME

EDITORS

GEORGE McKENNA was born in Chicago in 1937 and attended public schools in the city. He received a bachelor's degree from the University of Chicago in 1959, a master's degree from the University of Massachusetts in 1962, and a Ph.D. from Fordham University in 1967. He has been teaching at City College of New York since 1963. He is the author of several books and articles, including *American Politics: Ideals and Realities* (McGraw-Hill, 1976), and *A Guide to the Constitution: That Delicate Balance* (Random House, 1984). He has also edited a number of works, including other books of readings published by the Dushkin Publishing Group. At present he is writing an American government textbook for Dushkin, to be published in 1989.

STANLEY FEINGOLD was born in New York City in 1926. He attended high school in the city and received his bachelor's degree from the City College of New York. He received a graduate education at Columbia University and taught political science at City College. From 1970 to 1974, he was given a special appointment as Visiting Professor of Politics at the University of Leeds, England. At present he is Visiting Professor at Westchester Community College, a unit of the State University of New York. He edited, with George McKenna, the first four editions of this book.

AUTHORS

DAVID L. BAZELON has been Chief Judge of the U.S. Court of Appeals for the District of Columbia circuit since 1962.

WALTER BERNS is professor of political science at the University of Toronto. Among other works, Professor Berns is the author of *The First Amendment and the Future of American Democracy*.

WILLIAM BRENNAN is an associate justice of the United States Supreme Court.

ZBIGNIEW BRZEZINSKI was national security adviser to President Jimmy Carter. He is now professor of government at Columbia University and senior adviser at the Center for Strategic and International Studies at Georgetown University.

McGEORGE BUNDY was special assistant to the president for national security affairs from 1961 to 1966. He is currently professor of history at New York University.

GEOFFREY COWLEY is a staff writer for the *Seattle Weekly*.

BARRY CRICKMER is a senior editor of *Nation's Business,* a monthly magazine published by the Chamber of Commerce of the United States.

WILLIAM J. CROTTY is professor of political science at Northwestern University. He was a consultant to the McGovern-Fraser Commission on Party-Structure and Delegate Selection. Professor Crotty is the author of *Political Reform and the American Experiment.*

JAMES C. DOBSON was a member of the Attorney General's Commission on Pornography.

CHRISTOPHER DODD is a United States senator representing Connecticut.

G. WILLIAM DOMHOFF is a professor of psychology and sociology at the University of California, Santa Cruz.

ELAINE DONNELLY is a conservative activist who has testified before Congress on behalf of the *Eagle Forum.*

ELIZABETH DREW is a political analyst, television commentator, and a Washington correspondent for the *New Yorker.*

The late JOHN EAST was a United States senator from North Carolina before his death in 1986.

GREGG EASTERBROOK is a writer who contributes regularly to *The Atlantic Monthly* and other publications.

GEORGE GOLDBERG is an author and a member of the New York State Bar.

BARRY GOLDWATER is a United States senator from Arizona.

ANDREW GREELEY is a Roman Catholic priest and a professor of sociology at the University of Arizona.

LOIS HAIGNERE is a research associate and assistant director of the New York State Comparable Pay Study at the Center for Women at the State University of New York at Albany.

BEVERLY W. HARRISON is a professor of Christian ethics at the Union Theological Seminary in New York.

HENDRIK HERTZBERG is a contributing editor of *The New Republic.*

ROBERT JASTROW is a physicist and professor of Earth sciences at Dartmouth College. He is also the founder of the Goddard Insitute for Space Studies.

The late JACOB JAVITS was United States senator from New York for 24 years. He was also an author and lecturer.

MAX M. KAMPELMAN is a Washington lawyer who was selected to head the US delegation to new arms talks with the Soviet Union.

GEORGE F. KENNAN was US Ambassador to the Soviet Union in 1952. He is now Professor Emeritus at the Institute for Advanced Study at Princeton University. His books on foreign relations and Soviet policy, which include *American Diplomacy:1900-1950* and *Russia and the West Under Lenin and Stalin* have won many awards including the Pulitzer and Bancroft prizes.

JEANE KIRKPATRICK was the US Ambassador to the United Nations under President Reagan.

EVERETT CARLL LADD,Jr., is professor of political science and director of the Social Science Data Center at the University of Connecticut. He is the author of many books, including *Ideology in America* and, with Charles D. Hadley, *Transformations of the American Party System*.

SAR A. LEVITAN is research professor of economics and director of the Center for Social Policy Studies at George Washington University. He is also the author of more than thirty books.

DONAL E.J. MACNAMARA is a criminologist and director of corrections programs at the John Jay College of Criminal Justice in New York City. He is the author of *Corrections* and other books and articles.

ROBERT S. McNAMARA was secretary of defense from 1961 to 1968 and president of the World Bank from 1968 to 1981.

THURGOOD MARSHALL is an associate justice of the United States Supreme Court.

CHARLES MURRAY is a senior research fellow at the Manhattan Institute.

BENJAMIN NETANYAHU is the Israeli ambassador to the United Nations. His older brother, Colonel Jonathan Netanyahu, was killed during the Israeli rescue mission at Entebbe airport.

CONOR CRUISE O'BRIEN is a contributing editor of *The Atlantic Monthly*. He is also the prochancellor of Dublin University.

GARY ORFIELD is a staff member of the Brookings Institution, engaged in basic research in governmental affairs. He is the author of *Congressional Power: Congress and Social Change*, from which the selection in this book was taken.

DAN RATHER is the anchor and managing editor of the *CBS Evening News*.

RONALD REAGAN is the fortieth President of the United States.

GERALD SMITH was chief of the US delegation to the Strategic Arms Limitation Talks from 1969 to 1972. He is also the author of *Doubletalk:The Story of SALT I.*

JOSEPH SOBRAN is a syndicated columnist and senior editor of the *National Review. He is also the author of The Conservative Manifesto* (Empire Books, 1983).

RONNIE STEINBERG is director of the Program on Comparable Worth at the Center for Women in Government at the State University of New York at Albany. She is also the project director of the New York State Comparable Pay Study.

MARTIN TOLCHIN is the congressional correspondent for the *New York Times.*

SUSAN TOLCHIN is a professor of public administration at George Washington University.

ALAN TONELSON is the associate editor of the *Wilson Quarterly.*

JAMES Q. WILSON is professor of government at Harvard University and the author of *The Amateur Democrat, Negro Politics,* and *Varieties of Police Behavior.*

JAMES E. WOOD Jr. is Simon and Ethel Bunn Professor of Church-State Studies and director of the J.M. Dawson Institute of Church-State Studies at Baylor University. He is also the author of *Religion and the State* (Baylor University Press, 1985) and is the founding editor of the *Journal of Church and State.*

INDEX

Civil Rights Act of 1964, 215, 221, 223
Civil Rights Commission, 209, 212, 214
"colorblindness," doctrine of, 199
Commission on Obscenity and Pornography, 246, 247
Committee for the Re-Election of the President (CREEP), under Nixon, 44, 52
committees of Congress, changes in, 72, 73, 75, 76
Common Cause, 51, 53, 57, 58, 59, 62, 65
communism, and Central America, 298
comparable worth: 214-226; definition of, 217, 218; and job evaluation, 217-219, 222, 223; objections to, 215; problems created by, 225; study concerning, 218, 219
Comparable Worth: The Myth and the Movement (Johansen), 227
Congress: and abortion, 263, 267; and the budget process, 78-80; changes in, 74-75; committees of, 76-78; role of, in health and safety regulations, 114-115; impact of lobbies on, 80-81, 84; members of, as upper class, 18; influence of PACs over, 67; vs. presidential authority, 89-109; public financing vs. political action committees' financing of elections to, 48-60; recommended reforms of, 83-85; in Sixties and Seventies, 181; and social policy, 90-94, 124; stereotypes of, 86-88; role of, in opposing Vietnam War, 91; role of, in Watergate, 91
Congress and the Common Good (Maass), 95
Congressional Budget and Impoundment Control Act, 78
congressional calendar, 84-85
congressional campaign financing, legislation regulating, 52-53
congressional campaign spending, ceiling on, 84
Congressional Club, 49, 66
congressional committees: changes in chairmanship of, 73, 75, 76; proliferation of, 75-80; power of, 72, 75
Constitution: and affirmative action, 210, 211; Brennan on judicial defense of, 133-139; and congressional vs. presidential power to declare war, 96-109; and death penalty, 180, 181, 184-188; and protection of pornography through First Amendment, 244-258; power of Supreme Court to interpret, 126-132
Consumer Product Safety Commission, inefficiency of, 113-114
convention, reforming power of delegate selection to, 31, 43
conviction rates, 159, 160
corporate community: campaign contributions by, 51; involvement of, in government, 20-23; and political action committees, 51-53; political influence of, 17
cost vs. benefit, of government regulations, 115-117
County of Washington v. Gunther, 217
Court of Last Resort (Gardner), 193
Courts on Trial (Frank), 193
Cowley, Geoffrey, and controversy over comparable worth, 214, 215
Cox, Archibald, 55, 57, 62
Cranston, Alan, 221

Credentials Review Commission, 36
Crickmer, Barry, on disadvantages of government regulation, 110-117
crime: causes of, 167-168, 171-172, 177-179; and controversy over death penalty, 182-196; effect of deterrence on, 156-179; organized, and pornography, 249, 257; statistics on, 156, 157, 171; types of, 172-173
criminals, and controversy over morality of death penalty, 182-196
criminologists, and capital punishment, 190
Crotty, William J., in defense of political party reforms, 30-40
cruel and unusual punishment, and death penalty, 181, 184
Cuba, 293, 295, 299, 349
Curbing the Mischiefs of Faction (Ranney), 47

Dahl, Robert, 29
dairy industry, political action committee of, 52
Darwin v. Beason, 278
death sentence, and American juries, 185, 186, 187
death penalty: case against, 189-196; and Constitution, 184, 185; defense of, 182-188; and racial discrimination, 180, 181, 185, 191-193; vs. rehabilitation, 183
Declaration of Independence, 198
Decter, Midge, 209
defense budget, and Congress, 82
defense powers, of Congress vs. President, 96-109
degrading pornography, 250
delegate selection, Democratic party reform of, 31, 34, 36, 43
democracy, effects of political action committees on, 48-69
Democratic convention in Chicago, 30, 32, 33, 43
Democratic party, accomplishments of reform within, 34-40, 43-44
deregulation, under Reagan, 111, 120-123
deterrence: and capital punishment, 183, 186, 191, 192; effect of, on crime, 156-170, 174-175
direct election of president, 44, 46
disability insurance, 233
discrimination: and comparable worth issue, 214-226; racial, and capital punishment, 180, 181, 185, 191-193; reverse, and affirmative action, 200-212
Dobson, James C., on pornography and First Amendment protection, 253-258
doctrine of "color blindness," 199
Dodd, Christopher, argument against aid to the Contras, 292, 293, 298-300
Domhoff, G. William, on existence of power elite in America, 14-23
Donnelly, Elaine, on need for federal regulation of broadcast medium, 140, 141, 148-153
double screen defense system, 321, 322, 323
Down Syndrome, and debate over abortion, 264
Drew, Elizabeth: on effects of political action committees on democracy, 48-60; Samuelson's criticism of, 61-69

East, John P., in defense of aid to the Contras, 292-298